Stanley Kubrick at Look Magazine

Stanley Kubrick at Look Magazine
Authorship and Genre in Photojournalism and Film

Philippe Mather

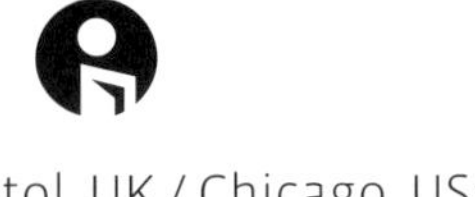

intellect Bristol, UK / Chicago, USA

First published in the UK in 2013 by
Intellect, The Mill, Parnall Road, Fishponds, Bristol, BS16 3JG, UK

First published in the USA in 2013 by
Intellect, The University of Chicago Press, 1427 E. 60th Street,
Chicago, IL 60637, USA

A catalogue record for this book is available from the
British Library.

Cover designer: Holly Rose
Copy-editor: MPS Technologies
Cover photo: © Estate of Philip Harrington. Courtesy of the Library
of Congress, LOOK Collection.
Production manager: Jelena Stanovnik
Typesetting: Planman Technologies

ISBN 978-1-84150-6111

Printed and bound by Hobbs, UK

Table of Contents

Acknowledgements

There are so many individuals who have helped me over the past ten years to produce this book that I find myself unable to list all of them, but I trust they will forgive me. I would like to single out a few people and organizations that provided significant technical, financial, intellectual or moral support, or a combination thereof: The Campion College President's Research Award Committee, the University of Regina President's Fund Committee, my colleague Dr. Philip Charrier from the University of Regina, Dr. Gary Rhodes from Queen's University – Belfast, Dr. Mario Falsetto from Concordia University, Dr. Gene D. Phillips from Loyola University – Chicago, Barbara Orbach Natanson from the Library of Congress, Melanie Bower from the Museum of the City of New York, Phil Grosz and SK Film Archives LLC, Richard Daniels from the Kubrick Archives at the University of the Arts – London, Felipe Diaz from the Saskatchewan Filmpool Cooperative, my publisher Jelena Stanovnik at Intellect Books, the anonymous peer reviewer at Intellect, my parents, Bruce and Pierrette Mather, and my wife, Angeline Chia.

Introduction

Authorship and Genre

In late February 1948, a 19-year-old photojournalist from *Look* magazine was sent to cover the Ringling Bros. and Barnum & Bailey Circus at their headquarters in Sarasota, Florida. The resulting photo-essay, published in the May 25, 1948, issue of *Look* and titled "How the Circus Gets Set," is a social study providing information concerning the resources required to run a circus, including 1,400 employees and 900 animals, from April to October each year. We learn that the winter months are a time for renewal, as the circus remains in "its 200-acre winter quarters in Sarasota, where these candid [*sic*] pictures were taken." The essay features flash photographs focusing on the women of the circus, acrobats and aerialists seen rehearsing, relaxing or waiting for a practice. A recently published photography book has made a surprising claim concerning this photo-essay, particularly its pictures of aerialists and a low- angle shot of a chimpanzee on roller skates being held on a leash by a statuesque ex-Folies Bergères performer (Crone, 2005, 91). It is suggested that these images foreshadow the 1968 science-fiction film *2001: A Space Odyssey*, a film as far removed from a circus as one could imagine. Yet the chimp and the circus performer are compared to characters from *2001*'s "Dawn of Man" sequence, with Moonwatcher as the chimp who is controlled by a being further along on the evolutionary chain. The relative sense of spatial disorientation and weightlessness achieved by the aerialists and a somersaulting bareback rider also convey the futuristic notion of defying gravity (Crone, 2005, 81).

Superficially, this unusual comparison between a late-1940s photo-essay and a late-1960s Hollywood film is justified by the fact that the director of *2001: A Space Odyssey*, Stanley Kubrick, was also the young photographer who was assigned by *Look* magazine to capture images for the circus story. However, the implied influence of an early career in photojournalism on a later, and much better known, corpus of feature films, would require a sustained and detailed argument. Indeed, Stanley Kubrick's reputation as a cinematic auteur and audio-visual artist is primarily based on 12 feature-length fiction films that he directed between 1955 and 1999. He is admired as a fiercely independent filmmaker, an autodidact who neither attended film school nor worked his way up through the film industry. Less well known is the fact that prior to making films, he spent almost five years working as a photojournalist, publishing over 1000 photographs in *Look* magazine. This book's guiding thesis is that the *Look* magazine photographs can shed light on the aesthetic and ideological factors that shaped the development of Kubrick's artistic voice, as well as our own understanding of his later film work. Moreover, since Kubrick was at a formative stage in his career during his tenure at *Look*, it will be argued that this represented an alternative to formal schooling in the visual arts. This will be supported by close textual analyses of Kubrick's photo-essays, as well as explorations of the contexts in which this work was produced.

Scholarship on Kubrick's work has largely focused on the "mature" films, beginning with his third feature, *The Killing* (1956). This book seeks to establish precise developmental connections between the *Look* photographs and Kubrick's three documentary shorts as well as his first two feature fiction films. The object is to uncover the publicly accessible historical sources of the Kubrickian worldview, a worldview that has been identified by critics as a means of interpreting his later films, but whose origin has seldom been studied as such. Furthermore, the single major research effort conducted thus far on Kubrick's photojournalistic career has adopted a curatorial approach bent on studying individual photographs outside the magazine context, which eschews the critical matter of editing multiple images in a narrative context (Crone, 2005, 6). Our goal will therefore not be to search for lost masterpieces but to gauge the extent to which the process of selecting still images in accordance with a shooting script, in the collaborative environment of a general interest photomagazine, shaped Kubrick's emerging talent in combining words and images for storytelling purposes. Analysing the influence of photojournalism on Kubrick's later film work should enhance our understanding of his approach to narrative structure, as well as his distinctive combination of pragmatic and aesthetic categories such as fiction and documentary, fantasy and realism.

While the critical literature on Stanley Kubrick's fiction films is fairly extensive, his photojournalistic output remains relatively unknown. Studies on Kubrick's cinema generally make only passing comments on his training as a photographer. For instance, Norman Kagan briefly claims that Kubrick's career at *Look* merely allowed him to "experiment with the photographic aspects of the cinema," overlooking photojournalism's narrative and editorial aspects (1). Thomas Allen Nelson provides a questionable rationale for ignoring Kubrick's *Look* output, suggesting that the documentary nature of photojournalism was so formulaic that it represented an aesthetic straitjacket, impeding the future filmmaker's creative self-expression (3). In contrast, Michel Chion correctly identifies the importance of the documentary aesthetic in Kubrick's feature fiction films, although he declines to investigate the *Look* photographs (12).

One exception is Vincent LoBrutto's 1997 biography of Kubrick. This text highlights the importance of the *Look* photographs in terms of both their scope and quality, and provides some useful background information for a more thorough examination of Kubrick's photojournalistic work (LoBrutto, 19–69). Another important exception is a major curatorial effort conducted, since 1998, by the Iccarus group, based in Munich at Ludwig Maximilian University's Institute of Art History. It has resulted in a travelling exhibition, a catalogue, several articles and most recently, a book edited by Iccarus founder Rainer Crone, *Drama and Shadows*, which presents approximately 400 photographs printed from the original *Look* magazine negatives stored at the Library of Congress and at the Museum of the City of New York. It should be noted that members of the Iccarus group tend to downplay contributions from the social and historical context in analysing Kubrick's personal signature. For instance, they present Kubrick's work outside the magazine context, including unpublished photographs, in effect making curatorial decisions designed to recover a voice assumed to be compromised by the journalistic situation (Crone and Von Stosch, 21). Also, when acknowledging influences, they focus on comparisons with established art photographers such as Henri-Cartier Bresson, Walker Evans and Robert Frank, rather than with Kubrick's colleagues at *Look* (Crone and Graf Schaesberg, 24). Michel Chion points out that this curatorial approach overlooks the fact that Kubrick himself never organized exhibitions nor published books based on his photographic work during his lifetime, and that these photos were designed to be published in a magazine where they interacted with a written text (12). This book follows up on Chion's comment, examining Kubrick's photographs in the light of *Look* magazine's mission to inform and entertain its readers, and considering how that mission, in turn, informed Kubrick's intelligent yet accessible films. It should be helpful at an initial stage to properly understand how Kubrick's published photographs functioned in the context of *Look*'s photo-stories.

This book is divided into two sections, authorship and genre, which broadly refer to the production and the reception, respectively, of Kubrick's work. In terms of authorship, the issue of agency is examined by focusing on the influence *Look* magazine had on Kubrick's later development as a filmmaker. This may be controversial to the extent that most critical approaches to Kubrick's oeuvre tend to adopt traditional conceptions of art based on various features of romantic aesthetics, including assumptions regarding the filmmaker's authorial control and creative independence, as well as his unique artistic identity, which is felt to emerge in spite of, rather than as a result of, contextual factors. When critic Alexander Walker asks, "What is it that makes Kubrick the kind of director he is?" the notion that the filmmaker's photojournalistic training may provide an answer is never explored, perhaps due to a lingering auteurist prejudice against the collaborative natures of filmmaking and photojournalism that undermine the assumption of a singular, self-contained voice, or indeed an artistic genius (7). This book's take on authorship will focus instead on a sociology of production, including a consideration of the discursive contexts in which artists work, particularly their work routines, as an indirect means of shedding light on the reader's activity. This should demonstrate the usefulness of examining the objective and publicly accessible factors that shape our cultural conception of a discursive intention.

A traditional art historical approach to Kubrick's photographs may lean towards the notion of "innate genius," and only acknowledge artistic mentorships as a means of assigning value and legitimizing the analysis of photojournalistic work (Crone and Von Stosch, 22). Instead, it will be argued that a focus on less noble personal influences and broader social factors can, ironically perhaps, help to achieve a fuller understanding of Kubrick's creative output and its development. Scholarship on Kubrick's early films, in particular, should be enhanced by a thorough examination of his photo-essays, including the contexts in which they were made. It is important to simultaneously acknowledge the enduring social relevance of the auteurist approach to interpreting texts and emphasize the need to place it in a larger ideological framework. Our analysis would be limited if it did not adopt a balanced approach to social theory and merely focused on certain features of the romantic model of authorship, such as the conflation of the artist and his work, the assumption of unfettered self-expression and the use of auteurism as an evaluative strategy. Ignoring the social context would undermine our ability to conduct an effective study of both personal and public factors, and ultimately fail to do full justice to the semiotic issues at hand. Instead, the question of individual agency will be located more productively within a sociology of production, also taking into account relevant social, psychological and cultural discourses and practices (Staiger, 40–43). One advantage of a sociology of production is that it acknowledges the fact that both photojournalism and film production are collaborative efforts that take place within an industrial context. Considering authorship as a site of discourses further allows for multisemic or contradictory readings of texts, which would otherwise be made impossible by auteurism's assumption of a coherent authorial statement (Staiger, 47).

Engaging in close textual analyses of Kubrick's *Look* photo-essays will prompt us to consider different ways of conceiving of the sources of agency, especially as a relationship between agency and structure. This exploration will help to reveal the emergence of the Kubrickian brand name or signature. It will be suggested that to situate the discursive intent exclusively in an individual consciousness, the "spirit of the age" or a specific artistic tradition is less helpful than attempting to integrate these various influences into a broader explanatory scheme (Fish, 13). In assessing the growth of Kubrick's voice as a visual artist, we will therefore include relevant biographical issues, the production contexts at *Look* magazine, the rivalry with *Life* magazine, the evolution of photojournalistic technology, the immediate post-war artistic, economic and ideological climate in New York City, etc.

In order to map these influences, the book's first section will begin by examining the significance of Kubrick's apprenticeship at *Look* from the perspective of developmental psychology, since he worked for the national photomagazine at a transitional and formative stage in the lifespan. The opening chapter will thus argue that the combined influence of mentors, such as Kubrick's father and his art teacher, peers such as his darkroom buddies, and popular narrative visual media such as comic books, photomagazines and movies, went a long way towards shaping the teenager's aesthetic sensibility. The next four chapters adopt a sociological model, developed by George Ritzer, who argues that an agency-structure integration is more productive than positing a singular agent, either free from influence or necessarily in conflict with the institutional contexts in which he worked, or a mindless robot reflecting society's concerns (Ritzer and Goodman, 406). Examining areas of common interest and thus potential influence between *Look* magazine and Stanley Kubrick should be the most constructive approach.

While romantic and humanist critics are committed to an individualistic conception of the expressive artist, post-structuralists argue that the human subject is determined by a host of external and constraining factors that undermine his/her autonomy. These factors have even led theorists to question the very existence of the author as an autonomous entity, other than to serve specific discursive or ideological functions (Foucault, 124). Similarly, sociologist George Ritzer describes a polarized and sometimes acrimonious debate in his field. This debate opposes theorists who claim that sociology should only focus on large-scale phenomena and those who favour analyses of individual behaviour (Ritzer, 12). Ritzer proposes instead an integrative sociological model that combines two different methods of describing levels of social reality

	OBJECTIVE	**SUBJECTIVE**
MACROSCOPIC	I. Macro-objective Examples: society, law, bureaucracy, architecture, technology and language	III. Macro-subjective Examples: culture, norms and values
MICROSCOPIC	II. Micro-objective Examples: patterns of behaviour, action, and interaction	IV. Micro-subjective Examples: perceptions, beliefs, the various facets of the social construction of reality

Figure 1: Ritzer's major levels of social analysis.

(cf. Figure 1). The first method is the macroscopic-microscopic continuum, which refers to the scale of the social phenomenon, ranging from an individual interacting with others, to larger groups, organizations and world systems, such as capitalism. The second method is the objective-subjective continuum, which concerns the distinction between social phenomena that have a material existence and those that exist in the realm of ideas (Ritzer, 25).

Combining these two continua creates four levels of social reality. Ritzer is quick to add that "the real world is *not* divided into levels of social reality, but it can be understood better with the explicit utilization of these levels" (24). His model functions, therefore, as a heuristic device. In terms of scale, for instance, formal organizations, such as *Look* magazine, represent an intermediate level referred to as mesoscopic (Ritzer, 223). Also, a given social phenomenon may manifest itself in several levels of social reality: Ritzer mentions the family as an institution endowed with both objective and subjective dimensions (25). Finally, the analyst is encouraged to examine the dialectical relationships between all four levels of social reality (Ritzer, 27).

Chapters 2 through 5 thus attempt to apply Ritzer's model to Stanley Kubrick's career as a photojournalist (cf. Figure 2). The second chapter focuses on the macro-objective level, namely the formal organization of *Look* magazine as a commercial institution. It is argued that *Look*'s hierarchy was, to a certain extent, mitigated by a relatively collaborative production process:

	OBJECTIVE	**SUBJECTIVE**
MACROSCOPIC	I. Macro-objective *Look* magazine: organizational *structure*	III. Macro-subjective Photojournalism: photo-essay genre at *Look* magazine
MICROSCOPIC	II. Micro-objective *Look* magazine: organizational *culture*	IV. Micro-subjective Kubrick genre in photography and film

Figure 2: Sociological analysis of Kubrick's career at *Look* magazine.

a fact that allowed the organization to take on a high school graduate as an apprentice, and provided Kubrick with a highly stimulating and educational experience. He was able to learn from and enjoy the individual and collective mentorship of *Look* magazine's talented staff of photographers, writers and layout artists. Chapter 3 describes the work culture at *Look*, particularly standardized work routines, as the micro-objective level of social reality. The flexibility of *Look*'s organizational structure expresses itself through the practice of group journalism, sometimes referred to as a craft system, which provided each member of the team the opportunity to contribute in several stages of the production process. A young Kubrick was therefore both required to internalize *Look*'s editorial style and encouraged to develop his authorship by offering suggestions on a photo-essay's layout, for instance. Ritzer's macro-subjective level is examined in Chapter 4, specifically *Look* magazine's conception of the photo-essay genre. It is argued that once Kubrick entered the film industry, he continued to apply the lessons learned during his "college years" at *Look*, including the magazine's norms and values that he had to adopt and implement in order to work successfully as a photojournalist. In this regard, a textbook on photojournalism published by the editors of *Look* immediately prior to Kubrick's employment reveals a specific set of formal, stylistic and thematic conventions that define the photo-essay. Lastly, Chapter 5 discusses the micro-subjective level by speculating on Kubrick's conception of the photo-essay genre, based partly on interviews with Kubrick as well as detailed examinations of his photo-essays. Of particular interest are essays published by *Look* colleagues that are echoed in Kubrick's own work, revealing the consistent thematic and stylistic tropes characteristic of post-war American photojournalism, which may be broadly described as a slightly heightened form of realism. Throughout this section, we try to follow Ritzer in examining the relationships between the four levels of social reality, by asking ourselves: how was Kubrick's artistic identity affected by *Look* magazine's organizational structure and culture, and by the photo-essay genre; and how did Kubrick's work, in turn, reflect itself or impact on these three levels?

Genre might be said to represent the reader's perspective in the book's second section, although it should be clear that genre can also function as a production blueprint for authors and that readers may, conversely, consider authorship as an interpretive strategy akin to a genre. Initially, we can identify the different kinds of articles or magazine genres in which the photos appear, as well as the specific nature of the relationship between the editorial text and the pictures. Comparative textual analyses of the photo-essays and the films needs to develop a system of correspondences between the codes and conventions of the photojournalistic and cinematic media, based on knowledge of magazine genres, on the one hand, and the Kubrick film genre, on the other. Genre has always competed with auteurism as an approach to meaning, because it displaces the origin of said meaning to a social space consisting of a set of labels that set up horizons of expectations, which are adopted by readers. A significant aspect of genre as a reading strategy is that its concerns are mainly semiotic, as compared with auteurism's evaluative dimension. It will be productive, therefore, to analyse distinctions between spot news and documentary or staged photographs, for example, as they speak to Kubrick's later interest in creating a kind of heightened realism in his films, even those belonging to fantasy genres. He always displayed a keen concern in establishing a plausible ambience, in order to facilitate the viewer's suspension of disbelief in his fictional narratives. Finally, one must guard against the temptation to apply one's knowledge of the "Kubrick genre," an after-the-fact construct based on a series of thematic and stylistic features culled from Kubrick's better-known work as a filmmaker, which is then used as an interpretive grid to read the photographs. Indeed, this may create the impression that Kubrick's artistic voice was always already fully formed, and that it simply expressed itself in several related media. Instead, this study makes an opposite claim, namely that Kubrick's identity as a creative person was the result of a process, and that it emerged gradually as it integrated a series of complex influences located in a specific cultural and historical context.

Chapter 6 will thus begin with an examination of photojournalistic genres according to their semantic, syntactic and pragmatic characteristics, borrowing from Rick Altman's theory of genre (1999, 207). A semantic analysis of the celebrity profile, for instance, would focus on the presence (or absence) of expected features such as a full-page glamour shot as an opener, images of the star resting at home, engaged in promotional activities, dating other stars, etc. If an essay were to present groups of people engaged in similar activities in specific institutional settings, then we would likely be dealing with a social study. A syntactic analysis would highlight the structural relationships between the essay's component parts, such as thematic oppositions between the public and the private in the celebrity story, or the combined use of narrative and rhetorical form in the social study. A pragmatic analysis would attend to the reader's engagement with photojournalistic discourse, in response to the magazine's use of realistic or documentary tropes (candid versus staged images), and its combination of information and entertainment value.

For example, Kubrick was assigned to photograph a social study about the new medium of television, providing instructive behind-the-scenes information, along with cheesecake content for male readers. The two-page essay titled "Ken Murray Tries Out TV Talent" (*Look*, May 9, 1950) contains five photographs, and presents vaudevillian Ken Murray as he auditions 250 "girls" for his variety TV show: they had answered an ad asking for "beautiful girls – no experience necessary". We are told that Murray's definition of "talent" boils down to "wholesome, natural" good looks, "the kind of girl you'd bring home," which the unpublished images suggest was partly linked to the women's cup size (Panzer 2005b, 442). Not surprisingly, Murray's sponsor was the Anheuser-Busch brewery, the maker of Budweiser beer. The opening photograph is a medium-shot of model Corky Brewster, seen in profile, smiling for the CBS television cameras (cf. Figure 3). Banks of studio lights are visible above her head, a camera to her right and a TV monitor to her left. The cameramen are almost invisible in the dark background. This image of modern technology would be revisited in *2001: A Space Odyssey* (1968) through the use of video monitors, providing multiple perspectives on a given subject, which also rhymes with the theme of the double, or the mediated nature of modern man. The CBS camera eye is also rearticulated in *2001: A Space Odyssey* as the computer HAL, who represents Kubrick's version of the cyclops from Homer's epic poem *The Odyssey*.

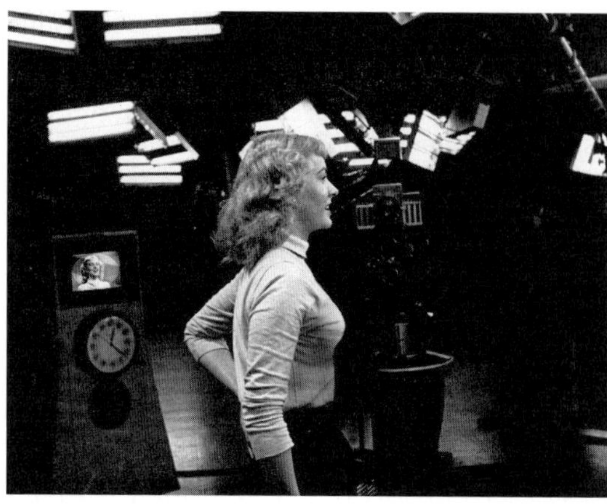

Figure 3: "Ken Murray Show"(1950).

Right below the opener is a medium shot of Ken Murray standing next to a camera, looking slightly to the right, wearing a hat and smoking a cigar in the studio. He is also identified by the caption as "a famous judge of girls," whom we might contrast with Humbert Humbert, the infamous character from Kubrick's film *Lolita* (1962), based on Vladimir Nabokov's novel. The second page includes three photographs, beginning with a frantic dressing room scene of contestants applying "the special make-up required to withstand the merciless, flat lighting necessary in television." A relaxed Murray leans against the same camera as on the previous page, minus the cigar, looking at model Cindy Cameron who smiles to a different camera off-frame. The last image provides us the second camera's head-on view of Ms. Cameron, with a wide roll-bar highlighting her face.

Chapter 7 shifts the generic focus to the photographic medium, arguing that the photo-essay is a fundamentally hybrid form combining photography and film, and that this mixed legacy contributed to Kubrick's eventual switch from photojournalistic production to filmmaking. It begins with a discussion on the nature of photography as well as the discursive functions of the photo-essay, such as photography's narrative aspects, its ability to trigger a fictional mode of reading and the semantically supplemental or oppositional relationship between word and image. This is followed by a historical examination of the photo-essay in the context of related, contemporary media, which contributed to blurring the distinction between photojournalism and film, and thus perhaps hastening Kubrick's departure from *Look*. The growing presence of serial photographs in newspaper journalism, including the use of the "machine-gun camera" from the mid-1930s onwards (a precursor to the motor drive), the layout style of family photo-albums, the popularity of the photo-novel and movie story magazines, the influence of newsreel documentaries and neo-realist fiction filmmaking in Europe and America, all point to an evolution in popular visual culture favouring moving pictures at the expense of still photography. Another symptom of the pictorial magazine's economic love affair with the cinema was the frequency of movie tie-ins, stories selected according to current Hollywood movie releases. For instance, Kubrick's July 4, 1950, story titled "12 Children – $75 a Week" is a two-page essay focusing on the Bova family from Stamford, Connecticut, and how they cope with six boys and six girls, ranging from 1 to 19 years of age. A comparison is explicitly made with the contemporary Hollywood film *Cheaper By The Dozen* (1950, Walter Lang), starring Clifton Webb as the patriarch of the turn-of-the-century Gilbreth family. *Look*'s editors no doubt hoped that the essay would benefit from the film's popularity, and from pointing out that such large families do not only exist in the realm of fiction or in a bucolic past. The Bovas live in a three-bedroom house, and 36-year-old mother, Stella, does all the cooking, cleaning and washing, and serves meals in two shifts. The eldest daughter does the ironing. The six photographs feature mostly smiling family members (a norm for family photos or home movies), and the body text argues that while their routine is strenuous, they "think it's fine."

Chapter 8 proceeds to develop a system of "transmedial" correspondences between the codes and conventions of the photojournalistic and cinematic media, based on a diagrammatic characterization of film form proposed by scholars David Bordwell and Kristin Thompson (Bordwell 1997, 168). A medium's formal systems (narrative, categorical, rhetorical, abstract, and associational forms) interact with the medium's stylistic system (mise-en-scène, cinematography, editing and sound). The resulting comparative analysis of film and the photo-essay highlights both similarities and differences between the media, including efforts made by magazine journalism to emulate film techniques, in an attempt to tap into the popular appeal of moving images and the glamour associated with Hollywood. These efforts apply especially to aspects of the photo-essay's stylistic system, in order to make up for the absence of a mobile frame and a soundtrack. The use of series photographs, in particular, may be viewed as the aesthetic equivalent to a long take or a camera movement, which leads us to hypothesize that Kubrick's later predilection for long takes as a filmmaker may find its origin in photojournalistic practices. Music and sound effects could not be conveyed in print form, however, voice-over narration and dialogue would be included as captions or in the body of the photo-essay's text. This appears, for instance, in Kubrick's two-page photo-essay titled "Off Guard in an Art Gallery" (*Look*, March 30, 1948), when he was assigned to cover the preview of a Salvador Dali exhibition at the Bignou Gallery in New York City, on November 25, 1947. The spread's bottom half uses two headlines to organize the Kubrick photographs thematically: "some came to look …" on page left, and "some came to talk …" on page right. This separation identifies two social functions of art show openings: the second one providing *Look*'s editors with an opportunity to supply likely dialogue for pictures featuring people engaged in animated conversations. According to one caption, Dali speaks "machine-gun French" with a small group that includes the wife of jeweller Pierre Cartier. In another picture, Dali talks to a wealthy Argentinian countess who owns five of his paintings. The Greek painter Aristodimos Kaldis is seen whispering something to his partner, and the caption adds that "critics, priests, socialites, actors mixed with plain millionaires." The closing photograph is isolated from the rest, printed as a "bleed picture" (i.e., extending to the edges of the page for added impact) and is a medium shot of Dali making a hand gesture. The "scythe-mustachioed artist" is quoted in the caption as he responds to criticisms of recurring motifs in his work: "Look at Raphael – Madonnas, Madonnas, Madonnas!" Related to dialogue is acting, which

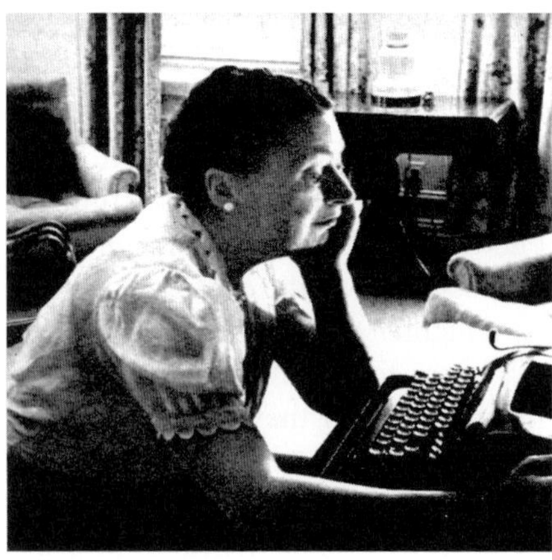

Figure 4: "Lady Lecturer" (1950).

our comparative analysis reveals to be the single most difficult dimension of filmmaking for a photojournalist to master. While the job of writing music or even photographing a film can be assigned to a specialist (the composer or the cinematographer), directing actors to deliver a sustained performance is a key responsibility of a movie's director, one that is not normally delegated. Unfortunately, it is a strictly dramatic or theatrical skill that Kubrick was not required to develop at *Look* magazine, and led to disappointing reactions upon the release of his first feature-length fiction film, *Fear and Desire* (1953).

The last chapter engages in a form of aesthetic archaeology, identifying photographic moments in Kubrick's films that are analysed as traces of his journalistic background. It is thus argued that the legacy of *Look* magazine reveals itself in a number of stylistic practices, such as the freeze-frame, the inset photograph, the zoom, long shots in which human figures are dominated by the setting, symmetrical compositions, frames within frames, deep space and available light. These practices highlight film's photographic pedigree, as well as others that point to a specifically journalistic origin, including the non-narrative structure of Kubrick's documentary shorts. The narrative fiction films also feature descriptive montage sequences, didactic narration, signs commenting on the action, and an ironic use of sound and picture combinations, all techniques rooted in the documentary photography one finds in post-war pictorial magazines. For instance, *Look*'s February 28, 1950, issue includes a profile of author Emily Kimbrough photographed by Kubrick and titled "Lady Lecturer Hits the Road." On the photo-essay's concluding page, a medium-shot of Kimbrough seated in her hotel room shows her leaning forward with elbows on the table, staring at the typewriter, in search of inspiration for a *New Yorker* story, a book or an article (cf. Figure 4). This image will be recycled in Kubrick's 1980 film *The Shining*, when Jack Nicholson's character also suffers from writer's block, but with a more dire resolution (Castle, 198). Naturalistic lighting is used in both cases, underscoring a consistent stylistic approach over a 30-year period. Such examples would only be coincidental if they were not so prevalent and did not form a systematic pattern. This book's project is to uncover the photojournalistic pattern underlying Stanley Kubrick's filmic oeuvre.

Chapter 1

Psychosocial Context: A Formative Period. Stanley Kubrick at *Look* Magazine in the Lifespan

A fundamental premise for this study is the banal yet crucial notion that a young person's formative years usually have a lasting impact on his or her professional development, yet most auteurist accounts of Kubrick's career either downplay or ignore this early period in his life. I therefore turn to basic concepts in developmental psychology that offer the advantage of focusing on commonalities between people rather than unique individual qualities (Bocknek, 16). In the case of an artist such as Stanley Kubrick, there can indeed be a temptation to eschew social-psychological concerns and assume, based on the perceived quality of his later films, that he was an exceptional individual who was mostly self-directed, primarily influenced by internal goals. The popular expression "no man is an island" suggests a different emphasis, and one may reasonably argue that it is more informative to consider the extent to which Kubrick conformed to a profile of the typical middle-class teenager. This approach will make it easier to properly assess the impact of Kubrick's years at *Look* magazine, and highlight the formative dimension of that life period. His tenure at *Look* coincides with the college years, specifically the period 17 to 22 years of age, identified by Daniel Levinson as the early transition to adulthood in terms of psychosocial development (Berk, 447). This period is also described as "more influential than any other period of adulthood," largely due to its transitional function in the lifespan (Berk, 435).

The young adult's development is the result of a complex interaction between personal talents and several factors included in the social-historical environment, such as cultural mores and family experiences (Bocknek, 23). Glen Evans and Millicent Poole describe two major kinds of "developmental frames," namely demographic variables (age, gender, parents' socio-economic status) and biographical factors such as type of school attended, work experiences and leisure activities (8). All of these frames vary in terms of their degree of generality: some apply to many young people, others are more specific. Among the most significant biographical factors, Gene Bocknek distinguishes between interpersonal relationships and intracultural expectations (Bocknek, 35). Important interpersonal relationships will naturally include family members, but also peers and mentors, both of which contribute in shaping and orienting career plans.

It is no secret that adolescents are directly affected by their peer group, and Bocknek argues that "fellow adolescents also provide reinforcement for experimentation with ideas, mores, and manners" (69). Although described as a loner in high school by biographer Vincent LoBrutto, Kubrick did nurture key friendships during his late adolescence and early adulthood, which helped him in identifying what he was most interested in (26). Between 1942 and

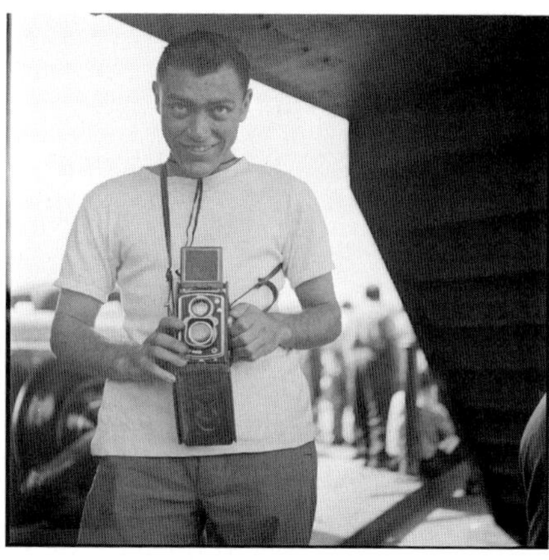

Figure 5: Alexander Singer caught by Kubrick with a Rolleiflex, June 1946.

1944, the Kubrick family lived at 2715 Grand Concourse in the Bronx, where 14-year-old Stanley met neighbour Marvin Traub, who shared a passion for photography and had his own darkroom: "When they weren't in the darkroom, they were out taking pictures and creating assignments for themselves as photojournalists" (LoBrutto, 12). LoBrutto adds that the showy tabloid photography of Weegee "was an early and significant influence on the fledgling adolescent photographers" (12). They likely saw Weegee's work in *PM Daily* and perhaps also at the Museum of Modern Art exhibition entitled "Action Photography" in 1943 (Naremore, 6). Evans and Poole point out that the media, as socializing influences, can also be considered important developmental frames (8). Kubrick photographed Frank Sinatra for *Look* magazine in October 1949, an assignment that may have brought back memories of Traub and himself getting "backstage passes to Sinatra concerts, where they would take pictures of the skinny Italian kid with the magnificent voice and snap photos of the screaming girls and adoring boys who dreamed of being Frankie" (LoBrutto, 15).

Kubrick remained friends with Traub and later photographed him for one of his early *Look* magazine assignments. Soon after entering Taft High School, he met another like-minded shutterbug with whom he spent many hours in the darkroom. Bernard Cooperman was a fellow member of the school's photography club, and they both worked on the Taft newspaper and magazine, documenting sports events and school plays (LoBrutto, 18). As with Traub, Kubrick and Cooperman went about town on spontaneous photography assignments, including a baseball game described by Cooperman in a way that may very well refer to Kubrick's photo-essay "Kids At A Ball Game," which appeared in the October 16, 1945, issue of *Look* (LoBrutto, 18).

Among Kubrick's peers in high school, it was Alexander Singer whose influence stood out (cf. Figure 5). As LoBrutto puts it, Singer "was a critical force in focusing Kubrick's destiny as a film director" (27). Singer later became a filmmaker himself, but unlike Kubrick, his background was in painting, not photography. Already familiar with Hollywood fare, Kubrick was introduced to European art cinema on trips to the Museum of Modern Art's film theatre with Singer (LoBrutto, 55). Kubrick was likely impressed by the fact that Singer "wrote stories and illustrated them for the *Taft Literary Art* magazine" (LoBrutto, 27). Kubrick was always in the process of learning how to express himself with still photographs, but it is through the combined influence of peers and exposure to *narrative* visual media (comic books, photomagazines and movies) that his ultimate vocation as a storyteller gradually emerged.

Singer graduated from Taft in June 1945, six months before Kubrick, and he was the first to consciously choose film over painting as a profession: "Singer's decision had a significant influence on Stanley Kubrick, who was quietly watching his friend's metamorphosis" (LoBrutto, 55). Singer began by writing an ambitious 125-page adaptation of Homer's *The Iliad* and illustrating it with 900 continuity sketches, and managed to get it to Metro-Goldwyn-Mayer (MGM) executive Dore Schary thanks to Kubrick's connections at *Look* magazine (LoBrutto, 55). When informed that MGM would not produce *The Iliad*, Singer wrote and storyboarded a simple, 20-minute story that he planned to direct, with Kubrick as cinematographer (Baxter, 34). According to Singer, Kubrick was so impressed by the thoroughness of his friend's work that he was bitten by the directorial bug, and now decided that he would not simply collaborate on a film project, he wanted to be the author (Baxter, 35). In what may have been a key moment in his life, "Stanley Kubrick used Alexander Singer's presentation of a director's cinematic ideas as a catalyst to inspire him to create, direct, and produce his first film" (LoBrutto, 57).

Singer received an assistant director credit for Kubrick's first film, *Day of the Fight*, and introduced the director to his composer friend Gerald Fried, who wrote music for Kubrick's first four feature films as well as *Day of the Fight* (Baxter, 38). Singer then made training films in the Signal Corps' photo unit, as part of his military service between 1950 and 1952, when he met James B. Harris, a young film distributor (LoBrutto, 109). He introduced Kubrick to Harris, who eventually produced three Kubrick films, *The Killing* (1956), *Paths of Glory* (1957) and *Lolita* (1962). This quick survey of three influential peers in Kubrick's late teens and early twenties should not be surprising, as it illustrates the contributions made by interpersonal relationships in a young person's development. It also highlights the extent to which Kubrick's emerging identity and worldview as an expressive person can usefully be described as a patchwork of influences resulting from the intersection between his personal aptitudes and social milieu.

The other significant type of interpersonal relationship in a young adult's life concerns mentors. There is a lingering tendency among older adolescents to continue the childhood process of modelling adults, that is, identifying with and imitating adults in their social roles (Bocknek, 192). Young adults gradually shift away from this dependency, becoming more autonomous and relating to peers as partners or competitors (Bocknek, 137). Daniel Levinson's theory of adult development identifies the mentor as a key influence in facilitating the young adult's conception of himself in the adult world (Berk, 448). This conception is called the dream, which guides the young person in his life decisions and can be most effective when it is precisely conceived or constructed (Berk, 448). Mentors may assist the

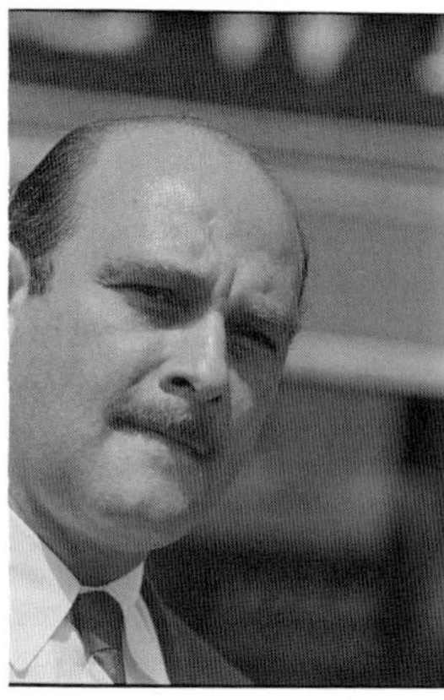

Figure 6: A Stanley Kubrick portrait of his father Jack, Summer 1946.

young adult in identifying and realizing his dream by functioning in three capacities: "as teachers who enhance the person's occupational skills; guides who acquaint the person with values, customs, and characters in the occupational setting; and sponsors who foster the person's career development" (Berk, 448).

Peers may act as mentors, although mentors are generally older colleagues at work, relatives, neighbours or friends (Berk, 448). There can be little doubt of Jack Kubrick's influence on his son, specifically in sharing his love of photography and chess (cf. Figure 6). Jack was an amateur photographer who, according to Kubrick's widow Christiane, "was passionate about photography and this passion was communicated to Stanley at an early age" (23). Biographer John Baxter adds that "for his thirteenth birthday Kubrick received from his father a gift that was also to have a far-reaching influence, a Graflex camera" (20). In a 1966 interview, Kubrick himself describes this influence in terms of developing problem-solving skills: "I became interested in photography [at the age of] 12 or 13. And I think that if you get involved in any kind of problem solving in depth on almost anything, it is surprisingly similar to problem solving of anything else. I started out by just getting a camera and learning how to take pictures, print, build a darkroom, all the technical things, then finally trying to find out how you could sell pictures and become a professional photographer" (Bernstein 2006, 314). It could be argued that acquiring problem-solving skills can more easily be attributed to the discipline of playing chess, and in any case the young Kubrick's hobbies neatly dovetailed into each other. As Kubrick explained it, "chess is an analogy. It is a series of steps that you take one at a time and it's balancing resources against the problem, which in chess is time and in movies is time and money" (LoBrutto, 19).

Jack Kubrick not only introduced his son to fascinating hobbies, but he and his wife Gert appear to have imbued Stanley with a great sense of self-confidence, a personal characteristic that certainly affects one's professional development (Berk, 472). As mentioned above, the Kubricks' socio-economic status played an important role. According to psychologist Stephen Hamilton, "several studies have found that more democratic and affectionate practices favoured by middle-class parents are more effective … in inculcating the attitudes and personal styles associated with middle-class status than the more authoritarian styles common among working-class parents" (124). Hamilton adds that parents who have complex jobs requiring judgement pass on the corresponding values to their children, specifically the importance of "becoming independent and creative" (125). The feeling of self-efficacy that follows from this style of upbringing can also be supported by an appropriate mentoring relationship, and Kubrick himself has acknowledged the impact of one of his teachers at Taft High School, Herman Getter, in contrast with the otherwise uninspiring context, which the school provided (LoBrutto, 30–31). Getter was the art teacher at Taft High, and is described by LoBrutto as an "encouraging influence on Stanley Kubrick's artistic nature …, a man whose primary goal as an educator was to motivate and inspire …, who concentrated on developing talents within his students rather than imposing a prescribed course on them. He created a stimulating environment for a young artist's mind" (28–29). In addition to being a teacher and a mural painter, Getter was a "lover and student of cinematography" who produced several films demonstrating art technique and held a patent for his invention the Project-O-Slide, used by physicians to review various aspects of medical procedures (LoBrutto, 29).

In his 1992 interview with LoBrutto, Getter related an early conversation he had with the young Kubrick, who expressed concern that he may not be able to graduate from Taft unless he took art as a major (LoBrutto, 29). Getter offered to look at Kubrick's artwork (drawings, watercolours, etc.) in order to confirm his eligibility for the major in art: "[Kubrick] said: 'Oh, I don't do that, I'm a photographer.' I said, 'Well, that's art.' When I said that, his eyes lit up! He suddenly found someone with whom he could talk" (LoBrutto, 29). If true, this brief episode would have been a significant revelation for the teenage Kubrick, who could now consider one of his hobbies in a different light, namely as an expressive medium that was valued not only by the commercial publishing industry, but also by society's loftier pursuits of art and learning. This revelation would presumably have preceded any trip to the Museum of Modern Art's photography exhibitions, and also affected Kubrick's conception of related media such as film. In fact, Getter showed Kubrick and classmate Alexander Singer his 16mm films as a means of discussing the technique and aesthetics of motion-picture photography (LoBrutto, 30). Both Kubrick and Singer were thus allowed to graduate thanks to Getter's supervision (LoBrutto, 29). During the production of *Spartacus* (1960) and after the release of *Barry Lyndon* (1976), Kubrick would reply to letters from his former teacher, expressing gratitude for the "stimulating film discussions" that Singer and himself had enjoyed in his class, as well as for being "an inspiration to him at a time when it was most critical" (LoBrutto, 30–31).

Psychologist J. J. Arnett points out that "emerging adults may be inspired to pursue a particular work path by the example of someone they admire. Teachers are mentioned quite often as providing such inspiration" (155). Mentorship implies a personal relationship; however, it is possible to admire and be influenced by someone by observing from a distance, particularly through the media. This person would not qualify as a mentor per se, but it does suggest a spectrum of constructive influences ranging from individuals to groups of people. Role models may thus be found in famous media personalities, as well as mentors in the strict sense, and collective forms of mentoring. Stanley Kubrick may have been inspired by the public work of Weegee to sell a picture to *Look* magazine in April 1945. He also received help from Herman Getter at Taft High School, and arguably from Photography Department Head Arthur Rothstein at *Look* magazine. Finally, the staff at *Look* constituted a kind of collective mentorship, also known as the "Bringing Up Stanley Club" (LoBrutto, 41).

The specific role of *Look* magazine in Stanley Kubrick's apprenticeship is analysed in the next chapter, but it should be clear from the above examination of peers and mentors that "what goes on inside people is only for conceptual purposes separate from the others with whom they are in contact. And no one can be understood without reference to cultural milieu, ethos, and expectations" (Bocknek, 34). Broadening the notion of mentor to include collective efforts at providing a nurturing environment should point towards developmental frames, which characterize the sociocultural context in which a young individual grows. These frames include intracultural expectations described by Gene Bocknek as "not society's highest aspirations for the individual but rather the way it defines psychosocial competence for any given stage" (37). For the life periods combining late adolescence and young adulthood, this competence includes the ability to make effective choices in school and at work, to achieve emotional independence, found a family and build a career (Bocknek, 35).

Choices in school were relatively limited, as the curriculum and pedagogy at Taft High were mostly traditional and uninspiring. However, Kubrick did manage to capitalize on some of its offerings: teachers such as Herman Getter and Aaron Traister did stimulate the budding artist, as did participation in the school's photography club and swing band, not forgetting contact with a few like-minded classmates such as Howard Sackler, who would later write the screenplay to Kubrick's first feature, *Fear and Desire* (Baxter, 25). Upon graduating from Taft in January 1946, young Kubrick was in a bind: the son of a doctor, he was expected to enter college, but was denied due to his low grades and to preference being given to returning servicemen on the G. I. Bill (LoBrutto, 33). He began taking night classes in the hope of qualifying eventually for college, but other factors conspired to lead Kubrick into an alternative form of schooling. It should be noted that until he was hired as an apprentice by *Look* magazine circa April 1946, he remained committed to pursuing a higher education, perhaps hoping that the freedom to choose his own major would prove more stimulating than Taft's prescribed curriculum.

The expanding post-war economy in the United States created a social context in which young people were more likely to search for full-time work immediately after high school, particularly since they typically married young and felt pressure to provide for their families (Arnett, 145). Kubrick was 19 when he married high school girlfriend Toba Metz, and they moved to Greenwich Village (Baxter, 31). Furthermore, only 20 per cent of young adults aged 18–24 had obtained some college education in America in 1946 (Arnett, 121). This figure would rise steadily, but Kubrick's road to university had been blocked long enough for him to consider learning on the job. Generally speaking, "the events of leaving school and getting a job are classical normative life span events," which supports the argument that Kubrick's years as a young adult were normative, not idiosyncratic (Evans & Poole, 74).

College was simply a way to get a formal education, and a young person could also receive a different kind of education that might be more appropriate to one's chosen profession. For instance, Grade 12 students have indicated that work experience programs "taught them people skills, job preparation, and business skills … that better prepared them for the job market upon graduation than did school" (Lerner, 161). Kubrick echoes this sentiment and highlights the fact that his tenure at *Look* coincided with the formative college years: "I was [at *Look*] for four years until the age of 21. And, of course, that would have been the period I'd have spent in college, and I think that what I learned and the practical experience, in every respect, including photography, in that four-year period exceeded what I could have learned in school" (Bernstein 2006, 316). High school students have also reported that working had a feedback effect, teaching them the importance of getting an education (Lerner, 161). Again, Kubrick makes a similar observation: "Getting out of school, I can't remember what was the particular turning point, I began to read and, within a relatively short period of time, caught up with where I probably should have been had I had a modicum of interest in things in high school. . . . I felt that I caught up pretty quickly when I became interested in things in general" (Bernstein 2006, 316).

Even though he refrains from identifying the "turning point" when he became "interested in things in general," the change in Kubrick as a learner coincided with his working years at *Look* magazine, and it has been observed that "many young people who do not learn well in school are diligent and adept learners in the workplace" (Lerner, 349). It could be argued that *Look* magazine's influence on Kubrick is enhanced not only by virtue of the fact that he was already passionate about photography, but also because he was doing his best to "catch up" and compensate for a sense of underachievement in school.

Gene Bocknek's model of adult development discusses three main factors: interpersonal relationships, intracultural expectations and intrapsychic issues (35). Intrapsychic issues concern a person's sense of identity, his or her own changing self-perception that shifts as a result of experiences with other individuals and negotiations with sociocultural expectations. My assumption has been that a belief in one's own ability, for instance, is necessarily affected by the personal and social contexts in which one grows, especially when we consider a relatively impressionable period in the lifespan. In other words, interpersonal, intracultural and intrapsychic issues are variables that "exist in constant dynamic interaction with one another" (Bocknek, 34). Not surprisingly, studies reveal that a wide range of psychological changes occur during the college years: as they gradually enter adulthood, young people develop improved reasoning skills, broaden their values and moral sense, and demonstrate an increased interest in "things in general," such as history and literature (Berk, 436).

Research indicates that no matter what kind of college (or the equivalent) is attended, psychological development occurs as a result of combining learning with extra-curricular opportunities and constructive contact with peers and other adults (Berk, 436). This does not minimize the significance of *Look*'s impact on Kubrick, but rather highlights the fact that late adolescence and early adulthood are formative periods regardless of where one spends them. Students themselves describe the college years as a time of great personal growth, related not to the quality of courses taken but instead to learning how to do many things for oneself for the first time (Arnett, 138). Becoming more organized and responsible is thus largely a consequence of the realities of leaving home, paying rent, juggling a part-time job with academic studies, and so on. These experiences impact on an emerging adult's identity and self-confidence, determining the development of self-concepts and orientations, that is, tendencies to particular ways of acting (Evans & Poole, 81). For instance, an individual's eventual preference for "self-directed action" (planning, problem-solving) or "other-directed action" (taking direct instruction, copying others) is not exclusively determined by that person alone (Evans & Poole, 82). Kubrick's predilection for problem-solving can thus be attributed not simply to chess-playing but also to the social context in which he worked and learned, as it "plays an important role in the expression of self-concept and a decisive formative and enabling role in the expression of orientations" (Evans & Poole, 82).

Biographers have made it clear that Kubrick's talent for photography had already been demonstrated by the time he sold his first photograph to *Look* in April 1945. However, this chapter has argued that the magazine's influence was more significant for his future career as a filmmaker, for two mutually reinforcing reasons. Firstly, it provided a four-and-a-half year professional experience, which was more than the culmination of his youthful experiments as a high school shutterbug, and which did more than nurture his interest in taking pictures. *Look*'s socializing influence cultivated discipline, responsibility, planning, problem-solving and a host of other valuable attributes that aided the success of Kubrick's career. It also required him to learn and polish specific skills concerning photographic story-telling, and to adopt the realist language of post-war magazine journalism, which provided a career-defining foundation in aesthetics. Secondly, these many life-lessons in how to work and conduct oneself professionally occurred at a crucial stage in Kubrick's growth as an individual. If it is indeed the case that the late teens are "more influential than any other period of adulthood," then from a developmental perspective, the impact of *Look*'s mentorship and training becomes all the more significant, one that should be virtually impossible for Kubrick scholars to dismiss. Not only did Kubrick's tenure as a photojournalist coincide with the college years, but *Look* magazine was in fact nothing less than the young man's substitute film school.

Chapter 2

Macro-objective Analysis: *Look* Magazine's Organizational Structure

Our sociological analysis of Stanley Kubrick's tenure at *Look* magazine begins with the macro-objective level of social reality, which concerns *Look*'s organizational structure. Sociologist George Ritzer lists the major components of the ideal-typical bureaucracy according to Max Weber: offices or departments are organized into a hierarchical system, with specific areas of expertise requiring participants to obtain appropriate training; the salaried staff does not own the means of production but is provided with the technology to do its job, and the organization is bound by rules recorded in writing (Ritzer, 83).

Gardner Cowles and the Ideology of *Look*

Look's hierarchy/structure

Look magazine was published by Cowles magazines, Inc., and founded in 1937 by Gardner (Mike) Cowles, a successful newspaper publisher from Des Moines, Iowa. The top of *Look*'s hierarchy included Cowles as editor-in-chief, along with associate, executive and managing editors, an art director and a picture editor. This was followed by several departments, each with its own head: ten writers and ten photographers, a women's department, art department, picture and editorial research, which added up to 103 permanent staff in 1946 (Cooperman, 151). In terms of its organizational structure, there does not appear to have been anything unusual about *Look* when compared to other magazines. Initially, *Look* was published in Iowa, along with its parent publications, the *Des Moines Register* and *Tribune*. Success led Mike Cowles to move the operations to New York City in 1940, which further formalized the organization's structure, with specialized departments and employees (Cooperman, 130).

This stratification was exacerbated during the war years, under the management of top editor Harlan Logan, who increased the number of committees and launched a book department and additional research departments, which were not directly related to the magazine (Cowles, 101). This created tensions with some of the other editors, but Cowles did not intervene, partly because he was absent during those years, having been asked by President Roosevelt to work for the Office of War Information (Cooperman, 145). He also felt that Logan's editorial approach, which favoured didactic and patriotic features, improved *Look*'s image for advertisers, one that had been originally conceived as relatively lowbrow and sensationalistic (Cooperman, 136). Cowles also appreciated Logan's professional approach, although the disproportionate amount of bureaucracy led to some inefficiencies and frictions with staff (Cooperman, 137). When the war ended, Cowles returned to *Look*, discontinued the extra-curricular departments and dismissed 58 non-essential employees. Harlan Logan resigned and was replaced by Dan Mich on November 26, 1946 (Cooperman, 149). With the exception of a three-and-a-half year hiatus, Mich was *Look*'s executive editor from 1946 to 1965, a period Cowles describes as its Golden Years (Cowles, 120). Stanley Kubrick's arrival at *Look* thus coincided with the transition from Logan to Mich as top editor. It bears mentioning that Kubrick joined *Look* during Logan's tenure, because although credit has been given to picture editor Helen O'Brian and managing editor Jack Guenther for his hire, it is possible that Logan may have suggested Kubrick's appointment as apprentice himself, or at least approved it. Indeed, the October 1, 1946, issue of *Look* includes an article written by Logan titled "The Hope of American Education," part of a series that recommended teaching arts at all levels and offering students as much experiential learning as possible, including apprenticeships, which is precisely what was being done for one of his young employees.

The transition from Logan to Mich brought about no change in the organization's structure as such, only a different editorial approach and production method, which necessarily affected the magazine's internal politics and the staff's morale. It thus fell on the top editors, particularly Cowles, to establish a particular organizational culture through the people they hired to implement effective production methods. According to Cowles, *Look* defined itself partly in opposition to its main competitor, *Life* magazine, known as the "Big Red One" (194). Published by Time, Inc., *Life* enjoyed far superior resources than *Look* (250 staffers, 28 bureaus worldwide, etc.), which allowed it not only to publish on a weekly basis, but also to follow breaking news more closely. *Life* could therefore outspend any of its rivals, which led *Look* to develop its own forte in well-researched, photographed and edited feature stories (Cowles, 194). Despite the increasingly professional approach favoured by *Look*'s administration during and after the war years, it may still have come across as a family operation in comparison with *Life* magazine.

It has often been observed that *Life*'s administrative style was more authoritarian than *Look*'s. John Billings, *Life*'s managing editor from 1937 to 1944, allegedly "ruled the magazine like an autocrat. … He did the layouts himself and edited all the copy" (Hoffer, 135–6). Similarly, Wilson Hicks, *Life*'s picture editor from 1937 to 1950, "favoured a rather strict separation of powers, … and was particularly negative and vocal in his belief that a photographer was too emotionally involved in the making of images to be of value in their editing" (Schuneman, 91). Mike Carlebach has claimed that Hicks was a hard taskmaster, and that photographers at *Life* were expected to implement editorial decisions: it had to be done *Life* founder Henry Luce's way, or else … (Carlebach). Photojournalism at *Life* was thus an editor's medium, not a photographer's medium. Author George Leonard, who was a senior editor at *Look* from 1960 to 1971, refers to *Life*'s approach as "the production-line method," whereas *Look* "employed what might be called the craft system" (Leonard, 17). These differing administrative styles appear to have directly affected the magazines' modes of production as well as their editorial content and tone. *Look*'s system, also referred to as "personal journalism," would produce inconsistent but surprising results, whereas *Life* was consistent and predictable: "*Life*'s production line yielded a reliable level of professionalism, issue after issue. *Look*'s craft system depended on the abilities of individual senior editors, and those abilities varied considerably" (Leonard, 19).

Look's personal journalism had an impact on the degree of involvement of photographers in particular. Stanley Tretick, a staff photographer at *Look* from 1961 to 1971, states that photographers had a lot of input, and that he was able to work on stories that interested him (Tretick). Similarly, Cal Bernstein, who was a *Look* photojournalist from 1959 to 1961, states that there was a lot of freedom at *Look*, and that the production process was collaborative (Bernstein). Paul Fusco was a staff photographer at *Look* from 1957 to 1971, and claims that *Look*'s strength was that everyone had a voice (Fusco). Fusco worked for *Life* after *Look* folded, and discovered that not only did Henry Luce's voice permeate all the stories that were created, but that he was no longer allowed to work on the layouts, as he had been at *Look* (Fusco). In contrast, *Look*'s executive editor Dan Mich allowed a story on the Berlin Wall to appear in the January 15, 1963 issue, even though he disagreed with foreign editor Bob Moskin's thesis: "That was the greatest compliment Dan could have given me. He published my article even though he disagreed with it. That was what *Look* was all about" (Cowles, 199).

Look's tone/ideology

When Kubrick joined *Look* in 1946, the magazine was about to complete a final shift in tone and modus operandi. Cowles' initial idea had been to produce a monthly, feature-oriented picture magazine printed on inexpensive paper, targeting a downscale audience (Cowles, 59). *Look*'s first managing editor, Vernon Pope, required stories to be edited for a mass readership: "Pope would instruct the staff to slant all material for the hypothetical average American, 'Sadie Glutz.' His standard saying was, 'If Sadie can't understand it, then it's no good'" (Cooperman, 76). *Look* thus started as a relatively brash, sensationalistic tabloid magazine, which achieved excellent sales at the newsstand, but also created an image that alienated many advertisers (Cowles, 62). *Look* was quickly converted to a biweekly, and efforts were made to raise the level of its content by adopting a policy that would change the publication to a general interest, family magazine (Cooperman, 115). Most notably, a series of essays on civil liberties published in the Fall of 1937, focusing on racism, freedom of religion, child labour, slum life, and so on, drew praise from the general press at the time and led to a tradition of doing civil rights stories, particularly in the 1960s, when *Life* was hesitant to deal with such issues (Cooperman, 118). "Where *Life* passed judgements generally aligned with those of the power elite, *Look* raised questions the power elite had never thought of" (Leonard, 19).

The move towards respectability included a sharp reduction in sensationalistic material and an increased ratio of text-to-images in order to attract more advertisers, as well as efforts to achieve subscription-based income rather than rely on newsstand sales, which led to a less brash, quieter tone: "The magazine no longer had to shout its presence on the dealer's rack" (Cooperman, 127). However, Cowles' decision to move the *Look* offices to New York City in 1940 and hire Harlan Logan as managing editor may have led the magazine too far down the path of respectability (Cooperman, 131). While Logan hired a new art director and made sure the writing improved, "the brassy tone of the Pope era was giving way to a quiet grayness" (Cooperman, 136). Cowles himself would admit that *Look*'s wartime essays, while patriotic and contributing to the magazine's prestige, "were often dull and boring. They were particularly lacklustre in contrast to *Life*" (Cowles, 100). This sentiment resulted in a post-war editorial readjustment to what became *Look*'s hallmark style, which Cowles attributes to the new managing editor, Dan Mich: "Mich's editorial philosophy was much closer to that of Vernon Pope than Harlan Logan. Like Pope, he was anxious to surprise, enthral, delight, and inform the reader" (Cowles, 101).

It is this philosophy that Stanley Kubrick worked under, and provides a useful context from which to evaluate the future filmmaker's well-researched and entertaining movies. It has been argued that *Life*'s Henry Luce wanted to focus on the news and educate more than entertain, whereas Cowles felt that "picture stories should be inherently interesting," a distinction that can have aesthetic implications to the extent that it qualifies photojournalism's realist or documentary impulses (Cooperman, 84). While the distinction is admittedly broad, it does relate to some of Kubrick's later pronouncements on film aesthetics, particularly the notion borrowed from Stanislavsky that while realism is good, "interesting" is better (Strick & Houston, 131).

In terms of their political ideologies, scholar James Guimond has argued that the two photo-magazines were similar in many respects, sharing a basic optimism in and commitment to "capitalist realism," and providing a showcase for the values of the American middle-class (152–3). Among the differences, Guimond finds that *Life*'s photo-essays were often sensationalistic and showy, their editorial comments brash, even chauvinistic, whereas *Look*'s essays were visually subtler, and editorially calmer, more liberal and willing to identify social problems in the United States: "By American standards of the time, *Look* had better taste and considerably more 'class' than *Life* did" (153). This contrasts with *Look*'s more humble, lowbrow beginnings.

Cowles' ideology/personal comments on SK

Vincent LoBrutto describes Cowles as "a lifelong Republican with liberal ideas," a rather vague characterization that might also apply to Kubrick's films, if we consider their tendency to combine a masculinist discourse with sharp criticisms of the political and military establishments (35). Perhaps Kubrick was a lifelong Democrat with conservative ideas, but in any case he was always reluctant to identify his political leanings in interviews, other than admitting to a belief in parliamentary democracy and the need for the State to ensure both public safety and social freedoms (Ciment 2003, 163). In his memoirs, Cowles suggests that his own intermediate or qualified political stance resulted from the combined influences of the top two editors of the *Des Moines Register* and *Tribune*, his father Gardner Sr. and Harvey Ingham (12).

Cowles describes his father as a conservative man who began his career in banking prior to building a newspaper empire, and was elected as a Republican to the Iowa legislature in 1899, where he remained for two terms (9). Mike Cowles and his older brother John, who would later become *Look*'s Chairman of the Board, worked at the family newspaper during summers, where "they 'apprenticed' in all departments, learning Cowles brand of journalism from the ground up" (Cooperman, 34). Ingham was a friend of Gardner Sr., even though he held liberal views such as opposing slavery, war, the excesses of big business, and supported the labour movement and internationalism (Cowles, 12). Cowles makes it clear that Ingham "became my idol and one of the most important influences in my life. … He also profoundly shaped my sense of an editor's role" (Cowles, 21). Although Cowles does not acknowledge this, he may have seen a bit of Harvey Ingham in *Look*'s executive editor Dan Mich, a man once described as "totally fearless, a crusader for the poor and the powerless, an avowed foe of entrenched power – and Republican programs. Intolerance of any sort infuriated him" (Rosten, 23). Even though he remained principally involved in the business side of *Look*'s affairs, Cowles' journalistic openness to opposing views trickled down to the editorial staff, who always felt free to pursue their own voice (Bernstein). Editor Leo Rosten has stated that he knew of "no magazine where the 'boss' was less partisan, more reasonable, and more determined to publish the widest possible spectrum of opinions" (22). It has in fact been argued that *Look*'s editorial line was liberal, despite Cowles being a moderate Republican, and that *Look* had a policy of presenting a balanced view as a means of reaching a wide audience (Carlebach). Rosten further claims that "*Look*'s spacious editorial policy flowed from the ease, the diversity, and the rock-bottom democracy of those who created each issue. These qualities Cowles respected, and he encouraged them by his own example" (22).

Cowles' influence on Kubrick, as founder and editor of *Look* magazine, was thus indirect, and concerned the identity of the photo-magazine itself. Had Kubrick sold his first photograph to the *New York Daily News*, as he considered doing in April 1945, or even to *Life* magazine, his future development might have been different (LoBrutto, 20). Indeed, the *New York Daily News* was a tabloid, and *Life* magazine was a weekly that covered the news, whereas *Look* was a fortnightly focusing on feature articles. If Kubrick had worked for the other two publications, he might have been directed towards spot news photography, and not had the same opportunity to contribute to the longer photo-essay format, which shares a closer affinity with fiction film.

Stanley Kubrick's own impact on the *Look* organization, including its top administration, can only be assessed after the fact, based on documents that may have deliberately sought to highlight the association between the magazine and its former staff photographer, now an accomplished and celebrated filmmaker. For instance, *Look* founder and editor Mike Cowles' memoirs, published in 1985, include a Kubrick portrait of boxer Rocky Graziano waiting before the call to the ring: "Stanley Kubrick, a filmdom great, in his teens was a *Look* photographer.

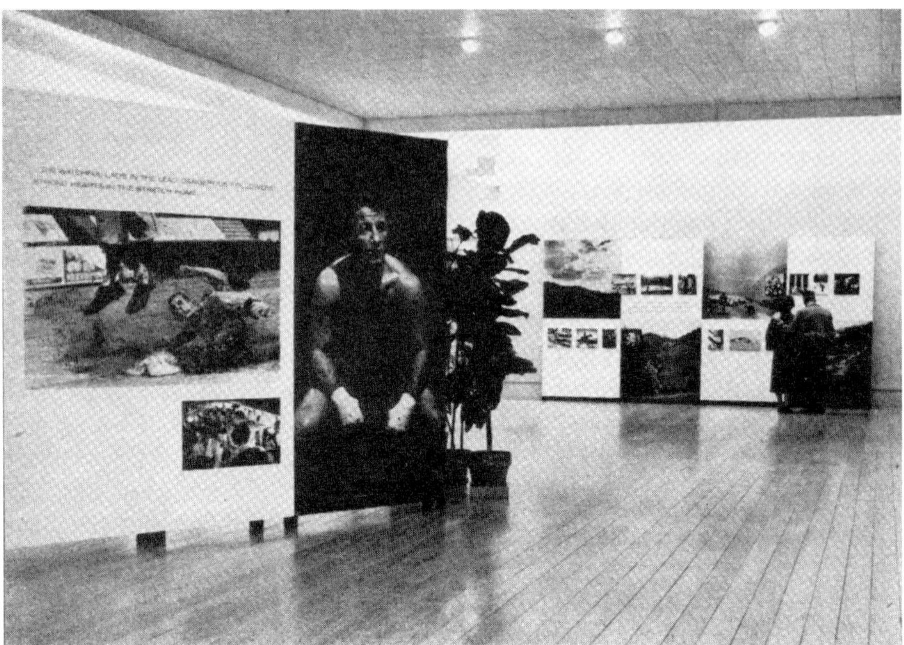

Figure 7: 1957 *Look* magazine exhibition, including Kubrick's portrait of Rocky Graziano.

Here he caught Rocky Graziano in pre-bout tension" (147). Cowles does not mention that the same portrait of Graziano, first published in the February 14, 1950 issue of *Look*, was selected in 1957 for a nationwide travelling exhibition of photographs titled *Look at America*, jointly curated by the American Federation of Arts and *Look* magazine. The April 30, 1957 issue of *Look* includes an article on its last page explaining that the exhibition featured 185 enlarged prints divided into ten themes. The Graziano portrait, named *Rage in his fists*, was printed six by eight feet high for the exhibition, and is one of only two photographs that appear in the article (cf. Figure 7). However, Kubrick's name is not mentioned in the credits, unlike Bob Sandberg's, who was still on *Look*'s staff in 1957. To emphasize the quality of the exhibition, the text informs us that it took months to select "from the thousands upon thousands of memorable *Look* photos." Either to justify an artistic look at photojournalism outside the magazine context or to indicate an appreciation for the contribution of photographers to *Look*, the article concludes with a statement that implicitly concerns Kubrick: "*Look* photographers are more than skilled picture-takers. They are observers, interpreters, students of human nature. They are visual communicators … pictorial reporters."

Paths of Glory was only released after the photo exhibition's run, on Christmas Day, 1957; thus Kubrick's name was not yet a prestigious, marketable commodity that *Look* would have been keen to exploit. The fact that his work continued to be selected by *Look* editors in commemorative publications without regard to the photographer's identity should confirm its enduring impact on Kubrick's "Alma mater." In fact, *Look* did publish a picture book in 1958 based on the *Look at America* exhibit, titled *Our Land, Our People*, with two Kubrick photographs included. A preface also points out the time-consuming process that led to the selection of 157 photographs (Hamilton & Preston, 14). Significantly, a technical appendix at the end of the book mentions the names of all the photographers, as well as technical information regarding the lens aperture, shutter speed, camera and film type used for each picture (Hamilton & Preston, 209–11). This suggests that the photographers' names may have appeared in the travelling photo exhibit as well, in which case observant cinephiles may have noticed Kubrick's name and identified the director of *The Killing* and perhaps *Killer's Kiss*.

In 1975, four years after *Look* folded, Abrams, Inc. published *The Look Book*, a 400-page commemorative book showcasing some of the best articles and photographs that had appeared in *Look* magazine's 34-year history. Three pictures taken by Kubrick are included, although only the aforementioned portrait of Graziano is attributed to its photographer. Printed full-page as a bleed-picture, with the descriptive caption "the numbed daze of despair," is Kubrick's first published photograph of a newsstand in the Bronx after President Roosevelt's death (Rosten, 59). It is not insignificant that this early photographic effort by Kubrick should be granted an almost iconic presentation, since the photographer's identity may not have been known to editor Leo Rosten. In other words, the picture was chosen strictly for its intrinsic quality, combining a historic moment with an expressive composition.

Another indirect reference to the impact of Kubrick's work in Cowles' memoirs concerns a lost advertising contract: "After a lengthy sales effort, ... we convinced Campbell Soup to become a *Look* advertiser. But just before its schedule of insertions was due to start, we published an issue containing a black and white photograph of artist Peter Arno in his studio sketching a nude model – not a frontal view, as later became common in *Playboy*, but a discreet, semi-back view. That was the end of the Campbell Soup business for some time to come" (113). The offending picture was a full-page photograph taken by Kubrick and published in the September 27, 1949 issue of *Look*. Kubrick would later renew his dealings with public controversy with the European ban on *Paths of Glory* and the X-rating of *A Clockwork Orange*.

Executive editor Dan Mich

Aside from Cowles' role as founder of *Look* magazine, the person most responsible for setting the tone and the organizational climate of *Look* would be the executive editor (cf. Figure 8). Dan Mich served in this capacity from 1946 until his death in 1965, with a three-year hiatus in the early 1950s (Cooperman, 152). He had been a managing editor under Vernon Pope and Harlan Logan, until promoted by Mike Cowles when Logan resigned in November 1946. Cowles attributes much of *Look*'s success to Mich's editorial style, which he describes as flexible, not bound by a formula (Cowles, 190). Mich seemingly wanted

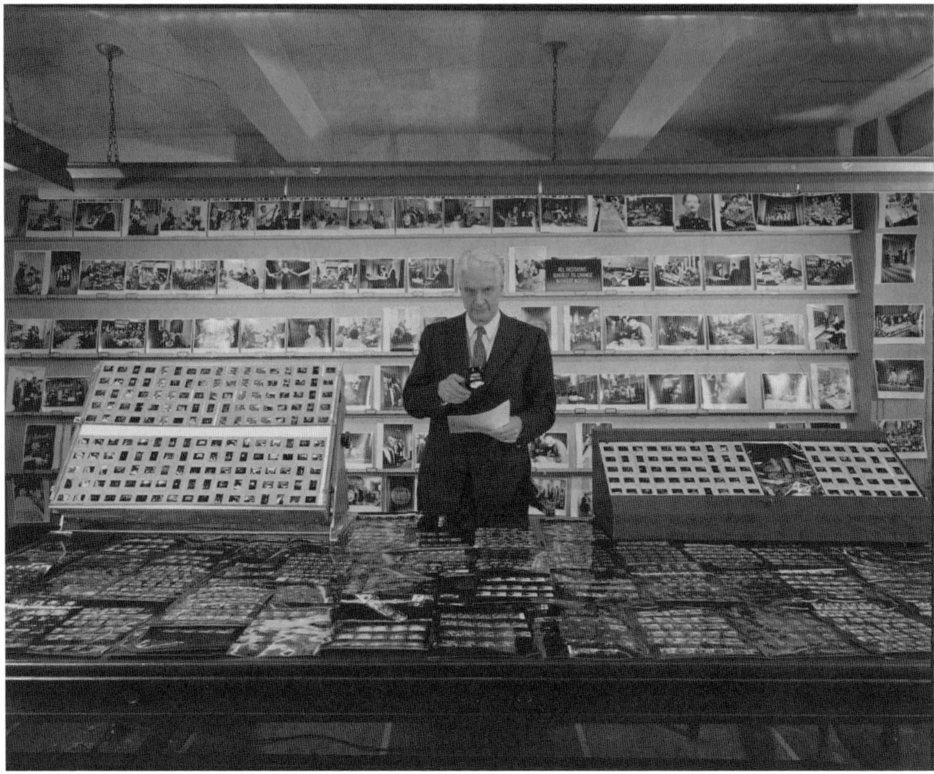

Figure 8: Arthur Rothstein portrait of *Look*'s Executive Editor Dan Mich (1958).

magazine stories to be "a personal dialogue between the writer, photographer and editor," and encouraged editors to create less didactic stories than had been produced during the war years, focusing instead on informing the reader with an entertaining twist (Cowles, 102). Although Mich's approach represented a return to some of the populist values espoused by Pope, he did not "instruct the staff to slant all material for the hypothetical average American" (Cooperman, 76). Instead, he was keenly aware of the demographic range of *Look*'s readership, and argued that "there is no such thing as a mass audience. ... Mass communications boils down, as conversation does, to one individual talking to another" (Cowles, 199). The speaker in this conversation was the story's writer, not simply *Look*'s executive editor. The writer was also encouraged to communicate his or her point of view, in a way that would be easy for any reader to identify, if not agree, with. In the words of senior editor George Leonard, the story's writer should be saying: "This is who I am, this is what I found, and this is what it means to me" (Cowles, 199).

Thus, Mich's key contribution was developing a brand of personal journalism that distinguished *Look* from *Life* magazine: "In *Look*, an education feature is not a pictorial essay on teaching systems. Instead, one finds a closeup portrait on a specific teacher, a specific pupil. Religion would not be an abstract preachment. It would be a minister, his family, members of his congregation" (Cooperman, 176). According to George Leonard, *Look* "was personal to a fault," in contrast to *Life*'s cool, impersonal, detached stance, which revealed itself emblematically in a recurring photograph: "An entire organization with all its equipment – say an army tank battalion – would be spread out on a concrete tarmac and photographed from a high angle. In these pictures, the human individual was shown as I suspect *Life* really saw him – as a chess piece that had its proper and clearly delineated role to play in an organizational or ideological scheme" (Leonard, 18).

Responses to Kubrick's later film style would typically reference chess and intellectual distance as well, except that such broad characterizations are descriptively inadequate and require further qualification. Indeed, Kubrick's films remain emotionally engaging, in part because they never eschew plausible representations of human, interpersonal relationships. If Kubrick's films do tend to adopt a lofty, cerebral perspective, they owe their emotional impact to a grounding in, if not a foregrounding of, the kind of "human interest" psychology that Dan Mich required of *Look*'s writers. Even though the typical *Look* story may have been "personal to a fault" and contained its fair share of "schmaltz," it remained for Kubrick a helpful means of mastering effective storytelling techniques (Tretick).

This tendency towards the sentimental at *Look* may be attributed to Mich who, according to Leonard, "favoured the underdog. He was fiercely partial to the poor, the weak, the downtrodden, the dispossessed, the victim of prejudice or injustice of any kind. This partiality was not in the least intellectual or philosophical. It came from the heart" (Leonard, 20). Kubrick has stated that while he did not "mistrust sentiment and emotion," he also refused to make films that ingratiated themselves with the audience if it meant sacrificing "a true picture of life" for a falsely hopeful message (Cahill, 198). He nevertheless admired the craft of a Frank Capra, whose photojournalistic correspondent may have been Dan Mich. Moreover, in his advice to writers, Mich emphasized the importance of researching a topic thoroughly, striving to "learn 10 times as much about it as would seem necessary for the space allotted" (Schuneman, 128). This systematic approach sounds similar to Kubrick's modus operandi when researching projects such as the aborted film *Napoleon*.

Mich allegedly "couldn't bear to see any animal hurt or killed," but he was no softy as an administrator, his authority and influence was unmistakable (Leonard, 20). Freelance photographer Andrew St. George sold a story to *Look* on Fidel Castro, and reported that Mich "had the appearance of a Renaissance archbishop and wielded approximately the same power" (Leonard, 20). *Look* photographer Cal Bernstein was impressed by Mich's strict policy of not accepting subsidies from companies when the magazine chose to do a story on them, and by his refusal to allow celebrities to select their own pictures (Bernstein). Photographer Paul Fusco observed that Mich was demanding but fair, and respected his journalistic instincts as to what would sell the magazine and keep readers away from television (Fusco).

Since Mich was "king of all he surveyed, … *Look* staffers spent hours trying to figure out [his] pet likes and dislikes" (Leonard, 20). While Mich held the power of veto on any given story, photographers were free to contribute to most phases of the production process, and *Look*'s high published-to-killed ratio, approximately 90 per cent according to Cal Bernstein, was an added encouragement to follow one's muse. Dan Mich's editorial process was relatively fluid and informal (Cowles, 188). In contrast, *Life* magazine's picture editor Wilson Hicks favoured a strict separation of powers, photographers seldom being granted editorial control (Schuneman, 91). *Look*'s editorial board met once a week, and accepted input from everyone on the board, including the picture editor. Staff members were invited on occasion to pitch story ideas. The exact number of assignments initiated by Kubrick himself is hard to know, and while a 1948 interview published in *The Camera* magazine suggests that half of his assignments were based on his own ideas, the percentage was likely lower (Stagg, 40). However, it is common practice among newspaper editors to use their photographers' areas of interest in determining assignments (Bolack, 27). Given Kubrick's own interest in sports and jazz music (he was a drummer in high school), it is no surprise to discover that he photographed several boxing and baseball stories, as well as some nightclub jazz performances.

Mich's tenure at *Look* is inextricably bound with that of Fleur Cowles, an ambitious journalist who had previously worked in the fashion and advertising industries (Cooperman, 153). She married Mike Cowles on December 27, 1946, shortly after Mich had been promoted to executive editor and Kubrick to staff photographer. Fleur quickly became the supervisor of *Look*'s Special Editorial unit, a.k.a. the woman's section including food, fashion and home living (Cooperman, 155). She eventually became an associate editor, and launched the revolutionary *Flair* magazine in February 1950, although it had to cease publishing a year later due to unusually high production costs. Fleur Cowles' involvement with *Look* was significant both in terms of the magazine's politics and its editorial betterment. Mike Cowles had recently made efforts to improve *Look*'s presentation: new

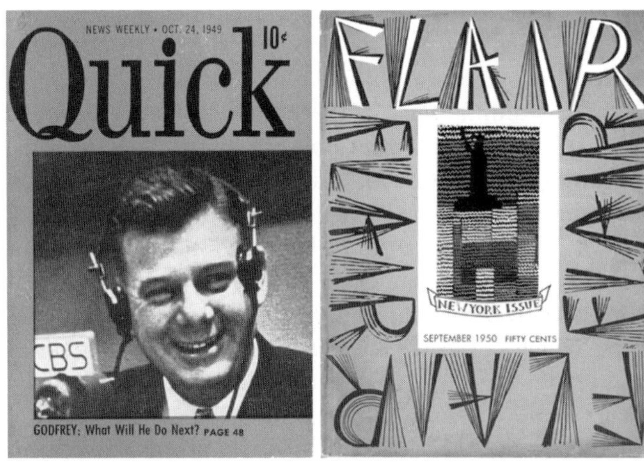

Figure 9: Issues of *Quick* (1950) and *Flair* (1951) magazines.

paper was used, parts of the magazine were printed by letterpress instead of rotogravure, and Merle Armitage, a type expert and book designer, was hired as the new art designer (Cooperman, 155). With Fleur Cowles in charge of a consolidated Special Editorial section, *Look* could confirm its transformation from a barbershop tabloid to "America's Family Magazine." Fleur had an eye for talent, and congratulated Kubrick on his portrait of German expressionist painter George Grosz in an office memo (Phillips 2005, 268). She also used a Kubrick portrait of Montgomery Clift for the September 1950 issue of *Flair*, the "New York Issue."

Fleur Cowles directed the woman's section as an independent unit, and it appears that her management style alienated some of the staff and created tensions with other editors, including Dan Mich (Cooperman, 156). Mich's decision to leave *Look* in July 1950, a month prior to Kubrick's own departure, was due to three factors: running disagreements with associate editor Fleur Cowles, an opposition to the publication of the weekly news magazine *Quick* as well as *Flair*, which he felt were diverting resources from *Look*, and an attractive offer from *McCall's* as editorial director (Cooperman, 167). Since the new executive editors proved to be relatively unsuccessful replacements, Cowles eventually managed to convince Mich to return to *Look*, on January 25, 1954 (Cooperman, 168). It should be noted that *Flair's* last issue had appeared in January, 1951, and that Cowles discontinued *Quick* after the June 1, 1953, issue (cf. Figure 9). Fleur divorced Mike Cowles in the summer of 1955 and moved to Europe, acting as *Look's* foreign correspondent (Vachon papers, Box 3, Folder 12). Mich was now free to edit *Look* as he saw fit, and the staff welcomed his return (Cowles, 120).

Technical Director of the Photography Department: Arthur Rothstein

As a member of the photographic staff, Kubrick's immediate boss would have been his Department Head, Arthur Rothstein (cf. Figure 10). The likely influence of Rothstein on Kubrick's development as a photojournalist cannot be easily dismissed. Rothstein was a former photographer for the Farm Security Administration (FSA), and achieved notoriety recording the plight of rural folk during the depression, as did John Vachon who was also hired by *Look*. Carl Mydans was another FSA alumnus who worked for *Life* magazine, and has commented on the FSA's influence on publications such as *Life*, *Look* and *Paris-Match*, that is, on photojournalism worldwide (Mydans). These photo-magazines inherited many of the FSA's techniques and interests, such as the format for assignment sheets, which were based on a model developed by the FSA's photography section Head, Roy Stryker (Barth). Gary Cooperman notes that "picture magazines of the late-1930s made extensive use of the honest, documentarian approach which Stryker had helped to pioneer" (17). Miles Barth, who curated an exhibition on Rothstein's documentary photography in the Fall of 1994 at the International Center of Photography in New York City, has stated that Rothstein learned much from Roy Stryker, particularly in his capacity as manager of *Look's*

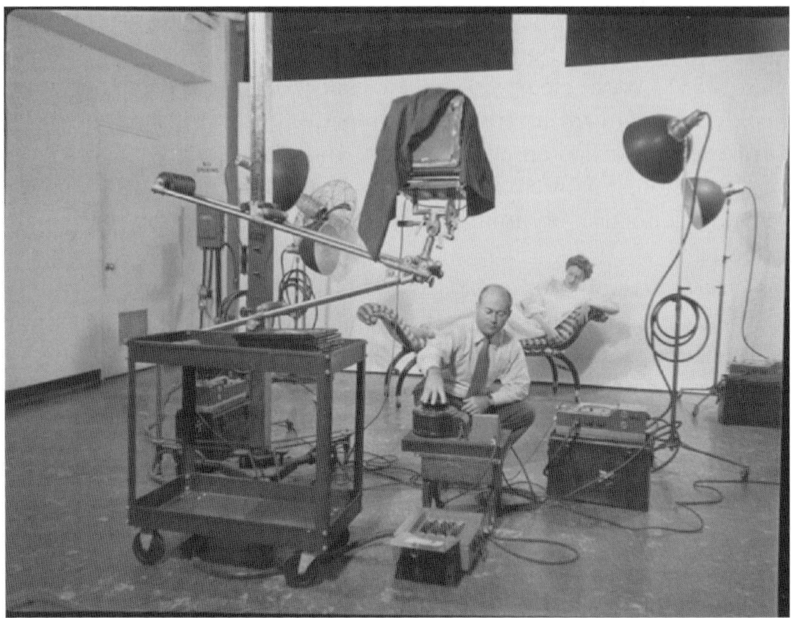

Figure 10: Self-portrait of Arthur Rothstein in the *Look* photo studio (1952).

photography department (Barth). Rothstein also organized exhibitions of his own work based on his reputation as an FSA photographer, was well connected with photography luminaries such as Beaumont Newhall and Edward Steichen, and much sought after as a teacher (Barth).

Professor of Journalism John Peterson confirms that Rothstein was a teacher and a mentor at *Look*, and that he formed many photographers such as Steve Shames and Chester Higgins (Peterson). He adds that Rothstein's textbook on photojournalism has been used in many journalism schools, and that his legacy is thus ensured thanks to his writings (Peterson). *Look*'s Paul Fusco has also praised Rothstein's abilities as an instructor, including the way he allowed photographers to work independently (Fusco). In an interview published in 1978, Rothstein himself cited Stanley Kubrick as one of his apprentices: "The greatest satisfaction an older photographer can have in his work is helping younger photographers achieve something. I helped Kubrick in his early days when he was a staff photographer at *Look*" (Rupp, 38). It is common practice for photography directors to assign experienced "photographers to serve as mentors to younger staff members" (Bolack, 36). Rothstein shared at least ten different assignments with Kubrick, and the young photographer was certainly smart enough to know when he had an opportunity to learn. Peterson also describes Rothstein as a problem-solver, another quality that Kubrick would have appreciated: Rothstein managed to get separate electrical supply to the photo studio from the rest of the *Look* building, to avoid the shifting voltage when the elevators ran.

The six-stage photo-essay production process at *Look* magazine, as described by Rothstein in his textbook *Photojournalism*, includes many opportunities for a picture editor or a director of photography to interact with his or her photographers. During the third stage, when the photographer is assigned to a story, part of the picture editor's job is to inspire and stimulate his photographers (Rothstein, 131). Editors expect photographers to demonstrate initiative, creative thinking and an eye for the unusual, which could certainly apply to Kubrick (Rothstein, 131). In return, "the photographer expects the picture editor to give him as much information as possible before going out on assignment, to fight for his rights, and to make him a part of the editorial operation" (Rothstein, 131).

The fourth stage is location shooting, when the writer and the photographer travel together "in the field," using the shooting script as a guide. Departures from the script often occur, which requires a certain flexibility. Kubrick would later comment on being able to adjust to "the reality of the final moment" and take advantage of an opportunity, even if it meant exposing weaknesses in the script (Strick & Houston, 134). Rothstein mentions the importance of coverage, the notion that since film is cheap, one might as well shoot as much as possible from various angles, to provide the layout artist with a greater range of options (12). This logic is virtually identical to Kubrick's practice during his film career, made infamous in particular by his numerous takes of certain scenes, which drove some actors to exhaustion (LoBrutto, 431). Rothstein also discusses the manipulation of images, a controversial issue in journalism, as a means to produce more effective photographs: he argues that "in order to make a scene more forceful it is sometimes desirable to distort or accentuate the effect by photographic means" (121).

Rothstein staged his famous 1936 photograph of a bleached steer skull in the South Dakota Badlands by moving the skull ten feet for dramatic effect. He was accused by some of faking the photograph to make conditions look worse than they were (Rothstein, 20). The staged photograph is a staple of the photojournalistic medium, highlighting its long-standing combination of documentary and fiction. Kubrick would continue to make this a central feature of his film style, always seeking to find the interesting or slightly surreal element embedded in a realistic situation (Strick & Houston, 131). Re-enactments and staging photographs "forces the photographer to become not only a camera man but also a scenarist, dramatist, and director as well" (Rothstein, 121). Rothstein's willingness to stage a documentary photograph for the camera's benefit may thus have impressed Kubrick, who was compared to a sponge, in terms of his ability to learn, by a film editor that he consulted in the early 1950s (LoBrutto, 73).

The dramaturgical and cinematic references underscore the parallels between photojournalism and film, which continue in the fifth stage of production of the photo-essay, assembly, that includes the selection of pictures and the layout. The film equivalent is editing, and photographers were not normally included in the layout process, although *Look*'s modus operandi was relatively generous. Rothstein mentions some basic principles in photographic layouts, which can be shown to have impacted on Kubrick's film editing practices. He mainly emphasizes the importance of creating various contrasts in order to avoid monotony: contrasts in scale, tone or subject can maintain reader interest (Rothstein 1979, 173). Rothstein's reference to contrasts in lines (verticals, horizontals, diagonals …) is reminiscent of Sergei Eisenstein's theories of montage, which he would have been introduced to in the late 1940s from reading Jay Leyda's translations of the Soviet filmmaker's essays (LoBrutto, 37). Kubrick was also interested in Eisenstein's theories, an influence that is noticeable in his early documentary films (Duncan, 25–8), as well as in a scene from his first fiction film, *Fear and Desire* (Chion, 17). Ironic contrasts achieved through editing would become a staple of Kubrick's later work.

Given all these cinematic references, it should be no surprise that Rothstein had an interest in motion pictures, and he owned a collection of film books, which Kubrick borrowed and even annotated (LoBrutto, 37). The papers of Arthur Rothstein at the Library of Congress include a page Xeroxed from Rothstein's copy of *Film Technique* by V. I. Pudovkin in which a passage concerning point-of-view editing has been underlined by Kubrick. The excerpt from Pudovkin's book is part of a three-page, typed document written by Rothstein circa 1980, about Kubrick at *Look* magazine: "At that time, more than thirty years ago, we had three things in common: a passion for chess, photography and film-making. Stanley was a much better chess player, but I knew a little more about films" (Rothstein).

As a photographer, Rothstein perfected the technique of including signs in his compositions, using them as built-in captions that comment on the action. For example,

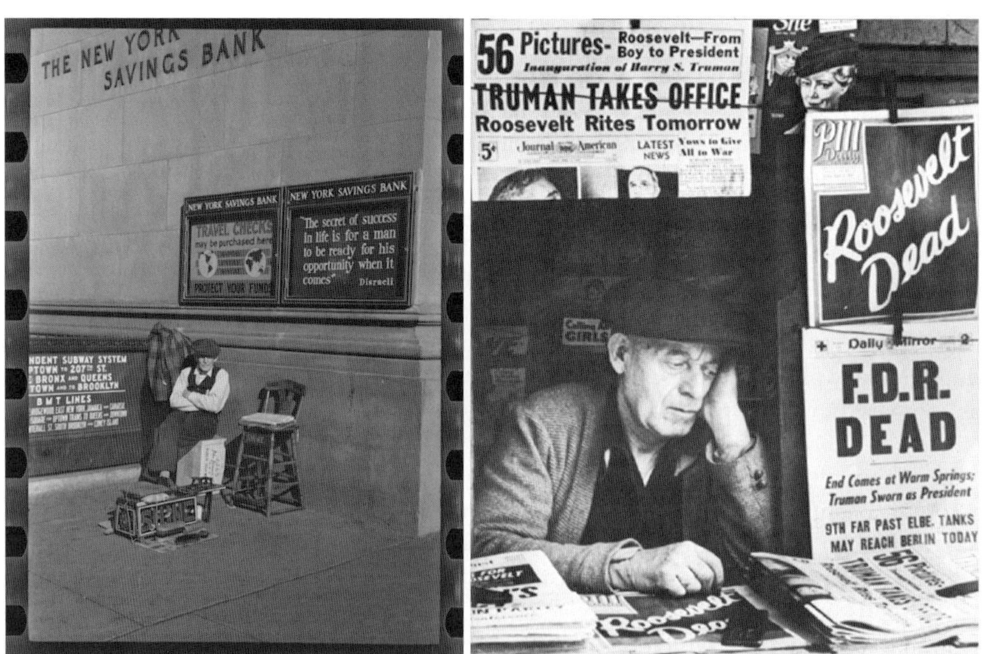

Figure 11: "Bootblack" (Arthur Rothstein, 1937) and "FDR Dead" (Stanley Kubrick, 1945).

Rothstein produced a short series of photographs in December 1937 titled "Bootblack," featuring a shoeshine man at the corner of Fourteenth Street and Eighth Avenue in Manhattan (cf. Figure 11). The shoeshine stand is set up in front of the New York Savings Bank, under a sign quoting, somewhat ironically, former English prime minister Benjamin Disraeli: "The secret of success in life is for a man to be ready for his opportunity when it comes." This is a staple of photojournalistic practice, and was obviously internalized by Kubrick prior to his period at *Look*, since it is explicitly used in his first published image of the depressed newspaper salesman: the titles announcing FDR's death provide a context for the man's emotional expression.

Another technique is to create an additional frame within the photograph as a highlighting device. Rothstein applied it to a January 1937 portrait of the family of a migratory fruit worker in Florida, with the wife and two of the five children framed by the window of their automobile. Kubrick took a similar portrait of a large family in Stamford, Connecticut, for the July 4, 1950 issue of *Look*, in which seven children look at the photographer through the three windows of their 1933 Plymouth (cf. Figure 12).

Long shots of men dwarfed by the creations of modern engineering is another popular theme that Rothstein explored in his June 1942 high-angle photograph of four men installing a large, circular generator at the Tennessee Valley Authority's Cherokee Dam (cf. Figure 13). This image resembles Kubrick's high-angle portrait of three men posing in front of Columbia University's massive cyclotron, for the May 11, 1948, *Look* issue (Crone, 223).

Symmetrical compositions featuring big city nightlife is also a photojournalistic trope, with Rothstein capturing Dallas' theatre row by night in January 1942 (cf. Figure 14). Kubrick took a similar shot of Chicago from a higher angle, for an April 12, 1949, photo-essay, looking down State Street with its glitzy theatre marquees (Duncan, 16).

Rothstein did not forget Kubrick's contributions to *Look* after the younger man retired from photojournalism. For the twelfth revised edition of the *Leica Manual*, published in 1953, Rothstein contributed an article describing the advantages of the small, 35mm camera for

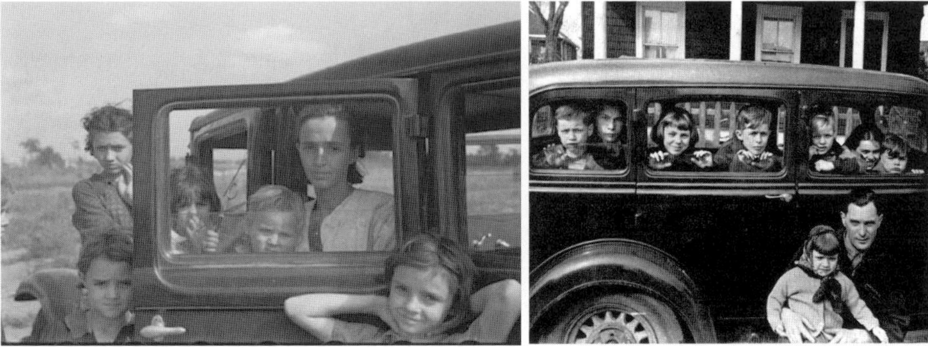

Figure 12: Arthur Rothstein, FSA (1937) and Stanley Kubrick, *Look* magazine (1950).

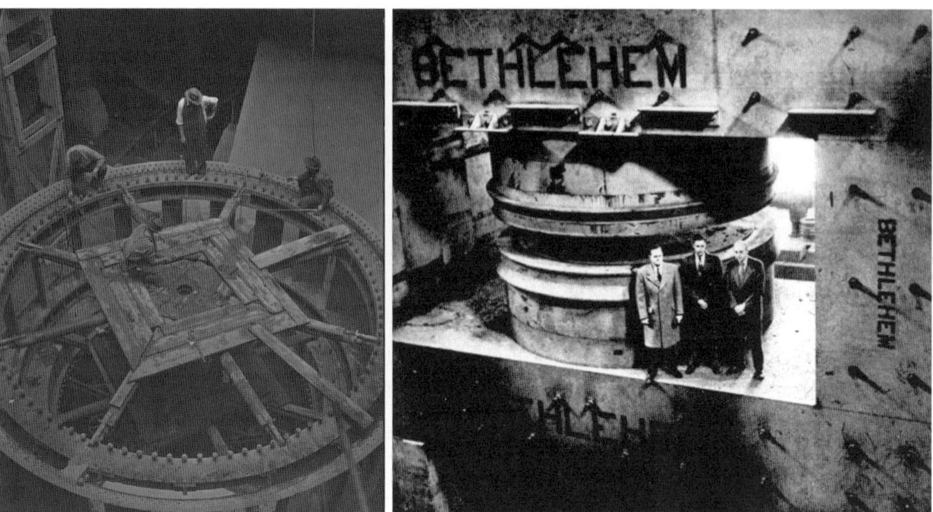

Figure 13: Arthur Rothstein, FSA (1942) and Stanley Kubrick, *Look* magazine (1948).

photojournalists. It includes a Kubrick photograph of weary subway riders, which appeared in the March 4, 1947 issue of *Look*, to illustrate the Leica's ability to obtain decent exposures in poor lighting conditions. The caption includes Kubrick's name, along with an implied compliment for the photographer: "A slow shutter speed requires a steady camera when photographing under natural light conditions" (Rothstein, 227). Moreover, after *Look*'s photographic library was donated to the Library of Congress in 1971, Rothstein wrote to lawyer William Elwood about establishing the monetary value of the *Look* collection. Dated July 10, 1977, Rothstein's letter includes the following comment: "Note the large number of photographs by Stanley Kubrick who has become one of the most famous film directors. These most certainly have considerable value" (Rothstein Papers, Box 5, Folder 11).

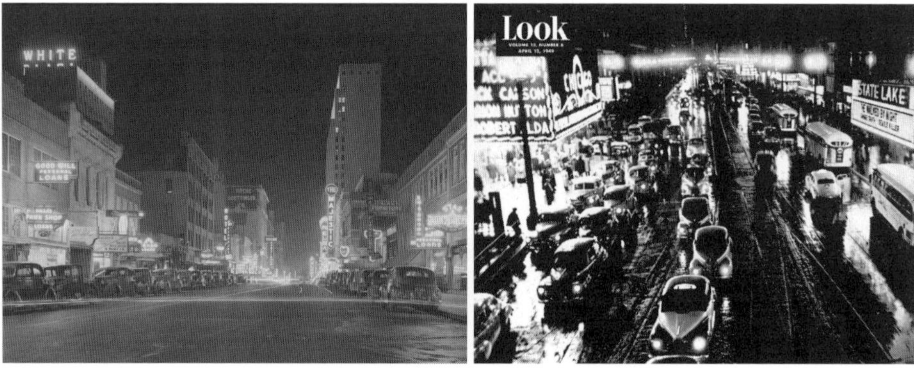

Figure 14: Dallas, 1942 (Arthur Rothstein) and Chicago, 1949 (Stanley Kubrick).

Apprenticeship

Kubrick has observed that the four and a half years he spent working for *Look* magazine represented his college years, adding that "travelling all over America, seeing how things worked and the way people behaved, gave me some useful insights plus important experience in photography" (Walker, 14). He has also referred to his first six months at *Look* as an apprenticeship, after which he was granted the status of staff photographer (Bernstein 2006, 315). His initial appointment as an apprentice must have been an unusual decision for *Look*, who clearly did not have a formal programme for high school graduates. Kubrick acknowledges his indebtedness to picture editor Helen O'Brian, who was aware of the youngster's academic situation, and offered him the apprenticeship, with the approval of managing editor Jack Guenther (LoBrutto, 34). *Look* was not risking much, given Kubrick's starting salary of $50 per week, and the opportunity to mould a young, talented photographer into the ideal employee (Panzer 2005b, 410). *Look* had prospered during the war years, as its advertising revenue almost quintupled between 1940 and 1946, from $1.3 million to $6.4 million (Cooperman, 147). Furthermore, O'Brian has stated that Kubrick "had the highest percentage of acceptances of any free-lance photographer I've ever dealt with," confirming that the staff at *Look* had become aware of the teenager's photographic eye (Stagg, 40). Comparing *Look*'s brand of apprenticeship with formal programmes, which have been developed in the United States and Germany, can provide us with useful information regarding the likely influence the New York photo-magazine had on the young visual storyteller. Moreover, the relative informality of *Look* magazine's arrangement with Kubrick both gives an indication of the organization's flexibility and can serve as a bridge between the macro- and micro-objective levels of social analysis.

Based in part on the photographic archives at the Library of Congress and at the Museum of the City of New York, we can determine that Kubrick's initial contract with *Look* magazine likely covered the period from April to October 1946. He would then have signed a new contract as a full member of the photography department, but since *Look* magazine had a six-week lead time between submitting assignments and publication, Kubrick's name did not appear on *Look*'s masthead until the January 7, 1947, issue. Despite his quick promotion to staff photographer, he clearly remained in a learning mode, absorbing each new experience afforded by his official position at *Look*, effectively extending his six-month apprenticeship by an additional year or so. Formal apprenticeships usually last between two and four years, and apprentices earn between 40 per cent and 60 per cent of the journeyman rate, with wages increasing by 5 per cent every six months (Cantor, 127). Kubrick has stated that his "highest salary was $105 a week," although *Look* journalists travelled first class and supplemented their modest income by making creative use of their expense accounts (Ginna, 18).

In the United States, apprenticeships were unregulated until the Apprenticeship Act was passed in 1937, the year *Look* was launched. Given the ad hoc nature of Kubrick's hiring, it is unlikely *Look* magazine formally registered him as an apprentice with the New York State Department of Labor. But a smart 17-year-old with supportive parents would have made sure that the conditions of his employment were clearly put down in writing. Such an arrangement would no doubt have benefited both parties: Kubrick's own education was on hold, and he had shown a penchant for experiential learning; *Look* would have been eager to use all available creative talent, given the fierce competition with *Life* magazine. In an analysis of cooperative education, Dr. Jeffrey Cantor outlines the mutual advantages of such programmes: "Employers benefit from the opportunity to recruit and pretrain future employees, which can reduce labor costs and improve overall business … [and] learners gain real feedback in on-the-job situations to ensure eventual job competence, thus increasing self-confidence" (7). Other benefits for learners include "practice in interpersonal relations skills, … feedback through performance assessment … [and] exposure to working role models in real situations" (Cantor, 8). It is important to bear in mind that Kubrick's lack of motivation in school does not mean that he was entirely self-directed and impervious to any form of schooling. Stephen Hamilton has written on education and employment in the transition to adulthood, pointing out that "many young people who do not learn well in school are diligent and adept learners in the workplace" (Lerner, 349).

In addition to work opportunities, formal apprenticeships require employers to provide instruction, usually delivered by a community college (Cantor, 114). It could be argued that *Look* magazine instructed their young protégé in at least three ways: by tailoring his early photography assignments, and by providing him with a copy of their in-house textbook, as well as individual and collective forms of mentorship. As a freelancer, Kubrick's photographs appeared in five articles (cf. Appendix I). As an apprentice, the photographic archives in New York and Washington, D.C., indicate that between April and October 1946, Kubrick's assignments focused on street photography and candid camera subjects. The nature of his assignments broadens from 1947 onwards, and his first major out-of-town job is an unpublished story on an orphanage in Lake Bluff, Illinois, submitted to *Look* on January 20, 1947.

During the apprenticeship, Kubrick's street assignments included mothers shopping with their children, Bryant Park in Manhattan, the Palisades Amusement Park, Bronx street scenes and the subway system. Candid camera subjects also included a woman trying on a hat in a clothing store, a dentist's waiting room and the subway. Kubrick may well have suggested some of these assignments himself, since he already had some familiarity with street photography, but the change in the types of assigned jobs suggests that *Look* initially wanted their junior photographer to perfect his craft and develop some chops as a professional shutterbug. Understandably, *Look* may also have wanted to reserve its more prestigious assignments, involving travel and celebrities, for its established staff, leaving young Stanley to demonstrate some creativity in the streets, parks and subway world of New York City (Bolack, 39–40). *Look* had an experienced group of photographers who had secured their professional reputations in the 1930s with organizations such as the Farm Security Administration, including John Vachon and Arthur Rothstein.

It has been argued that "the socialization of news photographers to professional and organizational demands begins in journalism textbooks, which include detailed instructions on how to photograph news events" (Bolack, 10). Kubrick did not have the opportunity to attend a journalism school, but *Look* magazine published its own textbook on photojournalism in 1945, titled *The Technique of the Picture Story*. A copy of this book, written by *Look*'s executive editor and art director at the time, Dan Mich and Edwin Eberman, would most likely have been supplied to Kubrick to familiarize him with some of the requirements of his new job, especially in his capacity as apprentice photographer. The book's seventh chapter, titled "Producing the Picture Story," provides a characteristically didactic list of ten "general rules for the writer-producer," and describes the production process in 28 illustrated steps, which involves every department at *Look* magazine (Mich, 194). The practical relevance of this textbook to Kubrick's new job is clear, and exemplifies apprenticeship at its most effective, that is, when students are taught how to relate their learning to work.

A third mode of instruction is mentoring, a job that was likely shared informally among members of the *Look* staff, since the magazine did not have an official apprenticeship programme. However, it is possible to make a distinction between individual mentors whose position at *Look* would have naturally led them to supervise Kubrick's work, and a collective form of mentorship, which the *Look* team participated in for the first two years or so of their junior colleague's career. In terms of the magazine's organizational structure, a photographer would spend much time in the field with the writer assigned to produce a given story, but his or her immediate superiors would be the photography department's technical supervisor and the picture editor. Laura Berk points out that "the best mentors usually are not top executives, who tend to be preoccupied and therefore less helpful and sympathetic. Most of the time, young adults fare better with a mentor lower on the corporate ladder" (472). We know that Kubrick was indebted to picture editor Helen O'Brian, who was instrumental in getting him a job, but the position of technical supervisor, closest to a staff photographer in terms of rank, was occupied by Arthur Rothstein, an accomplished photographer whose work for Roy Stryker at the FSA was well known.

As mentioned previously, Kubrick was paired up with Rothstein on a dozen assignments during his career, which must have been an informative and encouraging experience. Jeffrey Cantor argues that "mentoring is recognized as an effective method of training workers and/or learners by providing them with a behaviour model" (170). Thanks to his supportive mentor, a "protégé becomes better integrated into the organization and gains a sense of belonging" (Cantor, 175). The technical supervisor was the photography department head or "chief photographer," whose duties were closely coordinated with those of the picture editor. In his own textbook titled *Photojournalism*, Rothstein describes the three main functions of the picture editor as: (1) obtaining all the required photographs from various sources; (2) supervising and administering the photographic staff; (3) selecting the photographs to be published (129). Rothstein is quick to add that not all picture editors are responsible for these three functions: they normally sit on the editorial board and assign photographers to specific jobs, but may not supervise the photographers directly or select photographs for publication (129). The technical supervisor can thus function as an assistant administrator, working more closely with the photographers, supervising the photographic studio and the storing of negatives, and so on. *Look*'s staff included ten photographers, as well as a darkroom supervisor.

While Herman Getter's mentorship of Kubrick at Taft High was not shared with the rest of the teaching personnel, a markedly different situation likely occurred at *Look*, with everyone chipping in as required to assist the apprentice photographer. This supportive environment may be described as a collective form of mentoring, one that is not unusual in news organizations. In a thesis on socialization in photojournalism, Michelle Bolack observes that a director of photography may assign "photographers to serve as mentors to younger staff members," and describes the case of a photographer who had joined the *Times-Picayune* (New Orleans) staff "three months earlier after working briefly at a suburban newspaper. He had no educational background in journalism or photography and decided to pursue photojournalism because he enjoyed taking pictures" (36). The new journalist reported that "the only way you can learn about this job is to be around people who know how to do it. It's a teaching staff, if you don't mind constructive criticism" (Bolack, 36). The parallel between this man's situation and Kubrick's suggests that the informal supervision of new staff is a common occurrence, one replete with opportunities to learn about life and work.

Both the size of *Look* magazine's staff and its management style point towards a relatively collaborative, family atmosphere, which is reflected in a short commentary printed in the contents page of the May 11, 1948, *Look* issue. This revealing piece informs us about Kubrick and his fellow photographers: "In a spirit of friendly co-operation, they formed a 'Bringing Up Stanley Club,' dedicated to reminding Stanley not to forget his keys, glasses, overshoes and other miscellaneous trivia. The subtle influence of this loosely organized advisory group has also brought an apparent change in the young man's clothing tastes" (C. Kubrick, 36). The commentary goes on to indicate that Kubrick needed no such help in photographic matters, which was no doubt partly written as a sign of confidence in and encouragement to their junior colleague. He is also described as a "two-year veteran," perhaps as a further means of acknowledging the end of his apprenticeship. The reference to a "loosely organized advisory group" confirms the *Look* staff's role in collectively mentoring Kubrick.

Conveying values relating to "scheduling, organizational policy and procedure, maintaining a professional relationship and decorum, dress, etc.," are among the tasks required of formal mentorships, and it appears *Look* magazine imparted these values on Kubrick in an informal way (Cantor, 181). It should be clear that *Look*'s organizational structure was flexible enough to allow the teenaged Kubrick to work in a supportive environment as a de facto apprentice and then as a bona fide staff photographer, with colleagues providing him with models of adult behaviour. This experience helped him to learn about teamwork and communication, which no doubt proved crucial in his future development as a filmmaker, given the fact that Taft High may not have assisted specifically in developing collaborative skills, other than playing in a swing band and working on the *Taft Review*.

Comparing Kubrick's informal apprenticeship at *Look* magazine with two relevant case studies of formal programmes may shed additional light on the likely benefits for a teenager of working and learning at a national photo-magazine. Stephen Hamilton has studied the German apprenticeship system extensively, suggesting ways in which it could be adapted to the American educational context (Lerner, 349). He begins by pointing out that employers in the United States seldom hire teenagers for careers in skilled trades (S. Hamilton, 22). Youth without college degrees are usually relegated to the secondary labour market (unskilled services), an experience from which young adults gain little beyond some general worker skills and social skills (S. Hamilton, 24). Hamilton adds that "since the end of World War II, when returning veterans were given preference, U.S. craft apprenticeship has been predominantly for young adults rather than youth. The median age of U.S. apprentices is 25, compared to 18 in West Germany" (39).

These facts underscore the exceptional quality of *Look*'s decision to hire a 17-year-old. Granted, a six-month contract represented no more than a $1200 expenditure for the magazine, but the editors must have seen something in Kubrick to make them overlook the standard presumption of "youthful instability" (S. Hamilton, 24). So what do primary labour market employers look for in job applicants without college degrees, if they consider them at all? Hamilton lists the following worker virtues: punctuality, diligence, responsibility, receptiveness to supervision, "skills in social interaction and the ability to continue learning," as well as higher order skills such as "curiosity, problem-solving skills, and thoughtfulness" (14–15). This may be a tall order for most teenagers, but Kubrick was clearly passionate about photography, and his perceived talent by *Look* editors may have proven to be the trump card, which supplemented his other qualities as a worker. *Look* was certainly not obliged to hire a college "reject," but they did nonetheless, and probably not "out of pity," as Kubrick once claimed (Gelmis, 81).

In contrast to the situation in the United States, "apprenticeship is the most common experience for West German youth and their primary bridge from school to career" (S. Hamilton, 32). We are informed that "apprentices typically spend four days of each week at work and one day at school for three years" (S. Hamilton, 51). Effective apprenticeship programmes in Germany pursue the following goals: (1) Exploit the workplace as a learning environment; (2) Link work experience to academic learning; (3) Give apprentices the dual roles of learners and responsible workers; (4) Foster relationships with adult mentors (S. Hamilton, 16). As a result, "the majority of West Germany's older youth spend more time learning in workplaces than in schools" (S. Hamilton, 61). The secret to the success of apprenticeships, which can be usefully compared with Kubrick's situation at *Look*, may be learning through relevant and well-defined goal-oriented tasks. Hamilton argues that the integration of learning with work experience is critical to the apprenticeship system's effectiveness (51). He adds that education must achieve a balance between information and action, that is, the information must be made relevant through applied exercises, an approach that stimulates youth to learn more, to seek out more information (S. Hamilton, 123).

Similarly, the staff at *Look* magazine was engaged in a very specific goal-oriented task, namely to produce a photo-magazine on a fortnightly basis. Kubrick was undoubtedly eager to participate in this effort by perfecting the craft of hunting down pictures for the purpose of creating a visually interesting and narratively engaging photo-essay. His lessons in visual aesthetics were thus guided by the practical requirements of journalism, and the prospect of seeing one's efforts published for millions to see must have been particularly stimulating and validating for any photographer. *Look* photographer Paul Fusco was hired in 1957 after having studied photography in art school; yet he described his first years at the magazine as a crash course in real world photography (Fusco, RYL 1871). Learning in this context was not theoretical, it was precisely aimed at doing a better job, or at least one deemed as such by the editors. Learning about all aspects of the photo-essay production process, including the importance of preliminary research, was another beneficial gain for Kubrick in terms of his appreciation for the collaborative nature of photojournalism. This clearly prepared him in his future projects as a filmmaker, given his later reputation for thorough research and meticulous preparations leading up to each film production. Without the practical experience of seeing how things were done at *Look* and understanding why, extensive research might otherwise have seemed tedious and unnecessary to a teenager.

A particularly instructive example of the educational potential of magazine journalism for teenagers and young adults is *Foxfire*, a student-run magazine based in Rabun County, Georgia. Started in 1966 by high school teacher Eliot Wigginton as an experiment to get students interested in learning English, it became a credit class and then a vocational elective programme.[1] *Foxfire* has published continuously since 1967, including book anthologies of the best articles from the quarterly magazine, whose editorial goal was to preserve "the vanishing culture of Southern Appalachia." When the first book was published by Doubleday in 1972, the editors of *Life* magazine took notice, and wrote a story on *Foxfire*'s teenage reporters, explaining that "the romance of journalism seized them. Moving out into the hills armed with tape recorders and cameras (and, as the project prospered, videotape equipment), they began recording pioneer skills for posterity" (63). Wigginton's pedagogical approach was based on the assumption that "what the students really needed was to become involved in productive, responsible activities that would consume their energies, [and] teach them something in the process" (83).

The parallel with Kubrick's apprenticeship at *Look* is revealing, particularly when we consider his views on an experiential or personal approach to education, which happens to coincide with Wigginton's teaching philosophy. Commenting on his education, Kubrick told Gene Phillips: "I think the big mistake in schools is trying to teach children anything. Fear of getting failing grades, fear of not staying with your class, etc. … Interest can produce learning on a scale compared to fear as a nuclear explosion to a firecracker" (1975, 12). Similarly, Wigginton complains that "we hold students in a state of enforced early adolescence through all of high school, ignoring the tremendous hunger all young people have to do important, significant work; to make a difference in the community" (237). Wigginton thus made it a point to treat the students as adults as a means of ensuring that they not only behaved as adults, but also gained in self-confidence at a critical time in their lives.

In terms of *Foxfire*'s modus operandi, "the magazine has no photographer or editor – all students handle every phase of their articles from beginning to end and gain some control over every skill required, from interviewing to transcribing to photographing and printing to editing to layout and design" (Wigginton, 238). Obviously, *Look* was a magazine that functioned by coordinating the work of specialized professionals; however, they also favoured a relatively collaborative process that allowed photographers to submit story ideas and comment on layouts. This approach would have provided the young Kubrick with a detailed understanding and familiarity with the entire photojournalistic production process, an educational experience that is both similar to and different from formal apprenticeships and vocational programmes. Working for *Look* was clearly a stimulating experience for Kubrick, who undoubtedly benefited from being the only apprentice around, that is, from being surrounded with competent and encouraging mentors who trusted him and showed confidence in him. It was indeed a job that turned out to be a substitute art school, combined with the commercial concerns of reaching a wide audience.

Note

1   http://www.foxfire.org/magazine.html, accessed December 15, 2010.

Chapter 3

Micro-objectivity: The Work Culture at *Look* Magazine

Our application of George Ritzer's four levels of social reality now turns to the micro-objective realm, which concerns *Look* magazine's organizational culture and how it impacts on the individual actor's socioeconomic status, social contacts, behaviour and patterns of action and interaction (19). Typical work routines are thus the main subject of authorship analyses as a "sociology of production" (Staiger, 40–3). Rather than insist on individual authorship, the production context is examined to gauge the creative contributions of the personnel working collectively on a particular photo-essay or a film, for instance. The collaborative nature of such work highlights the fact that all the agents concerned, including those at the top of the decision-making hierarchy, must take up specific roles to allow the institution to function effectively. The more rigid the organization's hierarchy and culture, the greater the chance for worker alienation, although this appears not to have been an issue at *Look* magazine, in contrast with *Life* and the well-publicized battles with star photographer W. Eugene Smith, for example (Willumson, 6).

Professional status

Kubrick's status with *Look* evolved over the six-year period between 1945 and 1950. He was selling pictures on a freelance basis while he was still in high school, during the summer and fall of 1945. He graduated from high school in January 1946, and began hanging out with experienced freelancers in *Look* magazine's "bullpen," waiting for assignments outside the picture editor's office (Baxter, 28). Due to a combination of poor grades in high school and preference being given to returning servicemen on the GI Bill, Kubrick could not be admitted to college. Aware of his predicament, picture editor Helen O'Brian offered the 17-year-old a position as apprentice photographer in April 1946, which allowed him to contribute more regularly to *Look* magazine. By November 1946, he had been promoted to a full-member of the photographic staff, his name appearing on the contents page for the first time in January 1947 due to the magazine's six-week lead. He remained in that position until late August 1950, when he decided to quit his job to focus on documentary filmmaking. Photo-essays he had worked on during the summer continued to appear until the end of the year.

It must have been a heady experience for an 18-year-old to become a bona fide staff photographer for the second largest photo-magazine in America. "He looked so young," reports Photography Department Head Arthur Rothstein, "that I was frequently called by people who wanted to be sure that Kubrick was really a LOOK staff photographer" (Rothstein Papers). The people calling in to verify the photojournalist's credentials were likely both surprised by Kubrick's age and by the fact that someone so young could be working for such a prestigious publication (cf. Figure 15). In the 1953 MGM musical *I Love Melvin*, Donald O'Connor plays a young *Look* photojournalist who is about the same age as Kubrick. In an early scene, he visits a zoo on assignment and twice flashes his *Look* magazine ID card when security guards stop him. Their response is an enthusiastic "Oh, yes sir!" even though the zoo is closed to the public. A teenage Kubrick must also have enjoyed flashing his own *Look* identification, and been tempted to use his impressive title as a pickup line. The perceived glamour of the media features in an ironic scene from *Full Metal Jacket* when Joker introduces Rafterman and himself as "reporters from *Stars and Stripes*" to a Lieutenant Cleves who was involved in an operation that led to the murder of 20 Vietnamese civilians. Cleves exclaims "Oh, I see!" and obligingly answers Joker's questions, punctuated with self-conscious smiles for Rafterman's camera, which contrasts with what he is describing as well as the gruesome backdrop, an open-air grave filled with 20 lime-covered bodies.

The public reputation and thus the social status of photojournalists have often been determined by their image in Hollywood movies, one that has evolved over the decades (Brennen, 425). The 1920s and 1930s were dominated by representations and a perception of news photographers as aggressive, ruthless and untrustworthy, not unlike today's paparazzi (Brennen, 436). This began to change after World War II, particularly with the establishment of the National Press Photographers Association in 1945: "The investigative, probing, public 'watchdog' press photographer of the 1950s and 1960s truthfully reflected the birth of a professional national identity with the emergence of the NPPA and the acceptance of a code of ethics" (Bridger, 11). Perhaps more than the question of public trust, the commercial success of magazines such as *Look* and *Life* and the acknowledgement of their influence as major news media would have encouraged the general public to respect their reporters.

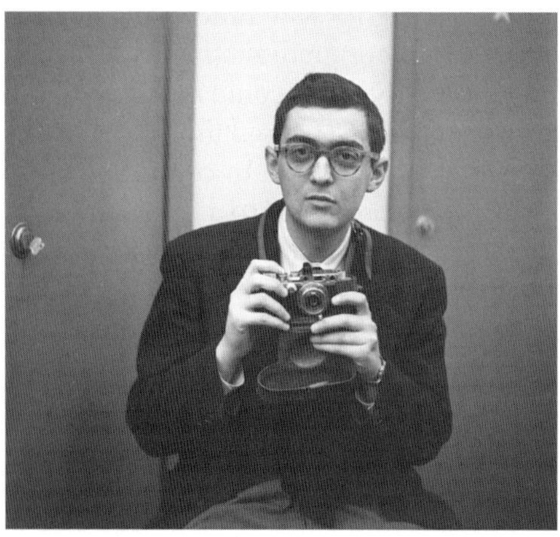

Figure 15: Arthur Rothstein portrait of Stanley Kubrick in the *Look* magazine offices (1948).

Life photographer Carl Mydans has stated that both *Look* and *Life* changed the public perception of photographers (Mydans). While photojournalists didn't receive a high salary (Kubrick's largest paycheque was $105 per week), *Look's* Stanley Tretick, best known for his photographs of the Kennedys, has pointed out that the magazine covered all their expenses, and that they always travelled first class and stayed in the best hotels (Tretick). As *Look's* ambassadors, they were provided with the trappings of status, befitting "America's Family Magazine." Another way of enhancing the status of photographers was to include a profile on *Look's* contents page. This was an opportunity for management to create reader interest in the production of the magazine, but also to promote its staff and express an appreciation for their hard work. Sometimes entitled "Behind the scenes with *Look*," these staff profiles also included writers and all of their photographers over a three-year period, from 1946 to 1948. As the magazine's junior member, Kubrick was the last to be singled out in this fashion, in the May 11, 1948 issue (C. Kubrick, 36).

Patterns of Interaction: Group Journalism

Like filmmaking, photo-magazine journalism was a collective enterprise, but there existed conflicting views about the most effective way to coordinate this group activity. In practice, *Life* and *Look* may not always have operated as antithetically as some writers have claimed, but there remained differences, which are worth noting, especially since *Look* magazine's preference for a collaborative method would have influenced the young Kubrick in a positive way. Mary Jane Hoffer explains that *Life* inherited the concept of group journalism from its parent publication *Time*, where it did not mean working together, but rather working within one's own speciality (research, editing, writing) and thus contributing to the overall project (122). This assembly-line mode of production made for a sleek, consistent and predictable level of professionalism (Leonard, 18). It was also based on a journalistic ideal of objectivity, and on the common concern among editors that "a photographer was too emotionally involved in the making of images to be of value in their editing" (Schuneman, 91). This argument about the photographer's lack of objectivity can easily be attributed to the editor's unwillingness to grant staffers any editorial power, and Kenneth Kobré has argued that *Life's* modus operandi made for a potentially alienating work environment for photographers, who had to put up with a shoot-and-ship system where they "had almost no control over stories after shooting them" (183). Wendy Kozol adds that "tensions periodically arose when photographers became frustrated by this exclusion" from the writing and layout of the photo-essays, which led to the resignation of even the most influential photographers at *Life*, such as Eugene Smith and David Douglas Duncan (40). On the other hand, *Life* writer Barbara Ellis, who worked with photographer Gordon Parks, claims that photographers were able to suggest story ideas, and that many tolerated their relative lack of editorial control "because to have their work displayed in *Life* was worth dying for" (Lovell, 105). A final reason for maintaining a strict separation of duties at *Life* may be attributed to its weekly publication deadlines and desire to cover spot news: with a lead-time of only five days, compared with *Look*'s six weeks, there was much pressure to ensure an efficient operation, even at the expense of staff morale.

In contrast, *Look*'s "photographer and photo editor, as well as the writer and art director, operated as a closely knit group, each contributing to the final story, without letting job titles limit each participant's input" (Kobré, 183). According to *Look*'s sports editor Tim Cohane, "the photographer voiced his opinions at each stage of the story's development" (Kobré, 183). Thus, "*Look* developed a system of photographer-writer teams for the production of major stories and essays" (Goldsmith, 2781). One reason for this system was to avoid possible resentment by photographers when their work would later be edited by people who were not in the field. Photographer Douglas Kirkland, who worked for *Look* from 1960 until 1971, argued that a "very good thing at *Look* is that the editor who creates the story goes on location with the photographer" (Rothstein & Kirkland, 97). Another reason for the collaborative concept was "to ensure the photographer had complete knowledge of the information that would be covered and the angle from which the story would be told" (Bolack, 26). *Look* magazine's modus operandi was to encourage photographers to establish relationships with writers in order to think in terms of the magazine's goal, which was to produce photo-essays, that is, narrative sequences of shots as opposed to isolated expressive pictures. Similarly, writers would be encouraged to think in visual terms, and, when preparing the shooting script, to "include any background information about the subject or setting that would help the photographer capture the environment" (Lovell, 53). The discipline required of photographers to not only consider visual and thematic links but also include storytelling concerns when taking individual photographs, is one that would undoubtedly serve Kubrick well when he later applied this skill to documentary and fiction filmmaking. In fact, *Look*'s director of photography Arthur Rothstein uses film as an analogy, to explain that photojournalism requires teamwork, and while it is theoretically possible for one person to be a film's producer, director, writer, cameraman, sound engineer and film editor, it would likely be inefficient (Rothstein & Kirkland, 94). It appears, then, that not only did people generally get along better at *Look* than *Life*, but that it was a smart way to take full advantage of the entire staff's knowledge and skills (Peterson).

An average of one out of ten assignments was shared with another photographer, and it is reasonable to assume that Kubrick learned much from working with his colleagues. The most common method identified by photojournalists "for learning new techniques and better ways to perform their jobs . . . [is] to observe and ask questions of fellow staff members" (Bolack, 35). In 1947, G. Warren Schloat Jr. was a newly hired writer who was paired with Kubrick, notably for the photo-essay "Life and Love on the New York Subway," which appeared in the March 4 issue of *Look* (LoBrutto, 38). Schloat, who was 33 at the time, had been a story editor for Walt Disney Studios, contributing to films such as *Snow White and the Seven Dwarfs* and *Dumbo*. Kubrick was interested by Schloat's background in film, and told him about his own plans as a future filmmaker. Interviewed by LoBrutto, Schloat also described Kubrick's candid-camera technique for the subway story, which involved a switch hidden in his pocket and a wire running up his sleeve (38). He may likely have received advice on the use of this apparatus from his colleagues at *Look*. The relationship between words and images defines the photo-essay form, and despite the collaborative nature of the work process at *Look* magazine, a breakdown of tasks and specialization remained. This had important consequences for Kubrick's development as a visual storyteller. According to biographer John Baxter, "Kubrick learned early the habit of looking to others for his narratives, and devoting his energies to illuminating them" (28). Almost without exception, Kubrick would later work with a writer on his film projects.

An example of a shared assignment is the photo-essay on the Philadelphia Beaux-Arts Ball, a social event that has been held every two years, on average, most recently organized by the American Institute of Architects. It began at Paris' École des Beaux-Arts in 1648, as a masquerade party to celebrate the end of the school year. The Philadelphia version started in 1949, and Stanley Kubrick was there along with colleague John Vachon to record the event. The story written by Patricia Coffin appeared in the September 13, 1949 issue of *Look*, although the Ball appears to have taken place on Saturday, April 30 (Vachon). Organized by Philadelphia's then Contemporary Art Association, the Ball raised $1400, and is described by the article as a diverse gathering of wealthy socialites, art students and "miscellaneous extroverts." The six-page essay includes ten pictures, each photographer contributing five, except that most of Kubrick's were printed larger than Vachon's. Kubrick's opener is a full-page medium shot of three costumed individuals representing Renaissance and Cubist Art. Most striking is the cubist character who wears a literal cube on his head as a mask, with a large eye drawn on one of its faces (cf. Figure 16). Fifty years later, Kubrick would create a brief montage of masks at the Somerton mansion in *Eyes Wide Shut* that appears to draw on the Beaux-Arts Ball story (Castle, 254). As with all photo-essays that were assigned to two or more photographers, John Vachon's work is seamlessly integrated with Kubrick's in the layout.

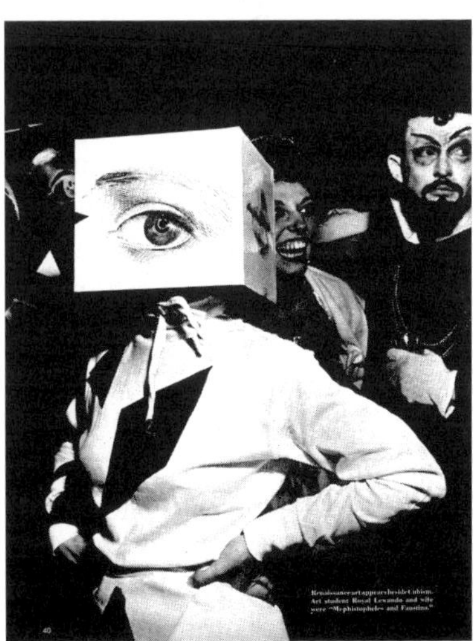

Figure 16: Philadelphia Beaux-Arts Ball (1947).

A more complex case is the July 19, 1949 article by Patricia Coffin entitled "Midsummer Nights in New York," which combined images by several photographers on different assignments . It is a commercial-free five-page photo-essay, which includes photographs by Kubrick, Arthur Rothstein, John Vachon and Phil Harrington. Coffin pulls together images of New York City nightclubs, Broadway shows, amusements parks, private penthouses and Times Square to argue that "Manhattan is America's busiest summer resort." Examining the sources of *Look*'s pictures reveals that the production of this photo-essay involved recycling images from several unpublished assignments, including three by Kubrick. Four of the 12 published photographs were provided by Kubrick, although a fifth one, attributed to Rothstein in the magazine's credits, is archived at the Museum of the City of New York in one of Kubrick's assignments at the Copacabana nightclub. Moreover, Kubrick's contributions, according to *Look*'s filing system, appear to have been culled from three different jobs: the *Kiss Me Kate* Broadway show (submitted December 6, 1948), "Nightclubs – Copacabana Girl" (submitted December 14, 1948) and possibly "Beatrice Pearson," officially filed on August 18, 1949, one month after the essay was published. Finally, a photograph of a performance at the Latin Quarter nightclub, from Kubrick's job "Nightclubs – Copacabana Girl," appeared in the November 26, 1951 edition of *Look*'s sister publication, *Quick*, for a follow-up article entitled "Are Night Clubs Old-Fashioned?"

Even though Kubrick was not assigned this specific story, it is his photograph of a performance at the Riviera nightclub, which was selected to be the opener and printed as a bleed picture, taking up three quarters of the two-page spread (16 by 13 inches). Anticipating the article in *Quick*, Manhattan's big nightclubs are described as "gaudy" and costly, which may prove problematic with a decrease in tourism income since 1948 and a growing preference for more intimate clubs. Kubrick's snapshot of the gaudy nightclub is situated at eye-level, right behind the first row of tables, encompassing a circular stage on the left with a female floor show and the audience enjoying a $5.50 dinner on the right. The photograph's angle provides a close view of both dancers and customers, which is ideal for the article's "ethnographic" purposes. The young performers wear flamboyant costumes and presumably engage in exotic Latin dancing. The drinking and smoking audience includes middle-aged men and women, and waiters are lined up against the wall, ready to jump into action as required. An unpublished image of the Riviera is included in Rainer Crone's *Drama & Shadows* (2005, 116).

The next spread begins with a large, vertically printed shot of two front row patrons at the Latin Quarter nightclub being entertained by a dancer on the edge of the stage, as she lifts up her skirt in traditional can-can fashion for their viewing pleasure. The middle-aged men smoke fat cigars and have turned their backs on the table to enjoy the show. In the foreground, the table is littered with various half-empty glasses and bottles of whiskey.[1] The second spread and the following page are divided into categories indicating the various types of night-time entertainment venues in Manhattan, according to this social study. Beginning with the Latin Quarter, the labels are: Big and Brassy, Garden, Theatre, Roof, Amusement Park, Penthouse, Perennial Swank, Private Pool. Under the "Theatre" category is a Kubrick picture of the opening number of *Kiss Me Kate*, a Broadway musical featuring two performers who appear in John Vachon's photograph of a garden party on the same page. The "Roof" section refers to the St. Regis Roof restaurant, patronized by two couples characterized as "cafe socialites" in the caption to a photograph by Arthur Rothstein (cf. Figure 17). Kubrick may have noticed this intimate, chiaroscuro picture of the four conversing around a table lit by candle-light, anticipating the imagery from his film *Barry Lyndon*. The dinner party is in the bottom half of the picture, with lights from Manhattan skyscrapers in the top half, visible in the background through the window. The caption explains that this sophisticated group prefers quiet "elegance to rowdy-dow entertainment," and that they must pay a hefty $6 for their meal, in addition to a $1.50 cover charge.

The last page's "Penthouse" label applies to a portrait of two actors, Beatrice Pearson and Murvyn Vye, having dinner at the Penthouse Club. Pearson had just finished filming the racially conscious film *Lost Boundaries* (1949, Alfred L. Werker), starring opposite Mel Ferrer in his film debut, while Vye had appeared as Merlin in the Bing Crosby musical *A Connecticut Yankee in King Arthur's Court* (1949, Tay Garnett). Kubrick's photograph was likely selected from the Beatrice Pearson assignment, and fits in with his colleagues' pictures of Times Square, the Palisades Amusement Park by night, Deborah Kerr walking out of the El Morocco restaurant, and a group of wealthy young people enjoying a midnight party at a private Mid-Manhattan pool. By including the Palisades, *Look* editor Coffin was no doubt seeking to round out this putative social study with an example of working class entertainment, although the glamourous penthouses and nightclubs clearly receive more layout real estate. The essay illustrates both the editors' ability to seamlessly integrate images from different photographers, and the technical proficiency of Kubrick's work when placed alongside that of established pros such as Rothstein and Vachon.

Life's Wilson Hicks and *Look*'s Arthur Rothstein were among the few to write about photojournalism as a distinct subject, and Rothstein's textbook outlining the production process was first published in 1956, revised three times and widely used in journalism schools.

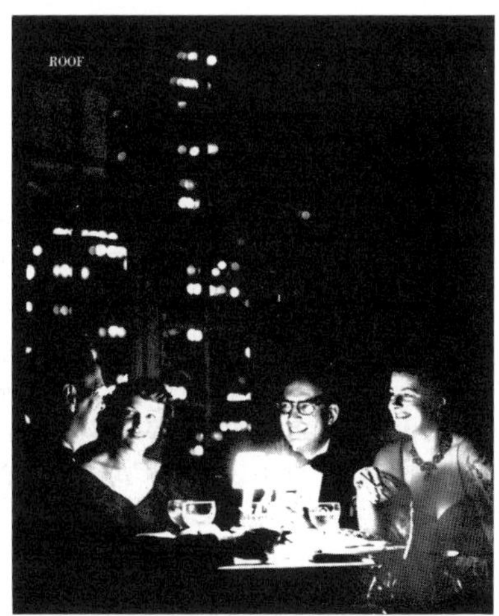

Figure 17: St. Regis Roof restaurant (A. Rothstein, 1949).

Rothstein identifies six stages in the process of producing a photo-essay, obviously based on his 24-year experience as *Look* magazine's technical director of photography (1979, 12–3). Many of these stages involved teamwork between the photographer and his fellow staffers, and thus potential influence in the work routine, particularly for a young and bright individual. In terms of its eventual impact on Kubrick's film production modus operandi, we may note that auteur film directors such as fellow New Yorkers John Cassavetes, Woody Allen and Martin Scorsese are known for surrounding themselves with a reliable stable of actors and a team of preferred collaborators, creating a kind of professional family environment. This practice can be read at least three different ways, pragmatically (people get along, performance is predictable), in terms of authorial control (chosen collaborators do what they're told) or even from a creative point of view (contributions from cast and crew are valued and included). This third aspect may be useful to consider as a corrective to the auteurist focus on individual vision, and Kubrick appears to have developed an ability early in his career not only to work collaboratively but also to demonstrate his appreciation for the work of others (with some notable exceptions, such as composer Alex North on *2001: A Space Odyssey*).

Story ideas

The first stage of photojournalistic production described by Rothstein occurred at the weekly board meetings, when possible topics for photo-essays were discussed. Referred to as the Editorial Plans Board, it included the executive editor, managing editor, two assistant managing editors, the art director and the picture editor (Cooperman, 180). In a two-month period, *Look* would screen approximately 800 potential stories from various sources before sending 250 to the Board for consideration, 200 of which had been supplied by *Look*'s own staff (Cooperman, 179). The ideas could originate from "staff researchers, writers, photographers, outside agencies, readers – almost anywhere" (Cooperman, 178). In selecting stories, the Board was also responsible for achieving an editorial balance, especially since *Look* was a general interest magazine: it had to cater to different audiences, ensuring that each issue featured family content, women's stories and so forth, including light essays designed to relieve pressure from more serious ones (Hopkins, 107). For example, the March 18, 1947, issue of *Look* included a grim essay entitled "State of the Nation" that identified "strikes, slums, immorality, crime, political corruption" as costly and destructive forces for which the nation had to find solutions. To offset this depressing piece, Kubrick was assigned a light subject, inspired by newspaper readership studies during the late forties indicating that children and babies were consistently among the most popular photographic categories (Kalish, 88). Entitled "Baby Wears Out 205-lb. Athlete," Kubrick himself singled out this particular story as being "pretty dumb," a rare distinction (Phillips 2002, 219). The four-page photo-essay was meant to illustrate the casual observation that a child's daily activities appear exhausting to adults. A 23-year-old college football player and ex-marine followed a 15-month-old toddler around an apartment, imitating his various bodily contortions.

Once a story was approved, the Board decided which editor to assign it to. It was almost always assigned to the person who proposed it, a policy that turned out to be "a great impetus to submitting well-thought-out ideas" (Cowles, 189).

Research

The second stage of photo-essay production concerned the background research, which the editor conducted in concert with research assistants. On the basis of this research, the editor decided whether a story could be pursued. It has been noted that "about five-sixths of a producer's time is spent on preparation for the piece with only one-sixth going for actual writing time" (Cooperman, 182). Kenneth Kobré recommends that photojournalists who take part in the research should "(1) pick an area of specialization; (2) make contacts with experts in the field; and (3) become familiar with the issues and new trends on the subject" (74). This echoes the researcher's duties listed by Kalish and Edom in 1951, which include "collecting facts and names, gathering background material, consulting encyclopedias and other sources, interviewing the people who know," and presenting the assembled information to the editor (38). While tedious, this work was critical for news organizations that had to double-check all facts for accuracy, to the satisfaction of their legal departments. University of Miami Professor of Journalism Mike Carlebach has pointed out that traditionally, researchers were women, and while he finds photographers and researchers to be more important than editors, they were typically considered lower on the totem pole (Carlebach). In any case, the importance of research is one that could not have failed to impress Kubrick, when one considers his meticulous approach to research as a filmmaker.

Photographer assigned

The third stage is when the photographer entered the picture. The editor consulted with the managing editor to choose a photographer. With a staff of ten photographers and twice as many writers, it was important to "select the right combination of talents for a specific assignment" (Cooperman, 180). The odd personality clash had to be factored in as well, since some photographers didn't work with some writers, which the editors were aware of (Fusco). *Look*'s Stanley Tretick claims that photographers and writers weren't paired up for too long a time, and that photographers didn't simply wait for an assignment, they would either suggest ideas themselves or ask to be assigned to a specific story (Tretick). He adds that stories were assigned in a loose, unsystematic way, and that photographers had a lot of input, there was a measure of choice in which stories they would agree to work on, depending on their interests (Tretick). Otherwise, it was the photo editor's job to determine which photographer would be most appropriate for a given assignment, based on their abilities and preferences (Kobré, 181). Kubrick's age was most certainly taken into consideration when he either suggested or was assigned stories about boxing, baseball, jazz music, the movies and universities, among other topics. This consideration of the photographer's interests provided Kubrick with many opportunities to meet and photograph Hollywood stars, thus laying some of the groundwork for his eventual move to California.

For instance, Kubrick took photographs of movie celebrities that were sometimes published as single portraits in articles dealing with other topics. Actress Gene Tierney appeared as a "mystery voice" on a January 1950 broadcast of the ABC radio quiz show *Quick as a Flash*, which was featured in the March 28 issue of *Look*. Kubrick's photograph is a medium close-up of Tierney smiling, standing next to the radio microphone with the show's host, Bill Cullen. The article's largest picture is an establishing shot of the six contestants during the radio broadcast, with the show's sponsor, Quaker Oats-Aunt Jemima, clearly featured. The last picture shows radio actors dramatizing the programme's questions, including Mercedes McCambridge, who had won the Academy Award for the best supporting actress in *All the King's Men* (1949) on March 23rd, just five days before the *Look* issue was published. Since *Look* had a lead-time of six weeks before going to the printers, it may be that McCambridge's picture was included on the basis of her having been nominated for an Oscar, even though she actually won the award before the magazine hit the news-stands. Another movie star who appeared in a yearly *Look* feature, the magazine's predictions for the coming year's influential personalities, is Robert Montgomery (cf. Figure 18). The January 3, 1950, *Look* issue includes a medium close-up photograph of the Republican Montgomery speaking into an ABC radio microphone, doing news commentary. Kubrick may have been interested in director Montgomery's bold experiment in point-of-view filmmaking, the 1947 film *Lady in the Lake*. Singer Doris Day appeared in an earlier instalment of *Look*'s yearly predictions, in the magazine's January 6, 1948, issue. Kubrick took a slightly low-angle medium shot of Day singing next to a faux Greek statue of a woman on a pedestal playing the castanets.

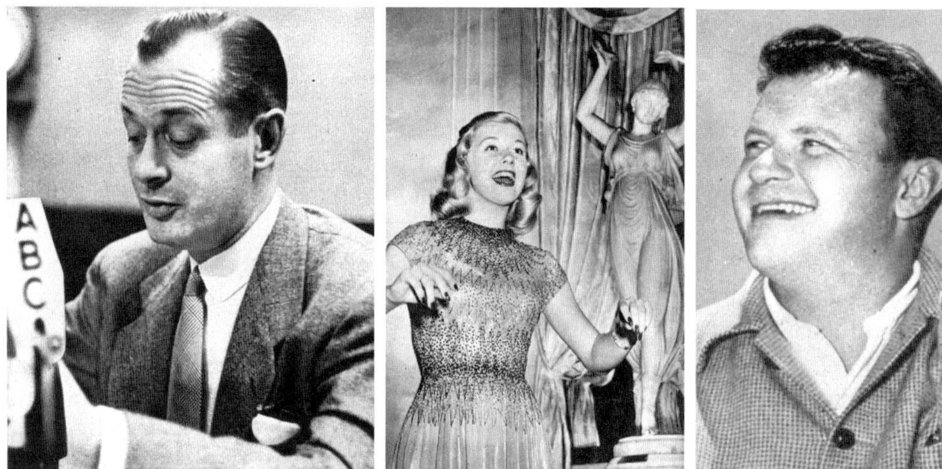

Figure 18: Kubrick portraits of R. Montgomery (1950), Doris Day and J. L. Mankiewicz (1947)

Day appears to be snapping her fingers as well, and the nature of photography is such that the statue seems just as alive (or frozen in time) as Day. Furthermore, the castanets are culturally linked to Spain, and one cannot help but think of Doris Day's signature song "Que Será, Será," which she would perform eight years later in Alfred Hitchcock's film *The Man Who Knew Too Much*. Composer Jay Livingston apparently got the idea for the song's title from the 1954 film *The Barefoot Contessa*, whose director, Joseph L. Mankiewicz, Kubrick photographed in 1947. Mankiewicz was asked to give advice to college freshmen in the October 28, 1947 instalment of *Look*'s regular feature "Meet the People." This feature consistently required medium close-ups, and Kubrick obliged with a portrait of Mankiewicz smiling and looking to his right. *The Ghost and Mrs. Muir* had been released on June 26, so Mankiewicz may have been promoting his new film when Kubrick took this photograph.

After the photographer was selected, he or she would go over the research with the editor, and they developed a tentative shooting script (Rothstein 1979, 120). Discussions covered suggested approaches to the story's "general theme, picture possibilities and anticipated space allotment," followed by travel arrangements and setting up appointments (Cooperman, 183). Part of the editor's responsibilities was to ensure that the photographer had as much information as possible in order to be thoroughly prepared for the assignment (Kobré, 181). When necessary, the editor also had to remind the photographer what kinds of pictures were needed, explain why some pictures may not be used, and remain open-minded and receptive to the photographer's suggestions (Kalish, 55). In this way, the editor would be able to stimulate and encourage the photographer's creativity, in order to obtain the best possible photographs and simplify the editorial process. In return, photographers would be expected to internalize the editor's style, or at least the publication's general approach (Rothstein 1979, 131). This would include thinking in terms of the story's overall narrative and rhetorical requirements rather than isolated artistic statements, as well as striving to catch strong lead-in shots to be used as openers (Hoffer, 127). It should be noted that the shooting script could be very sketchy, and was designed to be used as a guide only. It provided a framework or reference for work in the field, which could easily depart from what had initially been discussed. In fact, the concept of group journalism was essentially a matter of striking a balance between following work guidelines and the freedom to creatively explore one's evolving perception of a story (Hoffer, 126).

Location shooting

In the fourth stage, the writer and the photographer would normally travel together to capture the required visual and verbal material (in the case of interviews, for instance), with the shooting script in hand (Rothstein 1979, 120). Cooperman underscores the magazine team's relative editorial freedom in the field, arguing that "what occurs on location may be entirely different from what was expected and [the writer and photographer] are free to report as they feel the situation demands" (183). *Life*'s Carl Mydans reports that photojournalists had to develop the habit of stopping periodically to take notes, unless a writer was travelling with them (Mydans). *Look*'s Cal Bernstein claims that he travelled with a writer on 60 percent of his assignments, which was helpful since he wasn't systematic about note-taking (Bernstein). Mary Jane Hoffer explains that "while the photographer concentrated on capturing the mood of the story and composing his images, it was the writer's responsibility to identify the people, places and objects that he photographed, and establish a relationship among them. He made notes on … the exact date on which each picture was taken. He provided background information, as well as the facts of 'before' and 'after' to what we are seeing" (130). *Life* reporter Barbara Ellis adds that when going out on stories with photographers, she "handled the PR with those involved, smoothed the way for the photographer, logged every frame of what was going on, even if the shooter was using three cameras" (Lovell, 104). *Look* editor Leo Rosten claims that photographers went on assignment with "an enormous array of cases … loaded with an arsenal of equipment" and that they "might shoot forty rolls of film (1200 'frames') for a story that ended up using eight to twelve shots" (24).

According to the surviving prints and negatives at the *Look* archives in Washington D.C. and New York City, we can determine that Kubrick generally took several hundred pictures per major assignment, and more than 500 on seven occasions, including 1255 prints for the Walter Cartier boxing story (cf. Appendix I). In one of his earliest interviews, Kubrick even advised amateur photographers to take hundreds of pictures (Juntunen). From the 1255 archived prints, 18 were selected for publication in Kubrick's "Prizefighter" essay, which is in keeping with Leo Rosten's numbers (a dozen from 1200 prints), although it appears that the average number of pictures taken per job was on the rise during Kubrick's tenure at *Look*, just as the average number of photographs printed for each essay fell gradually with the evolution of graphic design for photo-magazines. For instance, Kubrick's colleague Frank Bauman took 210 photographs for an early forties profile of Ingrid Bergman, eight of which were used (Mich, 25). In contrast, only five pictures were selected for a *Look* photo-essay on fire fighters, from more than 3000 photographs taken by James Karales circa 1970 (Rothstein, 123). Therefore, the ratio of published to unpublished pictures was likely higher in the forties than it would be a decade or two later, despite the fact that one out of ten assignments was never published or yielded only one picture for a minor article. Among Kubrick's unpublished essays, for which pictures have survived, we might mention "Woolworth's Store" (607 pictures submitted in April 1947), the Jules Dassin film *The Naked City* (81 pictures submitted in July 1947) and "Showgirl Rosemary Williams" (701 pictures submitted in March 1949).[2] In the single portrait category, Kubrick's assignment to cover popular singer Peggy Lee included many pictures and distant travelling, work that was left on the "cutting room floor." Peggy Lee returned to her hometown of Valley City, North Dakota, and was welcomed as the local celebrity. Excluding the unprinted negatives, nine contact sheets stored at the Library of Congress contain over 180 photographs of Lee in a parade on Main Street, at a livestock show, doing a local radio broadcast, performing, and so on (French, 121). The single photograph published in the July 18, 1950, issue of *Look* includes a brief one-paragraph article showing Peggy Lee singing for North Dakota's governor while her husband accompanies on the piano.

Look's practice of group journalism also included sending more than one photographer on assignments, which might require multiple cameras, approximately 10 percent of all jobs. This represented a good opportunity for a junior photojournalist to learn from his more experienced colleagues, as mentioned in the previous chapter. For instance, the "Fight Night at the Garden" essay (February 15, 1949) was assigned to three *Look* photographers, including Kubrick. John Vachon was responsible for the high-angle establishing shot of the ring, which is reprised in the documentary *Day of the Fight*, and Kubrick's images of the ringside reporters are also present in the film's prologue. The essay's second spread is dominated by the only action picture, as one fighter bends over defensively to ward off his opponent's aggressive move. This image is situated in the centre of the spread and surrounded by reaction shots, as a means of replicating the placement of spectators around the ring. At the top of the page, a sequence of four images taken by Arthur Rothstein features a retired boxer's colourful reactions expressing "pain, surprise, boredom." Another spectator is made to look as if he is looking up to the fighters in the action picture, with the humorous caption: "The boys must be waltzing." The photographer for this picture and the one above it cannot be positively identified based on the contact sheets at the Museum of the City of New York, but it is a good example of the occasional *Look* job, which drew on the combined work of two or more staff photographers. In this instance, Kubrick was assigned to the ring, John Vachon focused on the Garden's turnstile and establishing shots while Rothstein took care of audience reactions.

Another shared assignment occurred in June 1948, when Kubrick and colleague Phil Harrington were sent to Macy's department store to photograph youngsters trying on the latest fashions. They took photographs surreptitiously, candid-camera style, through a "transparent magic mirror developed by Libbey-Owens Ford." This allowed *Look*'s photographers to capture the children's spontaneous reactions. The article published in the August 18, 1948 issue of *Look*, entitled "Bumper Baby Crop Starts School," begins as a social study on the wartime baby boom rather than a straightforward presentation of Fall fashions. We are told that six million babies were born in the United States in 1942 and 1943, and that this generation suffers from wartime problems such as absent fathers and multiple, inconsistent caregivers. One of the solutions mentioned, and a segue into the fashion part of this photo-essay, is to dress the children like other children so that they can feel as accepted members of their group. Implicitly, difference is not encouraged, in keeping with the widely held perception of the post-war era as one of conformism.

The hidden camera technique is another journalistic device designed to obtain interesting and colourful facial expressions, as opposed to strictly authentic, documentary events. Not surprisingly, *Look* plays up the realistic quality of this candid-camera approach, by claiming that the transparent mirror, for instance, is a way "to get true reactions" from the children, but their actual goal, one which Kubrick would adopt throughout his feature film career, was to get something striking or otherwise entertaining on celluloid. The three pages featuring the magic mirror shots include 16 photographs, nine of which were taken by Harrington, and seven by Kubrick. The results were printed in a serial fashion, highlighting the fact that the mirror likely dictated the camera setup, similar to Kubrick's later use of the front projection technique in *2001*'s "Dawn of Man" sequence. Consequently, the angle remains constant in all these pictures, with the photographer's responsibility reduced to capturing the right moment, if not the decisive one. Kubrick's snapshots reveal little Frank Gunther indulging in some mock pistol shooting as he tries on a western outfit, and young Sandy Lake attempting a partial split in her corduroy overalls. Rainer Crone points out that the children's enthusiasm, reflected in their playful expressions, contrasts with the dull school fashions (Crone & Schaesberg, 120).

Since all photographs and negatives for a given assignment were filed under the same ID number in *Look*'s catalogue, the only way to identify each photographer's work is from the "sources of *Look*'s pictures" listing in the magazine and the back of the contact sheets, which were usually stamped with the photographer's name and the date submitted. If the assignments were not published and the contact sheets were either not archived or not stamped, the negatives alone can only identify the photographer in a positive fashion if there is internal evidence such as a reflection in a mirror, which is very rare. Another exceptional case is when two photographers were assigned, and one of them took a picture of his or her colleague. This happened to Kubrick on the unpublished assignment "Sadler's Wells Ballet," when the famous troupe gathered at an English country house in October 1949, including Moira Shearer, Margot Fonteyn, Sir Frederick Ashton and others. Phillip Harrington was also assigned to this job, but the contact sheets, available at the Library of Congress, were not stamped. However, Kubrick appears in at least four pictures, thus identifying the photographer in those cases as Harrington (cf. Figure 19).

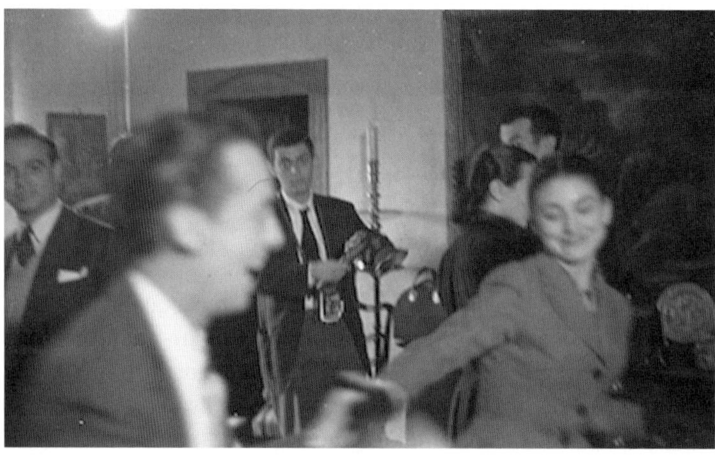

Figure 19: Kubrick caught setting up equipment by colleague P. Harrington (October 1949)

Picture selection and layout

The fifth stage of production was the assembly, including the editing of photographs and a preliminary layout. The photography lab would begin by printing contact sheets of all submitted camera rolls. For the 35mm format, this would represent at least one sheet per roll of film, adding up to over 40 sheets for 40 rolls, each sheet including no more than 30 frames of exposed film. According to Stanley Tretick and Arthur Rothstein, the photographer would be the first to look at the contact sheets (Rothstein & Kirkland, 99). The writer would then join the photographer and both would make "selects," that is, mark the contact sheets with an orange grease pencil, either with a check mark or by circling the chosen frames (Carlebach). The 60 to 100 selected photographs would be printed as 8" × 10" enlargements for further editing, in order to create the preliminary layout (Cooperman, 185). Paul Fusco adds that the photographer might give the dark room manager instructions about how to print the photographs, and that the printers would get to know the photographers' preferences (Fusco). The photo editor's job consisted in identifying the strongest photographs that could function as openers and enders, eliminating less relevant pictures in order to achieve an overall coherence, and keeping a variety of pictures to assist the art department in creating a layout (Hoffer, 133). According to Cal Bernstein, some of the major creative arguments concerned the lead picture, which would be printed larger than the rest and was meant to be both striking visually and encapsulate the essence of the essay, thematically and rhetorically (Bernstein).

Look photographer Douglas Kirkland observed that his main job normally ended here as the art director and the editor continued to work together on the layout, although he would have opportunities to comment during the preview stage, and his contribution was valued: "After the art director has completed the layout, the photographer generally has another look. … Fortunately at *Look* there is great respect for the picture and the photographer. If you don't feel you have gotten a 'fair shake' on a story, you can present reasonable variations which are certainly considered and frequently followed" (Rothstein & Kirkland, 98). The kind of work culture described by Kirkland suggests that Kubrick must have had opportunities to contribute at various stages of the editorial process, despite being the most junior member of *Look*'s staff. In fact, if the photographer was not immediately sent out on another assignment, he could participate in designing the layout: "After culling these prints further, we [the photographer-writer team] would devise a general layout scheme, including tentative title and subtitles. Then the two of us would sit down with one of the three art directors for a layout session" (Leonard, 18). In contrast, it seems that the photographer's opinion concerning the design and layout of an essay was rarely solicited at *Life* magazine, from a belief that photographers were too emotionally involved with their pictures and always disagreed with editors (Hoffer, 131). One of *Look*'s art directors, Allen Hurlburt, made a related argument regarding the usefulness of an objective eye, one who had not been on location and could perhaps more easily see what worked and didn't work pictorially, but he nevertheless insisted on a positive exchange with photographers: "Finished layouts are often a hell of a lot better than they started out to be because a photographer had a good idea that was better than mine" (104).

Look's art director William Hopkins claimed that the magazine's modus operandi included a meeting between the photographer-writer team and the art director, for a layout session that was not limited to questions of image placement; it also included a discussion of the essay's message or argument (Hopkins, 105). Both Cal Bernstein and Paul Fusco confirm that they were often involved in the layout of their essays, and that it was a collaborative and creative experience: there might be different views concerning the lead picture or the number of pages to allocate a story, but the magazine provided staff with much freedom to participate in the production process (Bernstein). The end result was one that could be described as a form of collective authorship, where all contributions added equally to the magazine's impact. For instance, curators at the Museum of the City of New York have argued that Kubrick's essay "Prizefighter" demonstrates *Look* art director Merle Armitage's "talent for visually sophisticated layouts juxtaposing small and full-page images in lively, asymmetrical patterns. … Armitage's crisp graphic design perfectly complemented Stanley Kubrick's striking photography, with its dramatic contrasts of light and dark" (Albrecht, 12).

A related topic that is seldom discussed is the thematic relationship between photographs and advertisements in a magazine photo-essay, as in Kubrick's "Mooseheart – The Child City" (June 8, 1948). The article's discussion of the important matter of food provision, illustrated by images of a child eating and the Mooseheart farm, is echoed by a full-page narrative ad for Borden dairy products, featuring Elsie the Borden cow and her family, as well as Del Monte tomato catsup. The caption for a sword dance picture mentions that students also help with housekeeping, which may be easier with Westinghouse electric home appliances. Two more full-page ads use family values as a pretext to exploit the dubious pleasures of marital infidelity in MGM's movie *Homecoming* (1948, Mervyn LeRoy), and cigar-smoking on a Sunday in Central Park for the Webster Tobacco Company. It is interesting to consider the influence of *Look* magazine's art director, Merle Armitage, on art directors working for *Look*'s sponsors, in terms of ensuring a coherent flow to the experience of reading the magazine's photo-essays. This process may also have impressed Kubrick, who certainly demonstrated an ability at portraying the commercialization of space, for instance, in *2001: A Space Odyssey*. Assisted by writer Clemenko and the rest of the *Look* team, Kubrick also created a de facto advertisement for the Mooseheart institution, and included commercial products in his essay on Columbia University, such as containers of Heinz white vinegar and Cow Brand baking soda, with labels facing the camera in his picture of the scientist setting fire to a piece of crumpled paper (Crone, 225).

Text and preview

The sixth and final stage was primarily the writer's task, drafting the headlines, text and captions for the photo-essay, once a preview of the completed layouts had been approved in *Look*'s conference room. The writer operated somewhat like a film's composer, preparing material and waiting for a rough cut to be delivered before adding text to the finished layout.

Cooperman points out that "the layout indicates exactly how much text and caption space [the editor] has to work with and the copy must be written to fit" (188). It appears *Look*'s staff always had an opportunity to comment on the layouts, since Vernon Pope's tenure as managing editor (1937–1942): "The common procedure was for Pope and other members of the editorial staff to put completed paste-ups on racks in the conference room for critical examination. Pope and Cowles made the final decision, but every worker had some say in the selection" (Cooperman, 76). Art director Allen Hurlburt confirms that the layouts were left "wide open for anybody to criticize who wants to. The layouts are in our conference room on the wall, and I've told photographers at the sessions we have together that if they have a comment or a suggestion on layout, to make it" (104). Cooperman adds that "many stories will stay on the wall for weeks before a final decision is made to use or reject the feature," depending in part on whether the story fits in with other articles being considered for a particular issue (188). If approved but not required for an upcoming issue, stories could be "filed in a special 'futures' cabinet" (Cooperman, 187). Based on the *Look* magazine archives in New York City and Washington, D.C., it appears that some stories were filed for up to a year, until circumstances allowed them to resurface and again made ready for publication. For instance, two of Kubrick's street photography assignments taken during his apprenticeship in the summer of 1946 were only published a year later ("While Mama Shops" and "Fun at an Amusement Park"), and his later profiles of Leonard Bernstein and Phil Rizzuto from August and September 1949 appeared in *Look* seven months later. In all cases, the final approval would be given by the editorial board after a preview meeting in the conference room (Cowles, 190). Essays would either be approved, "killed," sent back for modifications (including length) or filed for possible future use.

Even at the writing stage, *Look*'s production process appears to have been relatively flexible, for even though this was the domain of the magazine's editors, photographers report having been able to contribute to this phase as well. On the one hand, senior editor George Leonard explains that "when the completed layout was approved for publication, I would write both the picture captions and the text. The senior copy editor would work with me to improve the writing, but I had the privilege of approving all changes" (18). Photographer Cal Bernstein, on the other hand, claims that he wrote the text either himself or with the writer. Lacking direct information from Kubrick himself or his colleagues, it is difficult to gauge with certainty how much input he had regarding layouts and writing captions, but *Look* had an institutional tradition of being flexible in terms of roles and duties, in contrast with *Life* magazine. In fairness, it is important to mention that a handful of *Life*'s star photographers managed to obtain more editorial control than others, who may not have been interested in writing (such as Kubrick, perhaps), and Eugene Smith was among a small group of such individualistic auteurs at *Life*. In addition to the broad work culture differences between *Life* and *Look*, it appears that there may also have been a historical evolution in both magazines in terms of increased participation by staff in the editorial process, from the late thirties until the late sixties. For instance, Mary Jane

Hoffer claims that "over the years, as the role of the managing editor [at *Life*] became less all-encompassing and true cooperation developed, the individual talents of different photographers was recognized and they were given greater freedom in exploring their own ideas and particular approaches" (138).

Whatever Kubrick's direct involvement in the writing might have been, he was certainly an active participant in *Look*'s brand of group journalism, as he travelled with the writers who were responsible for the text, and was thus intimately aware of the content and "slant" of the essays he was working on. He was thus not only in a privileged position to discuss editorial matters with the writers, but could also play to the text through the way he photographed the stories. For example, sports editor Tim Cohane wrote a poignant story involving the manager of the Detroit Tigers, former Yankee third baseman Red Rolfe, for the September 26, 1950 issue of *Look*. Subtitled "the Heart of the Tiger," the profile focuses on Rolfe's battle with chronic ulcerative colitis, which sometimes made it difficult for him to attend practices, even though he always did. The five-page article's three large photographs, two of which overlap on both pages, possess an internal structure that both parallels the text and illustrates Cohane's words. In this case, the three pictures reveal Rolfe's intensity as he sizes up a young prospect, concentrates on the game from the dugout, and vociferously expresses his disagreement with the umpires, in a sequence that could be chronological. The text also leads us to read the photographs in terms of the manager's health, as the battle on the field becomes a metaphor for Rolfe's personal battle with illness.

The essay's opener shows the manager framed by a veteran scout for the Detroit Tigers and a young prospect with his back to the camera. Rolfe looks gaunt, older than his 42 years of age, as his steely expression focuses on the young player. The second photograph shows him leaning on his knee in the dugout, rather than sitting on the bench. The caption suggests that his "strict attention to the game" influences the entire team's attitude and concentration, a manifestation of the respect he commands. In the concluding photograph, the strain of his physical condition appears more evident as he waves angrily in the umpires' direction. Next to him, two men could function as stand-ins for the reader as they appear to express concern for Rolfe's state of mind. In fact, one man seems frightened by Rolfe's anger, while the other extends his arm, encouraging the manager to walk away from the field.

In contrast, Kubrick's profile of CBS radio host Arthur Godfrey is more complex in terms of its relationship between images and text. Radio remained the dominant live broadcast medium in the late forties, reaching a much wider audience than television. Arthur Godfrey spoke to an audience of forty million when he was featured in the February 1, 1949 issue of *Look*. Even though Godfrey had recently started hosting a television programme for CBS, most Americans knew him by voice only. Widely distributed photographs of Godfrey would represent an opportunity to put a face on an otherwise disembodied voice. The article by *Look* writer Jonathan Kilbourn informs us that Godfrey's popularity is due to his informal style, which gives an impression of authenticity. Godfrey himself claimed that, when on the air, he was just being himself.

He is credited with creating the "commercial-kidding" technique, in which he would gently poke fun at the product being advertised. This public persona endeared him to many listeners, and at first glance, one gets the sense that Kubrick's photographs seek to confirm Godfrey's folksy image by focusing on the radio man's family life in Virginia. Ironically, we are also told that Godfrey was only spending four days per fortnight with his wife and children, and that he lived in an apartment in New York City the rest of the time. This information casts doubt on the authenticity of Godfrey's public image, as do some of Kubrick photographs.

The article's second page is devoted to the 800-acre family farm, the largest picture featuring Godfrey being kissed on the nose by his horse. An establishing shot of the Godfrey mansion looks like Kubrick's own home in Hertfordshire, near London, after he moved to England in the sixties. The last picture is an over-the-shoulder shot of Godfrey with wife Mary sitting in the cockpit of their four-seater plane. Kubrick was a plane enthusiast as well as a licensed pilot, even though he eventually developed a fear of flying. The essay's closing spread includes an overlap picture of the Godfrey family enjoying a cartoon programme on television, with everyone looking off-frame left rather than at each other. It is a low-angle shot with the two children in the foreground, lying on the carpet, while the parents sit on a couch in the background. The left page includes a shot of Godfrey entertaining two couples on a sailboat, with no family member in sight, and the very last shot on page right shows a contestant on a talent scout radio show being supervised by Godfrey in the background.

This rift between the public and the private, fiction and reality, is seemingly mended in a typically ambiguous Kubrickian photograph, which opens the article. We are told that Godfrey often brings his work home by broadcasting from a small studio on his Virginia farm. The picture shows him sitting at a table with his son and daughter, wearing a headset and speaking into the CBS microphone. Are we meant to think that this hard-working man has found a way to combine his personal and professional lives, to truly be himself in public and make the audience feel he is "one of them"? The fly in the ointment is Godfrey's long-time assistant, Margaret Richardson, who appears on the left side of the picture, and might be mistaken for the wife in this "family portrait," were it not for the caption printed in small-type. This significant detail establishes a pattern that is underscored in the rest of the photo-essay.

Photo-magazines in the late forties were not quite as glamourous a medium as Hollywood, but they certainly represented a photographer's dream job. This chapter has argued that *Look*'s brand of group journalism allowed for a collaborative work environment, which was ideal for a young photographer's apprenticeship and development into a skilled professional. In contrast with *Life*, *Look*'s six-week lead-time allowed for a less formalized craft system, including the opportunity for photographers to submit story ideas, contribute to the selection and layout of photographs, and travel with writers on location to both shape the stories they were working on and learn more about their profession. This process helped photographers to think in terms of the narrative photo-essay form's requirements, including the importance of background research, as well as develop into well-rounded visual storytellers combining superior photographic skills and an ability to work with others to complete an important journalistic assignment.

One gets a vivid sense of the hierarchy at *Life* magazine from writer Barbara Ellis' account, one in which the top editors always had the final say, but that also included a pecking order in terms of the writers' and the photographers' seniority or influence. Ellis reports that "we treated photographers like gods, or at least movie stars. … To say that we reporters were in awe, for the most part, is an understatement. … To be assigned to work on a story with a noted photographer was real status. The photographer I learned the most from was Gordon Parks, who was a real master of available light, something I loved" (Lovell, 105–7). Like Parks, Kubrick favoured natural light and became a filmmaker, although he left the magazine business much earlier. Unlike Parks, Kubrick worked for an organization that was less stratified and was the only major magazine of the time to give a virtual carte blanche to its writer-photographer teams, allowing them to edit their own work without being imposed a specific editorial angle (Fusco). Referring to an essay published in the February 21, 1956, issue of *Look*, writer George Leonard explained that "if the subject of our story was a second-grade teacher in a small town in Illinois, we would stay in her classroom every day for several weeks, and frequently accompany her home. In this way we would not only get thousands of pictures and thousands of words, but also come to know her, her students, her family, and her colleagues in a close and personal way" (18).[3] For a bright teenager who was bored by traditional schooling methods, this hands-on professional experience would have been extremely beneficial, and one he could even report on in assignments dealing with similar forms of cooperative education.

For example, Radio station WTAG in Worcester, Massachusetts, organized a day-long promotional event involving 150 high school teenagers who had participated in a Radio Club course over a period of several months. The teenagers wrote, produced and performed material for an 18-hour broadcast day on WTAG. *Look* assigned 18-year-old Kubrick to cover the story entitled "Teen-Agers Take Over a Radio Station," a three-page essay containing seven photographs that appeared in the magazine's October 14, 1947, issue. The first page features a large photograph of a youngster on stage emceeing a quiz show live, with hundreds in the audience, including "glamourous guest" Gloria Swanson front row centre, looking much as she would a few years later in Billy Wilder's film *Sunset Boulevard* (1950). Kubrick took this picture from the stage in order to include both the radio host and the audience in the same shot. The captions inform us about two other photographs on this page, showing two students in the studio engaged in a "chatter programme" titled "Julie 'n' Johnny," and a teenage girl doing street interviews with support from friends and well-wishers. The next four pictures focus on a show entitled "Breakfast Party," during which the emcee encourages members of the audience to play a number of goofy games on stage. The last photograph is printed vertically, showing the host hugging a fellow teen radio club member in order to break a rubber balloon. The article points out that the shows were entirely produced by the students, and received national exposure thanks to the CBS network, not to mention *Look* magazine and their own teenage journalist.

Notes

1   *Drama & Shadows* also includes unpublished images from the Latin Quarter nightclub, mistakenly identified as the Copacabana (Crone 2005, 112, 117).
2   Five prints from the Rosemary Williams assignment are included in Crone's *Drama & Shadows* (107–111).
3   Pictures from this essay are featured in *Look*'s textbook *School Photojournalism* (E. Hamilton, 32–33 & 62–63).

Chapter 4

Macro-subjectivity: *Look* Magazine's Conception of Photojournalism

According to our diagrammatic representation of George Ritzer's levels of social reality, the macro-subjective realm would refer to *Look* magazine's conception of the photo-essay genre, as well as the norms and values that it expected its staffers to adopt and implement. It has been argued that "the socialization of news photographers to professional and organizational demands begins in journalism textbooks, which include detailed instructions on how to photograph news events" (Bolack, 10). Kubrick did not have the opportunity to attend a journalism school, but in 1945 *Look* magazine authored one of the earliest textbooks on photojournalism, titled *The Technique of the Picture Story*. A copy of this book, written by *Look*'s executive editor and art director at the time, Dan Mich and Edwin Eberman, would most likely have been supplied to Kubrick to familiarize him with some of the requirements of his new job, especially in his capacity as apprentice photographer. Even if Kubrick did not own a copy of the *Look* textbook, his published photo-essays are evidence of the knowledge of journalistic genres he acquired by collaborating with his colleagues.

In a foreword to *The Technique of the Picture Story*, the Director of the Division of General Education at New York University, Paul A. McGhee, explains that the *Look* textbook originated as a course taught by Mich and Eberman in the Fall 1944 semester at NYU's Washington Square Writing Center (Mich, 5). That two hard-working magazine executives should find the time to prepare and deliver a university course can seem surprising, and may speak to the *Look* editors' desire to both share their professional expertise concerning a growing journalistic medium and help to train a new generation of writers and photographers who may in turn want to join the *Look* organization. McGhee applauds the authors' "reflective and analytical approach to this new medium" of the picture-story, which is also in keeping with *Look* General Manager Harlan Logan's didactic and educational style of journalism (Mich, 6). Logan was in fact included in the acknowledgements, for guiding and goading the authors into preparing the textbook (Mich, 7). The Dean of the School of Journalism at Syracuse University, M. Lyle Spencer, provided an introduction in which he describes *The Technique of the Picture Story* as a pioneer book, and argues that while great picture-writers are perhaps only created on the job and in magazine offices, the practical fundamentals of the new visual language can be gained from the *Look* volume by "young men and women with ambition to become picture producers or writers. . . . The information essential to a successful beginning is between the covers of this book" (Mich, 13). Given the interest expressed by *Look*'s top editors in educating journalism students and the general public about the language of photojournalism, their willingness to take on a promising youngster as an apprentice photographer and providing him with a supportive work environment should be less surprising.

The following analysis will focus on five of the textbook's nine chapters, specifically those dealing with *Look*'s conception of the picture-story as opposed to its production methods, a topic that was covered in our previous chapter. *The Technique of the Picture Story*'s first and third chapters outline different types of photo-essays that budding journalists would want to be aware of, as well as the main forms of continuity (pictorial, narrative, thematic), which allow for a seamless mode of communication. The second and fourth chapters list the evaluative criteria used to gauge the effectiveness of individual photographs and to choose appropriate subject matter. The fifth chapter is entirely devoted to *Look*'s exemplary genre, the personality profile. Two other books written by *Look* employees will be cited in support of *The Technique of the Picture Story*, including photographer Earl Theisen's 1947 manual *Making Your Pictures Interesting*, and the 1958 *Look* textbook titled *School Photojournalism: Telling Your School Story in Pictures*. The underlying assumption here is that by internalizing the magazine's norms and values at a formative age, Kubrick would bring to his filmmaking career some of the mindset and procedures of *Look*'s brand of post-war American photojournalism.

Four basic types of photo-essays

The first chapter of *The Technique of the Picture Story* describes the major types of photo-essays in terms of the relationship between words and images, ranging from images being used for purely illustrative purposes, to picture stories that avoid words altogether. The intermediate cases include a balanced combination of picture and text, and a picture-story embedded within and running parallel to a text story. Photographs are used as illustration when the article's main argument is developed strictly through the written text, either due to the abstract nature of the topic or because an area specialist with no training in picture journalism was hired to write an article specifically for the magazine. In such cases, the photographs merely support the text by providing an extra visual appeal, but do not in themselves add to the argument or tell a story (Mich, 15). Among the examples cited is a posed photograph meant to illustrate an article on sex education, which reminds us of Kubrick's staged assignments for Evelyn Millis Duvall's pop psychology book *Facts of Life and Love*.

One of these assignments is the essay "What Teenagers Should Know About Love" (October 10, 1950), which includes staged photographs that Kubrick would recycle in his later film work. The second image illustrates the theme "love for an older man." A teenage girl leans on a mustachioed man's car in a medium-shot, smiling and looking downward, while the driver looks back at her with a smile. The caption reads: "Older men seem more romantic [to teenage girls], particularly if they are married. Most girls outgrow this phase." Here, a situation identified by the writer as a "phase" can implicitly degenerate into the taboo areas of paedophilia and incest, a topic that Kubrick would further examine by filming Vladimir Nabokov's *Lolita* in 1962 (Crone & Schaesberg, 178). The evocative power, indeed the ambiguity of images, allows for transgressive readings of photographs, which are not so innocently designed by the *Look* editors to illustrate a relatively less ambiguous text.

Duvall's contention that "most" teenage girls outgrow their attraction for married men is an implicit acknowledgement that some do not, thus potentially fueling "naughty" thoughts from *Look* readers as they consider Kubrick's suggestive photographs. The relationship of the photo-essays with the advertisements also reminds us of the deliberate editorial decisions, which were made at *Look* magazine on a continual basis. Kubrick's ambiguous photograph is framed by an ad for a Hoover vacuum cleaner on the left and Ovaltine beverage on the right. If we read these ads with the teenage-love essay in mind, the "mighty" Hoover vacuum cleaner might be gendered as male and associated with the married man in Kubrick's photograph, thus giving a new meaning to the ad's tagline "you'll be happier with a Hoover." Similarly, the man's temptation to return the teenager's affection might lead to some restless nights, as suggested by the Ovaltine ad's query: "How will you sleep tonight?" Luckily, Ovaltine promises a "drugless way to induce a good night's rest," supported by a close-up of a man sleeping.

The article's last photograph shows two teenage girls in a medium-shot, sitting close to each other under a tree in a wooded area, carrying three kittens. The rear section of a car in the background suggests the girls drove to this location to be alone and enjoy each other's company. According to the caption, the theme of this picture is "teen-age crushes." In a manner consistent with post-WWII values, Duvall's article argues that same-sex attraction is normal for teenagers, but that it must eventually be overcome, in order to allow for the "growth of normal love" for the opposite sex. Kubrick's photograph remains open to interpretation only if considered separately from the text, that is, out of context. It simply presents teenage same-sex crushes in a positive, even idyllic way, without the ambiguities found in some of the other photographs.

The Technique of the Picture Story also mentions an essay about famous union leader John L. Lewis as an example of the illustrated text (Mich, 18). The essay writers interviewed Lewis but it appears that no photographer was assigned to follow him for a day or more, as was the norm for personality profiles. Thus, a handful of medium close-ups were used to provide a sense of the man's character, primarily through his facial expressions when delivering a speech. Kubrick was also asked to obtain a family portrait of the newly elected Chairman of the Republican Party, Guy Gabrielson, at his summer home in New Jersey in August 1949. Published in the October 25, 1949 issue of *Look*, the portrait simply illustrates an article by Richard Wilson focusing on the politician's background, and the challenges facing a Republican party that had failed to elect a president since Herbert Hoover lost in 1932. In the photograph, Gabrielson is framed by his wife and son Guy Jr., with whom he relaxes on the front porch of their home (cf. Figure 20). Some of the unpublished shots available at the Library of Congress are more conventional portraits, with the subjects looking at the photographer, whereas *Look*'s editors chose to use a photograph in which the Gabrielsons

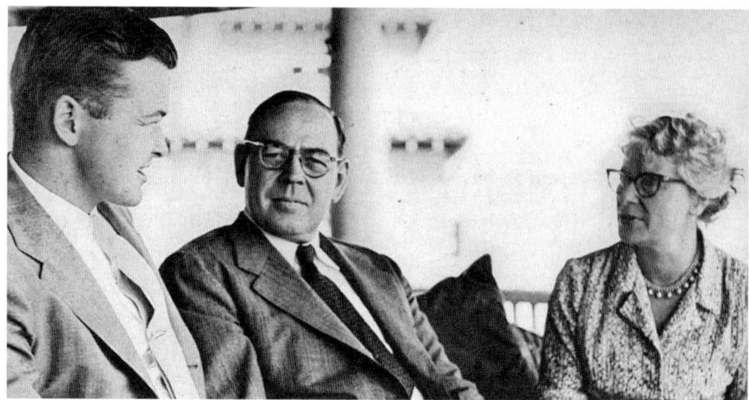

Figure 20: Republican Party Chairman Guy Gabrielson (centre), August 1949.

are looking at their son, engaged in a discussion. Combined with the use of a discrete long lens, which blurs the background, the photograph gives an impression of casual realism. The *Look* textbook points out the importance of obtaining natural-looking, unposed pictures: "The writer must learn to put his subjects at ease, get them relaxed in the presence of the camera" (Mich, 21).

At the opposite end of the spectrum is the "pure picture story," which includes no body copy but only a few discrete captions (Mich, 15). It can take the form of series photographs, which resemble still frames selected from a strip of motion-picture film. An instructive example that may have failed to achieve *Look*'s ideal of the pure picture-story is Kubrick's "First Look at a Mirror Bewilders the Baby" (May 13, 1947), a series of six pictures featuring a one-year-old interacting with his double. The photographic series is framed by the baby's two most extreme emotional reactions: a happy gesture greeting the fellow toddler in the first image, and unrestrained bawling in the last image. The emotional progression between these two states is not clear photographically, even though the *Look* archives at the Library of Congress indicate that Kubrick took at least 38 pictures, some of which could have expressed this idea of a growing frustration with the double. Thus, the narrative is constructed strictly through the captions, which could apply to a number of Kubrick film scenes in which our reading of the images is determined by voice-over narration, an obvious example being Humbert Humbert's diary in *Lolita* (1962). The arbitrariness of this series is highlighted by the fact that the editors felt it necessary to number the images from 1 to 6, suggesting that there is in fact no obvious visual sequence. Such numbering was a common photojournalistic technique in the 1930s and 1940s, but one that would seldom be used thereafter.

The *Look* textbook cites a similar example to illustrate the pure picture-story, an essay titled "Baby's First Flicker," which follows a two-year-old girl's reactions to a Mickey Mouse cartoon by including the child's possible thoughts as captions (Mich, 36). Mich and Eberman claim that "the article really requires no text, and a mistake was made in presenting it in the picture-caption technique" (37). Characterizing the use of captions as a mistake in this case is interesting for several reasons. The argument is that this essay is in fact a successful pure picture-story, one which does not require words because the images are self-evident and self-sufficient, and that the story is "told completely and simply by pictures" (Mich, 37). No explanation is offered to account for the mistake, however, such as the journalistic requirement for disambiguation, even at the risk of redundancies through separate channels of information. For instance, in *School Photojournalism*, the editors of *Look* advise students not to "trust in the reader's ability to draw his own conclusion: rarely can a photograph communicate completely without a caption" (E. Hamilton, 64). Moreover, the aforementioned "mistake" would continue to appear in pure picture stories, such as in Kubrick's "Bronx Street Scene" (November 26, 1946), in which two women comment on a friend's hairdo. It is not inconceivable, however, that this ideal of the purely visual story told without the aid of words was shared with the staff at *Look* magazine, and may have led to Kubrick's own interest in developing a new kind of film language freed from the constraints of spoken or written language: "I think that the scope and flexibility of movie stories would be greatly enhanced by borrowing something from the structure of silent movies where points that didn't require dialog could be presented by a shot and a title card" (Ciment 2003, 187). Kubrick's *Look* colleague Earl Theisen echoes these views in *Making Your Pictures Interesting*, when he states that "a truly successful photograph must be a self-contained unit in which no words of explanation are needed other than to say for identification who the persons are" (12).

An intermediate type of photo-essay, the "picture-text combination," is defined as "an article in which the storytelling is done by related pictures, arranged in some form of continuity. The text in such an article is important, but subordinated to the pictures" (Mich, 15). It is the most common type of photo-essay and represents "the modern picture magazine's most important contribution to the art of communication" (Mich, 15). A profile of Ingrid Bergman is used to illustrate the standard photo-essay, and is described as a carefully staged assignment, including a comprehensive shooting script (Mich, 23). Theisen specifically mentions *Look*'s shooting scripts, and recommends that amateurs may also wish to develop the discipline of preparing a script or at least formulating a plan prior to going on location for their vacation photo shoot, as a means of improving their visualization skills (29). The editors of *Look* concede that "scripts are important, but they should not be followed so rigidly that they become strait jackets," because the best pictures are often unplanned (Mich, 25). Similarly, Theisen argues that shooting scripts "are not intended to be hard and fast rules of procedures but directional helps so as to be an informative aid in the field" (29). He adds that "usually the best ideas are not dreamed up but shape up in front of the camera if the action is given free reign" (Theisen, 73). This sounds very much like Kubrick's modus operandi in rehearsing with actors and shooting dozens of takes, at least from *Lolita* onwards, when he would welcome improvisation in the hope that interesting new lines might emerge and add a surprising twist to a scene (Baxter, 159).

A good example of the picture-text combination that may require both planning and spontaneity was one of Kubrick's first street assignments as an apprentice for *Look*. During the hot summer months in New York City, kids, young and old, would entertain themselves by going to Coney Island or, between 1898 and 1971, across the Hudson River to the Palisades Amusement Park in New Jersey. Kubrick was sent there in June 1946, and he returned with at least 420 photographs, 26 of which were published a year later, in the June 24, 1947, issue of *Look*. Among the unpublished photographs, Kubrick's buddy Alexander Singer appears in several frames with a Rolleiflex, taking a picture of the photojournalist (cf. Figure 5). Titled "Fun at an Amusement Park," this is a four-page photo-essay uninterrupted by ads. The first spread's layout is unusual in that it is dominated by a cut-out photograph of a roller coaster, which overlaps on both pages, surrounded by smaller pictures. The faces of screaming riders unambiguously illustrate the essay's title. The first three pictures on the left focus on parents feeding or carrying their young children, followed by four slightly larger photographs on the opposite page listing some of the available games, such as shooting down "all the enemy German planes you want" or riding in bumper cars. The last image shows a woman and a soldier flirting at a handwriting analysis booth, a place where one "can meet some pretty interesting people" according to the caption. *Drama & Shadows* includes six unpublished photographs from this scene, which highlight more clearly the romantic nature of this young couple's meeting, and Kubrick's ability at capturing the many expressions of their burgeoning relationship (Crone, 215–17).

The second spread takes advantage of Kubrick's practice, common among photojournalists, of taking multiple shots of any given scene. The pictures are then arranged horizontally in a serial fashion, giving the appearance of stills selected from a documentary film. Four photographs depicting four different fairground activities are thus presented in as many strips, and identified in bold type as "Guess your weight; Tell your fortune; Ring the bell; Watch your step." The first strip shows a man claiming to correctly guess customers' weight for ten cents, which he accomplishes by merely observing in a clownish way. The second strip features Madam Zara, who has been telling fortunes at the Palisades Park for 22 years. The composition for these four medium close-ups is virtually identical, the only difference being the four women who seek answers "on love, marriage or success" and the fortune-teller's facial expressions. As a social study, this page indicates that only women consult Madam Zara, whereas only men attempt to ring a bell by hitting a stump with a large hammer, as pictured in the third strip. The caption points out the gender bias, observing that "showing off his strength is a man's weakness, a fact that has consistently made money for amusement parks." The men are in the foreground, facing the camera, with a small crowd of supporters behind them. The first two pictures show the men holding the hammers in mid-swing, whereas the next two shots show everyone looking up after the hit. The third picture differs by featuring a young boy who appears slightly challenged by the weight of the hammer, but who attracts a younger crowd of supporters, including two giggling girls. The final series continues this gender split with images of women encouraged to walk down a dark passageway, with rubber tubes scraping their ankles. All they can see are mechanical rubber mice moving in the distance, with predictable results. This adolescent humour would no doubt have appealed to the 17-year-old photographer, who used a flash to capture a full shot of a screaming woman lifting her leg to avoid the "mice," printed as a concluding full-page bleed picture, for dramatic effect. The contrast could be likened to a sudden close-up in a film scene.

The final intermediate type of photo-essay discussed by Mich and Eberman is the picture-story contained within a text story, which amounts to a text illustrated not by single photographs but by a pure picture-story or by a picture-text combination (15). The embedded story thus enjoys a certain independence, but is also related to the larger essay, representing both a variation on the illustrated text and a form of mise-en-abyme. The *Look* editors provide the essay "Painless Childbirth" as an example, a medical article written by an expert on "continuous caudal analgesia," which is "broad and general, partially historical, somewhat statistical" (Mich, 42). It was decided to illustrate this essay with a self-contained sequence of images following one woman's experience of giving birth thanks to this new medical procedure. Surprisingly perhaps, none of Kubrick's assignments appear to have been edited in this manner, with the possible exception of his first published photograph announcing President Roosevelt's death via a newspaper stand, which concluded a biographical summary of FDR's life with pictures from different sources. Another exception may be series photographs included with standard picture-text combination essays. Such series do not really constitute a story in the sense articulated by Mich and Eberman, since they are merely chronological sequences of images with no particular beginning and ending point. One interesting case, however, appears on the opening spread of the essay "Lady Lecturer Hits the Road" (February 28, 1950), a profile of best-selling author Emily Kimbrough on the lecture tour. Hugging the entire length of the page's right edge is a strip of six medium close-ups of Kimbrough eating grapefruit for breakfast and answering questions at the same time, which the Library of Congress contact sheets reveal to be an unedited, consecutive sequence of pictures taken by Kubrick with his 35-mm camera. This kind of candid serial imagery was a common layout option used by *Look* magazine, inspired by photojournalism's motion-picture leanings, and is singled out in the *School Photojournalism* textbook as a means of allowing the subject to express his or her personality (E. Hamilton, 33). However, the fact that neither the picture editors nor the layout artists felt it necessary to modify the picture sequence at all speaks to the photographer's seemingly effortless ability in capturing a perfectly varied range of facial expressions for this profile. Despite the lack of picture-story contained within a text story in Kubrick's published work, he must have been aware of the technique and certainly produced corresponding cinematic examples such as the violent film within a film in *A Clockwork Orange* when Alex is being brainwashed.

Seven forms of continuity in the photo-essay

Titled "Picture Continuities," the third chapter of *The Technique of the Picture Story* outlines the various kinds of visual and thematic relationships between images in a photo-essay, effectively defining the photojournalistic version of film's "continuity editing." In fact, the chapter begins with a comparison with motion pictures: "Many of the problems involved in constructing picture articles are similar to those involved in making movies" (Mich, 78). Earl Theisen adds that even though photography lacks the motion pictures' continuity of action, it is desirable for photojournalists to capture key moments in an event's unfolding in order to "suggest a sequence of thought" and enhance "the vicarious projection of the reader into the photograph" (34). The *Look* editors admit that it is not always possible to practise "personal journalism" to the letter, by using the same individual in all pictures to provide visual continuity, which is why other forms of continuity are required to unify photo-essays and supply some coherence (Mich, 78). These alternatives include literal or narrative chronology, visual comparisons and contrasts, thematic groupings and layout design.

The first type of continuity is a "simple chronology" in which a series of views on a single subject are presented in chronological order but with no specific or implied narrative (Mich, 78). The simple chronology is illustrated by two examples in the *Look* textbook, including a personality profile which incorporates private family photos obviously not taken by the magazine's staff (Mich, 80). In the August 5, 1947 issue of *Look*, Kubrick provided 12 pictures for a three-page essay on 15-year-old Polish war orphan Jack Melnik. Titled "I Found Freedom in America," the article's pictures are laid out plainly, like a family photo album, and numbered chronologically. Kubrick took 12 out of 13 published pictures, excluding the first one showing Jack after he was liberated by American GI's in 1944. It is slightly overexposed and was likely taken by the US Army in France, providing the magazine profile with photographic evidence of Jack's wartime experiences. The second example of a simple continuity is a two-page *Life* spread depicting the day in the life of a 16-month-old baby in Washington Square, Manhattan (Mich, 82). The layout begins with baby Dana leaving the apartment and ends with the girl dirtying her dress from eating ice cream, and the pictures are numbered to indicate a clear sequence, although there is no narrative progression per se other than an apparently random, before-and-after series of events. Kubrick produced a number of similar street photography assignments, including an unpublished candid camera series on the benches at Bryant Park, and the *Look* editors once again point out that this particular kind of job may not benefit as much as others from a detailed shooting script (Mich, 83).

The second type of picture continuity identified by the *Look* textbook is a properly narrative chronology, one where events are deliberately presented as a story, not a casual slice of life (Mich, 86). An eight-picture sequence of Frank Sinatra rehearsing a movie kiss with co-star Gloria DeHaven, under director Tim Whelan's supervision, is used to point out separate narrative stages: careful preparation, suspense as Sinatra is pressured to "make it special," and a gag ending when DeHaven swoons (Mich, 88). This form of continuity came naturally to Kubrick, whose last published essay as a freelancer was "A Short-Short in a Movie Balcony" (April 16, 1946), a stunt that he set up at the expense of fellow High School photographer Bernard Cooperman, who got slapped for making a move on an attractive classmate (LoBrutto, 25). The third and most common form of continuity, according to Mich and Eberman, is the repeated identity, that is, including the same person, object or place in all pictures (90). A person repeated in every image functions as a strictly visual link, which helps to hold a personality story together, for instance. Kubrick's July 19, 1949, portrait of Montgomery Clift, titled "Glamor Boy in Baggy Pants," is a five-page essay with nine photographs, all of which feature the movie star, except for two in which he interacts with fellow actor Kevin McCarthy and his family. The repeated identity technique also allows photo-stories to use structuring principles other than chronological order, as illustrated by *Look*'s wartime profile of a "Flying Nurse," much like Kubrick's documentary film short *Flying Padre* (Mich, 90). In the absence of a single character, a *Life* magazine essay about ladies evening wear in Broadway plays relies mainly on the clothes as a unifying factor, as well as similar shot sizes and a grid-like layout pattern (Mich, 92). Kubrick's "Life and Love on the New York Subway" (March 4, 1947) is unified by the location, even though the essay is further subdivided thematically.

The fourth "how-to" form of continuity is a precisely identified sequence of photographs, sometimes numbered, designed for didactic, step-by-step self-help articles, demonstrating how something should be done. The *Look* textbook adds that "the how-to treatment is more frequently employed in the participant-sports field than in any other," slowing down the action to analyse a golf swing, for instance, with the help of "magic-eye camera sequences" (Mich, 96). In the era's journalistic lingo, "magic-eye" actually referred to a modified motion-picture camera, although this was seldom explained in the photo-essays, as if to preserve the magazine's Hollywood-like aura of "special effects." Kubrick once used a so-called "machine-gun camera" (a modified 35-mm Bell & Howell Eyemo) to produce freeze-frame action pictures of Brooklyn Dodgers pitcher Don Newcombe throwing the ball in the camera's direction (April 11, 1950). Also used for didactic purposes is a fifth method of continuity, parallel or contrast, in which pictures are lined up axiologically to indicate the right and the wrong way of doing something (Mich, 100). This may be presented as an actual or speculative "before and after" sequence, or even as an objective, scene-by-scene comparison between a play and its film version, for instance (Mich, 98). The textbook presents a *Life* essay in which Patrick Hamilton's play *Angel Street* is compared to George Cukor's film adaptation *Gaslight*, and characterizes the compare and contrast technique as "ingenious," which may explain why *Look* magazine went on to exploit it in future issues, as in Arthur Rothstein's "How Europe Looks Two Years After V-E Day" (May 13, 1947). Parallel or contrast is a fairly common structuring device, since it can "put over editorial points simply, speedily and vividly" (Mich, 79). Contrasts are explicitly used in Kubrick's essay "Chicago, City of Extremes," published in the April 12, 1949, issue of *Look*: a lake-front park is opposed to a garbage-cluttered slum area, a cheap market to a fancy shop, and a homeless person eating a sandwich to a wealthy couple dining at a fine restaurant. Kubrick would continue to use comparisons as a filmmaker (usually ironic contrasts), at various levels of the filmic discourse: within a shot, between shots and between scenes. Soldiers in *Dr. Strangelove* engage in combat under a sign proclaiming "Peace is Our Profession;" Alex in *A Clockwork Orange* fantasizes about a biblical orgy while the prison chaplain believes that the inmate is deep in prayer; parallel montage in *Paths of Glory* contrasts officers in the chateau with soldiers in the trenches; achronological editing in *The Killing* compares the same key event from different points of view.

The layout artist's design may constitute a sixth form of continuity, based on an "arrangement of borders, boxes, panels or typography to give visual cohesion to an article which may or may not possess it otherwise" (Mich, 79). The art director's expertise is thus required in the case of conceptual essays or when the selected photographs are visually dissimilar. Kubrick's photo-essay "The 5 and 10" (September 2, 1947), about shoppers at a discount department store, illustrates the usefulness of a deliberate layout. The first spread begins with a large "bleed" picture in the top left corner, and is then dominated by horizontal strips of photographs organized by theme, some of which are serial in nature, similar to the Palisades Amusement Park essay. The opening spread's design is similar to one analysed in the 1951 book *Picture Editing*, in which the authors describe a layout "built around a large key picture with all others the same size," adding that it is "an unusual picture page treatment," although the evidence from *Look* magazine suggests otherwise (Kalish, 155). The spread thus includes four strips of four pictures each, featuring medium-shots of patrons at the stationery department, the toy counters, the household wares and undergarments sections. The first three strips include different subjects, so the layout helps to support the thematic separation by department, in contrast with the fourth and last strip, focusing on a woman wearing shades who examines underwear being sold at 35¢ a pair. She and another woman appear to discuss the matter, unaware of the photographer's presence, reminding us of Kubrick's earlier candid piece titled "Bronx Street Scene."

The seventh and last continuity device mentioned by Mich and Eberman is thematic development, which is presented as the need to highlight logical relations between pictures for rhetorical purposes (104). It is also pointed out that all seven techniques are almost invariably used in combination in order to strengthen each article's argument (Mich, 105). A typical combination that was often applied to Kubrick's photo-essays is a narrative progression contained within an overall thematic structure. A health-related social study titled "Childhood's Most Neglected Disease" (April 27, 1948) exemplifies this pattern in a useful way. Described by Vincent LoBrutto as "a sensitive photo study," this story focused on young victims of rheumatic fever being treated at a sanitarium in Chicago (40). Rheumatic fever is referred to as the leading fatal disease among children in the United States, a situation that would change considerably with the use of antibiotics in the 1950s. Framed by two large-sized pictures, the article includes a total of ten photographs illustrating the various forms of therapy applied to the youngsters. The second page focuses on the medical treatment received, while the third overlapping page shows some activities that children are encouraged to participate in during their convalescence at the hospital. The opener, printed as a bleed picture, is a medium-shot of a shirtless little girl with her arms stretched out in front of her, flexing her fingers to demonstrate muscular control. The photograph appears to use natural light from a window, which highlights the patient as she reaches out to grab her doctor's open hands, seen on the left edge of the frame. The dramatic picture introduces us to the plight of vulnerable children who become dependent upon adults other than their parents when they suffer from serious ailments.

Combining thematic grouping and narrative progression, the second page illustrates precisely what the medical treatment entails, beginning with a photograph of the same girl waiting in a reception room decorated for children. She then watches a boy submitting to an electrocardiogram. Seeing others go through tests makes the procedure less intimidating, we're told. The next two pictures show other girls getting checked for streptococcal germs and taking blood tests. To prevent infections, "parents are allowed to visit their children only once every month," an unfortunate situation that is offset by the hospital staff's "kindliness." A social worker, who visits the children daily and keeps parents informed, is seen smiling with a young boy. The last picture introduces a contrast between the medical technician's gear, as he places an X-ray screen in front of a young girl, and the explanatory caption, which points out the popularity of the fluoroscopic test among children due to the use of chocolate-flavoured barium sulphate. The technician wears large protective gloves and a thick apron to shield him from the radioactivity, whereas the skinny young girl is wearing nothing more than pyjamas.

The last page provides three examples of activities, which recovering children are encouraged to engage in, described as "occupational therapy." A smiling woman shows a cart filled with books from the Hospital's library of childhood favourites to an enthusiastic, bespectacled boy. The second picture features five children receiving schooling from a teacher who was specially trained by the Chicago Board of Education. Books provide a visual link between these two pictures, and with the exception of the X-ray technician, the caregivers in this photo-essay are all women. The concluding image is a large photograph of two girls happily playing with a doll house, meant to contrast with the article's opening shot of the helpless youngster. The social study's narrative thus provides a positive and hopeful progression from a concerned little girl and children required to receive various forms of medical tests, to more cheerful faces reading and playing as the Hospital staff takes care of them. Undoubtedly, publishing feel-good stories about children did not hurt *Look*'s sales at the newsstand, not to mention the image of all the featured individuals and companies.

Evaluative criteria for individual photographs

The textbook's second chapter identifies five aesthetic goals that photographers are required to aim for. This is prefaced by two general rules that beginner picture-story producers are advised to follow: to show people doing what they normally do in their own environment, and to narrow the focus to a single person whenever possible (Mich, 46). *Look*'s focus on personal journalism is made clear, although showing people doing normal things might be qualified, to the extent that personality profiles often thrive on unusual individuals, either celebrities or eccentrics. The evaluative criteria are then listed as: "1) storytelling quality; 2) photographic quality; 3) impact; 4) simplicity; 5) beauty" (Mich, 46). It is argued that a picture must possess a minimum of three out of these five qualities to be considered "good," that is, useful for the purpose of producing a magazine picture-story (Mich, 46). While the authors admit that rules "are made to be broken" and that "human judgments differ on photographs," they maintain that any picture-story producer who departs from their guidelines "is reducing his chances of success" (Mich, 46).

It is claimed that a magazine photograph's most important aesthetic property concerns storytelling: "Storytelling quality is virtually always an essential, because each picture must move the story along in relation to the picture preceding or following" (Mich, 46). This statement does not make it entirely clear whether a storytelling quality should be immanent to each individual photograph, or whether it is sufficient that it arise from the juxtaposition with other photographs, although Earl Theisen states that "while each photograph is a complete unit in itself, there is no picture that does not go directly to the point of the story" (Theisen, 68). Also, Mich and Eberman use a single shot of a street battle taken in Germany in 1919, to illustrate the narrative drama inherent in a wide, establishing view of armed conflict that includes ongoing hand-to-hand combat and injured soldiers, all in the same image. In any case, it is understood that photographers should be thinking in terms of multiple images revealing visual progressions and narrative sequences, rather than single, timeless, entirely self-contained art photographs. One of Kubrick's fashion assignments demonstrates this attention to narrative relations within and between images. One might think that fashion jobs are limited to showing models posing, when in fact an implied story could often add interest to the mise-en-scène. The August 17, 1948, essay "Will This Be the New Look for Men?" includes two shots illustrating the convenience of wearing a convertible coat. The first image shows a businessman wearing the topcoat version of his new coat and boarding a plane in Los Angeles, where the temperature is 65 degrees. The model walks down the airplane staircase in the next photograph, sporting the winter coat version with an alpaca lining and collar, as the temperature has dropped to 15 degrees in New York. Each picture has a built-in narrative potential, and implies a straightforward temporal ellipsis when combined with the other picture.

A more elaborate example of storytelling quality can be seen in Kubrick's essay "The Boss Talks It Over with Labor" (March 30, 1948). On June 23, 1947, the US Congress passed the Taft-Hartley Act, sponsored by Republican Senator Robert Taft, whom Kubrick would follow on the campaign trail two years later. Also known as the Labour-Management Relations Act, this federal law was designed to curb the power of labour unions. Five months after the Act became Law, the general manager of a company that produced kitchen appliances in Connersville, Indiana, decided to talk to his 2500 employees in groups of 100 on company time about the new labour law, allegedly "to regain the old fashioned intimacy of the small plant." The four-page photo-essay is framed by two large pictures showing the beginning and the end of the boss's speech, two key stages in any narrative. The opening shot appears to indicate that the boss's attempt to generate good feelings by talking in a friendly manner is successful, judging from the male audience's facial expressions. The caption to the concluding shot, however, describes the group as "poker-faced men," perhaps as a means of introducing narrative suspense before the workers vote informally on the labour law. The employees were asked to vote before and after the speech, in order for management to gauge the effectiveness of boss Eric Johnson's rhetorical skills. Below the article's opening photograph is a medium close-up of a worker about to vote against the Taft-Hartley Act, ironically contradicting the caption's claim that "voting was secret." The essay's closing photograph shows employees leaving the room after Johnson's lecture, with the boss silhouetted in the foreground. Unpublished contact sheets of this picture indicate that Kubrick sought to capture this particular image in a cinematic fashion, as workers are seen in consecutive shots, gradually disappearing through the back doors.

Photographic quality is the second criterion for a good picture, although the textbook does not provide a precise definition and simply defers to the photographer's technical expertise (Mich, 47). The authors do highlight the photographic qualities of a *Life* magazine portrait of American shipbuilder and industrialist Henry J. Kaiser, which include "interesting composition, good lighting, [and] extreme sharpness of detail" (Mich, 59). Unfortunately, what makes the composition "interesting" is not explained, neither are "good lighting" nor "sharpness of detail" defined, although we can describe the photograph's lighting as high key and its focus as sharp. Luckily, *Look* photographer Earl Theisen has more to say about photographic quality, specifically lighting and camera angle, which helps us to determine what the magazine's standards were. He lists three rules regarding lighting: "Make lighting seem natural; do not use tricky effects unless emotional effect is desired; use lighting that makes photographs easy to look at" (43). This boils down to a late-1940s conception of realism in lighting, which balances the need for clear communication, a sense of naturalism, and the photographic technology available at the time. For instance, noting that both rotogravure and the half-tone printing methods tend to increase contrast, Theisen observes that "most photographers use flashbulbs in sunlight to eliminate extreme contrast in the interests of good reproduction" (48). This is in keeping with the Hollywood practice of using reflectors on location in order to avoid deep shadows under the movie stars' eyes, which was also implemented by cinematographer Carlo Montuori when filming the landmark Italian neo-realist film *The Bicycle Thief* (1948). Despite his predilection for natural light, Kubrick himself also used flashbulbs outdoors in daytime, for instance, in unpublished photographs from the Ringling Brothers circus story (Crone 2005, 209). One of the colour Kodachrome prints from that assignment, available at the Library of Congress, shows a female assistant's arm on the left edge of the frame holding up the flash as Kubrick takes a picture of lady gymnasts standing on a bright red circus trailer (cf. Figure 21). At night or indoors, Theisen advises against the use of harsh flash photography on the grounds that it is "unfriendly, shocking," except when applied to crime-related subjects (44). Hard light thus becomes appropriate when it fits the code of realism of certain topics, such as crime and boxing. The *School Photojournalism* textbook also singles out a "strong play of light and shadow" as a quality that helps to make photographs "as vivid and eye-catching as possible" (E. Hamilton, 19). One cannot

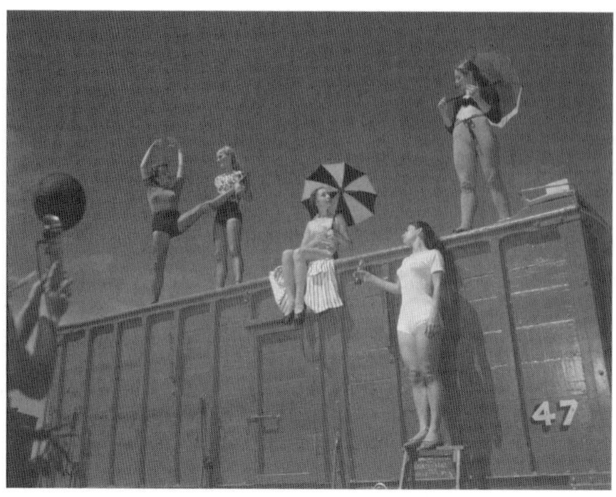

Figure 21: Members of the Ringling Brothers circus in Sarasota, Florida (March, 1948).

help but think of the teenage Kubrick's hero Weegee when it comes to flash photography, and the influence of film noir on photojournalism is hard to ignore as well. Kubrick used low-key underlighting for some posed or staged photographs, such as the low-angle shot of a woman receiving a telegram about a relative's medical operation in the essay "Do You Have Imaginary Illnesses?" (September 17, 1946). His use of low-key underlighting in the scene with Sherry at Val's apartment in the film *The Killing* is probably the most explicit (cf. Figure 22).

Theisen's discussion of camera angle takes on a cinematic tinge, when he contrasts "continuities" designed to illustrate "the various stages of a dance, sports event, or other action," with most other photographic situations (65). He acknowledges that series photographs, such as Kubrick's portrait of Milton Berle entertaining his daughter (June 21, 1949), would be discontinuous and visually confusing if the angle were not identical or

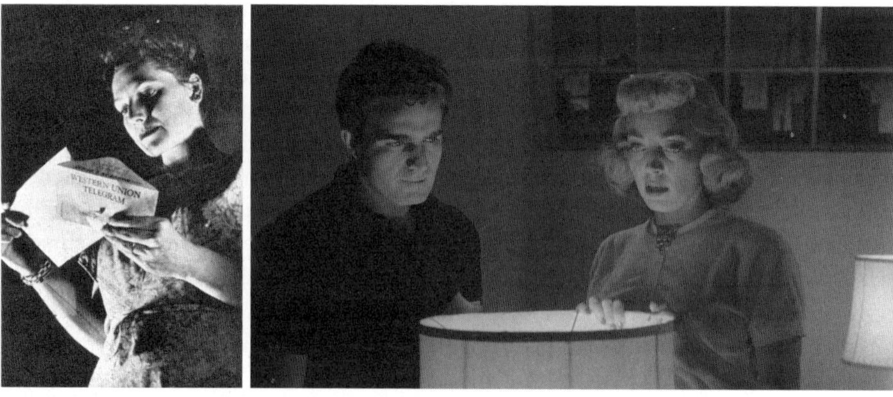

Figure 22: Film noir underlighting in staged photo-essay (1946) and The Killing (1956).

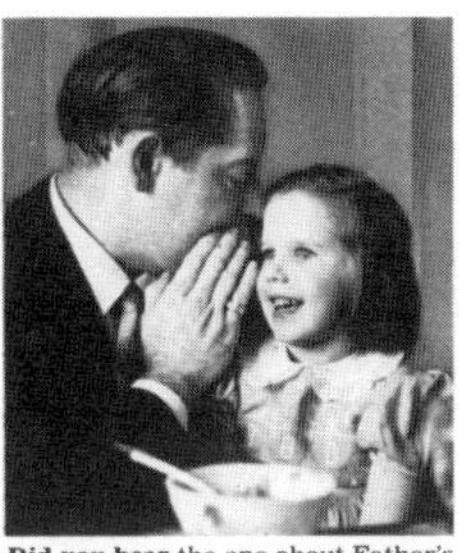
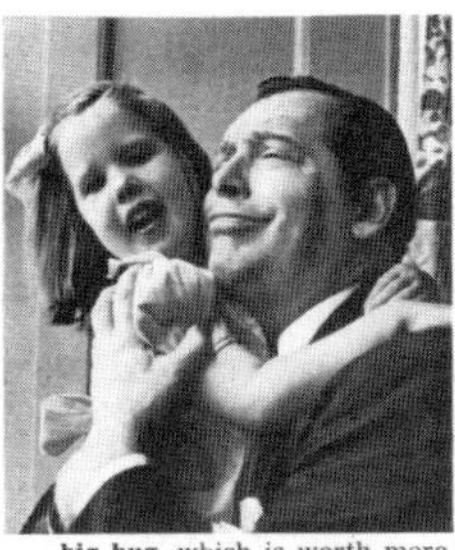
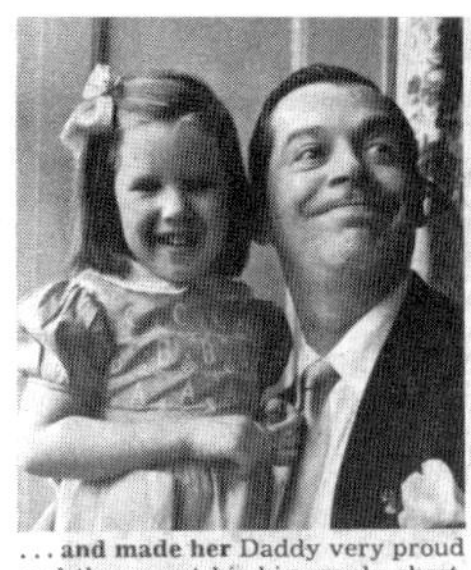
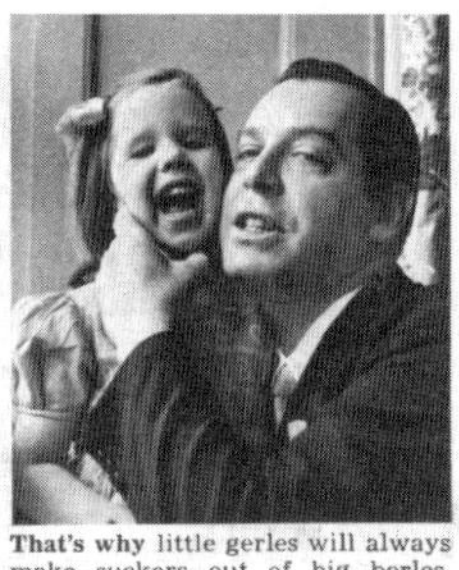

Figure 23: Kubrick portrait of Milton Berle and his daughter Vicki (April, 1949).

at least consistent, similar to the effect of a jump cut in film (Theisen, 65) (cf. Figure 23). Otherwise, the majority of photo sequences require a variety of camera angles in order to avoid a monotonous layout, a requirement that allows the photo-essay to emulate aspects of cinema's mobile frame, as suggested by Theisen's claim that "on *Look* magazine the camera is considered an instrument that is mobile, flowing with the dictates of the action" (63). Kubrick would most certainly avail himself of the mobile camera in his film career, in addition to the long take from a fixed camera position. However, it is deemed essential that the flexibility of viewpoints promoted by this ideal of mobility must not become unduly obtrusive or call attention to itself (Theisen, 64). Theisen thus introduces the notion of invisible editing, an important component of photojournalism's code of realism, which includes an unheightened form of didacticism, seamlessly communicating information about an essay's topic: "The instructive contents are introduced casually and included in a way that does not interfere with the activation of the picture. … It is imperative that while a picture must be informative the reader must never be aware of the fact" (74). For instance, Kubrick's essay "Deaf Children Hear for the First Time" (May 25, 1948) contains pertinent news about the development of hearing aids by inventor Leland A. Watson, whose device would receive a patent in 1952. The information is conveyed effortlessly thanks to radio and opera star Risë Stevens, who hosted a party in her New York City apartment in which 12 deaf children were outfitted with Watson's hearing aids. The two-page article is dominated by a medium close-up of Ms. Stevens on the left side of the picture, singing in a motherly way to a group of children wearing the special earpieces. The youngsters look up appreciatively at the star of the CBS Family Hour, who also appeared in the Hollywood movie *Going My Way* (1944, Leo McCarey) with Bing Crosby. This moment is singled out as the highlight of the soirée, according to the editors of *Look*, by virtue of the size and prominent placement of the image. The remaining three pictures on page left flashback to an earlier part of the evening when the children have their hearing aids fitted by Watson, Stevens and the children themselves. The second page includes three photographs showing the children getting used to their hearing instrument. Two girls hold up the device like a walkie-talkie, and in the essay's only critical image, a boy winces as the hearing aid produces feedback in his earpiece. The novelty wore off for some of the children who removed their earpieces before the end of the party. The concluding image shows a group of eight laughing children, while the caption informs us that they played games with Ms. Stevens, banged on the piano and ate cake and ice cream. This article likely contributed to maintaining Risë Stevens' popular image in the media, as well as publicizing Mr. Watson's useful invention. As for Kubrick, his skill at taking eye-level pictures of children once again proved engaging.

The third desirable quality in a photograph is emotional impact (Mich, 47). In fact, Theisen lists "visual impact" as *Look* editor Dan Mich's preferred quality for a publishable picture: "On the *Look* staff we hear a great deal about the word 'impact' these days. It is that quality of a photograph which stops the reader, that makes the photograph impelling and vital, and it is usually this shot that merits a big blowup in reproduction" (10). Crime photographer Weegee is identified as a freelancer whose middle name is "impact" because of the way he specializes in "human reactions to violence," including "fires, murders, suicides, riots" (Mich, 67). Regardless of the kind of emotional reaction elicited, such as laughter or anger, the object is to avoid leaving the reader indifferent, similar to the advertising industry's primary goal. It is also similar to the evaluative criterion "intensity of effect," listed as a valuable quality in film form (Bordwell 1997, 78). The *Look* editors claim that such an effect is easier to achieve in candid images, but that it remains the picture-story producer's responsibility to aim for and obtain that quality in staged photographs as well (Mich, 47). Theisen acknowledges that most published photographs are, in fact, what he calls "posed action," but advises that they should be conceived as re-enactments involving motion, rather than static poses, in order to introduce a natural quality and avoid a stiff portrait (78). As long as sharp focus is maintained, it is best to create the impression that the subjects are not acting for the camera but engaged in some other activity. Theisen also recommends that re-enactments remain in good taste, and mentions specifically that "most editors abhor anything in a photograph that remotely resembles a gag," which does not necessarily appear to be the case at *Look* magazine (81). Kubrick's "A Short-Short in a Movie Balcony" (April 16, 1946) was a gag disguised by the editors of *Look* as a candid moment captured with an infra-red camera, whereas Montgomery Clift's drinking binge in "Glamor Boy in Baggy Pants" (July 19, 1949) was a partly autobiographical mise-en-scène identified by the caption as a pure gag, no doubt in order to reassure Clift's fans and his agent.

It is fair to say that Kubrick has demonstrated his ability in creating an emotional impact in both his staged films and his candid photographs. In fact, Kubrick's portrait of Frank Sinatra smiling at a shy young girl in a school auditorium is printed full page in *Look's School Photojournalism* as an example of a vivid, striking image: "A visit to school produces spontaneous response from two small girls in the audience. Notice how girl at center is focal point due to her keen reaction and the fact that she is singled out by many eyes in the room directed toward her. The photographer has avoided the obvious pitfall: a stiffly posed group, looking toward the camera" (E. Hamilton, 16). It is further argued that while staged photographs must strive for authenticity and avoid exaggeration, drama and emotion enhance their communicative value, including their rhetorical effectiveness, that is, their ability to identify a social problem such as inadequate funding in the school system and convince the reader that something must be done about it (E. Hamilton, 36). Similarly, the horror of war as depicted in George Strock's photograph for *Life* magazine of American soldiers lying dead on a beach in Buna, New Guinea, can have an educational impact regarding the need to avoid armed conflict of any kind (Mich, 61). The authors of the textbook also include a picture depicting an injured airman being carried out of his plane to illustrate conflicting emotions, as "the expression on the hurt boy's face and the tenderness of his comrades speak more eloquently of the human tragedy in war than a volume of words" (Mich, 62). Kubrick has tapped into these emotional extremes when he included a close-up view of Vincent Cartier carefully applying Vaseline on his twin brother Walter's face prior to a brutal battle in the ring, in the essay "Prizefighter" (January 18, 1949). A number of situations in *Full Metal Jacket* also involve an apparently incongruous combination of caring and violence, such as when Joker spends time teaching Gomer Pyle how to lace his boots and make his bed, soon followed by Hartman's relentless verbal abuse and humiliation of the hapless recruit.

Simplicity of mise-en-scène is the fourth quality to be sought in an individual picture according to the *Look* textbook, including an avoidance of cluttered compositions, "complicated backgrounds, mottled patterns, confusing shadows and overcrowded rooms," a rule that should apply in 99 per cent of cases (Mich, 47). Theisen confirms that "to have impact a photograph must bid for attention through simplicity," which requires the photographer to get rid of non-essential details that would otherwise dilute and confuse the essay's main idea, making it "difficult to hold the reader's attention" (56). Striving to eliminate distractions is therefore a way to serve the story and ensure a clarity of communication, and we may recognize that Kubrick's meticulous and controlled film style owes something to the photojournalistic discipline of pursuing a simple and direct form of expression. The *Look* editors illustrate the desired simplicity with a chiaroscuro medium-shot portrait of a Chinese scholar reading a book lit by an oil lamp set on the table in front of him, followed by W. Eugene Smith's stark picture titled "Grave of unknown Marine in the graveyard" (August 1, 1944) (Mich, 75). Smith took the shot from a low angle in order to use the overcast sky as a neutral background, similar to the way Kubrick would frame the Jantzens in "Family Full of Health" (August 19, 1947), to isolate the athletes' bodies from their surroundings as they performed elaborate exercise routines. In contrast, a cluttered picture of Sinatra being mobbed by autograph-seekers is deemed successful, since the visual confusion is appropriate for this scene, in addition to the usefulness of "such minute details as pencils, notebooks, rings" (Mich, 53). Less successful is a portrait of a youngster eating corn on the cob, due to the distracting background of a storefront sign over the boy's left shoulder (Mich, 56).

Provided the photographer has noticed the presence of "irrelevant" visual information, the obvious solutions are to vary the angle or stage the scene in a desired fashion. When this is not possible, there remains the option of cropping a picture, a common practice in photojournalism decried by some art critics as causing grievous injury to an artist's vision, ignoring the photo-essay's collective mode of authorship. *Look*'s editors acknowledge that "appropriate cropping for publication or any other communicative purpose presents an editorial as well as an artistic problem: [one] must be equally considerate of both meaning and general attractiveness," but argue nonetheless that one "can always clarify the message of the picture by cropping out the non-essentials" (E. Hamilton, 55). We might say that photo-magazine editors are primarily concerned with the "studium," the poor relative in Roland Barthes' analysis of photography, which focuses on dominant cultural interpretations of photographs as they relate to the producers' discursive intentions (1981, 27). Art critics are more interested in the "punctum," a kind of personal and idiosyncratic surplus value they bring to reading photographs that turns them into good objects, by providing an additional source of aesthetic pleasure beyond the predictable signification of what Barthes calls the "unary photograph" (1981, 40).

The fifth and last quality identified by the authors of the *Look* textbook is beauty, which they fail to define but do illustrate with a number of examples and counter-examples. Their main recommendation is to focus on people doing things and avoid art salon genres such as landscapes and the still-life, including "such clichés as photographing a sunset or rain on cobblestones" (Mich, 47). A picture displaying the scenic beauty of the English countryside, for instance, "belongs in a story only if it does not impede action" (Mich, 69). A shot of skiers moving down a mountain can provide an opportunity to include a natural backdrop unobtrusively (Mich, 73). A backlit portrait of Hollywood star Veronica Lake by *Life* magazine's Bob Landry is considered beautiful yet "arty," and lighting that does not show a person's face clearly "should be used sparingly" (Mich, 68). Kubrick did not hesitate to include backlighting in his repertoire, as the portrait of Betsy Von Fürstenberg sitting on a windowsill (July 18, 1950) and the shot of a female student at the University of Michigan (May 10, 1949) lighting a classmate's cigarette indicates (Crone, 167).

Evaluative criteria for subject matter

In terms of photo-essay content, *Look* magazine's evaluative criteria are discussed in the fourth chapter of *The Technique of the Picture Story*, titled "Ideas for Picture Stories." The five prized qualities are "an interest that transcends spot news," a source for "picture impact," a "sharp focus" on the selected topic, a "focus on people, as opposed to things," and a "universal interest" (Mich, 106). These features were largely determined by the economic realities of magazine photojournalism. *Look*'s frequency of publication did not allow it to pursue spot news that might be quickly dated, whereas *Life* had the resources to both cover the news on a weekly basis and offer feature essays. This aspect of *Look* magazine's identity, the fact that its stories had to maintain "a vitality that cannot be sapped by news developments," dovetailed nicely into Kubrick's growing interest in film. The cinematic medium would necessarily involve long-term projects similar to major photo-essay assignments, allowing the young visual storyteller to make a significant statement rather than to mechanically report the news as it occurred (Mich, 106). For instance, Kubrick's essay "Dale Carnegie: He Sells Success" (May 25, 1948), about the noted author, public speaker and teacher, was timed to coincide with the publication of Carnegie's new book on stress management, *How to Stop Worrying and Start Living* (1948), whose title may have inspired Kubrick for his film *Dr. Strangelove or, How I learned to Stop Worrying and Love the Bomb* (1963). However, the photo-essay may be said to transcend spot news in the way it comments on the timeless power of rhetoric.

Carnegie had published the best-seller *How to Win Friends and Influence People* in 1936, a book specifically recommended by *Look*'s Earl Theisen not only for its "penetrating study of human nature" but also as a useful primer on salesmanship, which he considered to be an essential tool of the photojournalist's trade (Theisen, 144). Theisen explains that in handling people for a photographic sitting, one had to master an array of psychological tricks designed to get the subjects to do what you wanted them to do, by employing "a disguised technique of suggestion" as well as "the Socratic method of getting the subject to say 'yes' a couple of times to inconsequential things" in order to elicit their cooperation (20). Moreover, one of the main concepts in Carnegie's books is that it is possible to change other people's behaviour by changing one's reaction to them. There is a manipulative aspect to such concepts that Kubrick would have been familiar with as a chess player, and would have been encouraged to develop further in his dealings with photographic subjects. For instance, he has simultaneously criticized and adopted the "patzer" approach to chess, which consists in setting up traps by bluffing, acting so as to make the opponent make a premature move (Bernstein 2001, 45–6). He has also been known for playing mind games with his actors and collaborators in order to get them to deliver what he was looking for. Similarly, the Carnegie article's alliterative title, "He Sells Success," hints at an apparent contradiction in the rhetorician's approach, or at least another gap between intent and behaviour.

In the article "He Sells Success," *Look*'s staff writer Harold B. Clemenko interviews Carnegie during the graduation exercises at the New York City branch of Carnegie's Institute of Effective Speaking and Personality Development. One of Clemenko's strategies is to present Carnegie as a man of the people, a "country boy in the city." Kubrick's photographs tell a slightly different story. On the one hand, the photo-essay certainly includes pictures highlighting the positive impact Carnegie has had on his students, who display gratitude publicly for his guidance. On the article's fourth page, two identically framed pictures show Carnegie Institute graduates on stage with their teacher, thanking him for improving their sense of self-confidence. Captions to the article's closing pictures almost attribute supernatural powers to Carnegie, by suggesting that a bespectacled woman who leads a class song at the graduation exercises, no longer needs to wear her glasses, using them instead as a baton, thus "exhibiting victory over timidity." A topic that is not addressed in the article is the effect of Carnegie's teachings on students from different countries and ethnic backgrounds. Yet the essay opens with a large-sized photograph of Carnegie decorating a pupil from Hawaii with a garland of flowers, and the third page features a medium-shot of a Sikh man shaking his teacher's hand, thanking him for his success as an insurance salesman in New Delhi, India.

The more deceptive aspects of oratory emerge from pictures of Carnegie himself lecturing, as well as students engaged in a rhetorical exercise. A series of three pictures on the article's third page show male students reciting "Mary Had a Little Lamb," after being instructed to deliver it with anger. An appropriate scowl from one student is matched by another student's fists raised, then another one pounding the podium. Applying a tone that is at odds with the material, highlights the instrumental, one might say dishonest nature of rhetoric. Another series of pictures on the left page of the last spread shows Carnegie pointing his finger for emphasis during a speech, in a way that could be interpreted as menacing or manipulative, if we didn't know what he was talking about. In order to soften Carnegie's image, perhaps, another series of three shots showing Mrs. Carnegie listening to her husband provides a human-interest element.

The second evaluative criterion for picture-story content concerns ideas, which may lend themselves to visually interesting material, providing photographic opportunities that will possess the aforementioned quality of "impact." It is argued that writers in particular must train themselves to "think in terms of images" and learn "to visualize a story" as much as possible (Mich, 106). The challenge, therefore, facing traditional journalists working for a photo-magazine is to overcome their reliance on the written word, and not come to expect or assume that photographers will automatically jazz up their articles with creative pictures. *Look*'s editors admit that it is possible for a dull essay to be saved by superior photography, and provide the example of a *Life* personality profile of Russian émigrée fashion designer Valentina, which lacked originality as a magazine subject but benefited from an "imaginative use of lights and background" in order to produce an interesting story (Mich, 127). It is also possible to go overboard with a visual idea or concept, which starts as a gimmick or a gag and fails to move beyond that stage, as Theisen warns repeatedly: "One of the problems for *Look* and other magazines in getting stories in the fun or party categories is to find games and activities that will photograph" without looking silly or even ridiculous (125).

Kubrick's infamous "Baby Wears Out 205-lb. Athlete" (March 18, 1947) certainly falls into this category. It was premised on the idea that it might be visually entertaining to put a 23-year-old college football player and ex-marine through a new kind of boot camp, as he systematically aped a 15-month-old toddler's various bodily contortions during the course of an entire day. The captions consistently inform us that athlete Bob found baby Dennis' ad hoc exercise routines very tiring. The 12 photographs show Bob trying to keep up with the small boy as he squats, leans back on the couch, crawls up the stairs, does a somersault on the couch, rides his hobbyhorse, and so on. Although there is no internal evidence to support this, we are told that the photographs are organized chronologically, from morning until 4 pm, by which time Bob is "dog-tired." The second spread's first and last pictures feature Dennis looking at the camera, which he appears to find more interesting than his 205-lb. playmate. The first photograph shows Dennis leaning against the couch with his hand in his mouth: "Suddenly aware of photographer, Dennis stares at the funny man with the camera," explains the caption. In an intentionally humorous reversal, the last photograph's caption alleges that Bob lies on the floor to rest, while Dennis mocks his adult companion by imitating him and mugging for the camera.

Narrowing the scope of the essay to a manageable size is considered the third desirable quality: the chances of producing a successful photo-essay increase as one shifts the editorial attention from a small town to one block, and then from one family living in this block to a single member of the family (Mich, 106). Visually, one might argue that the narrowest focus would be a photographic series of the same object or person taken from the same vantage point, and that the relative difficulty in producing a photo-essay on a broad topic becomes a matter of editing a wide range of pictures and finding a thematic structure, which might contain this variety. During Kubrick's initial apprenticeship at *Look*, he was assigned a story titled "Street Conversations," which yielded 320 photographs (submitted August 23, 1946), 25 of which were marked with a grease pencil on the contact sheets now available at the Museum of the City of New York. None of these were published, although a different series of four pictures from this assignment appeared as the "Bronx Street Scene" (November 26, 1946), a good example of either giving up on a broad topic or narrowing the focus to a brief and simple story.[1] In contrast, *Look*'s editors were bolder in editing Kubrick's "Subway Story" (March 4, 1947), which featured 17 of 515 photographs (submitted September 25, 1946). In this case, the strategy was to organize the pictures thematically into three categories, thus allowing the magazine to print a more substantial and very successful essay. There is no doubt that Kubrick himself would go on to tackle ambitious projects, with films such as *2001: A Space Odyssey* and the aborted *Napoleon*.

The fourth stated quality is a focus on people rather than "things" (or ideas?), in keeping with *Look*'s approach to personal journalism, by which it distinguished itself from chief rival *Life* magazine. Senior editor George Leonard explains that "where *Life* was cool, *Look* was warm," and "personal to a fault. Even if I had wanted to, I would have found it very hard to depersonalize someone I had known intimately" (19). The focus on people was thus reflected in the popularity of personality stories, both celebrities and unknowns whose appeal might be based on eccentricities or other human qualities. Kubrick certainly photographed his share of personalities, ranging from composer-conductor Leonard Bernstein (March 14, 1950) to a family of weightlifters (August 18, 1947). It may seem paradoxical to suggest that Kubrick was influenced by *Look*'s humanist and sentimental approach to storytelling, if we consider common descriptions of his cinema as precisely the opposite: cold, rational, cynical, and so on. Apologists have offered a number of counter-descriptions, including the suggestion that Kubrick's films are not "cold," but rather "on fire with ideas" (Kolker, 8). If "cold" is synonymous with unemotional, adds film critic Jonathan Rosenbaum, "it simply is not true that Kubrick's films lack emotion. They are full of emotions" (248). Part of the problem is that we are dealing with a false paradox, due to a generalized tendency to polarize descriptions of a magazine's style, or indeed a filmmaker's. George Leonard simply overstated his characterization of *Life*, which was not always as aloof and impersonal as he implied, if we only consider the famous 1961 photo-essay on Rio de Janeiro favela resident Flavio de Silva (Parks, 200). Conversely, *Look* periodically displayed a controlled and even clinical visual style, particularly in its staged essays, which was not necessarily read as cold or oppressive.

Concerning Kubrick's mise-en-scène, the film director Sydney Pollack once made the following observation: "You can look at Stanley's films and say: 'There's a cool theatricality here that I admire but don't particularly respond to emotionally.' Now, if you're saying: 'In order to do that, was there some spontaneity that got missed?' Perhaps, I don't know. But in Stanley's opinion, and most of the world's, the trade-off was more valuable: what he got by creating this architecture in a very studied way was preferable to the slightly more spontaneous, closer to reality behaviour, let's say, that you see in most other movies" (Pollack). This represents another formulation of Kubrick's Stanislavsky-inspired maxim: "Real is good, interesting is better," which also resonates with film documentarian John Grierson's famous phrase: "The creative treatment of actuality." Enhancing or heightening the "real" was a cornerstone of the documentary movement in photography and film in the 1930s, and *Look* magazine (and Kubrick) certainly inherited this aesthetic approach. As Theisen points out, photojournalists worked hard to make staged essays look "natural," but that "look" always remained a convention, and resorting to personal journalism was a way of both facilitating the reader's identification with the story, since it featured interesting people, and forgetting about the constructed nature of the representation. By working at *Look*, Kubrick became steeped in the techniques of personal journalism, that is, how to create engaging portraits of people and tell their stories in a sympathetic way, but also how to photograph with "impact," to produce expressive images through re-enactments or by deliberately controlling the framing and content of each shot. This would serve Kubrick well in his film career as he strove to endow his films with strong emotional and intellectual dimensions.

The last important quality recommended by the *Look* textbook is aiming for a "universal interest," based on the fact that a mass-circulation magazine such as *Look* could only survive if it told stories that would register with a readership of over 17 million in 1948 (Cowles, 110). These numbers must have impressed Kubrick, who did not attend an art school that promoted the value of an artist's private vision, but instead worked for a commercial, professional magazine that valued the idea of informing and entertaining its readers. It could be argued that Kubrick always maintained a strong sense of the importance of entertaining a wide audience, as well as marketing, perhaps not in the same way as a Steven Spielberg, but at least to the extent that it impacted on his choice and treatment of subject matter. An example of "universal," or at least general, interest for an American photo-magazine in the late 1940s is the profile of attractive TV personality Faye Emerson. Television was still a novelty and was only starting to become a direct competitor to both Hollywood and magazines such as *Look*. Faye Emerson, Franklin D. Roosevelt's ex-daughter-in-law, became one of the most recognizable faces in TV land when she hosted two regular talk shows broadcast on CBS and NBC. Known as "Mrs. Television," it is claimed that the Emmy Awards were named after her. Her appeal was based on a combination of glamour, intelligence and a pleasant on-air personality. Eleanor Harris' article, published in the August 15, 1950 issue of *Look*, is titled "Young Lady in a Hurry," and gives the impression of an ambitious, independent and confidant young woman. Emerson's fame would fade in the late 1950s with the disappearance of prime time talk shows, but in the early part of the decade, she was "the First Lady of Television." She began her show business career in the 1940s by appearing in undistinguished Hollywood movies, but it seems part of Emerson's appeal among men was to wear dresses with consistently low necklines, which prompted some to say that she put the "V" in TV. *Look* took advantage of this popular topic of conversation by putting a colour photograph of Emerson on their cover, one of three covers that Kubrick made during his brief career as a photojournalist.

The photo-essay's opening spread begins with two vertical rows of four pictures each on the left page, meant to convey a sense of Emerson's busy schedule. The first row shows her standing on a TV stage with a camera to her left, sitting for a portrait between shows at the Roxy Theatre while on the phone, choosing a colour scheme for her Park Avenue apartment and being interviewed by Eleanor Harris while walking on a Manhattan sidewalk. In the second row of photographs, Emerson rehearses for a play with noted actor Sam Wanamaker (a few years before he left permanently for England, having been blacklisted by the House Un-American Activities Committee), introduces Sid Caesar on the Roxy stage, meets her new corporate sponsor at a press party and has a late night drink with TV personality Robert Q. Lewis. On the third and last page of the photo-essay, Emerson handles two phone calls simultaneously from her Fifth Avenue office. The Manhattan skyline offers an impressive backdrop as Mrs. Television sits in front of a window in a medium-shot. Despite the workload, Emerson is shown smiling in all these pictures, which make the contrast with the first spread's dominant picture all the more striking. A wide overlapping picture shows Emerson in a medium close-up directing a staff of technicians on an NBC studio set. The caption explains that "TV's queen" briefly lost her cool during preparations, but managed to get what she wanted. This photograph's grainy quality gives an impression of spontaneity, which contrasts with the carefully lit pictures on the first page. Emerson's extended arm pointing to something off-frame, for the benefit of a half-dozen people standing in the background, suggests a woman who commands attention and knows how to get things done. This behind-the-scenes look is meant to reveal an alleged temper, belying the on-air genial personality. While the article focuses on Emerson's drive and assertiveness, the overlapping picture seems to imply that there is a flip side to her positive personality. The "young lady in a hurry" may run over a few people in the process of achieving her goals.

The personality picture-story

As if to underscore the importance of the fourth evaluative criterion for photo-magazine subject matter, *The Technique of the Picture Story* dedicates its fifth chapter to a detailed consideration of the personality profile. The editors of *Look* argue that non-fiction personality stories were the most popular feature of national magazines, citing *The New Yorker, Life,*

The Saturday Evening Post, Collier's and *Liberty* as publications that always included biographies of one kind or another (Mich, 128). This popularity is attributed to a "tremendous human appetite for information about human beings," to which we might add an appetite for information on any subject that is made easily accessible thanks to the presence of a character as an entry point (Mich, 128). In other words, the character is a pedagogical device helping readers to learn about a topic by first identifying with this person. Naturally, such an instrumental or didactic use of the "person schema" goes beyond the personality profile *stricto sensu*, but it does highlight a continuity of purpose that *Look* magazine implemented on a fairly systematic basis, and which also happens to be a norm in narrative fiction with its widespread focus on a central protagonist (Bordwell 1989, 152). With the exception of *The Seafarers, Fear and Desire, Dr. Strangelove* and *2001: A Space Odyssey*, all of Kubrick's films feature a single protagonist, hero or anti-hero.

A subset of the personality profile, dealing only with celebrities, was singled out by smaller, specialized magazines focusing on the Hollywood film industry, and in 1974, Time Inc. launched the weekly *People*, two years after *Life* ended its 35-year run. *Look*'s approach did not limit its profiles to the rich and famous, but also included lesser-known professionals who achieved Andy Warhol's 15 minutes of fame due to the unusual nature of their business or because of their philanthropy. The latter case is illustrated by Detroit advertising executive Lou Maxon, who returned to his hometown of Onaway, Michigan, in Kubrick's photo-essay "Home-Town Hero" (October 25, 1949). It is argued that "picture magazines generally try to tell stories in terms of people – and in terms of *one person* whenever possible," and that the personality genre may be broken down into three types: (1) The well-known personality; (2) The little-known but eccentric and fascinating personality (hero or screwball); (3) The little-known but representative personality of general significance (an overworked doctor in wartime) (Mich, 128). Mich and Eberman go on to describe the production process on the personality story, which reminds us of Thompson's editor in *Citizen Kane*, who asks his reporters to talk to everyone whoever knew Kane well, and to find out the meaning of "Rosebud" (129). Napoleon may have been reporter Kubrick's Charles Foster Kane, considering the extraordinary lengths he went to in developing the daily card catalogue of Bonaparte's life, but failing to complete his project without the film studio's support (Castle, 496).

One of Kubrick's celebrity profiles almost ends up undermining the genre due to a subject who doesn't fit the stereotype of the celebrity. The two-page article on Miss America 1947, Barbara Jo Walker (March 16, 1948), presents Walker as an atypical Miss America, who prefers to spend her year studying rather than going on a whirlwind promotional tour to maximize her income from endorsements. Kubrick's camera follows Miss America in Cleveland, Ohio, as she attends the Methodist Youth Conference. The first page is dominated by a large establishing shot of the Conference audience listening to an address by church leaders, with Walker sitting in the first row. The second page consists of five photographs depicting Miss America in various settings at the Conference. The largest image, printed as a bleed picture, shows Walker sitting on the lower rung of a bunk bed in the girls' dormitory, looking up to chat with another girl. She obligingly signs autographs in a medium-shot, despite being besieged according to the caption. A more pleasant scene is a long shot of the convention dance instructor showing Miss America some folk dance steps, while other young delegates clap time. A light source allows Walker to stand out among a group of delegates, in a high angle shot showing them with their heads bowed during a session's final benediction. A slightly cheeky medium close-up features Miss America chatting with the President of the Methodist Council of Bishops, in front of a sign which points an arrow in her direction with the words "odd numbers." This refers to a theatre's seating numbers, but could be taken as a comment on Walker's status as an "odd" Miss America.

By virtue of being selected as Miss America, Walker was technically an instant celebrity, even though she deviated somewhat from her "role." In the field of show business, a celebrity is expected to be glamourous and behave accordingly, although it is argued that "the flaws and foibles of the subject are important in personality pieces," because "they provide many readers with the psychological satisfaction of being able to feel superior in some way to the celebrity about whom they are reading" (Mich, 157). This sentiment would be expressed again in chess-playing wrestler Maurice's speech in Kubrick's *The Killing*, when he tries to explain to Johnny that the gangster and the artist are alike in that "they are admired and hero-worshipped, but there is present an underlying wish to see them destroyed at the height of their glory" (Nelson, 38). Barbara Jo Walker was too much of a goody two-shoes to elicit such feelings, and *Look* could have chosen not to run the story, were it not for the undeniable glamour of the Miss America title. In comparison, it is less likely that a mere "little-known representative personality" would have appeared in the magazine if he or she did not "look the part" and was not "typical" of a large group (Mich, 129). The difference between *Look* and a film industry casting agency becomes blurred when the magazine editors openly admit to resorting to cultural stereotypes for their articles. It is difficult to discount the enduring influence of *Look* and the conservative ideology of post-war America on Kubrick's worldview and how it determined the types of characters he included in his own film stories. For instance, the gay characters in *Barry Lyndon* (soldiers in a stream) and *Eyes Wide Shut* (hotel desk clerk) come across as fairly anachronistic, single-note stereotypes or caricatures played for laughs, throwbacks to an era less tolerant of difference (Rosenbaum, 248).

In discussing *The Technique of the Picture Story*, I've attempted to indicate the extent to which *Look*'s editors had a didactic bent, which made them perfectly suited to take on a talented apprentice photographer, even though the organization wasn't formally set up to do so. The contents of the *Look* textbook outline some of the norms and values, which the editors would have expected someone in Kubrick's position to adopt, and contribute to as he gained experience and expertise. These norms and values include a knowledge of magazine genres, photographic continuity techniques, the aesthetic and conceptual values of single photographs and essay themes, and especially an ability to practise *Look*'s variety of personal journalism. The major types of photo-essays are identified according to word-image relationships, the most common being a balanced combination of photographs and written text, not unlike cinema's combination of image and sound tracks. A specific set of visual and thematic relationships between pictures in a photo-essay constitute the magazine version of film's "continuity editing," further highlighting intermedial links and photojournalism's ability to provide transferable skills to a filmmaker-wannabe. Kubrick also had to demonstrate his ability to achieve the magazine's aesthetic goals for picture-taking, which included narrative potential, the documentary qualities of sharp and deep foci, visual impact in terms of framing and mise-en-scène, and a clarity of expression at the service of journalistic rhetoric. This intensive professional "training" not only contributed to developing Kubrick's photographic eye, which became a virtual light metre,[2] but instilled in him an instinct for visual storytelling and vivid exposition, which were obvious assets for filmmaking. Regarding story content, the fact that *Look* required its staff to identify themes and ideas that were not limited by current events and to focus on "human interest" qualities must have contributed to Kubrick's relatively mainstream approach to subject matter, as it revealed a concern for reaching and entertaining a broad audience. Lastly, *Look*'s personal journalism was a perfect prelude to Kubrick's pursuit of narrative fiction film production, since he also went on to feature well-known personalities (Kirk Douglas, Jack Nicholson, Tom Cruise …), and had them perform eccentric roles (Dr. Strangelove, Alex DeLarge, Jack Torrance …) or representative character types (drill sergeant, corrupt politician, family doctor …). *Look* magazine's norms and values thus proved to be quite influential as they continued to manifest themselves throughout Kubrick's professional life.

Notes

1 Six photographs from this assignment appear on page 207 in Crone's *Drama and Shadows*, although the production date is incorrectly identified as May 1946, rather than August.

2 According to Sydney Pollack in the documentary *The Last Movie: Stanley Kubrick and Eyes Wide Shut*, Kubrick once asked his cameraman to read the light levels after a lunch break during the production of *Eyes Wide Shut*, even though the electricians denied that any changes had been made to the dimmers on the set. They then allegedly discovered a difference of 1/8th of an f-stop.

Chapter 5

Micro-subjectivity: Stanley Kubrick's Conception of Photojournalism and Film

I am influenced by absolutely everything I've seen.

Stanley Kubrick[1]

According to George Ritzer, the micro-subjective realm of social reality "involves the feelings and perceptions, the mental aspects of the actors' position in the stratification system" (19). Ritzer suggests that one way of considering the relationships between the actor and the larger society is through the notion of personal biography, which may focus on the objective and subjective aspects of career patterns, for instance (210). In principle, we should consider Kubrick's personal conception of the photo-essay genre and its relation to the film medium. Since Kubrick himself has said very little about his photojournalistic career, we must also look to secondary sources, such as the photo-essays he co-authored with his *Look* magazine colleagues. This chapter will therefore begin by considering Kubrick's own comments regarding the advantages of working for a major photo-magazine shortly after graduating from high school, especially the practical aspects of photo-essay production and their relevance for a future film career. Examining the concurrent influence of the film industry on *Look* magazine and its photojournalists will be followed by further observations from Kubrick on the production process involved in some of his early assignments, including collaboration with fellow staff members. This will lead into an extended analysis of thematic and stylistic dimensions of Kubrick's essays, which can be read in the context of similar work produced by his colleagues prior to and during his tenure at *Look*. The chapter will conclude with an examination of Kubrick's thoughts on photography and film aesthetics, centred around the realism versus formalism debate.

Apprenticeship at *Look* magazine

Until recently, Kubrick's best known comments regarding his career as a photojournalist were made to French film scholar Michel Ciment in 1980: he began by recognizing that "it was a miraculous break for [him] to get this job after graduation from high school," and acknowledged his indebtedness to picture editor Helen O'Brian and managing editor Jack Guenther, who hired him initially as an apprentice photographer at *Look* (Ciment 2003, 196).

Ironically, neither would remain with *Look* very long, as O'Brian left the magazine in May 1946, shortly after she had recommended Kubrick, and Guenther died tragically in a plane crash in October 1947 (Cowles, 202). It may be that Guenther's death contributed to the young photographer's eventual fear of flying, despite his youthful enthusiasm for aviation, since he had obtained a pilot's licence on August 15, 1947 (LoBrutto, 39). According to filmmaker Bob Gaffney, who shot the helicopter footage in Monument Valley for *2001: A Space Odyssey*, Kubrick gave up on flying due to an incident that occurred when he taxied on the runway one day, and "the plane bolted and took off with one side of the engine not firing" (LoBrutto, 297). An eerie foreshadowing was published in the August 5, 1947 issue of *Look*, when colleague Maurice Terrell photographed 19-year-old pilot Bill Lear, Jr., who had "survived the most harrowing experience of the flying fraternity – engine failure on take-off."

Kubrick then went on to comment on the practical aspects of his schooling at *Look* magazine: "This experience was invaluable to me, not only because I learned a lot about photography, but also because it gave me a quick education in how things happened in the world. To have been a professional photographer was obviously a great advantage for me. …" (Ciment 2003, 196). The key phrase, which Kubrick would never explicitly expand upon, is "how things happened in the world," which he had expressed in an even more elliptical fashion to Robert Emmett Ginna in 1960: "I did travel around the country, and I went to Europe and it was a great thing. I learned a lot about people and things" (Ginna, 18). An audio interview by Jerome Bernstein, recorded in 1966 but only made available in 2005, provides a bit more information but no clear insight into what Kubrick meant by the knowledge he gained from his four-and-a-half years at *Look* (Bernstein 2005). He does make the argument that the process of learning about photography as a teenager and obtaining a "fantastically good job at the age of seventeen" was a case of problem-solving (Bernstein 2005). The challenge was to find out what was required technically to take and develop photographs, to successfully submit pictures on a freelance basis and eventually be offered a job as an apprentice and finally a full-time staff photographer. He found out from reading camera magazines how to go about selling photo-stories, and proceeded to sell several pictures to *Look* (Stagg, 37). Kubrick criticized his high school for not providing students with practical problem-solving skills, and mostly limiting its pedagogy to rote learning (Bernstein 2005). He then points out that his tenure at *Look* represented his college years, with the difference that he acquired more knowledge and professional experience by working for the magazine: "That would have been the period I'd spend in college and I think that the things, what I learned and the practical experience, in every respect, including photography, what I learned in that four year period exceeded what I could have learned in school" (Bernstein 2005). He made similar comments to *Newsweek* in 1972: "By the time I was 21, I had had four years of seeing how things worked in the real world. I think if I had gone to college I would never have become a director. I would have wound up in some profession instead – science, law, medicine" (Zimmerman, 31). Thus *Look* became his film school.

The influence of film on *Look* and Kubrick

The historical relationship between photography and film is a complex one, but it is fair to say that the cinema was always a more glamorous medium than photojournalism, and that photo-magazines were happy to include articles about Hollywood stars and film productions, as well as develop a visual language inspired in part by the movies. Kubrick obviously enjoyed going to the cinema as a young person, as did most people in the 1930s and 1940s, but it is equally clear that *Life* and *Look* encouraged their staff to think and work in quasi-filmic terms, creating photo-stories that could easily be compared to movie storyboards. Kubrick reports that he attended movie theatres in the Bronx on a regular basis in his early teens, as the programme changed twice a week (Stang, 34). He would watch all the double features at the Loew's Paradise, the R.K.O. Fordham and the Thalia for Hollywood fare, and was introduced to international cinema at the Museum of Modern Art's film theatre (Bernstein 2005). To ensure that his film viewing was as comprehensive as possible, he would scan the newspaper *PM*'s listing of all films being screened in the five boroughs of New York, and "used to sometimes go out to Staten Island, just to see a film [he] hadn't seen" (Kohler, 252).

Kubrick shared this cinephilia with many of his *Look* colleagues, several of whom either owned many film books (Rothstein), had personal contacts with MGM (O'Brian), had worked for Disney (Schloat) or taught filmmaking at USC (Theisen). During Kubrick's tenure at *Look*, including his period as a freelancer, the magazine also forged relationships with the movie industry by covering important film productions or publishing profiles of new or established stars. Photographer Maurice Terrell went behind the scenes for an essay revealing production methods on western B-movies, a.k.a. horse operas (November 13, 1945). *Look*'s February 19, 1946, issue focused almost entirely on the American movie industry, including the magazine's Annual Movie Awards, articles by and about the President of the Motion Picture Association of America (Eric A. Johnston), a studio tour with actor Van Johnson, the best movie stills of the year, and so on. The contents page also introduced photographer Earl Theisen to *Look*'s readers: a veteran who had been on staff since the magazine's first issue in 1937, he was *Look*'s Hollywood correspondent, covering movie stars and producers, industry galas and premieres, and also taught cinematography at USC (Cooperman, 182). A year later, *Look* reprised the "Best Movie Action Stills" (February 18, 1947) with an essay on Hollywood studio still-photographers, including technical camera information about the published pictures, such as shutter speed and f-stop. The *Look* Movie Awards returned for the February 17, 1948, issue, along with a Maurice Terrell portrait of celebrated Hollywood DP James Wong Howe, who received the magazine's Achievement Award in cinematography. The caption explains that Howe had produced "some of the most thrilling fight scenes ever filmed" for *Body and Soul* (1947, starring John Garfield), by climbing "into the ring with the actors … with a hand-held newsreel camera." Nicknamed "low-key Howe" for his realist style of photography, James Wong Howe had been a boxing enthusiast like Kubrick, and included point-of-view axial shots of the fighters in the ring, a technique that was imitated by Frank Bauman in his staged photo-essay with Rocky Graziano's nemesis Tony Zale (*Look*, August 31, 1948), followed by Kubrick in his second feature film, *Killer's Kiss* (cf. Figure 24).

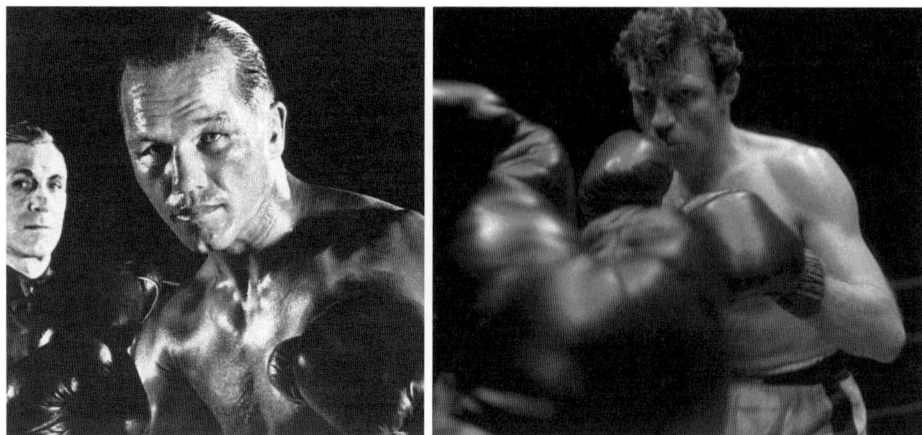

Figure 24: POV shots in *Look* magazine (1948) and *Killer's Kiss* (1955).

Two significant, albeit unpublished, Kubrick assignments further highlight *Look* magazine's ongoing interest in and commitment to covering related media such as film and television. Film producer Mark Hellinger's crime story *The Naked City* was being shot on location in New York City in the summer of 1947, and *Look* sent Kubrick to photograph the event. There are 81 pictures for this job in the archives at the Museum of the City of New York (submitted on July 31, 1947), including behind-the-scenes portraits of director Jules Dassin and cinematographer Bill Daniels (cf. Figure 25). Kubrick must have also remembered Ted de Corsia as the film's heavy when he hired him to play a corrupt policeman for *The Killing* nine years later. In its September 28, 1948, issue, *Look* featured a forgotten, early independent TV short directed by William Cameron Menzies, adapted from Edgar Allan Poe's story

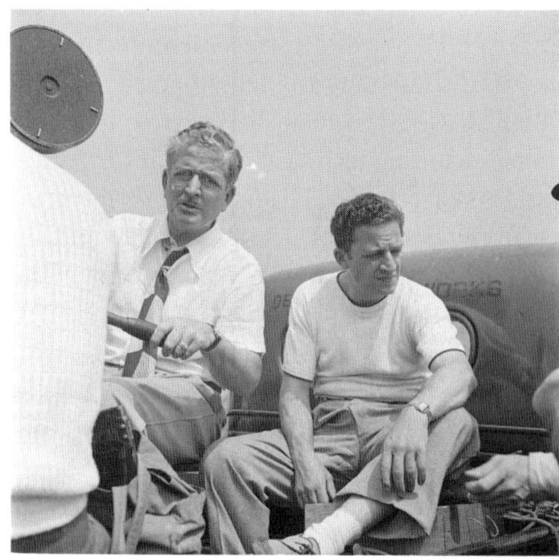

Figure 25: Bill Daniels (left) and director Jules Dassin filming *The Naked City* (July, 1947).

The Tell-Tale Heart. Shot in one day for $8000, the spartan production included mostly close-ups, some of which resemble Kubrick's compositions in *Killer's Kiss*, specifically when Davey lies on the floor with his face next to a Jack of Spades card (cf. Figure 26). Also forgotten is an unpublished social issue story titled "Families First," entirely staged with actors in several locations, which Kubrick photographed and submitted on April 28, 1948. The only information about this job is the summary provided online for the Library of Congress' *Look* collection, which states that "photographs show actors performing for a film or television show about a family or families. Includes family eating together; boys playing together; boys shoplifting(?); a policeman; a man in jail; teenagers dancing; families on their way to church(?); man and son at baseball game; parents with children."[2] The Library has archived 261 pictures on 35mm safety film, revealing an elaborate mise-en-scène, which suggests that this project may have been a government-sponsored documentary short, and that Kubrick functioned as the stills photographer rather than a behind-the-scenes journalist. No camera equipment, lights or crew are revealed in these photographs, whereas the "Naked City" job, in contrast, contained many pictures of bystanders interested by the location filming.

The January 17, 1950, issue of *Look* includes a letter to the editor from an independent Hollywood producer advertising his company's upcoming film *Champagne for Caesar* (1950, Richard Whorf), a satire of quiz-shows that premiered on May 11. The film included a phoney copy of *Look* magazine as a prop, with star actor Ronald Colman and title character Caesar the parrot on the cover. The letter suggests that the fictional events portrayed in the film "might well have warranted a cover on a national magazine like LOOK." Somebody at *Look* must have been taking notes, as the April 7, 1953, cover featuring Debbie Reynolds was designed in advance to allow for the MGM film *I Love Melvin*, released on March 20 and starring Reynolds and Donald O'Connor, to include an "authentic" *Look* cover as the film's central plot point. It was a great promotional stunt for both MGM and *Look*, underscoring the extent to which magazine photographers were, and still are, attracted to filmmaking, as people like Paul Strand, Robert Frank, Gordon Parks, Jerry Schatzberg and many others ended up working in both photography and film. Moreover, Kubrick's colleague John Vachon mentions seeing William Wyler's *The Heiress* in *Look* magazine's small, but comfortable, air-conditioned screening room where one could sit in easy chairs and smoke during free weekly previews of Hollywood films (Vachon). One would expect Kubrick to

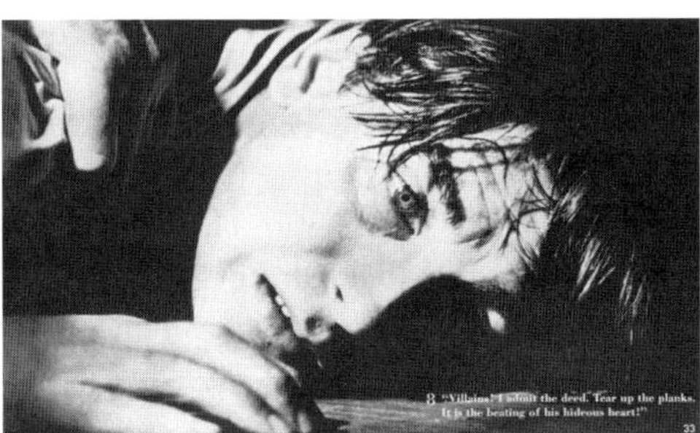
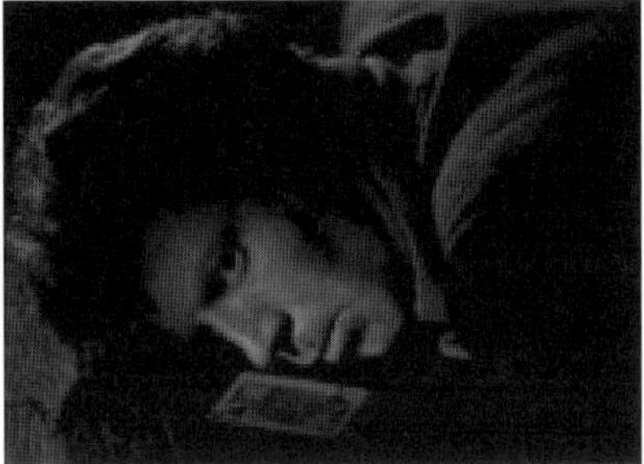

Figure 26: *The Tell-Tale Heart* (*Look* magazine, 1948) and *Killer's Kiss* (1955).

have attended these screenings, especially for a film such as *The Heiress*, released on October 6, 1949, which co-starred Montgomery Clift whom he had photographed earlier that year.

Photo-essay production process

There are but a few sources describing Kubrick's modus operandi in taking photographs on assignment for *Look*, but these may paint a portrait of the young photojournalist's conception of how to do his job, which can be supplemented with analyses of surviving contact sheets and negatives in the magazine's archives in New York City and Washington, D.C.. As a freelancer, it seems that Kubrick had already figured out when to stage a scene and when to wait for the moment. He apparently admitted to high school classmate Walter Trueman that he'd coaxed the newspaper salesman to adopt a dejected expression for his first *Look* photograph (June 26, 1945) of the newsstand on the day President Roosevelt died (Baxter, 27) (cf. Figure 11). Vincent LoBrutto's biography includes an interview with Kubrick's high school classmate and fellow photographer Bernard Cooperman, who recalls accompanying his friend Stanley to the baseball stadium: "I had no idea of what to do. I mean, I was going to take pictures of a baseball game. What he did was he just sat in front of a group of three or four kids facing the camera. They made faces at him and he just sat there until they finally forgot that he was there and he got great pictures" (18). Although LoBrutto does not mention the "Kids at a Ball Game" photo-essay (October 16, 1945), Cooperman's story may very well be a description of its production process. It appears as if Kubrick had good picture-taking instincts, even before joining *Look*. However, the patience required to stay put and keep clicking the shutter until something interesting happens is a discipline that Kubrick would have been encouraged to develop at *Look*, because series photographs had been a staple of photojournalism at least since Felix and Paul Nadar's interview with the French chemist Chevreul in 1886 (Newhall, 254).

During Kubrick's apprenticeship, he was assigned a number of street photography jobs, including a trip to the zoo. According to Mildred Stagg, who interviewed him for the October 1948 issue of *The Camera* magazine, "Kubrick was assigned to do a picture on how people looked to the caged animals. To find out he made the necessary arrangements with the authorities at the zoo at Prospect park in Brooklyn. In the monkey house there are both indoor and outdoor cages. The monkeys were in the outdoor cage, so Kubrick stationed himself in the indoor cage with his lens poked through the food slit. At first the monkeys were curious but after they were allowed to look in the camera they returned to hamming for their usual audience" (Stagg, 41). The *Look* archives at the Museum of the City of New York include 117 pictures of visitors outside the monkey cage, three of which were selected to illustrate the caption: "This is how people look to the monkeys". The angle remained the same on all these snapshots, the key being to capture interesting facial expressions to facilitate a humorous comparison between people and monkeys, a theme that Kubrick would explore in a more serious, satirical vein in *2001: A Space Odyssey* (Crone 2005, 194). One may imagine a 17-year-old Kubrick negotiating with zoo officials, leading to phone calls to *Look* for confirmation of the photographer's status. He admitted to Stang that on his subway story, a guard wanted to know what he was doing: "'Have you got permission?' the guard asked. 'I'm from LOOK,' Kubrick answered. 'Yeah, sonny,' was the guard's reply, 'and I'm the society editor of the Daily Worker'" (Stagg, 152).

Kubrick's "graduating" photo-essay as an apprentice, "Life and Love on the New York Subway" (March 4, 1947), was a considerable undertaking, with more than 500 archived photographs showing that he sometimes brought along his friends as extras, including high school classmates Alexander Singer and Toba Metz, as well as *Look* writer G. Warren Schloat, Jr.. Stagg reports that "to make pictures in the off-guard manner he wanted to, Kubrick rode the subway for two weeks. Half of his riding was done between midnight and six am. Regardless of what he saw he couldn't shoot until the car stopped in a station because of the motion and vibration of the moving train. ... For this series Kubrick used a Contax and took the pictures at 1/8 second. The lack of light tripled the time necessary for development" (Stagg, 152). Kubrick was also using the widest aperture that the 35mm Contax would allow, f 2.8. Schloat also revealed to biographer LoBrutto that Kubrick was using a candid camera technique, likely picked up from his *Look* colleagues: with the camera hanging from his neck, he ran a wire up his sleeve in order to trip the camera's shutter in his pocket without anyone realizing it (LoBrutto, 38).

An analysis of the published essay highlights the collaborative and complementary work of the photographer, writer and layout artist, and the extent to which a solid understanding of each other's tasks could produce a creative slice-of-life photo-essay. The essay consists of three double-page spreads containing a total of 29 photographs. Each spread forms one unit of design (Rothstein, 159). The first spread opens with an eye-catching full page "establishing shot" of Grand Central Station, printed as a bleed picture. Underneath the opening photograph is the headline, which also serves as the title of the photo-essay. Next to it is the "body copy," which announces the theme of the first spread. Hugging the bottom edge of the picture is the caption, beginning with a short phrase in bold type, followed by a complete sentence in regular type that comments on the photograph and adds information.

Thematically, the first spread focuses on overcrowding in the New York City subway during rush hour. Statistics are provided on the number of fares collected daily. The headline for the second spread, which runs down the middle of the page this time, identifies a new theme: picking out interesting personalities on the subway. The third spread is similar to the previous one in design, with a headline describing the closing theme, the subway as "flophouse." In terms of layout, the second and third spreads begin and end with a larger picture, which provides a formal frame. The picture in the top left corner is the reader's entry point, and the one in the bottom right corner acts as a transition in the second spread, and as a conclusion in the last spread. The second spread ends with a picture of a woman and a boy shot from behind, looking out the window at the head of the train. Visually it is a kind of off-screen glance inviting us to turn the page, which is likened to the train's next stop by the caption. The last picture features "two children slumber sprawled on their parents' laps," ending with the credit "photographed by Stanley Kubrick" (LoBrutto, 38). Rainer Crone could not resist comparing Kubrick's work to Walker Evans' photographs in the New York Subway, which were taken in 1942 but only published in 1966, long after Kubrick had retired from *Look*. We might instead consider the photojournalistic practice as the most relevant influence, and point to 20-year-old photographer Lisa Larsen's cross-country train essay "Travel Means Trouble" (*Look*, September 4, 1945). Although her career was cut short by cancer, Larsen won several awards for her work at *Life* magazine in the 1950s, after having apprenticed at *Vogue* during World War II, not unlike Kubrick. An interesting "upper-class" version of Larsen and Kubrick's essays is Walker Evans protégé Robert Frank's "The Congressional" (*Fortune*, November 1955) (Panzer 2005a, 46). Kubrick would revisit the New York Subway eight years later, in a scene from his second feature *Killer's Kiss*, when boxer Davy Gordon reads a letter from his uncle George. The candid quality of the photography remains intact (cf. Figure 27). This scene may also be compared to Alfred Hitchcock's *The Wrong Man* (1956), a film shot in a semi-documentary fashion in which Henry Fonda's character reads the newspaper on the subway.

Most of the pictures in this essay (23 out of 29) are cropped into a square format, in order to focus on the idea being expressed by the writer and photographer. A comparison with the 14 reproductions in Crone's book *Drama and Shadows*, which includes photographs left on the "cutting room floor," gives an indication of the editorial decisions that were taken (2005, 16–29). On the basis of this material, it is fair to say that Kubrick's work was not "manhandled," as critic Enrico Ghezzi feared (Sgarbi). According to *Look*'s Photography Department Head Arthur Rothstein, the editorial process remains a collaborative one, ideally, and photographers "should be consulted when the photographs are cropped and layouts made" (1979, 161). As a practising photographer himself, Rothstein was sensitive to the photographer's feelings concerning each photograph as "a sacred and profound statement," and so there is every reason to think that Kubrick was a willing participant in this process (1979, 159–61).

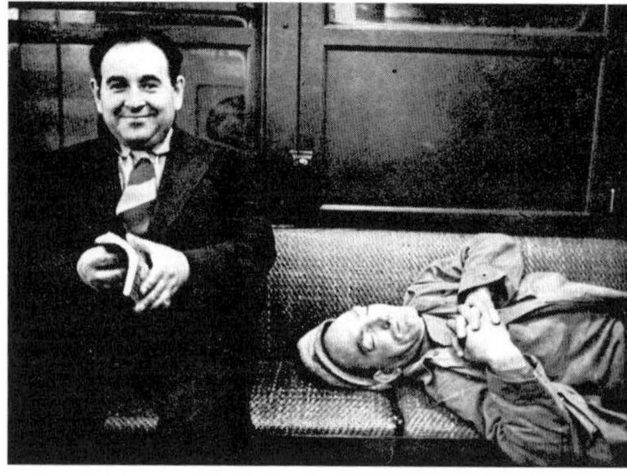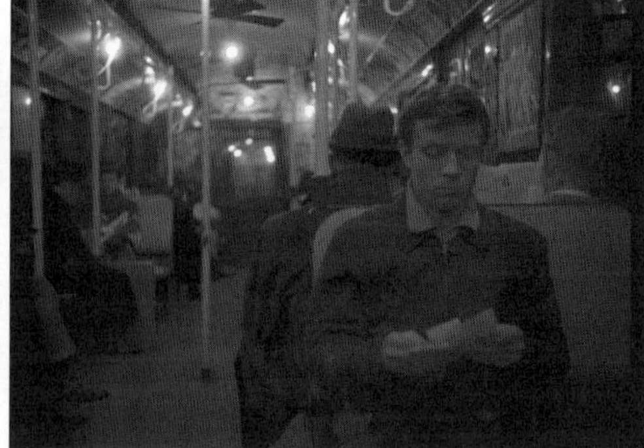

Figure 27: "The Subway Story" (Fall 1946) and *Killer's Kiss* (1955).

In fact, Kubrick described *Look*'s submission process for photo-essay ideas in a positive fashion. According to picture editor Helen O'Brian, "Stanley had the highest percentage of acceptances of any free-lance photographer [she'd] ever dealt with," and half of the candid stories he was assigned were his own ideas (Stagg, 40). Proposals for photo-stories would be typed up and five copies would be sent to *Look*'s Editorial Board for approval. Stagg adds that "Kubrick is maintaining the same high batting average as a staff photographer that he enjoyed as a free lance. He explains it by saying, 'The magazine's policy is so well determined that you seldom go out on a wild goose chase. When LOOK sends you out on a story the story is usually published'" (Stagg, 152). This indicates that Kubrick understood the magazine's policy and was able to supply well thought-out ideas that were often given the green light by the top editors.

Collaboration

As indicated in the above analysis of the subway story, *Look* staffers were expected to understand the overall photo-essay production process well enough to appreciate the complementarity of their respective tasks and duties, and contribute to the collective effort in an informed and efficient way. The March 5, 1946, issue's contents page includes an instalment of "Behind the Scenes with Look," which usually offered a brief portrait of a member of the magazine's staff. On this occasion, the editors decided to highlight the teamwork required to complete one of the featured articles, by identifying the stages in the production process and the number of people involved: "In all, 43 writers, editors, artists, photographers, researchers and layout men contributed directly to the article's completion." The editors further argued that "by its very nature, a picture-magazine is an example of close teamwork. In other magazines, which employ only the medium of the written word, an article may be largely the work of one writer. The picture magazine, however, employs both the written word and a multitude of visual devices, and each article represents the combined efforts of many persons." This argument also applies to feature filmmaking, and there is every reason to believe that *Look*'s organized yet flexible form of team-journalism made an impact on Kubrick's conception of how to work collectively with a group of creative people.

There is a tendency among critics to consider Kubrick to be the embodiment of the ultimate film auteur, an artist who personally made every major creative decision on all of his films. Admittedly, Kubrick himself has contributed to such a romantic, that is, individualistic, conception of cultural production by the way he has chosen to produce his films, far from the distracting, commercial centres of the movie industry. The official Warner Brothers website for the home video collection of Kubrick's films also fuels this form of myth-making with a quote attributed to Kubrick, expressing Alexandre Astruc's notion of the *caméra-stylo*: "One man writes a novel. One man writes a symphony. It is essential for one man to make a film." At times, Kubrick has also displayed a slightly defensive or cagey attitude in discussing influences for ideas on specific film projects, as if it might compromise his authorship and form the grounds for a legal challenge (Ciment 2003, 167). However, a balanced perspective must acknowledge the positive influence of collaborative production at *Look* magazine and its lingering effects, articulated in the concluding paragraph of Kubrick's brief essay "Words and Movies," first published in the Winter 1961 issue of *Sight and Sound*: "Nothing in making movies gives a greater sense of elation than participation in a process of allowing the work to grow, through vital collaboration between script, director and actors, as it goes along. Any art form properly practiced involves a to and fro between conception and execution, the original intention being constantly modified as one tries to give it objective realization. In painting a picture this goes on between the artist and his canvas; in making a movie it goes on between people" (Kubrick, 339). One can simply substitute the word "photo-essay" for "movie" to realize the impact of Kubrick's youthful training at *Look* on his subsequent career in visual storytelling.

Reciprocal influence of photojournalists

Opportunities for mutual influence between *Look* colleagues were the norm, not the exception, as photographers were constantly working with their magazine co-workers, whether travelling on assignment with a writer, discussing photo selections with the picture editor, layout designs with the art director or sharing a job with a fellow photographer. Kubrick was assigned to at least 40 jobs with other *Look* photographers, approximately one out of every ten assignments. Other than relying on magazine photo credits when the stories are published, the surviving photographs in the *Look* archives can only be identified, in the case of multiple-photographer assignments, if they include contact sheets with the photographers' names stamped on the back. The most significant and frustrating cases are three jobs that Kubrick shared with Phil Harrington over a five-month period during the last year of his tenure at *Look*. The unidentified contact sheets are all available at the Library of congress, and the third job, titled "Supermarkets," includes 195 negatives in the 2 ¼ inch format (the other two jobs are on 35mm safety film). Submitted on February 6, 1950, this unpublished essay appears to have been a joint promotional venture with a few grocery stores (Food Fair, First National Stores and Big Ben Market), judging from the prominently placed posters advertising *Look* magazine's recommended "hors d'oeuvres for entertainment, frankfurters for dinner, prepared meats for luncheon," and so on. The second and largest job, titled "Traveling saleswoman," includes 16 photographs by Harrington published on March 14, 1950, but the remaining 1368 photographs are unidentified.[3] The unpublished "Sadler's Wells Ballet" job, submitted on October 25, 1949, is perhaps the most interesting since Kubrick appears in a few pictures, indicating that Harrington is the likely photographer in those instances. One of these is a medium-shot portrait of Kubrick looking at his colleague while digging in his jacket's pocket for a flashbulb (cf. Book cover). Another shows

Kubrick setting up his tripod in a room with members of the ballet troupe milling about (cf. Figure 19). It is strictly impossible to tell whether all 187 photographs in this file are Harrington's or whether some, or none of these pictures, are Kubrick's. Thanks to internal evidence provided by Harrington, we can at least confirm that Kubrick was present and armed with a camera. Some of the outdoor pictures are deliberately staged and composed in depth, with members of Sadler's Wells sitting on the lawn for the camera's benefit. This sort of mise-en-scène is consistent with Kubrick's "wellesian" photographic style of the period, except that it also applies to Harrington, Frank Bauman, and virtually all of his colleagues at *Look*. Admittedly, the impossibility in identifying a photograph's "author" speaks in part to the technological nature of the photographic medium, but also suggests the degree to which work produced by different people could easily be integrated into a whole, pointing to a different kind of authorship, that of post-war American photojournalism. It is therefore a photographic genre, which Kubrick acquired at *Look* magazine, along with his colleagues, that largely determined the direction his filmmaking would take in the ensuing years, as opposed to the development of a uniquely personal, distinctive visual style.

Kubrick's conception of picture-magazine journalism was no doubt being shaped by his collaborative work with fellow members of the photographic staff, as they talked shop in the field or at *Look*'s offices at 511 Fifth Avenue, compared notes on their assignments, discussed the latest gadgets, and so on. During his apprenticeship at *Look*, Kubrick would learn by imitating the work of others, specifically those features that had proven successful aesthetically or popular commercially. In turn, his colleagues would learn from him as well. An interesting case is the portrait of German expressionist painter George Grosz, which stood out from other artist portraits in the "New York – World Art Center" feature (June 8, 1948) because it did not follow the norm of photographing an artist in his studio. Instead, Kubrick decided (or agreed) to make Grosz look like a businessman on a Fifth Avenue sidewalk (Crone 2005, 239). This unusual mise-en-scène may be a response to the conventional, studio-bound portraits of Jacques Lipchitz, Henry Koerner, Enrico Donati and others taken by *Look* photographers Bob Hansen and Arthur Rothstein for this assignment. It remains unknown whose idea it was to trade in the brush for a cigar, and the painter's smock for a pinstriped suit, although to sit brazenly next to a "No Parking" sign does fit the stereotype of the nonconformist artist. Kubrick's work may also have influenced *Look* magazine, as when responses to the "Dentist's Office" story (October 1, 1946) likely encouraged fellow photojournalist Jim Hansen to provide a follow-up instalment titled "The Dentist Suffers Too …" (May 13, 1947). An indignant dentist had sent a letter to the editor, which was published in the December 10, 1946, issue, complaining that Kubrick's waiting-room story was a "scare crow article," and suggesting that *Look* investigate "what is on the 'other side' of the reception-room door." The magazine's editors responded with a brief tongue-in-cheek essay explaining that "everybody sympathizes with the patient, but how about the reproachful grimaces the dentist has to face?" Jim Hansen's four photographs show patients compelled to "grimace" as the dentist sticks an apparatus in their mouths. This was followed by a much less cheeky "First Visit to the Dentist" (December 9, 1947), also photographed by Hansen, about a dentist and his assistant taking good care of 20-month-old, Shirley Temple-like, little Judy.

Feedback

The perception of Kubrick as a self-directed artist who is impervious to criticism is belied by filmmaker Curtis Harrington's report that Kubrick wept during a preview screening of *Fear and Desire*, after the audience laughed at Paul Mazursky's performance (Baxter, 54). This corroborates Kubrick's terse comment about the film, made in 1958: "Pain is a good teacher" (Stang, 36). It should be no surprise that photojournalists assess the quality of their work in some measure based on responses from their colleagues as well as readers (Bolack, 43). Kubrick received a number of public or official kudos during his tenure at *Look*, which no doubt helped him to gauge his performance. *Look* published 63 letters to the editor referring to photo-essays that Kubrick had worked on, which must represent a small fraction of the mail received by the magazine for those particular stories. It is possible Kubrick may have seen unpublished letters that also validated his contribution to the fortnightly publication. The content of the letters that appeared in *Look* ranges from general comments on the articles' subject matter, to agreements or disagreements with the principal arguments, as well as specific references to the photographs or even the photographer who took them. Displaying a standard form of journalistic balance and fairness, the magazine would often include both positive and negative reviews of their essays, and it is reasonable to speculate that *Look*'s management endeavoured to periodically select letters praising their staff, especially the junior members, as part of a morale-building strategy.

Among the letters merely offering personal observations about the photo-essay topics is a female reader who would like to "become friendly with Walter Cartier," the attractive young boxer chosen by Kubrick for his essay "Prizefighter" (January 18, 1949). Another woman complains that Cartier should study law instead of boxing, like his twin brother, wondering "why such perfection in anatomical detail would want to allow himself to be disfigured." Kubrick quickly learned about the advantages of casting photogenic individuals. Much less edifying is a reader from Chicago who complains that the "Chicago – City of Extremes" essay (April 12, 1949) features "a disgraceful coloured slum district," and wishes that people "who live in slum districts would clean up around their homes." Differing perspectives on Kubrick's "A Dog's Life in the Big City" (November 8, 1949) oppose the Executive Vice-President of New York City's ASPCA, hopeful that *Look*'s story "will make people more considerate of dogs," and a reader who sarcastically expresses no surprise that "city dogs need psychiatrists, if they lead such a pampered life." Even though Kubrick later owned dogs himself, his photographs suggest an amused or ironic stance regarding the wealthy owners of pet poodles and Dalmatians. The earliest review of a Kubrick photo-story concerns "A Short-Short in a Movie Balcony" (April 16, 1946), which contrasts a reader who identifies with the story's heroine and vows to slap the next wise guy who annoys her in a theatre, and a man who doubts the plausibility of the narrative's conclusion, arguing that "the average girl without a boyfriend doesn't react this way." *Look*'s claim that the photographer captured these allegedly candid images with an "infra-red" camera remains unquestioned.

Several of the clearly positive letters concern Kubrick's social studies on children's health topics, such as "Rheumatic Fever" (April 27, 1948), "Deaf Children Hear for the First Time" (May 25, 1948) and "Wally Conquers Polio" (October 12, 1948). Another comes from the New Orleans Jazz Club, who is "deeply grateful to LOOK for the timelessness and the quality of *Dixieland Jazz is 'hot' again*" (June 6, 1950). Kubrick was likely assigned this jazz story on the basis of his own musical interest: he had played drums in his high school's swing band, which featured female vocalist Eydie Gormé, who later went on to international fame (LoBrutto, 17). Kubrick may also have benefited from a "jazz connection" at *Look* magazine, since one of the two people responsible for hiring him, managing editor Jack Guenther, collected recordings of dixieland jazz. Executive editor Dan Mich inherited this record collection after Guenther died tragically in the October 24, 1947 United Airlines DC-6 plane crash in Bryce Canyon, Utah (Cowles, 202). *Look* music critic Joseph Roddy, who later interviewed the likes of Glenn Gould and penned the article "Dixieland Jazz is 'hot' again," accompanied Kubrick to New Orleans, when they visited jazz clarinetist George Lewis in his backyard. Unpublished shots of Kubrick on the drum kit are likely the result of Roddy mentioning that his photographer was a jazz drummer, and subsequently borrowing Kubrick's Rolleiflex to take pictures of the young photojournalist playing with these legendary musicians (Crone 2010, 274). Roddy returned to New Orleans with John Vachon 20 years later for George Lewis' funeral. The *Look* photo-essay "Jazzman's Last Ramble" (March 18, 1969) includes a picture by Kubrick of Lewis' young daughter Shirley dancing while her father played with his band, and a contemporary Vachon photograph of Shirley at the funeral (cf. Figure 28).

The earliest letter to comment on a specific photograph by Kubrick focuses on the last photograph of the subway story, titled "Life and Love in the New York Subway" (April 29, 1947). The tired father in the picture captioned "Sprawling Children" elicits the following hyperbolic description: "It seems unbelievable to me that a young man could possess such a weariness of the soul. In America, no one should be so burdened with despair. He has the look of Lincoln in his eyes, and a bit of the suffering Christ." As if to bring the reading back down to Earth, the editors respond to the letter with a strictly documentary appreciation of the picture's significance: "*Look* believes its New York subway riders will recognize the careworn expression as one belonging to those who take long subway trips with children." More in keeping with *Look*'s concern for journalistic objectivity is a letter from Republican Congressman Clarence J. Brown, expressing admiration for Kubrick's photographs of Senator Robert A. Taft in the essay "Taft Meets the People" (January 31, 1950): "The pictures which accompany the article have caught the spirit and the tempo of Senator Taft's campaign in an unusually accurate way." Perhaps the most unusual reference

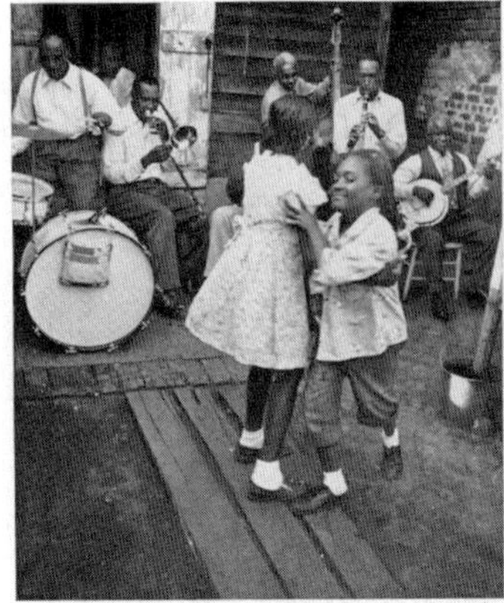

The treads of death, the hops of life, they were close in New Orleans. George's daughter Shirley (above, left) danced about the backyard 20 years ago as he worked. Then, in grief, with the music the same, only its cadence different, she wept (right) as he was carried from the church.

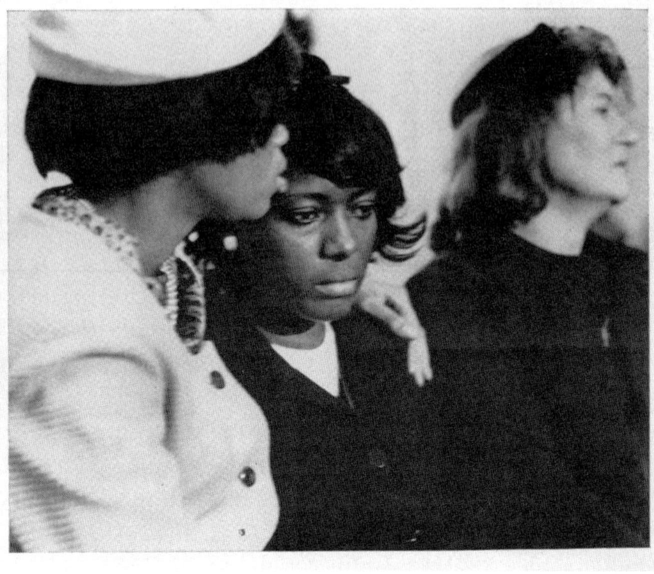

Figure 28: March 1950 photograph by Kubrick (left), and January 1969 by John Vachon (right).

to Kubrick's work for *Look* was a parody of the "University of Michigan" story produced by the editors of the University's student humour magazine, *Gargoyle*. The letter published in *Look* (August 30, 1949) features four photographs from the student parody, closely matching Kubrick's mise-en-scène but with an irreverent, juvenile brand of humour (cf. Figure 29).

Two appreciative letters mention Kubrick by name, including a particularly effusive one from Marlene Buttino in the August 30, 1949, *Look* issue, regarding the essay on Montgomery Clift, which had appeared a month earlier: "Many thanks for giving us that wonderful story and picture spread on Monty Clift. Three cheers should go to Stanley Kubrick, the photographer, for taking the best natural pictures of the most natural actor on the stage." Since the essay "Glamor Boy in Baggy Pants" (July 19, 1949) was mostly staged, the impression of realism conveyed by Ms. Buttino's letter indicates the degree to which Kubrick had mastered the photographic conventions for "naturalism," aided by Clift's ease in front of the camera, as a professional actor. Another fan of Kubrick's work was George Grosz, whom Kubrick had photographed for the article "New York – World Art Center" (June 8, 1948). Grosz sent a letter to *Look*, which appeared in the July 20, 1948, issue: "Only a few words to tell you how much I enjoyed seeing the photo of myself sitting on a chair on Fifth Avenue. I compliment you and your excellent photographer, Stanley Kubrick. ..." Such an acknowledgement from an established artist must have been quite flattering for a young photojournalist, confirming the high regard that Kubrick's bosses at *Look* had for their junior staff member. This regard is expressed by a short text on the contents page of the issue featuring the portrait of Grosz: "It must have been an artistic meeting of minds

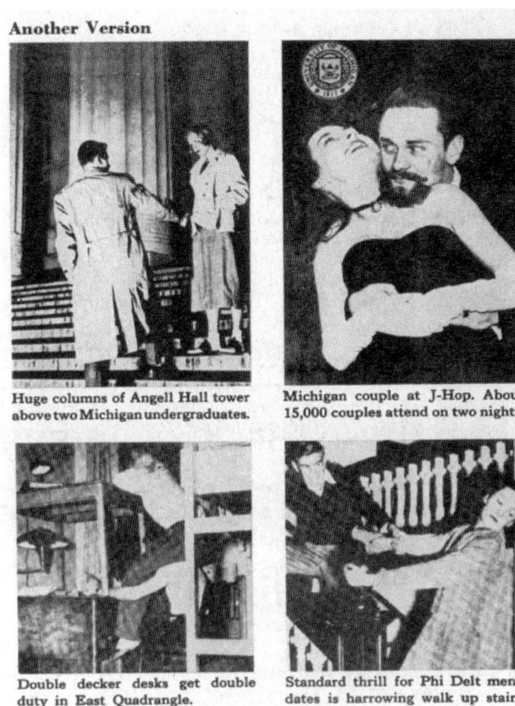

Figure 29: Student parody of Kubrick's "University of Michigan" story.

when painter George Grosz and young Stanley Kubrick agreed on the shot for the story, 'New York – World Art Center,' page 54, that would give them real Manhattan atmosphere. Grabbing a chair in his studio, Grosz followed the LOOK photographer down the elevator and out into the crowds on Fifth Avenue. As the artist straddled the chair, Stanley got his picture." Further underscoring the *Look* management's appreciation is an interoffice memo sent to Kubrick by Fleur Cowles, the magazine's associate editor and wife of *Look* founder Mike Cowles: "I think you just took the picture of the year … George Grosz parked on a chair in the middle of Fifth Avenue traffic (with a NO PARKING sign alongside) is IT!" Kubrick's mother Gertrude kept this memo in her scrapbook documenting Stanley's early professional achievements (Phillips 2005, 268).

Thematic tropes of photojournalism

Another way of ascertaining Kubrick's likely conception of the photo-essay genre is to compare his work, thematically and stylistically, with that produced by his colleagues at *Look* magazine. Recurring patterns as well as differences between photo-essays dealing with similar topics should not only give us a sense of what the *Look* modus operandi was and how much

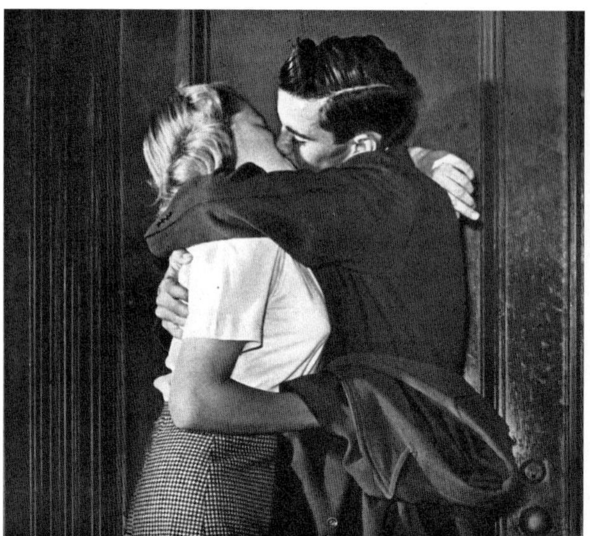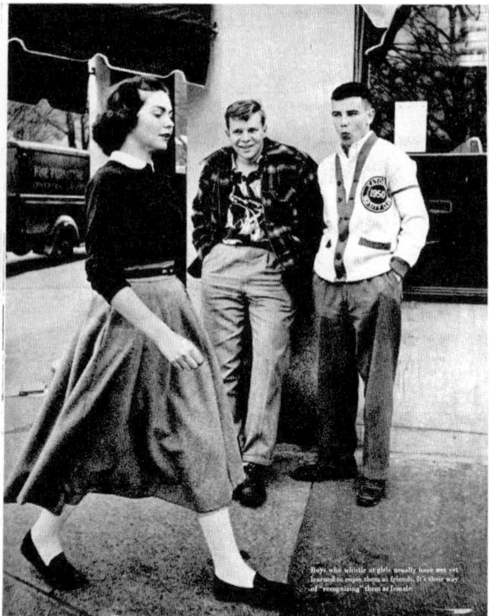

Figure 30: September 1946 photograph by George Heyer (left), and April 1950 by Kubrick (right).

variation was allowed or encouraged, but also confirm what Kubrick knew about these genres prior to applying this knowledge to his film career. Some of the common themes or sub-genres include street photography pieces, profiles of universities, travel stories, staged essays on teenage dating, sports personality profiles, big city nightlife, big rural families, and so on. In each case, focusing on essays produced prior to Kubrick's own efforts will help to identify the established norms that *Look* photographers were required to work from, including the magazine's junior staff member. For instance, George Heyer shot a staged photo-essay on teenage dating titled "Your Manners Are Showing" (September 17, 1946), published four years before Kubrick's "What Every Teenager Should Know About Dating" (August 1, 1950). In both cases the essay illustrates excerpts from a soon-to-be published guide to teenage etiquette targeting youngsters and their parents. They also open on a large photograph clearly establishing the theme of the article: Heyer shows teenagers kissing, and Kubrick features boys whistling at a girl (cf. Figure 30). Neither article depicts the preferred behaviour and instead indulges in providing "naughty pictures" of what teenagers should avoid doing, a convenient strategy justified by the essay's didactic purpose. The main difference is that the Heyer photo-essay's text is written in verse, rather than standard prose. We might note a full-page ad opposite Heyer's mildly sensationalistic opening picture, promoting *Look*-authored books *How to Keep Your Family Healthy* and *The Technique of the Picture Story*. Three years after "Your Manners Are Showing," Arthur Rothstein offered another staged photo-essay on teenage etiquette titled "Blondes Prefer Gentlemen" (August 16, 1949), based on a soon-to-be released book by the same name. Rothstein's mise-en-scène again focuses on social blunders instead of positive examples, beginning with a two-page overlapping picture of a shy boy who "acts the clam, bores his date" by not engaging in small talk. Rothstein's essay differs from the previous one thanks to a movie industry tie-in, as the actress who plays the girl is Joan Evans, a 15-year-old newcomer currently appearing in the Samuel Goldwyn picture *Roseanna McCoy* (1949). *Look* also included an article written by Goldwyn himself explaining how he discovered Evans and offered her a contract. Four months prior to the publication of Kubrick's teenage-dating essay, Bob Sandberg staged photographs for an article by *Look* editor William Houseman, "Adolescence: A Time of Trial and Tragedy" (April 11, 1950). Even though the theme is similar, it is not a promotional excerpt from a how-to book but a personality profile of 13-year-old Joan Feete from Larchmont, New York. It remains a staged essay, but the layout is less rigid than the grid-like pattern employed on the Heyer and Rothstein pieces, combining photographs of various sizes much like the Kubrick essay from August 1, 1950.

Kubrick staged some photographs to accompany the essay "Jealousy: A Threat to Marriage" (October 24, 1950) by "lawyer, writer and expert in family relations" Jacques Bacal, who authored at least 17 articles for *Look* magazine between 1945 and 1950. Fifty years later, Kubrick would revisit the topic of marital infidelity in his film *Eyes Wide Shut*. A previous attempt to deal with the theme of jealousy was made by photojournalist and FSA alumnus John Vachon, when he was assigned to stage Jacques Bacal's essay "The Other Woman Is Often the Creation of the Wife" (August 2, 1949). Both articles are similar in content, so it may not be surprising to notice two Vachon pictures replicated in the Kubrick essay, although with variations. The first common picture represents the trope of the "telltale sign," with the difference that the evidence is more incriminating in Vachon's mise-en-scène (a lipstick-smeared handkerchief) and meant to illustrate the man's vindictive attempt to hurt his wife, according to the caption. In Kubrick's essay, the woman notices a letter with "feminine" handwriting addressed to her husband, which in this case is supposed to depict an unduly obsessive and suspicious wife. The second picture features the couple walking down the street and the wife holding on to her husband's arm while he looks at the "other woman." In the Vachon version, the woman appears to be a stranger, and the caption argues that "though it is perfectly normal for a man to look at another woman, some wives cannot understand or forgive this" (cf. Figure 31). In the Kubrick essay, the other woman is presented as the man's secretary, while the caption explains that "to an abnormally jealous mate, even a friendly greeting exchanged with a co-worker may incite wild suspicions, resulting in bitter hostilities." The similarities are striking, and for *Look* to publish a second essay on marital infidelity or jealousy after 14 months suggests that this theme may have struck a chord with readers, and no doubt young Kubrick as well.

The travel essay was popular among photographers, because it allowed them to make extra money off their expense accounts, although travelling for extended periods of time could be hard on one's married life. One of Kubrick's outstanding photo-essays is certainly "Holiday in Portugal" (August 3, 1948), when he and editor Jonathan Kilbourn travelled to Lisbon and the fishing village of Nazaré. At least three major travel stories were published by *Look* between the end of World War II and "Holiday in Portugal," which we can use to determine the genre's conventions and gauge Kubrick's contribution. The first is Arthur Rothstein's "How to Drive Across the U.S." (July 22, 1947), which features Helen and

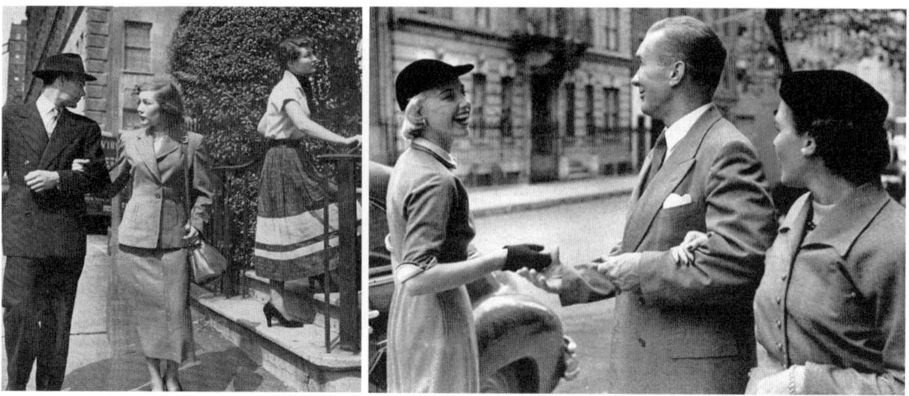

Figure 31: August 1949 photograph by John Vachon (left), and August 1950 by Kubrick (right).

Norman Scheffer and their four-year-old daughter Beverly on a cross-country road trip from New York to San Francisco. Since the locations change constantly, the first convention of the travel story is to use one or more characters as visual continuity devices. In addition, a middle-class white American family usually serves as a point of identification for *Look*'s target audience. Kubrick's Portugal story also follows a married couple from New York, but only to Lisbon and the surrounding countryside: the trip to the fishing village focuses on the local population exclusively. The *Look* editors obviously felt that the photogenic and exotic quality of Nazaré and its people compensated for the slight visual discontinuity. A more heavy-handed continuity device is numbering pictures, used for most images in both essays along with a strict grid layout to indicate the proper chronology. The only exceptions are the full-page photographs and the Nazaré pictures, as if time in this traditional fishing town followed a non-linear, mythical pattern. Sprague Talbott photographed "Honeymoon in Mexico" (September 30, 1947), combining the travel story with a celebrity profile, since the featured couple were both in show business. Betty Garrett was a Broadway actress and Larry Parks had been Oscar-nominated for the role of Al Jolson in *The Jolson Story* (1946), although he would be blacklisted in 1951 after appearing before the House Un-American Activities Committee. The article shows the couple in Tijuana and at Rosarito Beach, enjoying the local food and entertainment in no particular order, with large or full-page pictures of the beach framing the essay, a convention that applies to most photo-stories. Bob Hansen's "Honeymoon in Chicago" (June 8, 1948) is no exception, as it depicts an Arkansas couple's three-day visit to the Windy City, and conveniently segues into Kubrick's Chicago fashion pictures. Like fashion, travel stories never show poverty, in contrast with more critical essays such as Kubrick's "Chicago – City of Extremes" (April 12, 1949). Both Hansen's Chicago essay and Rothstein's road story conclude with travelling tips such as budgeting. The Scheffer's one-way trip to San Francisco, including lodging, food, gas, and so on cost them $275.

Kubrick also distinguished himself in the college story, producing excellent studies of Columbia University and the University of Michigan. The essay on Columbia prompted the editors of *Look* to write an appreciative piece on their young photographer, which appeared on the contents page of the May 11, 1948, issue (C. Kubrick, 36). Colleague Frank Bauman had produced a significant profile of the University of Notre Dame (November 26, 1946) prior to the Columbia essay, which likely served as a model for Kubrick. Bauman's photo-essay differs slightly from Kubrick's, by its use of a student as a protagonist and by opening with three large photographs on consecutive pages, the third one in colour, which was rare. In fact, the Notre Dame essay combines the college genre with a sports personality profile, since the student-protagonist is football star Johnny Lujack, featured in a medium close-up on the magazine's cover, looking like a Marine about to throw a grenade instead of a football. Lujack would go on to win the Heisman trophy in 1947, and play four years for the Chicago Bears. Moreover, the article was penned by *Look* sports editor Tim Cohane, who usually only wrote sports stories. Otherwise, the pictures are organized thematically to illustrate the University's scholarship, spiritual life, campus and social life, traditions and football team, not unlike Kubrick's Columbia and Michigan essays.

Tim Cohane also wrote a "pure" sports story, which prefigures Kubrick's two boxing stories starring Walter Cartier and Rocky Graziano. Photographed by Maurice Terrell and titled "What a Football Player Goes Through the Day of the Game" (November 23, 1948), this essay follows the University of Oregon's ace quarterback Norman Van Brocklin as he and his teammates prepare for a game against Stanford. Van Brocklin would later win the National Football League championship twice as quarterback, leading the Los Angeles Rams to victory in 1951 and the Philadelphia Eagles in 1960. The Cohane story explicitly adopts the "day in the life of" narrative structure, also employed by Kubrick for his two boxing photo-essays as well as the documentary short version of the Walter Cartier story, *Day of the Fight*. Terrell's photographs combined staged scenes such as the coach waking up his quarterback at 9 o'clock, and action scenes during the game itself. Included are similar events such as Van Brocklin getting dressed in the morning with his roommate, much like Cartier and his twin brother in Kubrick's boxing essay (cf. Figure 32), the coach taping the

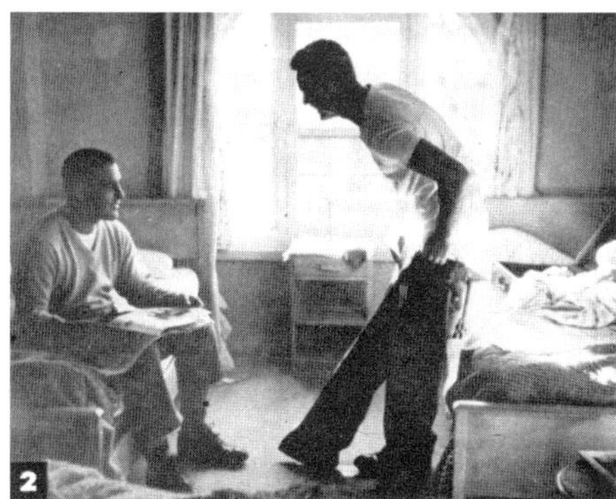
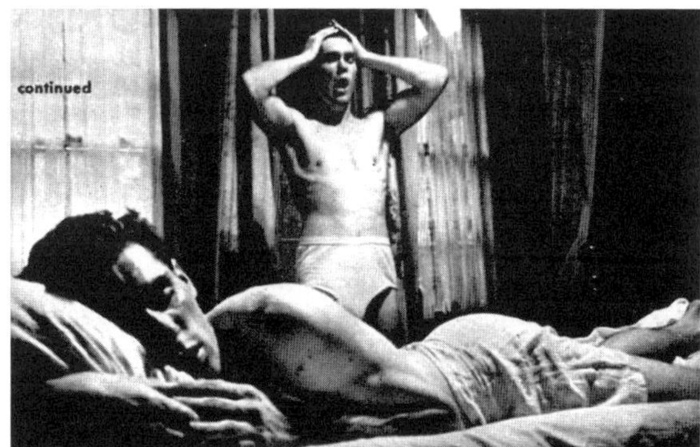

Figure 32: Taken by M. Terrell in November 1948 (left), and by S. Kubrick in January 1949 (right).

quarterback's ankles (as opposed to the fighter's fists) in the dressing room, and a relaxing shower after the game (although *Look* did not publish Graziano's shower pictures) (Crone 2005, 178). The only major difference concerns the layout, which is less varied in the football story: the first three pages use numbered pictures of equal size to confirm the chronology, along with arrows to identify Van Brocklin among his teammates. Kubrick's "Prizefighter" (January 18, 1949) contrasts full-page pictures with smaller ones in a productive fashion. In terms of preparing a shooting script for his sports personality profiles, it appears that Kubrick emulated the narrative structure of the Van Brocklin football story.

An interesting comparison emerges from two essays featuring top Republican senator Robert Taft, both written by *Look*'s Washington correspondent William Mylander, who was from Taft's home state of Ohio and had covered him as a journalist since 1925. The first essay, photographed by Doug Jones and titled "The Trouble with Taft" (October 15, 1946), combines candid photographs by Jones with a biographical overview embedded within the second spread, illustrated from other sources. Kubrick's essay, "Taft Meets the People" (January 31, 1950), does not include a pictorial biography and focuses strictly on illustrating Taft on the senatorial election campaign trail. Jones' portrait of Taft is comparatively informal, beginning with a large photograph of the senator in golfing togs. This is followed by a photographic series of six medium shots on the top half of the third spread showing the politician speaking in a relaxed setting. Kubrick mostly captures Taft at various meetings, looking very serious as he appeals to different constituencies who are not always sympathetic to the Republican platform. One exception is the opening photograph in which Taft literally reaches out in a friendly gesture to some office workers, in an effort to charm the voters and demonstrate that he is "a human campaigner." To the extent that both photographers had to identify scenes that revealed something authentic or simply laid-back about Robert Taft, Kubrick may have had the tougher assignment, since he could not count on casual moments on the campaign trail, only tense or awkward situations that spoke to underlying political differences.

The importance of surface appearances in show business might have impressed itself on Kubrick from his fashion jobs. An article on ladies' fashion involving several photographers sent on separate assignments was published in the January 3, 1950, issue of *Look*, and titled "The Mid-Century Look Is the American Look." In a bold and self-assured way, it claims to define the ideal of femininity for the whole world. Luckily for *Look*'s photographers, it turns out that this ideal is found in the United States, and stems from an American way of life based on "freedom, knowledge, purpose." The article goes on to provide the reader with five examples of American women who embody the ideal mid-century look, all Anglo-Saxon and upper-middle class ladies from 19 to 55 years of age. Kubrick was assigned in October 1949 to photograph the youngest woman, model Ann Klem, perhaps again on the basis of his being the junior member of the photographic staff. The caption informs us that Klem makes $20 an hour, and has earned as much as $500 a week. In contrast, Kubrick's highest salary at *Look* was $105 per week (Ginna, 18). While some of *Look*'s fashion pictures were taken in the magazine's studio against a neutral background, photographer Earl Theisen argues that "the posing in a fashion picture must suggest motion; the model must seem to be actually doing something," which explains the preference for embryonic or more developed narratives, such as Ann Klem's daily routine in Kubrick's essay (Theisen, 115). For a fashion story titled "Home Sewing Continues to be No. 1 Hobby of America's Women" (August 31, 1948), Arthur Rothstein produced studio photographs in colour, as well as action pictures featuring three college girls walking proudly by a campus residence wearing smart blouses and skirts they made themselves. One reason for the presence of narrative interest is to broaden the scope of fashion stories, because they "must capture the attention of persons not primarily interested in style. No magazine that caters to general circulation, as does *Look* in the family field, can afford to take space for material that is highly specialized" (Theisen, 108). Theisen could easily have been referring to Kubrick, who remained "famously uninterested in clothes" throughout his life (C. Kubrick, 29).

In the summer of 1950, shortly before leaving *Look*, Kubrick produced two notable personality profiles of young career women, featuring model and actress Betsy Von Fürstenberg (July 18) and television hostess Faye Emerson (August 15). The articles paint similar portraits of ambitious women who attempt to balance work and leisure, with generous layouts showcasing Kubrick's photography. A few months earlier, Jim Hansen had photographed Leila Hadley, the 24-year-old publicist for cartoonist Al Capp, creator of Li'l Abner, for the photo-essay "Career Girl" (May 9, 1950). The first sentence of Patricia Coffin's article describes Hadley as "a young lady in a hurry," which also happens to be the subtitle of Eleanor Harris' essay on Faye Emerson. The three main spreads of "Career Girl" are organized thematically to depict Hadley's work routine, organizing receptions for potential clients and spending her spare time. Coffin's main goal is to highlight the energy required for a single mother to entertain corporate guests as the promotional director of Capp Enterprises Inc., and to balance "a home and a job, expenses versus income." Coffin makes a comparable argument for Kubrick's profile of Betsy Von Fürstenberg, titled "The Debutante Who Went to Work." The essay's two spreads contrast work and leisure, even though the glamourous nature of Von Fürstenberg's business may not appear like work to most readers. The first page is dominated by a photograph of Betsy auditioning for the famous Broadway producer Gilbert Miller, in his New York City office. The opposite page shows Betsy sitting among a group of other debutantes, preparing for a reception hosted by former classmate Sandra Stralem at her family's estate. Below are three work-related pictures not by Kubrick, meant to support the article's claims regarding Von Fürstenberg's heavy workload. They include the cover of the French magazine *Elle*, a fashion shot and a set photograph from her Italian film *Women Without Names* (1949, Géza von Radványi). The opening photograph of "Career Girl" shows Hadley on the phone ordering groceries before rushing to the office, much as Faye Emerson works on two phones simultaneously in her office (cf. Figure 33). The closing photograph is a backlit full shot of Hadley in a translucent white robe, brushing her hair before dinner, similar to Kubrick's backlit picture of Von Fürstenberg with legs stretched in front of the window.

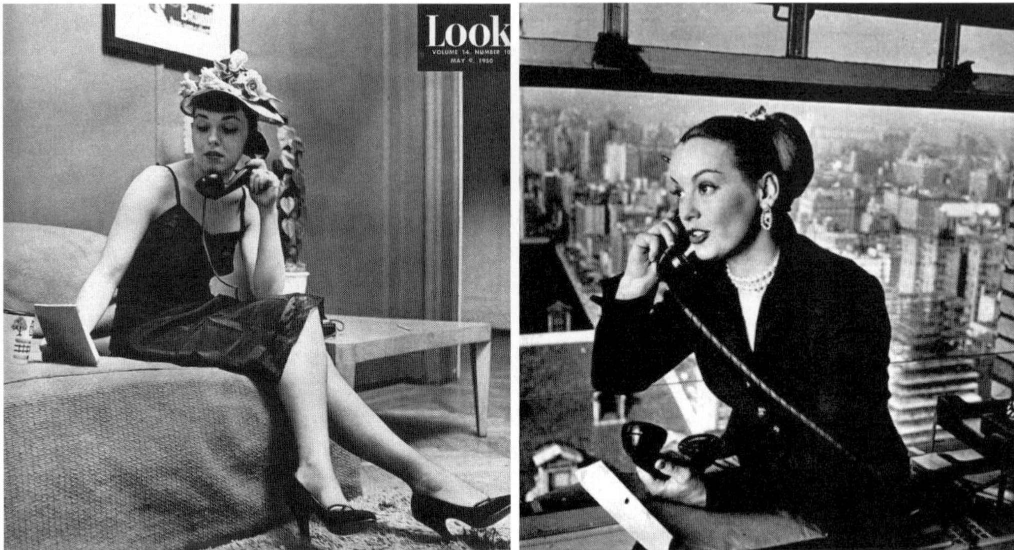

Figure 33: Taken by Jim Hansen in May 1950 (left), and by S. Kubrick in August 1950 (right).

Stylistic tropes of photojournalism

The question of Kubrick's photographic style is analysed in detail in Chapters 8 and 9, in terms of the transition from magazine journalism to filmmaking. For now, we can highlight specific features of that style and examine some of its potential sources within the pages of *Look*, which may once again indicate what Kubrick had in mind when he approached his assignments. The idea is to reveal indirectly what his conception of visual storytelling was, in the context of a social analysis of micro-subjectivity. The selected features include lighting, camera distance, angle, composition in depth, symmetry and photographic series used to suggest time (long take) or movement (zoom). Light is a defining feature of photography, and can also be discussed as an element of mise-en-scène. *Look*'s Frank Bauman photographed a story about a 17-year-old high school girl from Fort Worth, Texas, titled "Texas, Where They Dance" (April 1, 1947), which ends on a full-page exterior night-time shot of "Bugs" Kuhn with her boyfriend on graduation day, standing under a large building's portico. This shot anticipates two pictures from Kubrick's "University of Michigan" essay (May 10, 1949) by allowing the architecture to dominate the figures, and by using backlighting to create an intimate and secretive ambience (cf. Figure 34). Kubrick's Michigan story begins with a full-page shot of a teenage couple sitting on the steps of Angell Hall at night, with the building's large columns towering over them. The next spread includes a mildly subversive backlit shot of a young student lighting her classmate's cigarette. The transgression implied by backlighting in Kubrick's picture concerns traditional gender roles, whereas in Bauman it is simply a naughty allusion to pre-marital sex (Crone & Von Stosch, 26).

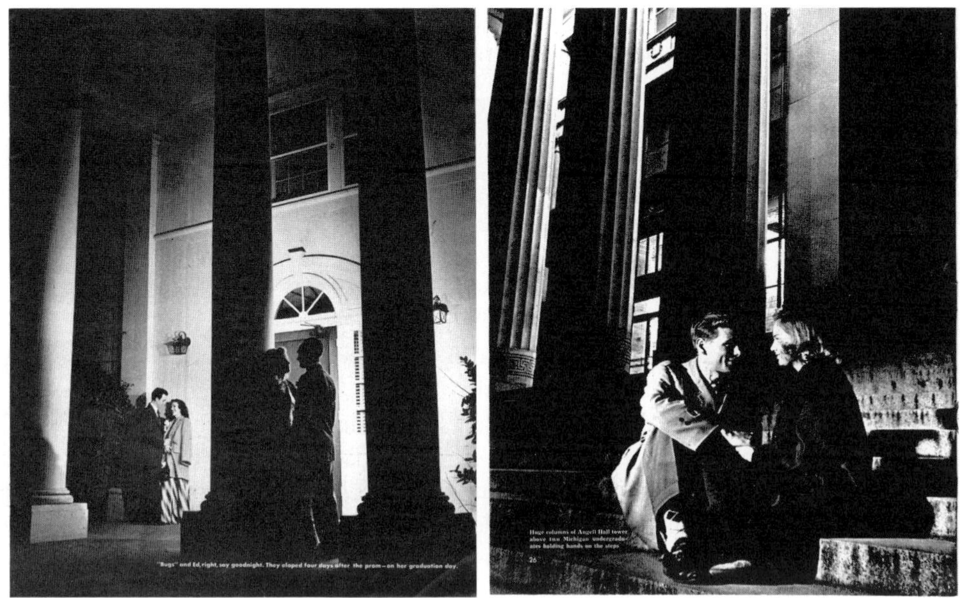

Figure 34: Taken by Frank Bauman in April 1947 (left), and by S. Kubrick in May 1949 (right).

Using setting to overwhelm characters for expressive purposes is an example of mise-en-scène, such as Bob Sandberg's creative shot of an engineering student in a co-operative programme at the General Electric plant in Schenectady, New York, in the article "Industry's Class of 1947" (January 7, 1947). Sandberg frames the student within a large circular piece of machinery that looks like a futuristic time portal (cf. Figure 35), an image that Kubrick will later explore in his film *2001: A Space Odyssey*, particularly when astronauts walk

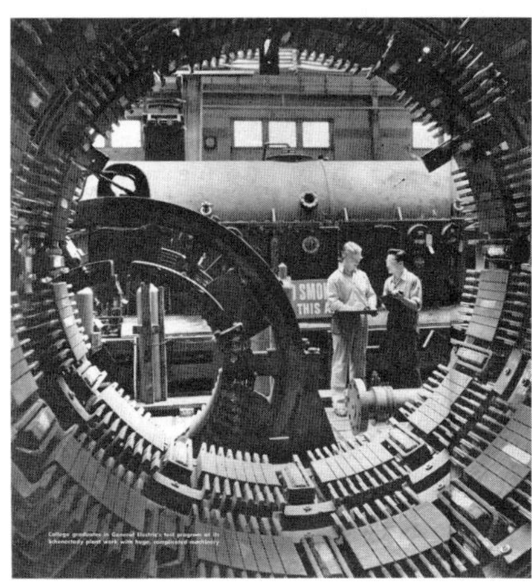

Figure 35: Photo by Bob Sandberg (January 1947).

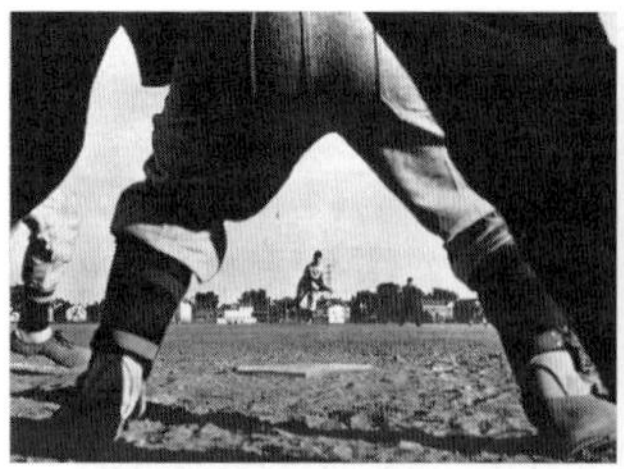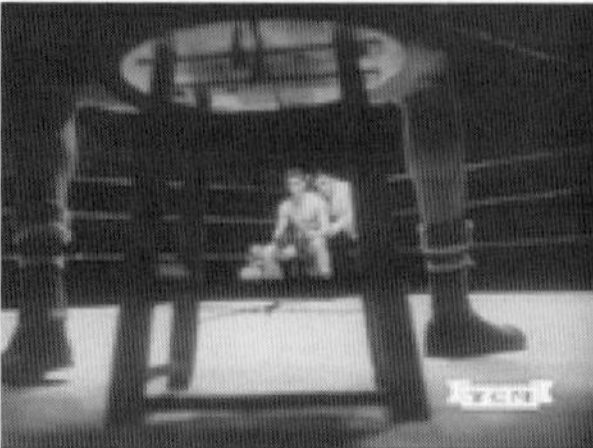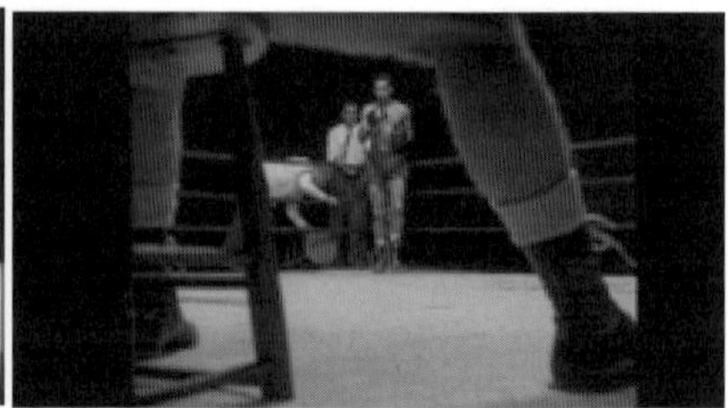

Figure 36: Photo by Bob Sandberg (August 1949), and Kubrick's *Day of the Fight* and *Killer's Kiss*.

inside circular passageways. Kubrick would also place small human figures next to a huge cyclotron in his profile of Columbia University (May 11, 1948), launching his ambivalent relationship with technology. Kubrick has often shown an interest in low camera angles, to create a sense of estrangement even though it may be justified by the desire to convey a child's perspective, for instance. In Frank Bauman's story "American Legion Junior Baseball" (August 16, 1949), the opening photograph is a striking low angle of the pitcher visible in the background, shot between-the-legs of the catcher and the home plate umpire. It places us in the action, as first-person participants in a physical sport, albeit at an unusual angle (cf. Figure 36). By necessity, ringside photographers are always shooting low-angle shots in boxing matches, which works to their advantage since it makes the athletes seem larger than life. Two virtually identical low-angle pictures of a boxer sitting in the corner of the ring, also shot between-the-legs of the opponent, appear in Kubrick's first documentary short, *Day of the Fight*, and his second feature film, *Killer's Kiss*.

Framing the image in such an overt fashion may come across as slightly flamboyant, but it does create a sense of depth by clearly separating foreground and background. Photojournalists working in black and white were especially keen to convey a dynamic or three-dimensional impression in their compositions, since they could not rely on colour to do the job, nor lighting in candid situations. Framing an image in depth, by capturing elements in the foreground, middle ground and background, was a common way of achieving this three-dimensional effect, particularly when combined with deep focus. *Look*'s Hy Peskin took a deliberately staged photograph of jazz pianist Stan Kenton and his band (January 8, 1946), by placing the piano and its player in the foreground, with the rest of the orchestra clearly visible behind the piano in the background. Kubrick created a very similar mise-en-scène in his essay "Dixieland Jazz is 'Hot' Again" (June 6, 1950) for a portrait of the Hot Five featuring pianist Art Hodes in the foreground, and the rest of the band behind the piano. The only notable difference is that Kenton offers a profile in Peskin's photograph, whereas Kubrick asked the pianist to look over his shoulder at the camera (cf. Figure 37). Another overt form of composition in depth is symmetrical framing, when the image features a vanishing point at the centre of the image, along a vertical line. Kubrick used this technique to good effect in his portrait of George Grosz, as if to suggest that the German artist was completely at ease in his adoptive city of New

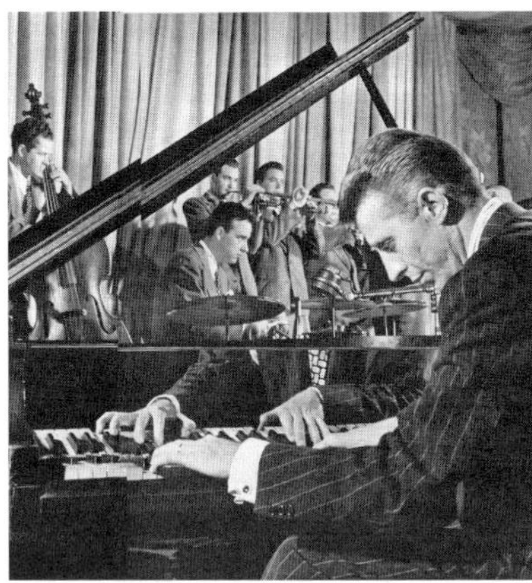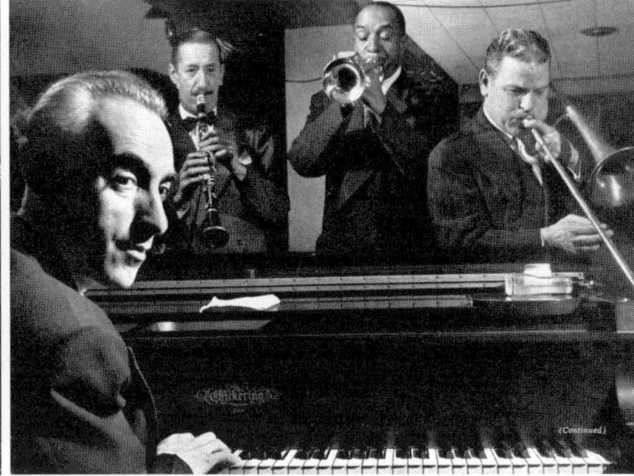

Figure 37: Photo by Hy Peskin (January 1946, left), and by S. Kubrick (June 1950, right).

York. Symmetrical compositions usually create an opposite impression, an overbearing, stifling sense of entrapment, which Kubrick tapped into for his feature films, such as *Paths of Glory*. His use of the oppressive resonance of symmetry may have been inspired by *Look* colleague Frank Bauman's essay "Basketball Come Home to New England" (March 1, 1949), about Holy Cross College in Worcester, Mass. The second spread includes three symmetrically composed pictures, particularly a high-angle view of the College's main dining hall, as well as a colonnade inside Memorial Chapel. Bauman's aesthetic choice may be intended to highlight the regimented nature of this Jesuit institution, and connote power and control.

Series photographs of a personality making a speech or engaged in some physical activity (comedians like Milton Berle, Sid Caesar or Jimmy Durante mugging for the camera) were extremely common in *Look* magazine, and underscore the fact that this film-like trope was utilized by photojournalists who often had the cinema in mind, at least implicitly. A clear example of series photographs is the second spread of the essay "Hot Drummers" (March 5, 1946), which may have been of interest to Kubrick the amateur jazz drummer. Hy Peskin, Frank Bauman and Earl Theisen took pictures of Ray Bauduc, Sid Catlett, Buddy Rich and Gene Krupa performing drum solos, which were arranged in four horizontal strips of eight images each, over the two-page spread. A narrow white interior margin separates the four strips, allowing for captions to characterize each virtuoso's style, akin to voice-over narration in a film. The next step would be to include dialogue in the captions, to emulate a "live," synchronized soundtrack, which was done for Kubrick's "Bronx Street Scene" (November 26, 1946). A particular case of series photographs is the so-called "magic-eye" or "machine-gun" camera, a modified film camera with a fast shutter allowing to freeze rapid action, used primarily for sports stories. Kubrick used it once to illustrate the Brooklyn Dodgers Don Newcombe's baseball pitch (April 11, 1950), much like Maurice Terrell had "filmed" Montreal Royals minor-leaguer Jackie Robinson, for the essay titled "Baseball's First Negro" (November 27, 1945).

Kubrick on realism

Most critics and scholars who have written about Kubrick's cinema have overlooked its journalistic or documentary underpinning, focusing instead on its slightly surreal or unusual qualities. This illustrates a tendency to polarize the discussion of film style, particularly in the wake of André Bazin's influential distinction between "those directors who put their faith in the image and those who put their faith in reality," that is, formalism versus realism (Bazin, 24). Kubrick himself may have contributed to this tendency with his aphorism "real is good, interesting is better," indirectly encouraging observers to downplay modes of realism and to conduct analyses of the variously defined "interesting" quotient, instead. In keeping with Bazin's approach, these analyses tend to be axiological, implying that Kubrick's distinctive, personal style (as defined by the analyst) is aesthetically preferable to the dominant alternative. Bazin championed realism, whereas Kubrick scholars often favour the "other" style, which is usually promoted as the sign of a unique, authorial expression. For instance, Luis M. García Mainar argues that Kubrick's cinema is characterized by "a combination of classical and more 'modernist' uses of stylistic options," which most writers present as a creative and playful critique of classical realist conventions (69). James Naremore identifies a specifically grotesque impulse in Kubrick's modernism, comparing him to Kafka and Welles when they include "deformed and disgusting representations of the body" (27). Kafka's literary work is also commonly described as absurd, existential and surreal, terms that can apply to aspects of Kubrick's films, although in both cases there is a propensity to eschew the realist basis that provides meaning to such significant "deviations." Kubrick's staged photographs have been favourably described as theatrical, yet he also developed candid camera techniques in keeping with *Look*'s journalistic nature (Crone 2005, 8). In a sense, Kubrick was exposed to, and applied the aesthetics of direct cinema *avant la lettre*. He appears to have learned the lesson that verisimilitude in representation, regardless of any narrative genre's specific conventions, is a key to ensuring the viewer's identification to the diegesis. Even the most absurd (*Dr. Strangelove*), supernatural (*The Shining*) or otherwise estranged (*2001: A Space Odyssey*) fictional worlds in Kubrick's work are grounded in an accuracy of detail and documentary realism, which are an equally significant characteristic of his film style, one that "lends an unfamiliarity to the real and an empirical life to the surreal" (Nelson, 89).

It is fair to say that Kubrick's aesthetic sensibility shifted slightly during his career, but that it never abandoned its rooting in the 1930s documentary project of photography and film, famously defined by John Grierson as "the creative interpretation of actuality" (Evans, 9). One might recall the fact that influential members of the photographic staff at the two leading picture magazines, *Life* and *Look*, had been trained by the Head of the U.S. Farm Security Administration's photography programme (1935–44), Roy Stryker, whose management style and aesthetic values continued to assert themselves through the work of his pupils. Among them was Arthur Rothstein, who became Technical Director of *Look*'s photography department on August 19, 1947, and John Vachon, who joined *Look*'s staff on November

23, 1948, and produced a photo-essay that received a complimentary review from Stryker himself. Vachon's "Harlem … New York's Tinder Box" (December 6, 1949) is an arresting pictorial essay very much in the FSA tradition, that prompted Stryker to write a letter to the editor congratulating *Look* for its "intelligent photographic reporting" (*Look*, January 31, 1950). Kubrick certainly inherited the values of the FSA group, most clearly expressed in an early interview he gave to the trade magazine *The Camera* in 1948, when he stated that "esthetically recording spontaneous action, rather than carefully posing a picture, is the most valid and expressive use of photography" (Stagg, 37). Obviously, Kubrick would soon revise this initial preference for candid rather than staged action, in order to take advantage of the photographic opportunities afforded by a heightened control of mise-en-scène. It bears mentioning that Kubrick's "revision" mostly affects the mode of production, possibly diverting attention from a continuity of purpose in terms of the intended effect on the viewer, which boils down to the critically important issue of verisimilitude or believability, particularly in narrative genres that deal with non-realistic subject matter.

This continuity of purpose is exemplified by Kubrick's views regarding the question of lighting, again first reported by *The Camera* in 1948: "When shooting indoors, Kubrick prefers to use the building's own lighting system, unless the illumination is too weak to permit photographing the natural movement of subjects" (Stagg, 36). Ten years later, Kubrick explained to *The New York Times* that "we are all used to seeing things in a certain way, with the light coming from some natural source. I try to duplicate this natural light in the filming. It makes for a feeling of greater reality" (Stang, 36). After the release of *The Shining* in 1980, Kubrick added that "in order to make people believe the story it's very important to place it in something that looks totally real, and to light it as if it were virtually a documentary film, with natural light coming from the light sources, rather than dramatic, phony lighting, which one normally sees in a horror film" (Molina Foix, 463). Kubrick's reference to the documentary mode, 30 years after leaving *Look*, indicates an enduring commitment to the realist aesthetic of late-1940s photojournalism, specifically at the service of improved viewer identification with the diegesis.

Much of Kubrick's obsession with details is directly linked to the issue of verisimilitude. Avoiding anything that might be perceived as "phony" or "fake" became something of a mantra for Kubrick, convinced as he was that in order to experience the emotional impact of a story, a viewer first had to believe in the "reality" of its fictional world. The story's credibility was nothing less than a prerequisite, one that Kubrick seldom ever compromised, and his own personal standards for plausibility were quite stringent. As Joanne Stang put it, "Kubrick is fiercely concerned with the accuracy of the small details that make up the backgrounds of his films because he feels this helps the audience to believe what they see on the screen" (36). When *Barry Lyndon* was released, Kubrick further underscored the reason for the importance of background research: "The starting point and sine qua non of any historical or futuristic story is to make you believe what you see" (Ciment 2003, 176). In the same way that he argued for the value of natural light, Kubrick spoke to the merits of filming in actual locations, unless they could be faithfully recreated on a soundstage: "I like shooting in real locations, because it is very difficult to recreate the realistic details you find there. This office, for example: you'd think it would be a very cheap set to build, but you'd never be able to have all the objects on the table set up as they are. You could spend hours trying to figure out why they are laid out in this way; but because they have been used, their messiness is impossible to duplicate. And that's what you get in real locations, an acute realism of details" (Walter, 23).

Perhaps the best illustration of Kubrick's adhesion to principles of realism as a guarantor of spectatorial identification is the argument he made at the time of the release of *2001: A Space Odyssey*, a film associated with a genre (science fiction) that is broadly linked to the fantasy mode. Kubrick explained that it was important to be scientifically accurate and to "use the factual elements as a means of building up dramatic credit with the audience, so that they are better prepared to open their minds to the more speculative and purely visionary aspects of the story" (Kohler, 246). In an interview with the French magazine *Positif*, he added: "I wanted the audience to believe everything that happens in the film. … [E]ach detail was important: we had to show actions that are part of everyday life in a way that would make the more challenging parts of the film more believable" (Walter, 16). Such was Kubrick's concern that viewers might dismiss *2001* for being fanciful, that he considered including a ten-minute documentary prologue, consisting of interviews with prominent scientists discussing the possibility of extra-terrestrial life in a deliberately serious fashion. This material was to be presented in 35mm black-and-white film, a decision consistent with Kubrick's view that black-and-white is more realistic than colour, an obvious nod to the impact of documentary photography (Reynolds, 149).

The same argument concerning the viewer's belief quotient applies to other fantasy genres such as supernatural horror, including films like *The Shining*. Kubrick reiterated the significance of creating an environment that is easy for viewers to relate to, by explaining that "in fantasy you want things to have the appearance of being as realistic as possible. People should behave in the mundane way they normally do. You have to be especially careful about this in the scenes which deal with the bizarre or fantastic details of the story" (Ciment 2003, 188). One is reminded of Tzvetan Todorov's cognitive definition of the fantastic as "that hesitation experienced by a person who knows only the laws of nature, confronting an apparently supernatural event" (25). In order to fully identify with the fictional character's ontological uncertainty about unfolding narrative events, it helps for the diegesis to be presented in a manner that invites the reader to apply theorist Marie-Laure Ryan's "principle of minimal departure," so that the story may be "conforming as far as possible to our representation of [the actual world]" (1991, 51). Kubrick was keenly aware of this psychological phenomenon, and generally allowed its requirements to dictate his aesthetic decisions regarding a realistic representation of the fictional world, which happened to dovetail with his own background in photojournalism. He recognized, for instance, the documentary-like quality of Franz Kafka's work, and identified him as an influence in filming *The Shining*: "This realistic approach was also followed in the lighting, and in every aspect of the decor it seemed to me that the perfect guide for this approach could be found in Kafka's writing style. His stories are fantastic and allegorical, but his writing is simple and straightforward, almost journalistic" (Ciment 2003, 186).

Most scholars appear to have overlooked the relational dimension of Kubrick's aesthetic, not appreciating the extent to which the surreal, grotesque, fantastic, absurd or simply intriguing moments in his oeuvre only acquire meaning when considered as a gestalt, in the context of a fundamentally realist discourse. While useful, Kubrick's aforementioned maxim "real is good, interesting is better" can be misleading, not only because it implies that the unusual is more significant than the mundane, but because it does not properly acknowledge their interdependency. The source of this proverb appears to be Constantin Stanislavsky, whom Kubrick referred to in a 1961 interview, mentioning that the Russian theatre director "made the point that, in addition to a performance being truthful and accurate and believable, that it also had to be interesting."[4] Kubrick further explained that it was not a question of seeking an arresting or exciting expression for its own sake, but rather to strike a balance between communicating ideas and appealing to the emotions. He felt that realism was "the best way to dramatize arguments and ideas," but that it was equally important to tap into the viewer's unconscious in order to provide an emotionally satisfying, but not artificially stimulating, aesthetic experience (Ciment 2003, 181). It may be described as a centripetal system requiring a balanced combination of rational, realist exposition of narrative information, with judicious intrusions of ambiguous, strange, surreal or supernatural actants and situations, depending on the genre. Perhaps the most straightforward expression of Kubrick's aesthetic approach was made to film critic Penelope Houston in 1971: "I have always enjoyed dealing with a slightly surrealistic situation and presenting it in a realistic manner" (114).

Our attempt to conduct a micro-subjective analysis of Kubrick's career at *Look* was based on the visual storyteller's own comments and likely thoughts concerning the relationship between photojournalism and film. It examined both published interviews with Kubrick and magazine photo-essays produced between April 1945 and December 1950, the period during which Kubrick entered into a professional relationship with *Look*. We have seen that Kubrick acknowledged the formative influence of his training as a photojournalist, one that determined the aesthetic language he would adopt for the rest of his filmmaking career. In 1989, he reiterated the importance of a photographic background for film and added that collaborating with specialists from relevant disciplines remained essential (Bouineau, 36). Thematic and stylistic analyses of essays produced at *Look* that anticipated Kubrick's own reveal a visual genealogy linking the work of the FSA photographers, pictorial magazines such as *Life* and *Look*, the *March of Times* documentary newsreels and the fictional feature films of Stanley Kubrick, from *Fear and Desire* to *Eyes Wide Shut*. Clearly, the commercial exigencies of producing work for a mass audience established themselves early in Kubrick's career, providing a grounding that strictly artistic aspirations may have overlooked. *Look* magazine's mission to inform and entertain its readers perfectly mirrors Kubrick's saying "real is good, interesting is better," and the filmmaker's insistence on adopting a scrupulously realist form, even when dealing with fantasy genres, speaks to the enduring influence of his photojournalistic training and to the notion that it is precisely its realist language that allows flights of the imagination to bear meaning.

Notes

1 In conversation with Renaud Walter. Interview first published in *Positif* 100, December 1969 (Walter, 17).
2 http://www.loc.gov/pictures/item/lmc2000009093/PP/. Accessed on November 17, 2010.
3 Crone presented one of these photographs as Kubrick's, but the identification remains unconfirmed (Crone & Von Stosch, 23).
4 http://www.guardian.co.uk/film/1999/jul/16/stanleykubrick. Accessed on December 8, 2010.

Chapter 6

Photojournalism Genres: A Semantic/Syntactic/Pragmatic Approach

As "America's family magazine," *Look*'s mandate was to inform and entertain its wide readership, thus to produce a clear, unambiguous, reader-friendly text giving "the impression that communication resides in the transmission of a message from a Sender to a Receiver" (Odin 1995, 227). However, in the same way that Stanley Kubrick could never guarantee the desired interpretation of his films, *Look* magazine's editors could only assume that their subscribers would adopt reading protocols relevant to non-fiction photojournalism, even if the reading was not entirely in line with the editors' discursive intentions. We have seen how *Look*'s management and staff, including Kubrick, defined the photo-essay as a mode of journalistic practice. We can now shift our attention to the reception end of the communication chain, by studying several conceptions of the photojournalistic medium as a set of interpretive strategies, applicable to distinct photo-essay genres such as portraits of artists and politicians, man-on-the-street enquiries, social studies, political or cultural events, features on American institutions, and so on. Hearing from *Life* magazine staffers and contemporary scholars should provide a broader context within which to gauge Stanley Kubrick's likely understanding of various kinds of photographic storytelling.

In order to highlight the notion that any historically grounded analysis of cultural production can ill-afford to ignore the communicational context in which this production took place, the abovementioned types of photo-essay genres will be examined in terms of their semantic, syntactic and pragmatic characteristics (Altman 1999, 207). A tripartite theory of signs may define syntax as the relation of signs to one another, semantics as the relation of signs to their referents, and pragmatics as the relation of signs to their interpreters (Morris, 111). The following analysis should underscore the interrelated nature of these complementary and mutually irreducible dimensions of semiosis (Morris, 131).

Semantic Features

Film theorist Rick Altman's initial distinction between semantics and syntax is based on a general theory of textual signification, which can be applied to photojournalism (1999, 224). The semantic level concerns the various lexical elements or building blocks that characterize the magazine photo-essay, such as the use of specific locations, character types, shot sizes, sizes on the printed page, descriptive text, essay titles and subtitles, and so on, while the syntactic level refers to the ways in which the lexical elements are structured (Altman 1999, 219).

Identifying a list of relevant elements is a useful first step in defining a genre; however, any unit of meaning is seldom if ever self-contained, and is usually also understood in structural terms, through its arrangement with other units co-present on a two-page spread, for instance. The impact of a close-up may be significant to the extent that it contrasts with an establishing shot printed on the opposite page, thus revealing the interconnectedness of semantic and syntactic features. For example, the opening page of Kubrick's essay on Rocky Graziano (February 14, 1950) contrasts a large close-up of the unshaven boxer in the locker room, and a much smaller medium close-up of Rocky at home playing with his baby daughter, images that are read in relation to each other and to the essay's subtitle: "He's a good boy now".

A magazine's own generic label is a semantic element that can serve as a means of classifying various kinds of photojournalistic articles and thus to establish a certain horizon of expectations for readers. *Life* magazine helped to establish one major generic distinction, which has applied to the field of photojournalism overall, that between spot news and features. Thanks to superior resources and a weekly publication frequency, *Life* magazine was better equipped than *Look* to compete with newspapers, radio and television as regards current news. Perhaps the most spectacular example of *Life*'s ability to follow the latest news was its decision to outfit a DC-8 as a flying editorial office, including a darkroom, in order to cover Winston Churchill's funeral in London, on January 30, 1965 (Lovell, 69). By then, however, *Life*'s efforts had almost become anachronistic, as general-interest photo-magazines were gradually losing their audience to television. In print form, spot news remains primarily a newspaper genre, often consisting of single photographs rather than the multiple images characterizing the photo-essay that *Look* specialized in. Moreover, reader interest in breaking news is directly tied to its timeliness, meaning that spot news photographs quickly become obsolete, and their generic value is then mostly relegated to the archives. In contrast, what feature photographs lack in timeliness they gain in timelessness, by focusing on the enduring appeal of slice-of-life, human interest topics (Kobré, 59). The value of Kubrick's picture of Frank Sinatra smiling to an extremely shy pre-teen girl (January 31, 1950) does not reside strictly in its topical reference to the popular crooner's effect on post-war bobby-soxers, but rather in a "universal" identification with the embarrassment of being singled out in a public venue, if not with the emotions of teenage idol worship in general. This photograph's continued appeal is confirmed by its presence as a full-page picture in *Look* magazine's commemorative volume, published in 1974 (Rosten, 270). By the same token, editors found it desirable to identify a newspeg, that is, an argument about a feature story's timeliness (Kobré, 132). For instance, Kubrick's profile of Columbia University enjoyed political currency thanks to Dwight Eisenhower's recent appointment as President of the institution. The Republican Party had been courting war-hero General Eisenhower in the hope that he might help them defeat Harry Truman in the November 1948 election.

Another example of the "timeless" approach to magazine journalism is illustrated by the sports photography genre. "In a sports feature photo, the photographer ignores the critical winning moment in favor of capturing the atmosphere of the event. Impressionistic pictures of this kind transcend the actual event and become a universal statement about the sport" (Kobré, 97). Kubrick's two major boxing stories focused on the athlete's perspective, Walter Cartier's disciplined regimen in "Prizefighter," and Rocky Graziano's comeback efforts in "He's a Good Boy Now." However, the experienced editors of *Look* magazine also knew that there was much drama and human interest in considering a sporting event from the audience's perspective, as a social and psychological phenomenon. Thus, Kubrick was assigned to cover Friday night fights at Madison Square Garden, in late October 1948, along with *Look* colleagues and former FSA photographers Arthur Rothstein and John Vachon. "Fight Night at the Garden" was published in the February 15, 1949 issue of *Look*, and includes 13 photographs over four pages. Only one image, shot by Kubrick, features the action in the ring, perhaps as a reminder that the boxing match itself is at the very least the pretext for this social event. All the other pictures focus on audience reactions to the match and the media coverage.

The essay begins with a full-page photograph by John Vachon that overlaps on the opposite page, an establishing shot of the ring surrounded by thousands of fight fans who disappear into the darkness of the stadium as they sit progressively further away from the centre of attention and the main source of light.[1] The opening spread is completed by the headline, body copy and four photographs by Kubrick showing radio and newspapermen covering the bought ringside. The text informs us that sports fans spent over a million dollars in 1948 to attend boxing matches at the Garden, and that "folks from every walk of life attend these Friday night fights. They breathe the atmosphere of the big time. Later they tell friends: 'I was there!'" The public interest in this social event justifies the media coverage by ABC radio and the Associated Press, and Kubrick captures the reporters in action.

During the late 1940s, the majority of *Look*'s photo-essays fell under the magazine's rubrics "American Spotlight," "World Spotlight" and "Strictly Personal." Other frequently recurring feature categories included "Sports," "Fashions and Beauty," "Food and Homemaking" and "Movies and Entertainment." The magazine's smaller yet enduring features were listed under the "Departments" section, and included "Letters to the Editor," "Meet the People" and "Photoquiz."

Thematically, *Look*'s top two rubrics represented a strictly geographic distinction between national and world affairs. Otherwise, the labels "American Spotlight" and "World Spotlight" were umbrella terms covering a wide range of topics including articles about art, political figures, institutions, the media, social studies, and so on. A different kind of generic distinction is revealed when we contrast the "Spotlight" rubrics and "Strictly Personal." Broadly speaking, the "Strictly Personal" articles focused on individuals, whereas the "Spotlight" articles illustrated social events or institutions. There were intermediate cases, such as articles that followed an individual attending a social event, and articles featuring a group of people. However, if we apply this basic thematic distinction between personalities and social studies to Kubrick's output and to *Look* photo-essays in general, it is clear that the two kinds of approaches are equally represented. It can thus be argued that social studies and personality features represented *Look* magazine's two main thematic genres.

Personality features can be divided into famous people (including the infamous) and heretofore unknown or little-known individuals. The latter category can be further divided into the unusual or eccentric and those who represent a trend or a particular social group (Kobré, 131). Stanley Kubrick was assigned to photograph his fair share of celebrities, including authors, politicians, actors, radio stars, band leaders, comedians, artists, musicians, and so on. He appears to have become quite comfortable working with celebrities, producing posed portraits and staged scenes as well as more spontaneous, candid pictures. Readers would expect both the insightful formal portrait that captured something of the celebrity's persona, such as Yousuf Karsh's close-up of Harvard University's President (*Look*, December 18, 1950), as well as naturalistic, casual moments revealing the real person behind the façade. The general assumption, however, was that a celebrity's persona would be similar (if not identical) to his or her "true personality." This idealistic assumption helps audiences identify with these larger than life personalities, to enhance the authenticity of their relationship with stars, that is, their fantasy. While Kubrick was not entirely responsible for the tenor of the celebrity profiles he worked on, there does appear to be a gently subversive streak running through many of these photo-essays, which sometimes takes the form of slight contradictions between the text and the photographs.

Movie stars are a continuing source of public fascination, and Kubrick was a regular filmgoer in high school and during his years at *Look*. In an interview with Michel Ciment, he identifies an assignment involving Hollywood actor Montgomery Clift as a positive experience (2003, 196). The July 19, 1949, photo-essay, written by *Look* staff writer Jack Hamilton, is titled "Glamor Boy in Baggy Pants," and stands out as a particularly unglamourous yet interesting celebrity profile. The five-page essay opens and closes with full-page photographs, illustrating two contradictory aspects of his persona: the lonely anti-conformist, and the man who "loves children." The opening page is a medium close-up of Clift licking his finger as he eats breakfast in a torn white tee shirt. The décor is Spartan and the lighting harsh, appropriate for a film noir set but not for a movie star in his home. Facing this surprisingly low-key image is a large picture of a dishevelled Clift on page right. Wearing a tweed suit with an unbuttoned shirt and a loose tie, hanging on to a crumpled raincoat under his arm, Clift appears to mock his profession's dress code. The caption reads: "Here, he's ready for a Saturday night party." He rather looks like he has just returned from a party, early the next morning. The next page includes two more pictures of Clift in his apartment: yawning as he reads a movie script in bed, cigarette in hand, and putting on a white dress shirt over his white tee shirt, while plaster can be seen peeling off the ceiling. This contrasts with the opposing page's concept of the squeaky clean American family, an advertisement in which the manager of the Cleveland Indians is served Wheaties for breakfast as the rest of the family looks on, smiling. The ad's high-key lighting and selective use of colour also enhances the documentary quality of Kubrick's photograph of Clift in bed, with its grainy texture and its exclusive reliance on natural light.

The essay's closing spread features an attractive shot of Clift on page left, sipping his morning coffee as he looks out the window, and a full-page photo of him on page right, playing with actor-friend Kevin McCarthy's son, while the boy's mother smiles broadly. The headline on page left declares that "Monty's as 'strong as an ox' and eats like a stevedore." One wonders whether this affirmation of Clift's masculinity is meant to offset the impression of sensitivity displayed by Kubrick's photographs, as the actor stares soulfully out the window or becomes the playful "Uncle" Monty. Page left also includes a smaller picture of Clift lying on the floor, drinking liquor straight from the bottle. The caption describes this picture as a "gag pose" suggested by Clift himself. While it is sadly ironic that the staged picture would foreshadow Clift's later unsuccessful battle with alcoholism, its position below the morning coffee picture creates a Kubrickian double. Both figures are left profiles, drinking from a cup or a bottle, and one gets the sense that these are perhaps two facets of Clift's personality. Kubrick would later explore the doppelgänger theme, as it allows to reflect on the struggle between reason and emotion, being and appearing, as well as the artifice of representation. The reflexive dimension of Kubrick's work may also be noticed in the last picture of the second spread, as Clift and Kevin McCarthy develop pictures in McCarthy's kitchen dark room. We can substitute a young Kubrick and his picture editor for the two actors, looking through 8″ × 10″ prints such as this self-referential one, to select the best ones for the story.

On the one hand, the distinction between the celebrity and the mere personality is a matter of degree, as it depends on name recognition. On the other hand, the reader's emotional and intellectual investment in the star or celebrity is different in nature to his/her interest in previously unknown personalities who appear as representatives of their own profession, social class, political interests, and so on. One such professional who worked behind the scenes and was not very well known beyond his local community is Lou Maxon. This Head of a Detroit ad agency is presented as a philanthropist rather than a strictly ambitious business person. The October 25, 1949 essay informs us that his company grossed 20 million dollars in 1948, and that during the Depression, he helped to feed over a hundred poor families in his home-town of Onaway, Michigan, outfitted local softball teams, bought band uniforms for the school and helped deserving students pay college tuition.

Titled "Home-Town Hero," the photo-essay focuses on the last day of Onaway's fiftieth anniversary Homecoming Week, set aside to celebrate the town's benefactor. The opening page features a large photograph of Maxon parading down Main Street on the back seat of a convertible, waving in Kubrick's direction, while the town's baseball team, band and youth follow behind. A smaller picture taken earlier the same day shows Maxon having an outdoor breakfast with a large group of guests. The second page includes a picture of Maxon sitting on an outdoor platform while a local merchant makes a speech, followed by a reaction shot of Boy Scouts and other youngsters listening. Maxon sits underneath a large-size poster of himself, and Kubrick took the picture as the ad exec was looking to his left, duplicating the pose in the poster. By timing the photograph in this reflexive way, Kubrick brings attention to its status as a representation rather than a candid, naturalistic picture. It may also remind us of Orson Welles making a speech in front of an oversized poster of himself, in the 1941 film *Citizen Kane*. As for the Boy Scout holding on to the American flag in the second shot, he winces from looking in the sun's direction, which makes him appear to disagree with the speech praising Maxon.

The third and last page also includes a reaction shot of children to speeches. The children of Onaway are the main recipients of Maxon's generosity, yet a low-angle shot of two young girls sitting on the grass shows them looking up to the speaker off-frame, seemingly perplexed by what they are hearing. They may simply be too young to appreciate the extent of Maxon's contribution to their lives, but the last photograph shows the businessman demonstrating his enthusiasm and commitment to youth by making a few practice swings on the baseball field, in shirt and tie. This essay on a local celebrity would no doubt have appealed to small-town America, compensating for *Look*'s habitual focus on New York City.

Social studies may investigate the inner workings of specific industries and institutions, explore urban or rural life in America and abroad, or they may be eyewitness accounts of cultural events enhanced by in-depth analysis. Some of the institutions and industries examined include health, education, show business, fashion and travel, and the cultural events may include sports, Broadway musicals and society balls. Education is an interesting case since, although Kubrick had been unable to pursue higher education, *Look* magazine undoubtedly took advantage of his youth to "infiltrate" a college relatively undetected, for two successful university profiles including one of the University of Michigan. Published on May 10, 1949, the nine-page essay written by Don Wharton includes 26 photographs, beginning with a full-page staged photo lit from the side as two undergrads hold hands, dwarfed by the building behind them, which enhances the intimacy of their tête-à-tête. On page right, exterior and interior views of the Law School use composition in depth and deep focus, recurring Kubrick devices. The exterior shot of law students walking in a campus courtyard between classes is split in half vertically: on the left, a full shot of four men shows them walking towards or away from the camera in the middle ground, while the right side is a medium close-up of two men, one in profile and the other facing the photographer. University buildings are visible in the background, along with leafless trees whose branches appear to grow from the two young students' heads, possibly another instance of Kubrickian compositional humour. The interior shot features a view of the dining hall in perspective, with a slightly angled line of sight, and one or two students in the background who appear to be staring at the photographer, amused at the prospect of appearing in the student newspaper, perhaps, if not *Look* magazine.

The essay is structured thematically, with the second spread including pictures of student life on page left and sports activities on page right. The social activities page is dominated by a frontal flash medium shot of a couple attending the social event of the year, a formal dance called the J-Hop, which is so popular it takes place over two evenings. Kubrick appears to have captured the couple abandoning proper, formal dancing etiquette, as the man stands behind his date with his arms around her waist while the woman leans her head back blissfully on his shoulder, smiling broadly. In addition to taking relatively candid photographs, Kubrick also enjoyed eliminating depth cues in order to make it look as if foreground and background elements were adjacent to each other, either for expressive or sometimes humorous purposes. This applies to a picture in the top left corner of the social activities page, featuring three female students in the Stockwell dormitory: deep focus combined with an empty middle ground and a flat backdrop makes it appear as if the woman in the right foreground is a giant, smiling at two small women occupying double-decker bunks in the left background, one of whom looks like she is standing on the other's head.

The dormitory photograph is followed by one depicting a scene "at an informal Theta Xi party," according to the caption, where female student "Pat Crotty lights Buzz Durant's cigaret" [sic]. Rainer Crone singled out this picture as presenting a reversal of social norms by having the woman light the cigarette, suggesting it was Kubrick's way of highlighting the article's mention of Michigan as the first major university to accept women in 1870 (Crone 2005, 12). In addition to this unconventional gesture in an immediate post-war context, the photograph also features expressive backlighting, to make the informal party at a frat house seem more risqué or film noir-like. Kubrick would later use backlighting in a rather ominous scene in *A Clockwork Orange*, for example, when Malcolm McDowell's droogs taunt and beat up a homeless drunkard.

The second spread's right page concerns sports activities, including swimming, basketball, football and winter sports such as making ice and snow sculptures. The article mentions that in 1950, only a quarter of registered students were women, which may explain the full shot of a man putting the finishing touches on a female nude. The caption explains that a "pulchritudinous snow lady greets visitors to one of men's dormitories."

The next page discusses how students' opinion on teaching is solicited. The dominant picture is a medium close-up of three dorm friends having dinner, including class president Val Johnson, who is referred to as a "Negro senior" by the caption. It also adds that "racial problems are diminishing at Michigan," implying that this is an ongoing issue, unlike Kubrick's article on Columbia University, which includes a picture of an Indian Sikh student with no mention of race relations. The bottom left picture features the Physics Department's small but still impressive synchrotron, another device from the atomic age that no doubt fuelled Kubrick's interest in a topic that led to the satirical film *Dr. Strangelove*. One of the remaining four smaller images was taken at the University hospital, and demonstrates Kubrick's practice of using a low camera height when photographing children, a technique he would later use in *The Shining*, while following young Danny on his tricycle. Moreover, the boy in the foreground is reading a book titled *Work and Play*, similar to Jack Torrance's phrase "all work and no play" from the same film.

The next page discusses the "Michigan approach," which ostensibly prioritizes undergraduate teaching, but is accompanied pictorially by little more than a fairly dull portrait gallery of university administrators. The only exception is a medium shot of the president, Dr. Alexander Grant Ruthven, holding on to one of the boxers he raises. Both dog and master are shown in profile, looking to the right and a source of light, likely a window. Kubrick may have been cheekily suggesting a visual analogy between humans and their pets, one that he would articulate more fully in his November 1949 dog story. Ruthven is also made to look as if he is looking approvingly at a full-page advertisement for Old Gold cigarettes.

The following two photographs on subsequent pages focus on the media, likely a topic of interest to Kubrick the photojournalist. Speech majors are shown reading a story on the University's radio station, and the city editor of the *Michigan Daily* newspaper critiques the latest issue with managing editor and boss Harriett Friedman, in the newsroom. City editor Dick Maloy leans over a copy of the newspaper while Ms. Friedman sits casually on the side of the table, smoking a cigarette. The newsroom is large, with a high ceiling, and Kubrick uses Wellesian deep focus reminiscent of the scene in *Citizen Kane* where Kane fires Jed Leland, by including a Royal typewriter in the foreground and other desks in the background. Indicative of a long-standing interest in journalism and a modernist penchant for reflexivity, Kubrick would revisit the newsroom set in his industrial short film *The Seafarers*, as well as in his feature *Full Metal Jacket*, whose protagonist is a journalist.

The decision to cover certain topics over others may also be a response to contemporary readership studies, which served the dual purpose of identifying popular genres among readers and establishing advertising rates for potential sponsors, on the basis of a predetermined list of generic topics. *Look* publishers John and Gardner Cowles were pioneers in this regard, when in 1928 they hired a young PhD graduate from the University of Iowa, George Gallup, to try out his new reader interest survey system on *The Des Moines Register* and *Tribune*, *Look*'s parent publications (Cooperman, 44). The famous Gallup Poll was thus first used by the Cowles brothers to determine the feasibility of picture journalism, and confirmed reader preference for "visual material over stories composed of solid blocks of copy" (Cooperman, 48). Thematically, readership studies from the late 1940s indicate a keen reader interest in pictures of children and travel, followed by various human interest stories and ending with special interest topics such as fashion and sports (Kalish, 88). A survey conducted by the Associated Press in 1977 provides similar results, with readers preferring human interest and feature pictures over spot news and sports (Kobré, 185). When broken down by gender, topics such as fashion and sports fare much better, perhaps explaining their continued presence in general-interest, family magazines such as *Look* and *Life*, although it is not clear to what extent editors were influenced by reader surveys.

What is clear from the published essays is that Kubrick was assigned to cover many of the popular topics identified by the surveys, including babies and children: kids at a ball game, a baby looking in a mirror, deaf children receiving hearing aids, a school for orphans, children at a clothing store, and so on. He was thus made aware of magazine genre formulas, and dealt with them creatively by systematically using low angles when photographing children, for example. This had the effect of making the subjects appear more active and placed them on an equal footing with adults. A particularly affecting example is the lead picture for the essay "Wally Ward Conquers Polio" (October 12, 1948), a low-angle shot of a five-year-old boy taking tentative steps while carrying a football, as his father beams with pride. Kubrick would continue to use low angles to enhance the viewer's ability to identify with children, most noticeably in the aforementioned film *The Shining* (1980), when Danny cycles through the corridors of the Overlook Hotel.

Some of photojournalism's top rhetorical tropes, or "good feature subjects," include kids imitating adults, animals acting like people and the incongruous (Kobré, 61). For the September 16, 1947 instalment of "Meet the People," Kubrick photographed six pre-teens being questioned about the subject of punishment, and made them look like a panel of experts sitting at a table behind microphones. In an essay on dogs in New York City (November 8, 1949), Kubrick featured four Afghan canines striking a glamourous pose on the back seat of a convertible. An August 19, 1947 article on a family of weightlifters includes a toddler doing chin-ups. Photojournalism's penchant for striking, eye-catching or unusual visuals certainly remained an aesthetic interest of Kubrick's who, short of providing surreal or freakish imagery in the manner of a Diane Arbus, always strove to go beyond the expected, while remaining grounded in the believable.

Syntactic Features

The syntactic dimension of magazine photojournalism refers to the ways in which semantic elements are organized into a structure that produces meaning. To the extent that the structure itself bears meaning, concerns about the logical priority of semantics over syntax is a chicken-and-egg problem, and for the purposes of our textual approach, syntax and semantics are considered complementary semiotic phenomena.

The generic distinction between personality profiles and social studies is primarily based on semantic characteristics, people in one case and institutions in the other. Another common generic system contrasts the photo-story and the photo-essay, referring this time to syntactic characteristics, namely narrative and rhetorical form. It should be noted that semiotically, these two distinctions are not unrelated, as I have been arguing. Indeed, there is a tendency for articles about people to adopt story form, and for articles about institutions to adopt rhetorical form, a tendency for which there may be a pragmatic explanation. However, from an analytical perspective, we can examine the story/essay distinction as a syntactic issue.

The Merriam-Webster dictionary defines the photo-essay as "a group of photographs (as in a book or magazine) arranged to explore a theme or tell a story." Telling a story is clearly not the same thing as exploring a theme or making an argument, even though one may combine formal strategies. In his encyclopedia entry on photojournalism, photo editor Arthur Goldsmith articulates the difference between the photo-story and the photo-essay in a helpful way. He recognizes three basic forms: the picture sequence, the picture story and the picture essay (Goldsmith, 2785). The picture sequence refers to a chronological series of photographs depicting a single event, whereas the picture story concerns a more complex event, covers a longer period of time and has a clear three-part structure (beginning, middle and end). In terms of narrative form, there is in fact no substantive distinction between the sequence and the story, since length or complexity do not change the fact that we are dealing in both cases with a story, that is, two or more causally related events. However, there is a significant aesthetic difference: Goldsmith compares the sequence to "a selection of stills taken from a strip of motion-picture film" (2785). This comparison underscores the mutual influence of photography and film, and the generic relevance of reading a sequence of pictures as if it were stills from a movie. For instance, in the June 11, 1946, issue of *Look*, a one-page sequence of 12 shots titled "A Woman Buys a Hat" is a candid series of medium close-ups of a woman at Ohrbach's clothing store in New York City. We see the woman's left profile as she sits on a chair, trying different hats, holding her chin on a few occasions as if to express her indecision. In the last frame, she suddenly looks in our direction, but it does not appear as if she has spotted the peeping tom. Kubrick biographer Vincent LoBrutto points out that "the twelve pictures look like frames from a movie sequence, maintaining continuity and depicting movement as the woman reacts to the hat choices" (LoBrutto, 35).

Goldsmith then defines the picture essay as a non-narrative report on a subject or theme. The types of non-narrative form involved are not explicitly identified, although Goldsmith implies that the picture essay may go beyond mainstream journalism by adopting a more personal, artistic mode of expression: Henri Cartier-Bresson's picture book *The Europeans* (1955) is mentioned as an example (Goldsmith, 2786). Authors commenting on photojournalism seem more comfortable describing story form, so much so that many characterizations of the photo-essay limit themselves to negative definitions, by stating that the photo-essay is not a story, that it does not use narrative form.

There appear to be three generally agreed upon non-narrative forms that best describe the photo-essay, and which may be designated as poetic form, categorical form and rhetorical form. Poetic form includes both abstract and associational forms, categorical form concerns thematic groupings and rhetorical form refers to argumentation strategies (Bordwell 1997, 129). Walker Evans' famous profile of "Chicago" (*Fortune*, February 1947) has been cited as an example of poetic form, which consists in "a free arrangement of different formats on one theme with only a small amount of text," and calls for "associative thinking on the part of the reader" (Lebeck, 230). It may be that the Evans portfolio inspired *Look* editors to invite the *Chicago Daily Sun Times'* Irving Kupcinet to write an essay on the Windy City, and have it illustrated by their own junior photographer. Titled "Chicago: City of Extremes," this five-page photo-essay appeared in the April 12, 1949 issue of *Look* and includes 11 photographs by Kubrick. Comparing both essays reveals similarities and differences in their use of non-narrative forms.

The Kubrick–Kupcinet essay makes a simple yet visually compelling argument, summarized by the title. The article runs through a series of social and economic contrasts that, for Kupcinet, define the city of Chicago. Hunting for visual contrasts in Chicago would certainly have been a choice assignment for Kubrick, who must have enjoyed looking for photographic examples of the rich and the poor, the highbrow and the lowbrow, the cheap and the expensive, the old and the new, and so on. Such a series of visual oppositions, while evocative, might come across as tendentious if contextual information was not provided by the written text.[2] The Walker Evans piece also includes visual contrasts, such as a dilapidated church in a slum neighbourhood and a massive Baha'i temple described as a "suburban Taj Mahal." The *Fortune* essay is generally more ambiguous, however, raising questions about Chicago's identity as a city.

Evans' penultimate spread, for instance, includes portraits of pedestrians on page left, mostly looking away from the spread's centre margin or gutter. On page right, a crowd lines up under the marquee of the Oriental theatre, also with their backs turned to the gutter. The busy Saturday night theatre outing contrasts with a Sunday afternoon picture of an alley, featuring abandoned peanut and shoeshine stands. Even though this spread is the only one to feature Chicagoans, the unusual layout, combined with the pedestrians' blank expressions, creates a sense of dispersion and disunity. Kubrick's photo-essay, on the other hand, is based upon a set of binary oppositions, which provides a clearer, if less subtle, kind of formal coherence. "Chicago: City of Extremes" opens with a striking high-angle, symmetrical composition looking down an avenue in Chicago's Theatre district by night, a perfect setting for marquees advertising noir films such as *The Accused* (1949, William Dieterle) and *He Walked by Night* (1948, Alfred L. Werker). While the *Fortune* essay's subtitle refers to Chicago as an energetic city, the excitement of nightlife is more palpable in *Look*'s lead photograph, and Kubrick would recreate a similar scene in New York City for a shot of leading lady Gloria crossing the street at night in *Killer's Kiss* (1955).

Poetic or associational form as exemplified by the Evans portfolio thus tends to be looser and more allusive than categorical or rhetorical forms, and the *Look* essay pursues the rhetorical logic of contrast fairly systematically. The second spread is dominated by two photographs illustrating the headline: "The beauty of the lake front rivals Paris, but the slums are the nation's worst." On the left page, a wide view of the lawn in front of Buckingham fountain in Grant Park contrasts on page right with back alleys in the slum area of the city's south side, littered with uncollected garbage. Smaller pictures at the bottom of page left oppose a strip-tease artist at the French Casino with a female nude statue in "swanky Drake Towers apartment" (Crone 2005, 36). Observant photo editors made use of abstract form in this instance, choosing a picture of dancer Midge Miller who adopts a pose similar to the statue's, thus enhancing the comparison. The caption amusingly reports that while Ms. Miller is engaged in a "daring strip tease," the wealthy apartment dweller "admires real art in her collection."

For the most part, Evans avoids glamourous images of the elite and their dwellings, focusing instead on signs of decay, on the effects of history upon wealth and ambition, which is a fairly common artistic trope. In particular, the second spread shows the 1933 Century of Progress Exposition site overgrown with weeds, and a solitary run-down townhouse in the old South Side, which is "pocked with slums" but "was once Chicago's Gold Coast." Conversely, the *Look* essay reveals a more classically balanced journalistic discourse, and its concluding spread, for example, features three pairs of contrasting photographs. The largest pair begins with a full shot of a homeless man eating a sandwich for lunch, sitting "among debris of demolished buildings" (Crone 2005, 31).[3] Kubrick appears to have used a fairly wide-lens, and asked the subject to pose for him by looking to his left. Crone points out that in choosing a slightly low angle, "Kubrick seems to enthrone his destitute subject, thus generating immediate empathy in the viewer" (2005, 30). On page right, a rich couple in the background thinks "little of paying $10 for lunch" at a fancy restaurant, relaxing while a cook cuts some roast beef for them in the middle ground, and a large dessert tray is displayed in the foreground (Crone 2005, 32).

The topic switches from food to clothing at the bottom of the left page, as a smaller picture of a street market shows items for sale from 1¢ to $30, while a more posh establishment "features dresses up to about $700" (Crone 2005, 38). Contrasts in housing is included on the last page, with an image of an African-American woman preparing a meal in a "crowded, ill-kept slum building" in Chicago's Harlem, Bronzeville (Crone 2005, 34). The contrasting image, not by Kubrick, is an exterior shot of a modest but clean apartment building with lawns and trees. The body copy ends with author Kupcinet deciding that, despite his opening complaints against Chicago's prudish censors, who forbade performances of Jean-Paul Sartre's play *The Respectful Prostitute*, he still loves the city of extremes. The closing credit states: "Photographed by Stanley Kubrick."

Rhetorical form in photojournalism has been defined as an attempt to construct an argument from a consistent point of view, which is documented and explained to the reader by each picture in the layout (Kobré, 151). This may be exemplified by the work of celebrated photo-essayist W. Eugene Smith, a *Life* magazine staff photographer between 1939 and 1954. Smith considered that the photo-essay functioned as a set of mutually reinforcing photographs that did not tell a story, but rather explained a situation and proposed a moral argument (Moran, 15). The famous essay "Spanish Village," published in the April 9, 1951, issue of *Life*, used rhetorical form as a means of influencing "public opinion in the debate over foreign aid to Spain" (Willumson, 115). Smith opposed aid to Franco, and expressed this view by highlighting the poverty of Spanish villagers and the repressive presence of the Guardia Civil, alleviated somewhat by religious faith and the influence of the Catholic Church. In addition to this argument, the essay's layout suggests "the life cycle of nature: from planting to harvest, birth to death" (Willumson, 112). This subtle progression in the imagery thus reveals a narrative or chronological structure rather than a rhetorical one, although ending the essay with a wake spanning the entire two-page spread may be read as a provocative call to action, to rescue the defenceless villagers from their oppressors. It should be clear that the photo-essay does not necessarily eschew narrative strategies, nor does the photo-story avoid arguing a point or using poetic form.

Kubrick's photo-essay "Holiday in Portugal" (*Look*, August 3, 1948) may be compared with Smith's "Spanish Village," in terms of its own distinctive mix of formal techniques, this time privileging narrative form. Before *Look* and *Life* lost their audience to television, the mandate of these general-interest magazines was to inform and entertain their readership, the entire family. As a rhetorical device, the "personality" approach to photojournalism was a means of making more abstract topics palatable to a wide audience. The use of narrative form would allow readers to effortlessly identify with the story's protagonist, a procedure that taps into "a culturally universal feature of humans' ways of making sense of texts" (Bordwell 1989, 153). While the most obvious example of the personality approach to photojournalism is the celebrity profile, a genre that single-handedly ensures the success of current speciality magazines such as *People*, Kubrick's only travel story makes an interesting use of personality journalism.

"Holiday in Portugal" was an important assignment for Kubrick. He and *Look* editor Jonathan Kilbourn spent two weeks in Portugal in May 1948, ostensibly following Manhattan drug-firm executive Bill Cook and his wife Janet on their European vacation. Twenty-two photographs were published in a five-page photo-essay uninterrupted by ads. The body copy explains the essay's structure at the outset: "On these pages the Cooks make their own comments on a pictorial record of their colourful trip." In terms of generic expectations, the essay thus taps into the exoticism of travelling to a distant land, presented as highlights from the Cooks' family photo album, captioned with personal commentary on their trip abroad. The captions were likely written by the editors of *Look*, but they are printed in quotes to maintain the fiction of a personalized account, a first-person narration that also functions as a realist trope.

The essay is also presented as a chronological narrative, beginning on the first page with the Cooks disembarking from their Trans World Airlines plane, and ending with "A last look at Lisbon." The Cooks appear in all seven pictures in the opening spread, as a means of ensuring visual continuity. Four small photographs in the top left corner function as a quick introduction, as the Cooks are shown on Lisbon airport's tarmac, relaxing in their hotel room, taking a stroll on the "broad Avenida, or Fifth Avenue," and enjoying an evening drink in a sidewalk café. Two more pictures at the bottom of the first page are printed in a slightly larger format, followed by a full-page image, thus creating a graphic crescendo in image-size akin to a filmic zoom-in. One of the two pictures again features the Cooks sharing a drink, this time at Estoril beach, echoing the night-time shot of the café at the top of the page, with Bill on the right and Jan on the left in both shots.

Dominating the spread is a shot printed as a bleed picture and overlapping on page left by two inches. It features strong washerwoman Izabel Ferreira ankle deep in the Mondego River, carrying Jan Cook for a laugh while two other women continue washing clothes, and with the University of Coimbra included as an impressive backdrop. The fiction of a family photo album is revealed through the presence of Bill Cook as photographer. He appears in the left middle ground, pretending to take a picture of his wife even though she faces the opposite direction. Bill is actually facing *Look* magazine's photographer, as if to indicate the real author of this photo album. If anything, Bill may be aping Kubrick's habit of featuring the Cooks with their backs turned to the camera. Moreover, if Kubrick were really the appointed family photographer, we might expect Jan Cook to look in his direction, whereas in fact both she and the washerwoman are looking slightly to the left. Rather than the family photo album, Kubrick's formal strategy suggests a different kind of illusion, that of the objective documentary, although ironically Hollywood narrative fiction also requires its performers not to acknowledge the camera. This photograph's relay of looks may be read as a characteristic Kubrickian ambiguity: a reflexive mise-en-scène paying lip service to the family snapshot, but primarily setup as self-conscious photojournalism.

The second spread begins with the photo album format, thanks to six small size pictures of the Cooks visiting various locations in and around Lisbon. Except for the commentary, our travellers then vanish from the remaining three quarters of the spread, which are devoted to a more straightforward travel pictorial, unencumbered by the presence of the American couple. Kubrick's highly formalized compositions in at least four of the opening pictures preclude any sense of spontaneity, or even warmth between the two married people. In fact, a running visual theme in the top three pictures is the physical distance between Bill and Jan Cook. Kubrick uses their bodies virtually as props to create depth in the image, requiring them to stand far apart. The result is stylized and elegant, albeit unnatural looking. In the first two shots, Kubrick has Bill sitting or standing in the foreground while his wife remains in the background, then reverses this pattern in the third shot. He also alternates Bill and Jan's respective positions within the frame, switching from left to right and back again. In the first picture, the Cooks are drinking espresso coffee in the Bussaco Palace, where they spent the night. It is an interior shot, with each person framed by symmetrical archways looking onto another building. Bill looks up to the right, artificially lit from below with slightly creepy results, while Jan enjoys a more natural sidelight. In the second shot, Jan and Bill stand stiffly inside the Cathedral of the Jeronymos in Lisbon, looking like characters from Alain Resnais' *Last Year in Marienbad* (1961). It is a ground-level shot, with Bill's back to the camera, much like the picture of Jan next to the windmill. But where the miller was looking in Mrs. Cook's direction, Jan now looks slightly away from her husband, as if avoiding his glance. Appropriately, the caption describes the Cathedral's "huge, vaulted corridors that echoed eerily when we talked." The third photograph is an exterior shot of the countryside, "dotted with olive trees and wild geraniums." Jan is visible in the foreground from the waist up, picking a geranium in profile, while Bill stands further away, also in profile, perhaps admiring the landscape. However, Kubrick uses deep focus to make it appear as if Bill has become *The Incredible Shrinking Man* (1957, Jack Arnold), standing next to the geranium and his wife whom he must now look up to. This may be Kubrick's way of making fun of Bill Cook's 6 foot 3 frame (Kubrick was 5′8″), which the concluding text mentions as a cause for admiration from the locals. The Cooks both stand as giants in a picture of St. George's Fort, looking rightward in a three-quarter profile. The Fort itself is in the background, but deep focus along with the theatrical convention of oblique staging allows for the Cooks' bodies to be turned slightly towards the camera while simultaneously creating the impression that they are looking at the Fort next to them, when in fact it is behind them. Sergei Eisenstein, whose writings Kubrick was familiar with, might have described this as a "conflict between matter and viewpoint (achieved by spatial distortion through camera angle)" (Eisenstein, 54).

Right below these six opening pictures, a headline announces the spread's main themes and suggests an order in which the pictures may be read: "Cooks' tour included palaces, bull-fight, and village of Nazaré." On the opposite page is a 10½″ × 8½″ establishing shot of a bullfight, a typical tourist vista and otherwise unremarkable picture. Lined up along the bottom edge of the spread, however, is an attractive series of six pictures featuring men and women working on the beach of the traditional fishing village of Nazaré, 100 kilometres North of Lisbon.[4] Five unpublished photographs from this series appear in Crone's "Drama & Shadows," with the observation that they "testify to the young photographer's respectful fascination with the people and their culture" (126–130). Crone goes on to argue that Kubrick was inspired by Henri Cartier-Bresson's ability at capturing "an essential human dignity in his subjects," although no specific evidence is provided (126). Ironically, *Look* magazine may have paved the way for noted photographers Cartier-Bresson and Edouard Boubat, both of whom travelled to Nazaré on assignment in the mid-1950s, several years after the publication of Kubrick's photo-essay.

The six photographs focus on the women of Nazaré, many of them widows dressed in black, creating a striking contrast with the bright, sandy beaches. One of these is a backlit shot of a woman in black, carrying a basin of clothes on her head, with the sun reflected on the shimmering surface of the water. The woman's face cannot be seen, her body silhouetted against a background almost equally divided in three parts: sand, sea and sky. Also backlit is a man wearing a beret and carrying a stick, leading two oxen on the sand. A woman who may be a grandmother looks after a young child, while a group of five women carrying basins appear to be leaving the beach, perhaps after washing clothes. One of the more striking shots features another group of five women, this time pulling in fishing nets. The nets are not visible in the picture, either because they are too far or kept beyond the edge of the frame. The women are leaning forward, away from the ocean as they pull on a rope at regular, two-metre intervals. Kubrick has composed the shot in depth with a vanishing point on the far left, with the woman closest to the camera on the right edge of the frame, and the others gradually receding into the distance. They almost seem to be engaged in a tug-of-war with nature, as the rope disappears into the sea, their collective strength all the more impressive given the lack of traction provided by the slippery sand.

The Nazaré pictures in this spread come across as more spontaneous than the rest. They remain well balanced and composed, but not as conspicuously staged as those involving the Cooks. For example, the Library of Congress archives include a dozen shots of villagers pulling in the nets, all from different angles, whereas there are five slightly different iterations of washerwoman Izabel Ferreira carrying Jan Cook, obviously posing for the photographer. As if to underscore the difficulty of taking pictures in Nazaré, one of the captions states that "this was the only place we visited where we found people who said, in effect, 'Why should we pose for pictures? What do we get out of it?'" Given the implied lack of cooperation from locals, which is belied by other unpublished photographs in Nazaré, such a statement might be a way of touting the *Look* photographer's skill at capturing images of the Nazareans, and to highlight the pictures' relatively candid, unrehearsed, realistic qualities. Instead, it may be argued that Nazaré is actually quite a photogenic village, and that subsequent tourist pictures, never mind those taken by Cartier-Bresson and Boubat, suggest that Kubrick's accomplishment is not exceptional. However, this spread is a concise illustration of Kubrick's versatility as a photojournalist, as well as an indicator of his penchant for combining realist and formalist aesthetics, which he would continue to pursue as a filmmaker. For example, we might parallel the Nazaré and Lisbon pictures with scenes from *Dr. Strangelove* (1964): the documentary feel of the hand-held imagery of Burpelson Air Force Base under attack, and the studied compositions of soldiers listening to Base Commander Ripper's orders prior to the attack.

The last page is dominated by a high-angle 10″ × 10″ shot "atop a dizzying stairway that leads down from St. George's Fort to the city itself." Again, the Cooks are physically separated by a dozen steps to benefit Kubrick's compositional requirements, with Bill pausing briefly in the left foreground while Jan catches up. This is a follow-up photograph to the previous shot of the couple looking at the Fort's staircase, presumably before they began their ascent. Kubrick again calls upon the theatrical convention of a character looking away from the putative object of his gaze, the spectacular view of Lisbon, in order to allow the viewer to see the character's reaction. An extreme version of this practice, which can be interpreted as rude behaviour on the character's part, may be seen in the classic noir film *The Big Combo* (1955, Joseph Lewis), in which the antagonist systematically speaks to the hero with his back turned to him. Only the audience gets to see the interlocutors' faces, in a frontal staging that undermines plausibility for expressive purposes. The two-dimensional nature of photography is also being put to use, since Bill is looking to the right at the top half of the image, which is where the city vista is located graphically, even though it is behind him if one reads the image by applying the rules of perspective. Bill thus becomes the *Look* reader's stand-in, inviting him or her to identify with his point of view as he admires the scenery, albeit somewhat indirectly. Kubrick will further exploit the notion of ambiguous point of view in his film career, particularly in the concluding Louis XVI apartment scene from *2001: A Space Odyssey*, when astronaut Dave Bowman sees himself grow old in stages.

One of the syntactic issues raised by this analysis of "Holiday in Portugal" is the relationship between text and photographs, and how the relative importance of each semantic element may determine an essay's generic identity and its associated reading protocols. Some have argued that photographs are more important than text in a photo-essay, especially if one considers the space occupied by images on the printed page (Hoffer, vi). Others, such as *Life* magazine's long-time executive editor Wilson Hicks, have claimed that both media complement each other in ways that undermine the notion of semiotic dominance (35). Karen Lange, a caption writer for *National Geographic*, has stated that uncaptioned photographs function as art, but if one adds text, they become photojournalistic, that is, conveyors of information (Lovell, 115). One might object that this depends upon the tenor of the accompanying text, but it certainly reflects a distinction between photo-magazines and photo-books, for instance. The photo-book tends to display single pictures with little or no contextual information, for strictly expressive purposes. Comparing *Look*'s essay "Holiday in Portugal" with Rainer Crone's presentation of the Nazaré photographs in *Drama & Shadows* is a good illustration of this distinction (Crone 2005, 126–131). We might add that the generic context is broader than the text's presence or absence, and its thematic focus on expressive qualities or informational content. Assigning photographs to a genre is also an institutional matter: "Photojournalistic photographs are photographs used by newspapers" (Scott, 99).

There is no denying the impact of written text, especially captions, on how we read accompanying photographs, in the same way that in cinema it is "the sound track that provides a base for visual identification, that authorizes vision and makes it possible" (Altman 1992, 62). Studies have shown that a slight majority of photo-magazine subscribers read only captions and do not bother with the text or body copy (Lovell, 111). Captions serve important pragmatic functions, which will be discussed below, including as points of entry for the text itself and as a means of suturing image and text. But in terms of journalistic expectations, the most critical aspect of the relationship between text and image may be the truth claim, which is being made, either explicitly or implicitly. Theorist Jean-Marie Schaeffer has argued that the photograph does not actually prove the word's veracity, but merely confirms it by not disproving the verbal text (140). He adds that the journalistic text does not really need the photograph to be understood, but its argument can be enhanced by the image's indexical nature, that is, its physical connection to the referent (Schaeffer, 142). Ironically, it is this very indexical dimension that, in principle, also provides the image with the power to disprove the written text should this text appear inaccurate. While image and text can indeed complement each other, chiefly by allowing the image to submit to and be anchored by the word, the photograph's polysemic qualities and its indexical nature can also reveal minor or major discrepancies between the two channels of information. This can lead to alternative or at least more complex readings of otherwise transparent journalistic essays, such as Kubrick's aforementioned ambiguous portrait of actor Montgomery Clift.

Pragmatic Features

Pragmatics concerns the relation of signs to their interpreters, which may be understood as the many discursive contexts that determine textual semiotics. Variations in time and space will affect our reading of a given photo-essay, by modifying the cultural and ideological context in which the reading takes place, which in turn can affect generic conventions. These conventions do not only represent photojournalistic production blueprints, but also a series of expectations, reading protocols or interpretive keys that exist not as empirical, textual constructs, but as mental dispositions in the cultural sphere. Three of the most significant pragmatic concerns in photojournalism include the medium's realist discourse, the distinction between information and entertainment values, and the issue of poetic licence, that is, the artful staging of documentary material. The relevance of these features to Kubrick's development as a visual storyteller will be made clear.

Realism in the photo-essay may be analysed in terms of both specific representational practices and the rhetorical effect of these practices, namely the generic expectations associated with the photojournalistic medium. Realist techniques adopted or developed by magazines such as *Life* and *Look* can be described as the journalistic equivalent to the Classical Hollywood Cinema's continuity system, the so-called invisible style of mainstream filmmaking (Thompson, 194). For instance, realist expectations for the narrative photo-essay required photographers to avoid pictures displaying a direct mode of address from the social actors, similar to the Hollywood dictate not to look at the camera (Kozol, 47). This enhanced the perceived candid quality of the snapshots, even if the pictures had been staged and not "caught on the fly." Non-narrative essays are more amenable to formal portraits, including a direct mode of address, tapping this time into a more self-conscious reading of documentary realism, which highlights the authenticity of the photographer's relationship with the human subjects. This particular technique is also used in portrait and art photography, indicating a distinction that is pragmatic in nature and not textual. Bridging the gap between narrative and non-narrative conventions of realism might result in slightly transgressive uses of the direct mode of address. In "Glamor Boy in Baggy Pants," Montgomery Clift never looks at the camera, suggesting that Kubrick's essay is not so much an authentic portrait, but rather an opportunity for Clift to play another role, an ironic reversal of the standard handsome-movie-star layout. The University of Michigan pictorial (May 10, 1949) includes a photograph of painter, curator and educator Jean Paul Slusser, shown lecturing to an art class. Kubrick chose to position the camera at the head of the classroom, with Slusser pointing in the photographer's direction from the middle ground and the students examining the object of their instructor's lecture from the background. This direct mode of address is both reflexive and slightly disconcerting, because the participants do not appear to be posing for the photographer, yet they are nevertheless looking in a direction that collapses the source of the viewer's gaze with an unknown object behind the frame, indicated by Slusser's gesture. The reader of *Look* magazine has been unmasked, and is being interpolated by the University art professor.

The photojournalistic version of the "zero point of cinematic style," as Noël Burch termed it, was also characterized by a relatively unobtrusive layout, one that sought to draw readers into the story and support the essay's argument by highlighting the images, not the patterns in which the photographs were arranged (Burch, 15). Layouts thus used a grid format that, for the most part, preserved the rectangular format of the photographs, thereby enhancing the impression that the pictures were unaltered, authentic records of a documentary event (Kozol, 43). Perhaps the dullest layout in *Look* was that used for the magazine's regular feature "Meet the People," which Kubrick often contributed to in his first three years at *Look*. "Meet the People" followed a very rigid formula: it was basically a man-on-the-street inquiry, asking people to respond to a set question, illustrated by rows of identically framed and printed medium close-ups, identifying the alleged authors of the answers published as captions. The May 13, 1947, issue of *Look* included 12 European war orphans arriving in New York, mostly from Czechoslovakia and Poland. They are all asked: "What Was Your Worst Experience?" The tragic answers are variations on the theme of losing one's parents in Auschwitz, Bergen-Belsen or Dachau. Seven of the pictured orphans are 17 years old, just a year younger than Kubrick at the time, and one wonders whether the photojournalist pondered on his own circumstances, given the fact that his grandfather Elias Kubrick was also a European immigrant, arriving in New York from Austria in 1902 (LoBrutto, 6).

The relationship between images and text is not only a syntactic matter, but also a pragmatic one, which, in the case of the realist photo-essay, consists in suturing the two channels of information into a coherent narrative or discourse: "texts explain, narrate, describe, label, speak for (or to) the photographs; photographs illustrate, exemplify, clarify, ground, and document the text" (Mitchell, 94). Producing a seemingly transparent, obvious, common-sensical and non-contradictory "readerly text" is the end result of a deliberate ideological strategy (Barthes 1974, 4). The goal is to create the impression that both the language and the content of the photo-essay are self-evident, unheightened and natural, that is, realistic. This impression, however, always remains no more than a rhetorical effect, but one that is used to reach the widest possible audience. It would be hard to deny that Kubrick's schooling in mainstream photojournalism influenced his approach to mainstream filmmaking, specifically his adoption of a viewer-friendly film language. At the same time, we might recognize that New York City after World War II witnessed a growing interest in the "writerly text," that is, non-classical or modernist modes of expression that media professionals, such as Kubrick's colleagues at *Look*, would have been familiar with. While these professionals were committed to a mainstream realist aesthetic partly for commercial purposes, it may be argued that the inherent opportunities offered by the photojournalistic medium for irony and various forms of discursive resistance between word and image would not have remained entirely unexplored.

For example, *Look* editors created a subtle, mild caricature of the top officers in charge of Strategic Air Command, in a satirical fashion that Kubrick would explore in *Dr. Strangelove*. In the June 22, 1948, issue, a series of five photographs taken by Phil Harrington show General Kenney from a low angle, standing over a globe and casually lighting a cigarette (rather than chewing gum like Kubrick's General Turgidson), while the captions reveal that he speaks of knocking out the enemy's capacity to wage war. In the January 15, 1952, issue, a large portrait of cigar-chomping General Curtis LeMay, overlapping a picture of a B-36 bomber, may very well have inspired Kubrick's portrait of the psychotic General Ripper from *Dr. Strangelove*. Finally, Kubrick's photo-essay on the fundraiser for the musical *Gentlemen Prefer Blondes* (September 27, 1949) includes a photo-sequence of composer Jule Styne offering a one-man performance of the musical in order to secure financial backing. Styne is shown belting out a tune on the piano, looking at his hands, touching his head with eyes to the ceiling, looking over his shoulder, simultaneously wiping his brow and holding his glasses in the other hand, and finally enjoying a glass of water. As if to underscore the composer's efforts, an advertisement for Bufferin analgesic tablets is laid out next to Kubrick's photo-sequence, including drawings of a man holding his forehead and drinking a glass of water, mirroring Styne in the last two photographs. It is not clear whether it is the musician or his audience who have developed a headache, a bit of humour from *Look*'s editors, which Kubrick would no doubt have appreciated. Kubrick may thus owe his later skill for expressing irony and the grotesque to his colleagues at *Look* magazine, at least as much as to Weegee and the Hollywood film noir (Naremore, 29).

The second major pragmatic feature in photojournalism concerns the distinction between information and entertainment values. To a certain extent, this lines up with the syntactic distinction between the photo-essay and the photo-story, the implication being that rhetorical form is generally more serious, less fun than narrative form. However, given the commercial reality of mass media, the ideal of journalistic expression is to combine news and entertainment in a seamless fashion, another manifestation of discursive suturing. Moreover, *Look* magazine's mission to inform and entertain its readers is later echoed, arguably, in Kubrick's intelligent yet accessible films, particularly in their distinctive combination of documentary and fictional approaches to visual storytelling.

It has been suggested that news and entertainment values led to the development of "two modes of journalism, informational journalism, which promoted a rational, intellectual discourse, and story journalism, which concentrated on emotion and unpredictability" (Kozol, 193). A 1951 manual on picture editing makes a similar distinction between "record" pictures, required for their informational content, and "emotional" pictures, which supply aesthetic qualities (Kalish, 41). It is nevertheless acknowledged that many pictures can be read two ways, and suggested that whether a picture functions as serious news or as frivolous entertainment, both items are valuable in journalism (Kalish, 79). Arthur Goldsmith, an editor for *Popular Photography* magazine, argues that hard news and sentimental features are actually two ends of a spectrum rather than separate categories (Kobré, 69). *Look*'s art director in the late 1960s, William Hopkins, spoke about the importance of achieving an editorial balance in a general magazine, with light stories meant to relieve pressure from heavy essays (107). This is well illustrated by *Look*'s November 8, 1949 issue, which includes noted freelance photojournalist Robert Capa's serious essay titled "Israel Reborn," and Kubrick's frivolous "A Dog's Life in the Big City," both announced on the cover page. Capa's eight-page photo-essay is engaging, as it chronicles the challenges faced by a new country, in the wake of a horrific war. The photographs show us new citizens arriving by ship, smiling and hopeful, as well as settlers working under difficult conditions to make a new life for themselves. The portrait of a carpenter carrying lumber is presented as a "Biblical figure," while an elderly man being helped off the ship is described as "one of many old people who come to die in the Promised Land their ancestors left over 2000 years ago." The essay thus combines hard information about the social and political situation as well as human interest stories to tug at the heartstrings. In contrast, "A Dog's Life in the Big City" focuses on New York City's idle rich, but remains a surprisingly interesting social study related to fashion, and written by Isabella Taves, journalist and wife of *Look* Executive Editor Dan Mich. The cover page explicitly promises to explain "Why City Dogs Are Happier," which is attributed to the extra care dog owners give their pets in the city and the availability of a myriad of services ranging from dog hospitals to dog walkers and sitters.[5]

The opening spread contrasts "a lost mutt" with high-class afghans and poodles. The mutt is granted a full-page bleed picture, as he poses with three young boys who found him and brought him to the ASPCA shelter. The modestly dressed boys look down at the dog, while immediately behind them, a man peers quizzically at the photographer through a barred window. On the opposite page, Kubrick takes a low-angle shot of six wealthy dogs being looked after in the checkroom of a fancy New York club "while their mistresses lunch." As if empathizing with the dogs' brief feeling of abandonment, the woman caring for the pets looks downward, seemingly depressed. Similarly, the last photograph on this spread shows a doorman from a ritzy Park Avenue apartment building walking a boxer down the surprisingly empty sidewalk. The doorman walks away from us, hanging on to the dog's leash with his left hand. The boxer follows obediently, although he turns his head towards the photographer in an almost reproachful way. Meanwhile, the lonely doorman strikes an almost tragic figure in this symmetrically composed shot looking down the sidewalk, as he dutifully if unenthusiastically does his job.

The second spread begins with a striking shot of four prize-winning Afghans looking out the back seat of a convertible. These are the kinds of dogs who are members of the Dog Bath Club on East 57th Street, enjoying a swimming pool and an air-conditioned kennel. On page right is professional dog-sitter Virginia Browne who boards "pets when owners are out of town." Browne is shown caring for a poodle on a bed while the author's Dalmatian sits on the floor. As a further sign of canine affluence, the article mentions the availability of psychiatrists "for maladjusted dogs," and Kubrick takes a low-level shot of a spaniel being fed ground sirloin by his master's butcher.

The concluding spread offers much body copy, under the headline "City dogs get deep affection, often expensive medical care." Lined up along the spread's top edge are four small photographs illustrating the issues of fashion and medical care. One close-up shows two vets working on a poodle simultaneously, with one's head emerging behind the dog's, while the following closer shot focuses on a small puppy whose head fits in the care giver's hands. The captions point out that despite the expense of using "miracle drugs" and modern equipment, maintaining a dog's health can make regular check-ups seem affordable. More interesting is a simple contrast, a patiently composed shot of a Great Dane and a miniature pinscher examining each other, muzzle to muzzle. The contact sheets indicate that Kubrick had to wait for the perfect moment when the dogs were facing each other. The archives also reveal a more extensive and mildly humorous study of women of leisure with their similarly groomed dogs. Only one example survives in the photo-essay, a low-angle shot of a "pretty owner" on a Manhattan sidewalk, whose hairdo matches those of her two poodles. This would undoubtedly have tickled Kubrick's funny bone. One measure of an assignment's success is how often it is recycled in subsequent issues. Kubrick's portrait of the Afghan dogs in the convertible and the two dogs facing each other later appeared in January 1950 issues of *Look*, in the popular "Photoquiz" feature.

A third pragmatic feature concerns two partly overlapping distinctions: journalism versus art, and candid versus staged images, the common understanding being that journalism does not (or aims not to) stage its imagery, whereas art photography is free to do so, since it is a subjective form of expression. The main differences between these twin concepts are as follow: from an analytical perspective, the journalism versus art distinction is modal or logical in nature, whereas candid and staged photography refer to representational practices, which can in fact be used in either of the aforementioned genres. From an evaluative perspective, there is a tendency within art circles to denigrate photojournalism as formulaic and assigned work, and a tendency within journalism circles to denigrate staged photography as manipulative and unethical.

The generic distinction thus refers to how the photographs are presented and how they are intended to be read, not how they are produced. Noted magazine art director Willy Fleckhaus expressed this idea, albeit in a prescriptive fashion, by claiming that "a magazine is not a museum, and a good magazine has no walls for pictures. The picture must be a part of the magazine" (115). In addition to magazine photographs being read collectively rather than individually as works of art, captions will usually confirm the appropriate reading stance. Jean-Marie Schaeffer has argued that the photojournalistic image employs a referential "witness protocol," which often depends upon the co-presence of an explanatory text for its proper application, failing which the photograph becomes mute and is read, as if by default, according to aesthetic art protocols (Schaeffer, 145). Schaeffer gives the example of Robert Capa's D-Day photographs when they are deprived of a journalistic narrative and displayed in a museum (146).

The notion that photographs are not inherently tied to a specific genre and may be recontextualized is one that has evolved since the emergence of photo-magazines as a new medium. Mary Panzer suggests that while photojournalism and art photography were relatively undifferentiated after World War II, to the extent that the same photographic work could easily be displayed in a news magazine or a museum, the distinction hardened in the 1960s and became dominant until "the lines began to blur again" by the turn of the millennium (Panzer 2005a, 25). A good example of this evolution may be the presentation of Stanley Kubrick's photojournalism as art, in the two historical periods identified by Panzer. Two years after photographer Edward Steichen curated the landmark exhibition *The Family of Man*, which opened at New York's Museum of Modern Art in 1955, the American Federation of Arts organized a travelling exhibition of photographs published in *Look* magazine, titled "Look at America." Poetry by Archibald MacLeish was used to introduce 185 photographs, organized thematically into ten groups, that travelled to a dozen American cities such as Atlanta, Memphis, Chicago, Minneapolis, Philadelphia, and so on. The April 30, 1957 issue of *Look* includes a photograph of this exhibition highlighting Kubrick's dramatic portrait of boxer Rocky Graziano, printed in an enlarged, eight by six foot format, and titled "Rage in his fists" (cf. Figure 7). *Look* produced a catalogue or book version of the exhibition the following year, with 157 of the selected photographs, including Kubrick's picture of Frank Sinatra speaking to a shy and embarrassed pre-teen girl, as well as the abovementioned portrait of Graziano (Hamilton & Preston, 82). The book's Preface justifies the project, as a generic departure from strict photojournalism, by explaining that photographs published by *Look* offer both "a dramatic visual record of how Americans live and what interests them" and reveal the photographers' individual contributions and personal styles, as skilled practitioners of a "creative art form," suggesting that their work can also be thought of in artistic terms as self-expression (Hamilton & Preston, 12).

In 2005, art historian Rainer Crone published *Drama and Shadows*, a collection of 400 Kubrick photographs organized into 31 photographic stories and divided into four broad categories. Unlike the *Look* exhibition, Crone's recontextualization of the photographs as art is based on a more strict separation between journalism and art, designed not only to highlight the individual artist's worldview, but also to promote a formalist aesthetic approach at the expense of documentary realism (Crone 2005, 7). Thus, a deliberate effort is made to rescue Kubrick's youthful work from its fate as impure, commissioned magazine fare, by practising a kind of substitute authorship wherein the curator sets out to recover – or create – a voice assumed to be compromised by the commercial context of photojournalism.

While candid and staged photography refer to production practices, the candid approach is more strongly associated with documentary, journalistic photography, thus the tendency to conflate certain camera techniques with a genre's nature. In fact, journalism's reliance on technology to implement the documentary ideal of objectivity has led to a shift in generic expectations in the last 50 years, according to what is technically possible. In 1948, *Life* photographer Eugene Smith, echoing similar thoughts expressed by *Look*'s Arthur Rothstein, explained that "the majority of photographic stories require a certain amount of setting up, rearranging and stage direction to bring pictorial and editorial coherency to the pictures" (Kobré, 302). Restaging events for the camera was thus not considered objectionable by photojournalists until the 1970s, particularly in situations where the photographs could not otherwise be easily obtained, and when there was no deliberate attempt to conceal the photographic method used. Only with the development of noticeably faster film and lenses, around the time Kubrick was filming *Barry Lyndon* by candlelight, did it become possible to photograph almost anything, and therefore more difficult to justify restaging documentary events on technical grounds. It bears mentioning that Kubrick learned his craft at a time when standards discouraging poetic licence were not so strict.

In contrast with Eugene Smith, Kenneth Kobré's textbook on photojournalism, first published in 1980, urges photographers to avoid the staged photo-essay, or docudrama, at all costs, because it allegedly confuses the reader and undermines the publication's credibility (Kobré, 165). While post-war photo-magazines displayed a relatively more liberal attitude towards staging visual material, standards for responsible journalism did exist, as revealed by several social studies published by *Look* in 1950 and photographed by Stanley Kubrick. These studies are noteworthy for being acknowledged by the editors of *Look* as containing staged photographs meant to illustrate the articles' arguments. One such photo-essay, appearing in the August 1 issue, had its photographic method precisely identified by *Look*: "All situations dramatized in photographs illustrating this article were posed and staged with the co-operation of students of the Katonah High School, Katonah, NY." The images were thus not being presented as candid, documentary photographs, even though they embraced the realist aesthetic prevalent in photo-magazines such as *Life* and *Look*.

The essay was designed to illustrate excerpts from a new book written by Evelyn Millis Duvall titled *Facts of Life and Love*, a popular psychology, how-to book for teenagers and their parents. One may surmise that Kubrick was assigned this job due to his age.

Titled "What Every Teenager Should Know About Dating," the first instalment of Duvall's book includes 12 photographs spread over six pages. Subtitled "A guide to the do's and don't's" of teenage dating, the article outlines the era's attitude towards romantic love, including the following recommendation, printed as a caption on the fifth page: "Standards of good taste keep thoughtful couples from showing affection in public. Offenders hold hands in corridors, kiss in public and even neck at parties." Ironically, while the corresponding photograph features two innocent-looking students carrying books, they are also shown holding hands. By including an image that illustrates what teenagers should not do, the editors of *Look* are cheekily having it both ways: criticizing poor manners and publishing slightly offensive material, at least according to Duvall's code. Instead of attributing this mildly subversive stance to Kubrick's identity as an unconventional artist rebelling against the platitudes of assigned work, it might make more sense to acknowledge the role of *Look*'s editorial staff. They were both familiar with the concept of irony and able to identify an opportunity to exploit a potentially titillating (albeit relatively tame) and thus commercial photographic situation.

At the top of the article's third page, a photograph illustrates the caption's argument that an invitation to go for a ride in an automobile can represent a hazard (for girls, implicitly) and that it is best to decline suspicious offers. The picture is staged in a naturalistic fashion akin to a film scene, with the students engaged in a conversation rather than posing for a still photograph. The concluding shot once again offers an apparent contradiction between image and words, as the teenagers display a much more liberal attitude than Ms. Duvall. The caption states that "a good-night kiss is often the customary way of ending a date but most boys and girls agree that the first date is too soon for such a display of affection." Kubrick's response is to provide *Look*'s readership with a close-up shot of a couple on the verge of breaking into the aforementioned kiss, made to appear more intimate and illicit through the use of backlighting.

The above examination of photojournalistic genres is based on a pragmatic and cognitive understanding of discourse, wherein readers of magazines react to the various textual features of photo-essays by applying their knowledge of relevant reading protocols, according to the social and historical context in which they have acquired this knowledge. My underlying argument, with respect to Stanley Kubrick, has been two-fold. First, in order to work successfully for *Look* magazine, the young photojournalist had to internalize this pragmatic knowledge of photojournalistic discourse and implement it in his own work, at the production end of the communicational chain. He thus had to familiarize himself with the various features of personality profiles and social studies, and realize the respective advantages of creating photo-stories versus photo-essays. Secondly, the goals and values of popular photo-magazines in the immediate post-war era combined a desire to inform and entertain its audience with a realist aesthetic allowing for both candid and staged imagery, a combination that in many ways characterizes Kubrick's later filmmaking career.

Mary Panzer has described a similar combination in the world of fashion photography, revealing the widespread impact of journalistic conventions, and the common tendency for its representational practices to spill over into other genres and related media, such as film. For instance, in a late-1960s effort to look hip, "[p]hotographer William Klein applied street photography to fashion work for *Vogue*, sending his models out into traffic, . . . with references to French *nouvelle vague* film" (Panzer 2005a, 22). The continued influence of cinema, exemplified in this case by the French New Wave's realist ethos, also reminds us of a reciprocal system of correspondences between media, one that finds expression in Kubrick's use of grainy, documentary-like combat footage in *Dr. Strangelove*, for example. A more recent photographic assignment by Nadia Benchallal, published by *Vogue Hommes* in 2003, is described as one in which the photographer "plays with the conventions of photojournalism, producing an essay that might be taken for a documentary account of the life of young men in rubble-strewn Ramallah, the Palestinian capital – except that this is a cast fashion shoot" (Panzer 2005a, 362). We might also compare this essay to a docudrama, or a fake documentary-like Peter Jackson's film *Forgotten Silver* (1997), which has the virtue of highlighting the conventional or constructed nature of the realist aesthetic. Moreover, it reminds us of the self-conscious presence or use of documentary codes in staged photo-essays such as Kubrick's aforementioned "What Every Teenager Should Know About Dating," and that there is often much overlap between genres and modes that may help a young photographer transition from magazine journalism to newsreel shorts and feature-length filmmaking.

Notes

1   A similar shot is included in *Drama & Shadows* as part of the Cartier job and incorrectly attributed to Kubrick (Crone 2005, 183).

2   The Library of Congress archives include over 1000 photographs for this assignment, although only a fraction of the original negatives have survived. A handful of duplicate negatives from contact prints were made for Rainer Crone's *Drama and Shadows* as well as for a brief article, which appeared in the *Chicago Tribune* (Panzer, 2005c).

3   The contact sheets at the Library of Congress reveal that Kubrick made 56 exposures featuring this man, on black-and-white Super XX Kodak safety film. The series starts with a long shot emphasizing the debris, ending with a medium close-up portrait.

4   The *Look* Archives at the Library of Congress include approximately 100 pictures of Nazaré by Kubrick, none of which feature the Cooks, suggesting they may not have travelled there.

5   The archives at the Museum of the City of New York include 346 negatives for this assignment, 11 of which found their way into the six-page photo-essay.

Chapter 7

Photography and Film: History, Ontology and Pragmatics

The relationship between photography and film has been the subject of several monographs, including Garrett Stewart's *Between Film and Screen*: his analyses have broadly focused on the photographic nature of cinema and the cultural perception of differences between these related media. They basically revolve around three binary oppositions: photography is associated with stasis, death and the real, whereas film is lined up with motion, life and illusion (Stewart, xi). This binary division proves to be asymmetrical, since film has the option of representing stillness as well as movement, although it seldom does so because it is a reminder of cinema's "photogrammatic basis" and of motion as an illusion. Thus, the paradox of film provides a life-like but phoney representation, whereas photography seems real or authentic, despite (or perhaps because of) its poignant, funereal qualities. This cultural perception is partly due to photography's link to documentary traditions and family photos, and with film's dominant association with narrative fiction, a perception that is put to good use in Stanley Kubrick's film *The Shining* (Stewart, 176–87).

The purpose of this chapter will be to study some key aspects of the relationship between these two media, in terms of their mutual influence and likely impact on the evolution of Kubrick's career, as he made a gradual transition from photojournalism to fiction film. Of particular interest are the parallel social, cultural and economic histories of photography and film, including the popular perception of film and photography's value and prestige during the immediate pre- and post-war era. This will be preceded by an examination of the ontology and pragmatics of photography and the photo-essay, as well as a comparative analysis of photography and film.

Ontology

Three topics that were undoubtedly central to Kubrick's thinking about his craft, and how it related to his future filmmaking plans, are the narrative dimensions of photography, its potential for fiction, and the semiotic complementarity or resistance between word and image. One of the defining features of a narrative is the presence of a chain of events, that is, at least two causally related events. If we consider traditional pictorial genres such as the portrait, the landscape and the still-life, we might conclude that a single image cannot tell a story. However, Marie-Laure Ryan reminds us that in 1766, G.E. Lessing had written about painting's narrative potential when it judiciously chooses to represent a "pregnant moment," which evokes both a sense of the past and the future (2004, 25). This may be likened to beginning a story *in media res*, hinting that something has led to the current state of affairs, and that consequences will follow. In fact, it was a common photojournalistic practice to not only cover story events sequentially, but also keep an eye out for a striking lead picture, one which could open the photo-essay as an attention-grabber, precisely because of its temporally evocative quality. For instance, Kubrick's photo-story of New York boxer Walter Cartier, titled "Prizefighter" (January 18, 1949), opens with a full-page soulful portrait of Cartier, waiting with his manager before entering the ring. The introductory portrait of the boxer is followed by a flashback to the morning of the same day, with a series of smaller pictures showing the many preparations leading up to the fight. In terms of narrative structure, the decision to begin *in media res* and thus to resort to a flashback is a strategy that Kubrick later used in his early films *Killer's Kiss, The Killing* (United Artists; US, 1956) and *Lolita* (MGM; UK, 1962).

A prior example of the expectant or pregnant moment can be seen in Kubrick's essay "Dentist's Office," published in the October 1, 1946, issue of *Look*. Using a candid camera technique, Kubrick presents 19 patients of all ages each sitting on a chair or on a couch, hoping that by holding their jaws the pain will go away, with an expression that makes them "look as if they want to be somewhere else." The elsewhere suggested by the patients' reflective gaze is situated not only in space but in time. Illustrating *Look* magazine's contention that "Americans are dutiful but nervous dental patients," the 19 characters are shown killing time, anticipating a near future when they will be able to leave the purgatory of the waiting room, and swiftly proceed onto the road to recovery (Von Amelunxen, 16). This forward-looking trajectory is a counterpoint to the photograph's more common function as a Bazinian death mask, locked into a moment from the past rather than the future. Ultimately, the pregnant moment remains a virtual quality, which relies on the viewer's interpretive activity in contributing an implicit chain of events. Failing that, a single photograph cannot be a narrative but only offer narrative potential thanks to evocative temporal or causal features. However, as soon as a second photograph enters the equation, the viewer is led to establish a relationship between the images, and thus to think in causal and narrative terms. Narratologist Gerald Prince has made a useful distinction between a minimal narrative, which represents a single event ("she opened the door"), and a minimal story, which requires the representation of two stages of an event that are causally linked (Ryan 2004, 36).

Clive Scott discusses the hybrid case of the photomontage, the simultaneously single and multiple image that can narrate to the extent that it encourages us to replace the usual pastness of the photograph in favour of an "emergent process" (243). One might argue that a similar effect can be achieved with composition in depth, whereby the various planes (foreground, background, etc.) of the image comment on each other, virtually constituting separate stages in an event. Kubrick's essay "How the Circus Gets Set" (May 25, 1948) opens with a full-page photograph, a deliberately staged low-angle medium close-up of circus President John Ringling North shouting orders to trapeze artists walking on a tightrope on the left of the image (Crone 2005, 85). Kubrick has created a slightly disorienting image by eliminating depth cues and framing the shot to make it appear that North is a giant speaking to miniature aerialists performing right next to him, when in fact they are far behind and above him. According to Rainer Crone, compositions such as this one indicate Kubrick's knowledge of Constructivist photography, which would have been accessible to him at New York's Museum of Modern Art, an argument that could also apply to Kubrick's colleagues at *Look* (2005, 76). As a result, the left half of the circus photograph shows trapeze artists who have been rehearsing (present perfect progressive tense), that is, an activity situated at least in the past and the present, while the right half focuses on North as he barks (present) or is barking (present progressive) orders, which implicitly should have an effect on the aerialists in the immediate future, as they are expected to implement their President's orders.

While the photo-essay often uses narrative form, in which case it may be referred to as a photo-story, non-narrative forms are also common. However, the fact that journalistic practice readily avails itself of stories is a useful reminder that narrative should not be conflated with the notion of fiction, since by definition, the documentary discourse of journalism is not supposed to represent imaginary beings, places or events. Moreover, photography's indexical nature contributes to its cultural perception as a strongly referential medium, thus its tendency to favour documentary rather than fictional enunciation. Nevertheless, there remain photo-magazine genres that exploit the psychological appeal of fiction, particularly fashion and explicitly staged photo-essays. Roger Odin points out a paradox in this regard, further complexifying the relationship between story and fiction: a single photograph appears more likely than a sequence of photographs to trigger a desire for fiction, allowing for a contemplative reading mode and for the viewer's imagination to take over, whereas the narrative sequence imposes a reading and curtails the viewer's fantasy (1987, 50).

This phenomenon may be illustrated with one of Kubrick's staged essays, titled "Jealousy: A Threat to Marriage" (October 24, 1950), a characteristically didactic how-to article written by Jacques Bacal, a lawyer specializing in family relations. Kubrick sets up clichéd yet ambiguous situations that a jealous mindset may misinterpret, material that he would return to in his last film, *Eyes Wide Shut*. The large, opening photograph shows the male employer and his young female secretary smiling at each other, while the wife has got her husband elbow-cuffed, and is poised to pull him away. The second picture shows the woman looking at her husband's mail, particularly an envelope "in strange feminine handwriting." In the fourth photograph, the husband reads the mysterious letter shown previously, perhaps not sharing his reason for smiling with his wife as she looks over his shoulder. The caption warns: "Shutting out an uncontrollably jealous person from ordinary activities produces an antagonistic reaction." Even though the article discusses jealousy from both partners, the photographs focus only on the suspicious wife, for the sake of narrative simplicity.

The third picture reveals the man sitting on his secretary's desk while she gives him a very flirtatious smile, and neither of them notices the wife in the background looking around the door. The caption functions as narration, informing us that: "Entering her husband's office unannounced, a jealous wife deliberately spying on her mate, expects to find him in an embarrassing situation." The photograph is composed in a less ambiguous fashion than the previous ones, and the caption suggests that this mise-en-scène is a representation of the wife's subjectivity, an expression of her fears comparable to the fantasy imagery in *Eyes Wide Shut*, depicting Alice Harford's virtual affair with a naval officer, as imagined by her husband Bill. Jealousy is a great source of dramatic conflict, and Kubrick made use of it early in his career. Among the jealous characters featured in Kubrick's films, we might note the dance hall manager Rapallo in *Killer's Kiss*, Humbert Humbert in *Lolita*, and Lady Lyndon in *Barry Lyndon*. Apart from the unopened envelope and reading the letter, there are no causal sequences in these four photographs. Instead of telling a story, they illustrate a narrative situation plainly identified by the article's title, thus allowing for the contemplative pleasure of fiction, the viewer's desire to look beyond the frame and fantasize (Odin 1987, 49).

The language of photojournalism is not limited to single or multiple photographs, just as the cinema is not limited to the moving image. There is a complex relationship between word and image, between the photograph and the written text, which a cinephile such as Kubrick would no doubt have compared to the motion picture's visual and acoustic tracks. He might have reflected on the nature of images and words, and considered the alternately complementary and conflictual relationship between these two channels of information. Is the photo-essay (or the film) the result of a seamless combination of photographs and text, perhaps highlighting a specific hierarchy between the two "substances of expression," or do contrapuntal and even resistant relations bear meaning as well?

It has often been observed that the expression "a picture is worth a thousand words" can be quite misleading, even if one does not necessarily agree that "practically every picture is nearly worthless without words" (Kalish, 127). The exact nature of the picture's linguistic value remains unclear, so if "a thousand words" refers to an abstract intellectual argument or an elaborate narrative sequence, the power of the single photograph would indeed be impressive. Photographs tend in fact to be indeterminate or ambiguous at best in terms of meaning, requiring contextual information in order to gather the aforementioned linguistic capital (Scott, 64). Only the image's descriptive power is relatively self-contained, and can prove more economical than words (Chatman, 125). Does the photograph work with verbal language or against it? It is a paradox: the photograph is both polysemic and indeterminate, powerful and weak, flexible and vulnerable. It acquires value when it confirms or proves verbal assertions made in the captions or the accompanying article, which means that it owes its value (i.e. its meaning) almost entirely to the text (Scott, 64). According to photojournalist Kenneth Kobré, words can completely determine one's interpretation of a photograph, especially if the picture is otherwise neutral. Even when an image is striking or relatively less ambiguous, the caption can still direct the viewer towards a desired reading (Kobré, 201).

A talented young photojournalist such as Stanley Kubrick would have been intimately familiar with the practical aspects of word-image relationships, as he actively contributed to the collective process of photo-essay production, including not only the selection and layout of pictures but also the combination of words and images. His training therefore extended far beyond the technical aspects of photography, and encompassed a wide range of editing and storytelling skills. One such skill would be the creative contrast or counterpoint between text and photographs, sometimes manifesting itself as self-conscious and subtle ironic commentary, thanks to the image's ambiguous discursive status. It has been argued that the photo-story's forte as a genre resides in exploiting the productive tension arising from gaps and discontinuities between still photographs, not to mention between photographs and the accompanying text (Campany, 84).

Examples of implicit ironic counterpoint can be found in a photo-essay on Republican senator Robert Taft, co-authored by Kubrick and writer William Mylander from the *Look* Washington Bureau. Taft was the son of President William Taft, who had succeeded Theodore Roosevelt in 1909. A staunch conservative, senator Robert Taft is best known for having written the Taft-Hartley Act in 1947, which has since remained the basic labour law in the United States. Kubrick travelled in Ohio in late October and early November 1949, following Taft who was campaigning for re-election to the Senate. More than 400 photographs from this assignment are now stored at the Library of Congress, nine of which were selected by *Look*'s editors for an essay titled "Taft Meets the People," and published in the magazine's January 31, 1950, issue.

Mylander's thesis is that while Taft may come across as a taciturn and intellectual individual, he does possess a sense of humour and campaigns hard to prove that he is, in fact, a man of the people. The opening photograph sets the tone by showing the senator smiling and leaning forward across a desk to shake hands with an office worker. One might say that Taft is making an effort to bridge the gap between himself and regular working people. As was his preference, Kubrick once again uses natural light coming from a window, providing the photograph with a sense of spontaneity and authenticity. This impression is qualified by the presence of Taft's wife Martha, who stands smiling at the picture's centre, framed by her husband and the office clerks, suggesting that her help or encouragement was required for the senator to extend his hand. In fact, Martha Taft was known to be an asset to her husband thanks to her gregarious personality.

Even though Kubrick took photographs of Taft delivering speeches, including dramatic ones such as Taft onstage silhouetted against theatre lights, *Look*'s editors chose to show the senator either listening to others or shaking hands, emphasizing his openness. The essay's second page includes two pictures of Taft waiting before being invited to the podium. The top half is dominated by a medium close-up of Taft sitting at a table in the foreground, looking to his right and away from an audience of farmers sitting in the background in a church basement. The visual separation between Taft and the farmers symbolizes the challenge facing the politician in his bid to win the approval of the working class. Taft's reluctance to support farm subsidies would prove to be a liability for the Republican Party in the American mid-west.

Another challenging audience would be unionized workers, since Taft's drafting of the Taft-Hartley Act was designed to curb the power of labour unions, and was described by Democratic President Harry Truman as a "slave-labour bill." A second medium close-up shows Taft studying his speech at a Lions Club luncheon, indicating a careful and studied approach. The caption, however, claims that the Senator tries to employ a personal approach to delivering speeches. To suggest a certain measure of success, the third photograph is a high-angle, over-the-shoulder shot focusing on a smiling elderly couple shaking hands with Taft, presumably at a reception after a speech.

The third page's headline states that "all comers get friendly reception," that is, Taft is approachable and willing to listen to anyone's concerns. This statement is supported by a photograph of Martha Taft being interviewed by a reporter, and a particularly interesting medium shot of the Senator making note of a voter's reaction after a meeting at the Dayton (Ohio) YMCA. Leaning unusually close to Taft is an African-American man with stains on his jacket's lapel, sporting a wry smile and a tired expression on his face. Taft simply writes something down on his little notepad, apparently oblivious to this minor invasion on his personal space. While the caption claims that Taft is being studious in noting voters' concerns, his body language appears to suggest that he is, in fact, ignoring his interlocutor. This would confirm stereotypes of Republicans being insensitive to the plight of African Americans, especially in the pre-Civil Rights era. On the other hand, Taft did bother to meet this underrepresented community. Meanwhile, in the background, another African-American man looks straight at the camera with an inscrutable expression. This is a good example of a photograph whose caption does not do justice to its ambiguous visuals, and we can imagine Kubrick, Johnny-on-the-spot, capturing this slightly awkward moment, regardless of whether or not it would be included in the published photo-essay.

Placed in a pragmatic perspective, the respective ontologies of the photographic and filmic images are a contributing factor in the communicational norms that determine the semiotic status of photographs (Schaeffer, 10). Borrowing from John Searle's speech-act theory, Jean-Marie Schaeffer distinguishes between two types of communicational norms or reading protocols: constitutive protocols that allow viewers to confirm the properly photographic identity of photographs, and normative protocols that affect the interpretation of photographs according to specific institutional contexts, while taking the photographic identity as a given (108). In terms of its constitutive protocols, Schaeffer suggests that photography enjoys a stronger referential or documentary quality than film, because its referent is explicitly and unambiguously located in the past, whereas film creates a temporal illusion by pretending that the referent is located in the present. Using the terminology of Peircean semiotics, Schaeffer argues that the temporal dimension of the photographic image has an indexical function based on our knowledge of its mode of production (the camera created an image as a physical and chemical imprint), whereas the mobile image of film has an iconic function since it resembles or imitates our experience of unfolding time, but can never be simultaneous with the time that is being referenced, in contrast with a live television broadcast, for instance (65). Ironically then, Kubrick's documentary short *Day of the Fight* (1951) can come across as more contrived and staged than his photo-essay "Prizefighter" (1949), even though both share similar narrative strategies and the same subject, boxer Walter Cartier.

Normative reading protocols basically refer to different photographic genres, understood not as actual photographs classified according to the genres whose defining features they exemplify, but as labels functioning as interpretive keys, suggesting a horizon of expectations concerning certain themes, visual styles, pragmatic functions or effects, and so on. Considering genres as normative rules rather than empirical categories allows for the same photographs to be read (by the same person) according to different protocols, in different institutional contexts, and avoids the essentialist assumption that texts can have only one meaning and belong to only one genre. On the one hand, Kubrick's much published photograph of boxer Rocky Graziano waiting for the summons to the ring can be a narrative episode in a magazine photo-essay, included among 14 pictures relating the day of the fight, specifically the point at which "the time of battle finally draws near" (*Look*, February 14, 1950). On the other hand, such an image may also be recontextualized as art photography, singled out as an expressive artist's personal portrait of a "mythic hero," in a coffee table art book celebrating the artist's vision and style (Crone 2005, 173). This is another manifestation of the previously mentioned susceptibility of the photograph to interpretive manipulation, whether through accompanying text (sports journalism versus art historical exegesis) or the exhibition context (daily newspaper versus art gallery).

Related to the ontology of photography and film is the question of overlapping or intersecting aesthetics, namely photographic and filmic genres that owe something to, or are inspired by the other medium. The formal and aesthetic parallels will be examined in detail in the next chapter, but a few key features may be identified at this stage, particularly as they appear frequently in the critical literature. Indeed, there is a tendency to describe the formal properties of the photo-essay in filmic terms, not simply as an illustrative analogy but to suggest a deliberate decision among photo-magazine editors to emulate the cinema whenever possible. For instance, photography historian Beaumont Newhall compared the pioneering work of late-1920s German photo-magazines to film production practices: "From his selection of the photographs [the photographer] built a well-structured, organic layout, with a large general view as an "establishing shot" – to use the language of the motion-picture editor – through details to a finale" (Newhall, 260). Thus, the magazine art director's work in creating a layout is compared to that of the film editor, specifically in implementing various features of the continuity system developed in Hollywood during the teens (Thompson, 194–213). For instance, analytical editing is the notion that one may resort to closer views or "details" of characters and objects once the narrative space has been defined in a wider shot. Kubrick's early photo-essay "Life and Love on the New York Subway" is a prominent example of this strategy and reveals other dramaturgical practices more commonly associated with film than documentary photography.

Published in the March 4, 1947, issue of *Look*, this essay ends with the sole credit "photographed by Stanley Kubrick," although biographer Vincent LoBrutto identified G. Warren Schloat, Jr., as a then newly hired writer who was paired with Kubrick for the subway story (LoBrutto, 38). It consists of three double-page spreads that use thematic development as a structuring principle and illustrate how the collaborative work between the photographer, writer and layout artist can produce a creative slice-of-life photo-essay. As mentioned in Chapter 5, the second and third spreads begin and end with a larger picture that provides a formal frame and a variety of image sizes comparable to cinema's analytical editing, whereby the larger image can both establish space and act as a transition to the next scene.

Kubrick also provides these photographs with a documentary quality by using a candid camera technique. One fortuitous shot of college students in the second spread includes a bespectacled young man in the right foreground, reading a textbook while standing. Behind him in the left background, two other young men sitting on a bench appear to be "helping" a female classmate with her homework, by leaning close to her. The contrast between the studious man focused on his book and the flirtatious boys focused on the girl would certainly not have escaped Kubrick's eye. Despite this and other slice-of-life moments, Rainer Crone prefers to highlight the dramatic aspect of these photographs by contrasting them with Walker Evans' documentary photographs in the New York Subway (2005, 16). Crone suggests that Kubrick's images go "beyond documentary photography to reach an almost theatrical quality. The subway becomes a stage where life is in limbo, its scenes transformed into allegories of hope and expectation" (2005, 16). One could argue instead that Kubrick's work adopts the era's photojournalistic aesthetic, which combined fly-on-the-wall, candid imagery with deliberately staged, "theatrical" scenes.

The last spread, for instance, includes several group pictures of commuters likely caught unawares as they attempt to get a bit of shut-eye, while other shots may have been staged once the train had reached the end of the line. An intermediate case might be carefully composed candid images, which take advantage of real situations, but enhance them through deliberate framing as opposed to capturing the moment on the fly. An example of this intermediate case may be the last spread's opening shot contrasting two men: one takes a nap by lying on the bench while next to him, another man reads a book. Crone chose to reproduce an unpublished version of this shot, in which the reader focuses on his book (2005, 22). In the published image, however, the man looks at the photographer and smiles, prompting the caption to state that "the wide-awake rider gives camera an I-know-what-you're-up-to grin." But has this man in fact unmasked Kubrick? It remains ambiguous, especially given the photographer's use of hidden camera strategies. What is clear is that *Look* magazine's selection is more reflexive and thus indicative of the photographer's presence than the view chosen by Crone.

Below this opening image are a series of shots featuring tired subway riders that look fairly spontaneous at first glance, an impression that may change upon inspection of the *Look* archives at the Museum of the City of New York. One picture is captioned: "Two more sleepers are lonely leftovers as train hits end of the line." It is carefully composed in depth, using a post to split the image vertically down the middle. In the left foreground is a man leaning against the subway car's window, while the right background shows another man sprawled on an empty bench. The train appears vacated, which, added to the shot's formal composition and the fact that 14 variations on this image can be found in the *Look* archives, leads one to speculate about the identity of the two sleeping individuals and thus the documentary nature of the photographs. Were the men perhaps friends of Kubrick's who agreed to participate in a staged shot? We know from LoBrutto's biography that Kubrick's high school friends were featured in the April 16, 1946 short movie balcony story (25). Other unpublished pictures from the subway story include shots of then-girlfriend Toba Metz, as well as fellow film enthusiast Alexander Singer, who also appeared in the Palisades Amusement Park assignment, submitted June 24, 1946. Whether they were staged or not, these images blend seamlessly together, reminding us of photojournalism's ongoing tradition of pictorial enhancements, which undoubtedly influenced Kubrick who would later incorporate documentary-style moments in his fictional narratives.

While a photo-essay's headline and body copy may remind us of film intertitles, captions are explicitly positioned on the printed page to offer both third-person commentary or narration and first-person dialogue for specific photographs, that is, those under or next to which they appear. *Life* magazine copy editor Joseph Kastner once remarked that the photo-magazine writer "produces a kind of sound track to be played as an accompaniment to the visual track, pictures" (126). This analogy between captions and the movie soundtrack can be illustrated with a brief piece produced during Kubrick's period as an apprentice photographer in 1946, at a time when the young photographer included a number of subjects immediately familiar to him, such as his high school English teacher. A series of four pictures titled "Teacher puts 'Ham' in *Hamlet*," featuring Aaron Traister from Taft High School in the Bronx, appeared in the April 2, 1946, issue of *Look* . This short essay capitalizes on the serial variations of multiple photographs, which suggest an unfolding narrative, highlighted by the captions that accompany the images. Traister would teach literature by doing readings of Shakespearean plays, and playing the various parts himself. A brief text under each photo includes a quote from the play's text, indicating an attempt to recreate the images and sounds of an event that falls short of being a documentary film of the teacher's performance. The photo novelistic technique of combining photographs with text as dialogue was not uncommon, but Kubrick's shooting practices seem to have encouraged the narrativization of his work.

A photo-essay obviously lacks cinema's mobile frame, but it does feature a series of images analogous to the film industry's storyboards. Multiple photographs do have the ability to tell a story, by virtue of the fact that they cannot be read simultaneously: the viewer must look at them sequentially, typically from left to right on a two-page spread, and thus establish a potential causal link. However, Roger Odin suggests that the resulting narrative tends to favour discourse over story, as a spatial layout is a more overt acknowledgement of enunciative manipulation, in contrast with film's "natural," relatively unheightened temporal succession (1987, 48). As noted previously, this explicit presence of discourse tends to limit the photo-essay to a documentary mode of enunciation, preventing it from being read as fiction. Only the single photograph, according to Odin, has the ability to tap into the viewer's desire for fiction (1987, 50). In this case, the analogy with film suggests that both media rely on a fetishistic mechanism of denial, in order to achieve the willing suspension of disbelief that characterizes the psychology of fiction. Odin explains that the fictional effect is achieved at the expense of the still photograph's indexical nature, and that the viewer transforms the photograph into a film, much like film itself creates an illusion of movement and temporal unfolding by denying its photogrammatic nature, that is, a series of still photographs (1987, 50). In contrast, *Life* magazine editor Wilson Hicks argues for what he calls an "overvalue phenomenon," which occurs when a combination of photographs and words "enhances their sense of reality," producing an "imaginative 'plus' [that] is multiplied in a picture story," such that the story's "narrative and descriptive content is so expanded by the viewer, imaginatively, that they take on something of a motion picture's fullness and fluidity" (23–4). The fictional effect described by Odin is therefore also accessible to the photo-essay according to Hicks, whose use of the film analogy underscores that medium's influence upon photo-magazine journalists, including a young Stanley Kubrick.

Another example of captions used as dialogue appears in the November 26, 1946 issue of *Look*, for a series of four pictures printed vertically and titled "Bronx Street Scene."[1] Kubrick may have shot this series with a telephoto lens, given the candid nature of the scene and the relatively close framing. The four photographs show two women examining the hairdo of a friend. The scripted captions suggest that the woman begins by telling her friends about the hairdo. She then turns around so they can examine the hairstyle. She lifts up her hair in the third shot to show the back of her neck, and is gone in the final shot, leaving the two friends to laugh about it and shrug their shoulders. It appears as if the mutual influence of photojournalism and film was, for the most part, a positive financial and aesthetic phenomenon, although David Campany points out that it was occasionally counterproductive, specifically when it led to a creative straight-jacket rather than offering new possibilities. By imitating film form too closely, especially continuity and flow, the photo-essay would miss an opportunity to explore some of its expressive strengths, such as stillness and gaps, and the productive tension arising between qualities of motion and stasis (Campany, 84).

History

Examining the cultural milieu in which Stanley Kubrick lived and worked in the 1940s, specifically the historical system of economic and technological influences on both the visual arts and the mass media should contribute to our understanding of Kubrick's growth as an expressive person, including his decision to resign from *Look* magazine and pursue filmmaking full-time. The following section focuses on the still emerging traditions of photography and film, particularly as they intersect in the medium of photojournalism and reveal common aesthetic and commercial interests. The hybrid nature of the photo-essay, and its appeal to someone like Kubrick who had an interest in both photography and film, becomes apparent when one considers older photographic genres that likely inspired the photo-essay's development.

One of the most striking early uses of photographs on the printed page, particularly once the halftone process allowed for photographs to be reproduced in newspapers, is the aforementioned interview of French chemist Michel-Eugène Chevreul captured by Paul Nadar and published in the September 5, 1886 issue of *Le Journal Illustré* (Newhall, 254). A series of 13 photographs of Chevreul being interviewed on the occasion of his 100th birthday is accompanied by captions under each picture providing the scientist's comments as recorded by a secretary (Hoffer, 99). Serial photography not only evokes motion pictures, but anticipates the appearance of cinema by at least a decade, if we include Eadweard Muybridge's photographic sequences from the late 1870s, showing a galloping horse. Moreover, the Chevreul interview prefigures both the photo-story and sound film thanks to the use of captions, indicating that Kubrick's essays "Bronx Street Scene" and "Teacher puts 'Ham' in *Hamlet*" have a distant parent, whose genealogy can be traced back to the late 1850s (Scott, 341). Clive Scott argues that the magazine photo-essay's closest relative was none other than the cine-novel, a promotional device used by the Hollywood film industry between the two World Wars, and designed to allow the cinema to reach rural communities, which did not have a movie theatre (184). The cine-novel's legacy continued after World War II in Europe, with the popular comic-book style photo-novel (Scott, 185). Thus, serial photography both precedes and parallels the development of motion pictures as a major entertainment industry, in ways that spill over into related media such as comic books, and other photographic genres like the family photo album and the cine-novel, a.k.a. the movie story magazine.

Family pictures had a significant influence both historically on the photo-essay and personally on Stanley Kubrick, a middle-class boy from New York City. Kubrick's father Jack had a private medical practice for 30 years and was also an amateur photographer, an ideal socioeconomic environment for a child to be exposed to the temporal and thematic sequential arrangements of photographs in family albums (LoBrutto, 8). Mary-Jane Hoffer astutely describes a likely generic cross-fertilization after the turn of the century, between family albums and magazine photo-essays: "This new involvement in picture taking, and particularly picture arrangement, helped to educate people and prepare them as the audience for the new illustrated magazines, which, encouraged by popular demand, put more and more photographs on their pages. The dawning visual literacy of the public may have encouraged the appearance of naive picture spreads as well, whose arbitrary arrangements are very reminiscent of the casual layout found in the familiar family album – quite possibly its inspiration" (Hoffer, 70). The gradual and widespread acceptance of photo-magazines in the 1920s and 1930s was therefore partly the result of a new enthusiasm for and popular involvement in photography. The layout for *Look* magazine's regular feature "Meet the People," characterized by regular rows of identically printed medium close-ups, resembles a portrait gallery similar to some family albums, an impression strengthened by the knowledge that during the Fall of 1946, Kubrick managed to include at least five significant friends and family members in three separate instalments of "Meet the People."

High school girlfriend and soon-to-be wife Toba Metz, for instance, is included in the December 10, 1946, issue of *Look*, inaccurately identified as a musician. Two issues later, a January 7, 1947, instalment of "Meet the People" features a portrait of Kubrick's second wife, the ballet dancer Ruth Sobotka, in profile, photographed by her future husband using studio lighting.[2] Opposite Sobotka is Kubrick's uncle David Perveller, identified as a "business man," although it is his younger brother Martin who would later do business with nephew Stanley by financing his first feature film, *Fear and Desire* (1953). Two of Kubrick's photographer friends also appeared in "Meet the People," including childhood darkroom buddy Marvin Traub, in the same issue as Toba Metz. In the November 26, 1946, issue of *Look*, fellow Taft high school graduate Alex Singer is identified as a freelance photographer hoping to produce magazine covers. Both Singer and Toba Metz appear in some of Kubrick's unpublished *Look* magazine contact sheets, particularly for those early street photography jobs such as the subway story, which were ostensibly assigned to help the young photojournalist develop some craft. Kubrick thus brought along friends to assist him during his period as an apprentice photographer for *Look* magazine, in effect combining his professional assignments with family pictures.

Movie story magazines were a "robust ancillary product of classical Hollywood cinema … devoted to article-length fictionalizations of feature films" (McLean, 3). Film scholar Adrienne McLean describes a range of movie stories in terms of their layout and relationship to the parent film, defining the movie story as "a concatenation of stills, other photos, and text, brought together under the primary relay text of the motion picture, that perhaps creates a space, literally and figuratively, in which third meanings can be added to films through compensatory or retroactive viewings as well as readings" (McLean, 12). McLean adds that, since these stories appeared before the films were released, "the 'prereading' of some of the films – not only of their plots but their mise-en-scène, their 'looks' – might easily have affected spectator response to the films themselves" (McLean, 6). Given the fact that the movie story magazines flourished from the late 1920s onwards, it is reasonable to assume that their visual rhetoric would have influenced the design of the photo-essay in *Life* and *Look* magazines, both of whom began publishing in 1937. Moreover, *Look* produced two significant movie stories during Kubrick's tenure, even though this never became one of the magazine's regular features: a "picture story" of the Laura Z. Hobson novel *Gentleman's Agreement* (June 10, 1947) and a "picture dramatization" of Willard Motley's novel *Knock on Any Door* (September 30, 1947).

The *Gentleman's Agreement* is a nine-page picture story featuring 19 photographs by Kubrick's colleague Maurice Terrell, accompanying a "5000-word condensation" of the novel, with key lines of dialogue under each photograph. The opening page explains that the story was produced jointly with Twentieth Century-Fox, in the Fox studios with their contract actors, although not those who were to appear in the film version, which premiered in New York City on November 11, 1947. This movie tie-in functioned as a kind of preview for the Hollywood film production, in contrast with the Lux Radio Theatre's 60-minute radio adaptation that also streamlined the plot but featured the same actors (Gregory Peck, reprising his role) and was aired on September 20, 1948, months after the film's release. Fox's Darryl Zanuck had allegedly paid $125,000 for the movie rights to Hobson's novel, and must have considered the joint project with *Look* magazine a valuable way to publicize the story he was producing.

Look certainly appeared to promote its relationship with the movie industry, and one can imagine Maurice Terrell relating the experience to his colleagues in New York, especially young film buff Stanley Kubrick. The date of *Gentleman's Agreement*'s New York City premiere coincided with *Look*'s November 11, 1947 issue, which included a four-page, twelve-scene parallel comparison between the magazine's picture story (described as a "picturization" and a "picture-condensation") and the Fox movie (cf. Figure 38). Other than the actors, the main difference between the two versions, as printed in the magazine, seems to be Terrell's use of a relatively low-key, film noir-type of lighting, which perhaps speaks to film director Elia Kazan and cinematographer Arthur Miller's decision to treat the delicate topic of anti-semitism in a more sober and unsensational fashion. In any case, they were given the opportunity to consider *Look*'s partially storyboarded version of the film they were shooting during the summer of 1947.

Knock on Any Door is an even more impressive commitment by *Look* to the picture dramatization of a novel, since it was not initially linked to a film project, yet was given 11 pages and 23 photographs by Frank Bauman. The editors argued that this special treatment was warranted given the importance of Motley's book as a "new social document – the story of how a slum child, through society's neglect, can become a murderer." The layout is similar to *Gentleman's Agreement*'s, with lines of dialogue in bold type highlighting the beginning of each paragraph, providing an easy entry point in order to read the photographs. It should be noted that three action scenes are conveyed by using partially blurred photographs, a technique then only used by art photographers to depict movement, whereas photojournalists generally remained influenced by the documentary dictates of Roy Stryker's FSA group and its concern

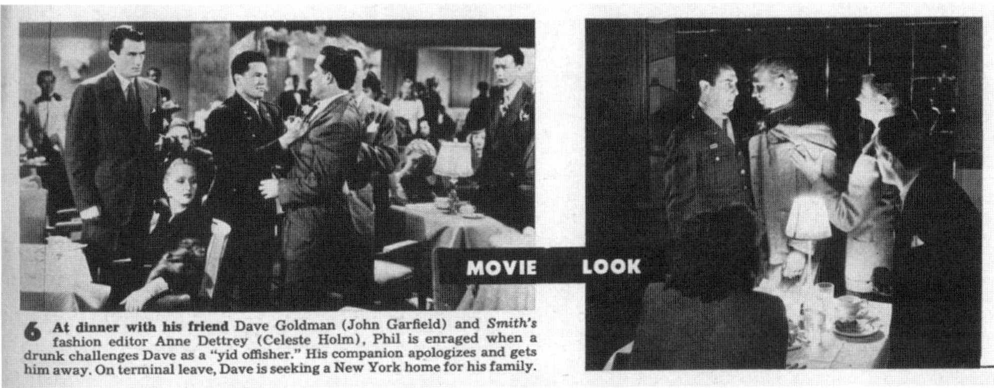

6 At dinner with his friend Dave Goldman (John Garfield) and *Smith's* fashion editor Anne Dettrey (Celeste Holm), Phil is enraged when a drunk challenges Dave as a "yid offisher." His companion apologizes and gets him away. On terminal leave, Dave is seeking a New York home for his family.

Figure 38: Film and photo-magazine versions of *Gentleman's Agreement* (1947).

for sharp focus. Frank Bauman was perhaps the most experimental of *Look*'s photographers, often working with strobe lights, multiple exposures and trying out all the latest gadgets.

On February 22, 1949, Columbia Pictures released a film adaptation of *Knock on Any Door*, produced by Humphrey Bogart and directed by Nicholas Ray. Three weeks later, *Look* published a four-page essay comparing the film and their own picture dramatization from 1947 (March 15, 1949) (cf. Figure 39). The text informs us that Bogart had read *Look*'s photo-story two years earlier, and been inspired to produce a film version of Motley's novel. He and his production team were then provided with copies of Bauman's photographs as part of their research. This time, the cinematographer adopted Bauman's noir style, to express the gritty feeling of Chicago's slums. The set design also appears to have followed the *Look* story more closely, perhaps in keeping with Bogart's initial interest in the magazine's treatment. However, there remained specific plot points that the film could not include due to Production Code restrictions, which were promptly identified by the *Look* article, notably a point-blank range shooting and an execution on the electric chair. It is hard not to think of Kubrick the cinephile making a mental note of cases where photo-stories were used as blueprints for the production of motion pictures, especially considering the fact that none other than Humphrey Bogart was inspired by the work of *Look* magazine's editors and photographers, and that Kubrick later engaged in such adaptations himself.

As we move closer historically to the debut of *Life* and *Look* in November 1936 and February 1937, respectively, the most significant influences on the two major American photo-magazines may be the European photo-magazines of the late 1920s, and the documentary movement of the early to mid-1930s. Photo historians sometimes downplay the importance of the European magazines on the grounds that *Life*, while it did not invent the photo-essay, was the publication that did the most to popularize it as a photographic

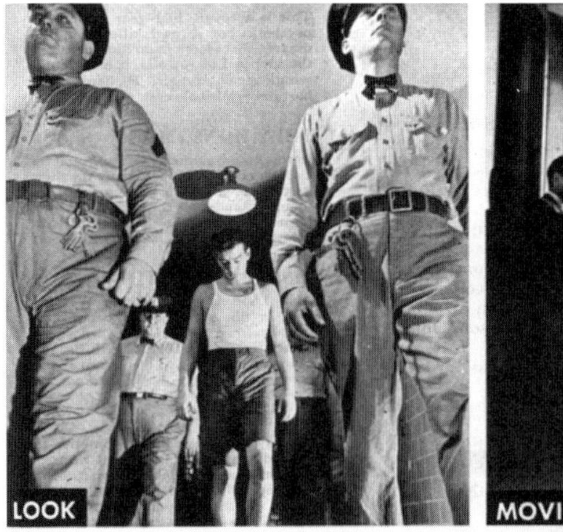

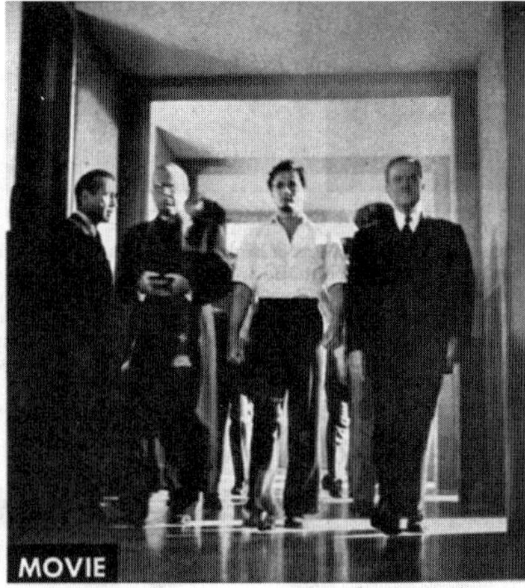

"**The last mile!** He looked at his pants cut off at the knees. 'Yeah, the suit I looked good in . . .'" Nick, the victim of slum life, marches to his death. His attorney vows that he will devote his life to help all boys like Nick.

Figure 39: Film and photo-magazine versions of *Knock on Any Door* (1947–49).

genre (Goldsmith, 2781). The fact remains that by 1930, the photo-essay was a well-established form of journalism in French and German magazines, including *Vu* and the *Berliner Illustrirte Zeitung*. Moreover, the publisher of the *Berliner Illustrirte*, Kurt Koff, has argued that both film and photo-magazines represent a similar, common response to modern life, thanks to the immediate and succinct expressive qualities of pictures: "It is no coincidence that there are parallels between the development of the cinema and of the *Berliner Illustrirte*. Life has become more hectic and the individual has become less prepared to peruse a newspaper in leisurely reflection" (Lebeck, 112).

Another parallel between the film and magazine industries is the exodus of talent from Germany, especially once the Nazis came to power in 1933. Film director Fritz Lang immigrated to France in 1934, and Kurt Korff was hired by *Life* publisher Henry Luce as a consultant. According to Ronald Lovell, "Korff played a key role in getting *Life* started, particularly in target audience, the photographers hired, and how photographs would be obtained and laid out" (Lovell, 96). This association establishes a direct link between the German and American magazines, further confirmed by the fact that during the production of *Look*'s experimental "dummy" issue in 1936, "there were foreign magazines around for the staff to examine … as aids for gaining a better feel of the picture story technique" (Cooperman, 75). In addition, Luce and *Look* publisher Mike Cowles were comparing notes on their respective dummy issues, with Time Inc. even making an initial investment in *Look* magazine, before it became clear that they were direct competitors (Cowles, 59).

Yet another link between print journalism and film was made when Time Inc. launched *The March of Time* newsreel series in 1935, convinced that visual reporting represented the future of journalism. Wendy Kozol argues that, with an estimated viewership of 12 million in 1936, *The March of Time* proved that "the desire for imaging reality outweighed the need for veracity," given the standard and accepted practice of staging or re-enacting events for the camera (Kozol, 29). As an avid film-goer, Kubrick would have been exposed to his fair share of newsreels, at a time when movie screenings routinely included short subjects. While the screen time devoted to newsreels could be justified on moral grounds, the newsreel producers still had to compete with animated cartoons as well as feature-length narrative fiction films, at least in terms of sustaining visual interest, which contributed to making re-enactments unavoidable. Staging events was also a common occurrence in documentary photography, one that FSA and future *Look* photographer Arthur Rothstein brought to light with his controversial picture of a bleached steer skull in 1936 (1979, 20). Photographic and filmic practices in both the fictional and documentary modes had more in common than might be expected, thus allowing a young photojournalist such as Stanley Kubrick to apply his image-making, editing and storytelling skills across related media fairly easily. It should come as no surprise that when Kubrick felt he had "graduated" from *Look* magazine, he first turned to *The March of Time* with a film project. High school friend Alex Singer had been working for Time Inc. as an office boy, but in the end Kubrick approached Radio-Keith-Orpheum (RKO)-Pathé as *The March of Time* was closing down due to competition from television (LoBrutto, 64).

Technological change affects the relationship between photography and film to the extent that it can determine expressive possibilities in each medium differently. One of the main reasons that audiences had to accept newsreel re-enactments was that film equipment in the 1930s remained cumbersome and slow to respond to news events. Such a limitation did not affect photojournalism to the same extent. Granted, there was a lingering tendency among photographers to work with the 9.5 lb. Speed Graphic camera, which used film holders allowing two shots on 4″ × 5″ film, mainly because the size of the negative generally allowed for better quality reproduction on a large magazine page (Kobré, 335). However, lightweight 35mm still cameras would gradually replace the larger models, particularly as the quality and speed of lenses and film stock improved. *Life* editor Wilson Hicks explains that the German Leica camera had originally been designed as a small exposure metre loaded with 35mm roll film (also known as "cinema film") in order to conduct exposure tests for the benefit of motion-picture camera shooting (40). Kubrick would later use a Polaroid camera to check exposure during the filming of *2001: A Space Odyssey*. The Leica's design improved steadily between 1924 and 1932, until it became a versatile instrument with significant advantages over the larger-format cameras. "Thirty-six pictures could be exposed on one loading of film, . . . [which] could be advanced almost instantaneously, allowing exposures to be made in rapid succession" (Hicks, 41). The ability to advance the film quickly was critical in producing sequence or serial photographs, a cinematic quality that appealed to Kubrick who made the Leica one of his standard cameras (Crone 2005, 4). Exposures were also made lengthwise rather than across the strip of 35mm film, thus producing a larger and higher quality image than a motion-picture frame. Finally, the Leica's compact size made it easy to carry and relatively inconspicuous, thus facilitating photojournalistic assignments that required swift changes in camera position or candid, spontaneous subjects.

The main technical difference between a still camera and a movie camera is the latter's ability to take two dozen still photographs per second. In contrast with large still cameras such as the Graflex, those using roll film could easily capture many stages of a single event, but neither were capable of breaking down a single movement (a falling object, a horse's gallop) into discrete images each having occurred less than a second apart. Motor-drive photography, which developed gradually during the 1960s, represents a hybrid technology, combining features of still photography and motion pictures, dramatized in Roger Spottiswoode's 1983 film *Under Fire* (Stewart, 46). Motor drives had not yet emerged in the late 1940s, but *Look* magazine was employing an alternative technology, primarily for sports assignments. The April 11, 1950 issue of *Look* includes a profile of Brooklyn Dodgers pitcher Don Newcombe, photographed by Kubrick. The essay's opening layout includes a sequence of nine pictures of Newcombe in a medium close-up, winding up for a pitch and releasing the ball. The grainy quality of the prints suggests frame enlargements from 35mm motion-picture film, and may thus be the first instance of Kubrick handling a movie camera in a professional context. A likely candidate would be the "Machine-Gun Camera" developed by George Yates in 1934, a movie camera adapted for sequence photography (Van Citters, 75) (cf. Figure 40). Yates was the senior photographer at *Look* magazine's parent publications, the *Des Moines Register* and *Tribune*. He adapted a 35mm Bell & Howell Eyemo to take 16 still frames per second, with a long lens and a 1/1,000-second shutter (Cooperman, 39). With its increased shutter speed, the Eyemo was able to freeze the subject's movements, thus avoiding the blurred imagery characteristic of motion-picture film and producing a picture sharp enough to be printed in a magazine. The sequence of photographs in *Look*'s baseball player profile is also printed in increasingly larger sizes, creating a cinematic zoom-in effect. Newcombe's face goes slightly out of focus as he follows through on his pitch, which suggests the use of a long focal-length lens with a shallow depth of field. This assignment appears to be the only time that Kubrick used the machine-gun camera, although it was often employed by other *Look* photographers for sports articles, sometimes identified by the captions as a "magic-eye" camera. Kubrick also used a standard Eyemo on his first two documentaries and for second unit filming on *The Killing* (1956) and *Lolita* (1962), suggesting that his introduction to the Bell & Howell camera made a positive impression.

George Yates' efforts in adapting the Eyemo reveal both the still camera's technological shortcomings and photojournalism's specific aesthetic requirements. The need to capture something of a sporting event's movement and speed motivated photographers to imitate the capabilities of motion-picture technology, yet they could not do so at the expense of the photo-essay's codes of realism, namely that any given photograph must remain in sharp focus and not include blurring that might compromise the image's readability. This particular requirement does not exist in art photography, pointing to parallel traditions in the intersection between photography and film, and revealing that throughout his career, Kubrick remained largely committed to mainstream conventions in photographic and cinematic expression. Even during the production of his visually most experimental film,

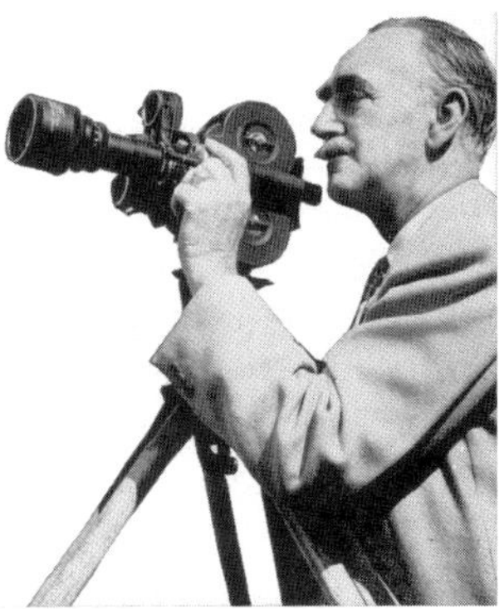

Figure 40: George Yates with the "machine-gun camera," a modified Bell & Howell Eyemo.

2001: A Space Odyssey, Kubrick displayed a documentary photographer's penchant for sharp imagery, almost to the detriment of cinematographic requirements. Interviewed about the making of *2001*, special effects supervisor Douglas Trumbull relates a revealing experiment: "One of the things that Kubrick wanted was this incredible high quality, super-super sharpness. And having been a stills photographer, he was interested in exploring strobe photography, with strobe lights going off on each frame of film, so each frame was absolute, pristinely sharp and clear, in infinite depth of field, f32 kind of shots. So all this super-tech equipment was brought in and John [Alcott] had strobes, a lot of power supplies and all this stuff, and that was when Kubrick and I discovered that super-sharpness is not what you want, blurring is what you want. Film is all based upon the expectation that a frame of motion is going to blur a little bit while the shutter is open" (Trumbull). In hindsight, it may seem surprising that Kubrick had not realized that his experiment would create an effect similar to stop-motion animation, known precisely for its stroboscopic quality, as in the films of Willis O'Brien and Ray Harryhausen, for instance. Moreover, it turned out that a controlled blurring of the image was an essential ingredient in creating *2001*'s Stargate, thanks to Trumbull's slit-scan photography. But Kubrick was a documentary photographer at heart, as implied by Trumbull, and during his tenure at *Look*, he also witnessed colleague Frank Bauman produce over a dozen assignments involving strobe lights, often combined with multiple exposures, in the magazine's studio. More than 15 years after his departure from *Look* (and beyond), Kubrick's aesthetic instincts remained grounded in, although certainly not limited by, photojournalistic values such as sharp focus as a guarantor of realism and the "zero point of cinematic style" (Burch, 15).

Both Kubrick and Yates were applying conventional photographic values to film technology, the only difference being that Yates was aiming for a printed magazine layout, whereas Kubrick had a projected motion picture in mind. Both were also attempting to "appropriate the techniques, forms, and social significance of other media and … rival or refashion them in the name of the real" (Ryan 2004, 31). Kubrick must have felt that there was something inherently unreal about the filmic image, that it was deficient in spite of the appeal (and the illusion) of motion, thus the attempt to make the cinematic image sharper. Kubrick thus carried into his film career *Look*'s mainstream response to photojournalism as an intersection between photography and film, in contrast with art photographers who were producing experimental photo-books, that is, artistic photo-essays that did not adopt a realist aesthetic. The photo-essay was a new photographic genre in the 1930s, and as such exemplified the principle of remediation discussed by Marie-Laure Ryan, namely "the formal logic by which new media refashion prior media forms" (2004, 31). Ryan provides the novel as an example, arguing that "the novel comes into its own, after the eighteenth century, by developing a compromise between the loose structure of oral epic and the tight climactic organization of drama" (2004, 29). One might then describe the photo-essay in a similar way, as a compromise between the tight, compact statement of the single photograph and the time-based medium of film. Timothy Corrigan offers instead a more specific characterization: "If the essay film inherits many of the epistemological and structural distinctions of the literary essay, the key transitional practice linking these two practices is the photo-essay" (47). The practices Corrigan refers to are not part of the mainstream; they do not include the standard documentary short nor the popular magazine photo-essay, that is, the genres that Kubrick worked in. He describes a parallel form of remediation between photography and film, one that applies to personal, lyrical, artistic forms of expression, specifically the work of Chris Marker. In fact, Corrigan's article appears in a book that focuses exclusively on avant-garde or art cinema texts, which explore the intersection between photography and film. Similarly, David Campany analyses photo-books by Walker Evans, Robert Frank, William Klein and Ed Van Der Elsken that combine the artistic convention of ambiguity with experimental techniques inspired by cinema, such as blurring and captions for first-person narrative diaries (Campany, 60–93). Such artistic work tends to foreground formal and stylistic affinities between the two media in an explicit fashion. The magazine photo-essay, in contrast, is designed to serve its rhetorical and narrative purposes in a relatively unheightened, self-effacing manner, thus "unconsciously" revealing the photo-essay's hybrid ontology. While photojournalism may not be as innovative aesthetically as art photography, it does have the advantage of disseminating its hybrid language more widely. In fact, the examples listed by Campany do indicate a fairly common interest within the art community in combining the techniques of photography and film that can be partly attributed to the development of the magazine photo-essay, especially when one considers that many art photographers were also photojournalists. For example, one of Robert Frank's mentors was Alexei Brodovitch, whose day job was art director at *Harper's Bazaar*, but also published an expressive documentary book in 1945 titled *Ballet*, which differed from his practice at *Harper's* and displayed cinematic influences (Campany, 75).

A social and aesthetic history of photojournalism and film must also consider commercial or economic factors, which encouraged the two media to overlap, particularly as the cinema and magazine industries had complementary interests and common competitors. Before television overtook radio as the dominant mass medium in the 1950s, general interest photo-magazines such as *Life* and *Look* had competed successfully with radio by tapping into the public fascination with images, a fascination that was enhanced by the popularity of motion pictures. Hollywood itself had also integrated some of radio's modes of production, with the development of sound film, highlighting a system of reciprocal influences that were deliberately encouraged by industry leaders as mutually beneficial. Movie star profiles, for instance, were an obvious way to both increase newsstand magazine sales and provide publicity for actors and their studios. *Look* magazine had correspondents in Los Angeles, including photographer Earl Theisen, who frequently covered Hollywood stars. Other movie tie-ins pursued by *Look* included photo-essays concerning films either currently in distribution or in production, and regular features such as "Photocrime," staged crime scenes inviting readers to solve a mystery. The only instalment of "Photocrime" shot by Kubrick, for the March 18, 1947 issue of *Look*, was actually a radio tie-in featuring actors from the CBS series *Perry Mason*. However, the magazine announced an editorial change that also represented a shift in its commercial associations: "Beginning with the next issue of LOOK, the Photocrime adventures of Inspector Hannibal Cobb will be photographed in the film city. They will be directed by Robert Siodmak, of *The Killers* fame, and enacted by Universal-International players." *Look* also collaborated with major film studios on projects that included references to the magazine itself. Thus, MGM's 1953 musical *I Love Melvin* was shot on location in New York City, starring Donald O'Connor as a young *Look* photographer who falls in love with Debbie Reynolds and ultimately succeeds in getting her on the magazine's front cover, the actual April 7, 1953, issue of *Look*.

By the mid-1950s, television represented a direct threat to both Hollywood and photo-magazines, as it offered live video broadcasts and film entertainment in the comfort of one's home, and competed with *Life* and *Look* for advertising dollars (Goldsmith, 2782). However, during Kubrick's tenure as a photojournalist in the late 1940s, television was still in its infancy, and magazine articles about the new medium revealed an almost innocent curiosity and even enthusiastic support. For example, one of Kubrick's last assignments, submitted on July 27, 1950 and published in the December 5 issue, well after he had resigned from *Look*, is virtually an advertisement for the CBS network, albeit anachronistically titled "How Radio's Top News Team Covers the World". Written by *Look* editor Hubert Pryor, it praises CBS' cutting-edge approach to television news reporting, declaring it the best in the business. The four-page essay begins with a close-up portrait by an unidentified photographer, of Edward R. Murrow, the pioneer TV news broadcaster whose reports on Joseph McCarthy in the mid-1950s would lead to the Senator's censure. This is followed on the next spread by a side view of New York TV newscaster Doug Edwards reading the news to a large CBS camera, while a man holds up cue cards for him right next to the camera lens. This is an interesting behind-the-scenes look at the making of a TV news broadcast, despite the fact that the contents of the prompting cards have been deleted for publication. Of note is the fact that Edwards, who became the first anchor of the CBS Evening News in 1948 until he was replaced by Walter Cronkite in 1962, was hired by Kubrick to narrate his first documentary film, *Day of the Fight*. Kubrick was in the post-production phase of his work on *Day of the Fight* when he met Edwards for his last *Look* assignment. The movies remained more glamourous than television, however, and their influence on magazines manifested itself in a number of ways, including the photo-essay's tendency to translate filmic techniques whenever possible. This points to an asymmetrical influence between media according to their relative degree of popularity. Synchronically, less successful media tend to incorporate, imitate or adapt the codes and conventions of dominant media. Diachronically, new media seek to make themselves backwards compatible by adopting the conventions of older, long-established media. Compared to film, the photo-essay was the new kid on the block as a mainstream genre, and so we find examples of magazine layouts, which may be described as cinematic. A common strategy, as has been discussed, was to print related images in a serial fashion, as a means of making the photographs look like frames selected from a strip of motion-picture film. Magazine art directors made this analogy literal, at times, by adding fake sprocket holes along each side of the photographs.

One particular assignment that may exemplify Kubrick's thinking about his shifting career objectives was the production of Jules Dassin's film *Naked City*, shot on location in New York City during the summer of 1947. Although unpublished, this behind-the-scenes look at the making of a Hollywood film was clearly inspiring for Kubrick, who submitted 2″ × 2″ Rolleiflex negatives in late July 1947, eighty-one of which are in the Museum of the City of New York. The film itself is significant for a number of reasons, starting with the fact that its title and subject matter were borrowed from the famous photojournalist Weegee's book "Naked City," published in 1945, which focused on night-time crime scenes in New York. Weegee had been a boyhood hero of Kubrick's, who later returned the favour by inviting him to work as stills photographer on *Dr. Strangelove* (Baxter, 185). But in 1947, Weegee was also covering the filming of Dassin's movie, and Kubrick caught him at work on a stepladder, wielding his trademark Speed Graphic with flashbulb (C. Kubrick, 38). While Kubrick often acknowledged his indebtedness to childhood mentors, he was now aiming his camera at filmmakers, specifically director Jules Dassin and cinematographer Bill Daniels, who won the Academy Award for best cinematography on *Naked City* (cf. Figure 25). Daniels was best known as Greta Garbo's cinematographer, and later became president of the American Society of Cinematographers. Dassin was less fortunate: in 1952, he was blacklisted by Hollywood, and forced to leave the United States due to the communist witch hunt conducted by the House Un-American Activities Committee. The post-war era in Hollywood witnessed a wave of gritty crime films later referred to as film noir, as well as documentary-style filming, which included *Naked City* and Henry Hathaway's *Call Northside 777* (1948). The documentary impulse was also strongly felt in Italy with the neo-realist movement, and Jules Dassin's film made a noticeable impact on Kubrick in at least two ways. First of all, the role of the heavy was played by Ted de Corsia, who would later appear as the crooked cop in *The Killing* (1956). Secondly, a follow-shot of de Corsia catching up with and overtaking a woman with a baby carriage was captured from inside a vehicle on the street, seen reflected on storefront windows in the background. Kubrick adopted this shooting strategy for his second feature *Killer's Kiss* (1955), which includes New York City street scenes shot in semi-documentary style, either with a hand-held camera or, in a clandestine fashion, from inside a moving car. The mutual influence between documentary photography and staged cinema can also be seen in the Academy Award–nominated documentary *The Quiet One*, directed by Sidney Meyers in 1948. Shot in New York City by noted street photographer Helen Levitt, it includes staged scenes and photographic inserts, which speak to a historically located, hybridized form of visual storytelling rooted in documentary realism that does not eschew expressive techniques (Dogra-Brazell). Film pioneer John Grierson's aforementioned characterization of the documentary as a "creative treatment of actuality" was, in effect, both endorsed and implemented by the major photo-magazines, including *Look*'s director of photography and FSA alumnus, Arthur Rothstein, who wrote about the importance of re-enactments in the production of picture stories (1979, 121).

The photo-essay is a journalistic genre that, for a number of aesthetic and historical reasons outlined above, is situated half-way between documentary photography and film, often revealing the influence of fiction film through its narrative structure, use of captions as dialogue, storyboard-like version of analytical editing and staged re-enactments. This chapter has argued that, as an active and full participant in the production of photo-essays for an important American magazine, a young Stanley Kubrick would have been influenced by the hybrid nature of photojournalism in the late 1940s, and acquired knowledge and skills allowing him to make a "natural" transition into mainstream filmmaking. In some respects, the photo-essay form may have been more appealing than film, since it combined photography's enhanced sense of documentary realism with the option of telling stories in a way that emulated the movies. It was also more affordable, and Kubrick was being paid for the privilege. Another advantage of the photo-essay was that it afforded the flexibility of the editor either noting relevant dialogue in the field or "dubbing" it in later, while the photographer was encouraged to think in silent movie terms, that is, by capturing images that were inherently narrative in their framing and sequencing, thus providing a potential redundancy of information as well as more options at the editing stage. This flexibility was put to good use by photomagazine editors, who could just as easily assign photographers to interview famous personalities or stage a photo-essay adaptation of a popular novel. Moreover, the magazine industry nurtured commercial ties with Hollywood, which even led to actual film productions based on the most successful photo-stories. All these factors underscore the notion that a professional photojournalist at a formative stage would not only realize the marketability of his skills in visual storytelling, but also later reveal the influence of a specifically journalistic background as he moved forward in his career in a related medium.

Notes

1 According to the archives at the Museum of the City of New York, these pictures were taken circa August 1946, and are included in a relatively unfocused *Look* job entitled "Street Conversations," which may have been specifically assigned to Kubrick as part of his apprenticeship, to help him develop skills in capturing scenes unobserved.
2 This picture suggests that Kubrick's biographers are mistaken when they claim that he first met Sobotka through David Vaughn "in late 1952" (Baxter, 59). It appears, rather, that he knew Sobotka in late 1946, given *Look*'s six-week lead time, thus prior to marrying his first wife Toba Metz in 1948.

Chapter 8

From Photojournalism to Film: Transmedial Correspondences in the Formal and Stylistic Systems

It has been noted that Kubrick's first documentary short, *Day of the Fight* (1951), was an adaptation of his 1949 photo-essay titled "Prizefighter," and that his second feature film, *Killer's Kiss* (1955), includes scenes and camera angles borrowed from his previous boxing stories (Schaesberg, 245). Although this visual and thematic focal point represents the clearest example of a direct link between Kubrick's early projects, a comparative textual analysis of his photo-essays and films might logically be based on a system of correspondences between the codes and conventions of the photojournalistic and cinematic media. Developing such transmedial equivalences should assist us in gauging Kubrick's growth as a visual storyteller, specifically in evaluating his likely ability to translate and adapt the languages of photojournalism and film, rather than learn a radically new form of expression bearing no relation to his work at *Look*. Employing this system of correspondences to conduct textual analyses may then highlight a consistent use of narrative, rhetorical and visual tropes, demonstrating the enduring influence of *Look* magazine's photojournalistic methods on Kubrick's career as a filmmaker. The inter-semiotic system will be based on the diagrammatic characterization of film form proposed by David Bordwell and Kristin Thompson in their textbook *Film Art* (Bordwell 1997, 168). Film form is first defined as "the overall system of relations that we can perceive among the elements in the whole film" (Bordwell 1997, 66). This overall system results from an interaction between the formal system and the stylistic system: the formal system refers to the discursive function that determines the organization of a film's images and sounds, and the stylistic system consists of "patterned and significant use" of cinematic techniques (Bordwell 1997, 168). This chapter will consist in applying the film form diagram (cf. below) to the medium of photography, thereby mapping a series of similarities and differences between media that will help us to identify those areas where Kubrick was able to make a seamless transition to film, and those where he either needed to adjust, adapt, or change.

<u>Film Form:</u>

Formal system	← interacts with →	*Stylistic system*
(discursive function)		(patterned use of techniques)
- Narrative		- Mise-en-scène
- Categorical		- Cinematography
- Rhetorical		- Editing
- Abstract		- Sound
- Associational		

Formal System

Bordwell and Thompson list five formal systems, each defined by its discursive purpose: narrative, categorical, rhetorical, abstract and associational form. While these systems were examined in Chapter 6 in terms of their relationship with photojournalistic genres, we now turn to their capacity to shed light on transmedial concerns. The purpose of narrative form is storytelling, that is, relating "a chain of events in cause-effect relationship occurring in time and space" (Bordwell 1997, 90). Categorical form consists in dividing a subject into parts or categories, usually loose, common-sense ones, in order to inform the audience by organizing our knowledge of the subject (Bordwell 1997, 130). Rhetorical form focuses on presenting a persuasive argument about a given topic, and the goal of abstract form is to "arrange the images so as to compare or contrast qualities like color, shape, rhythm, and size" (Bordwell 1997, 146). Finally, "associational formal systems suggest expressive qualities and concepts by grouping images" (Bordwell 1997, 154). It is important to note that, while these five discursive functions are logically distinct, they are not to be conflated with specific genres, nor are they used in a mutually exclusive fashion by individual films or photo-essays. In describing the features of each formal system, we may be tempted to establish equivalences between narrative form and fiction, rhetorical form and documentary, abstract form and the avant-garde, unless we bear in mind that these systems are formal, logical categories describing basic discursive functions ("theoretical" genres), as opposed to socially constructed, pragmatic genres, which are defined by different audiences for different purposes using a variety of different parameters (Altman 1999, 207). The following analyses shall point out the frequent co-presence of formal systems within the same text, such as the use of story form in a documentary photo-essay and poetic or abstract form in a fictional photo-story.

Narrative form

While acknowledging that verbal language is more versatile than pictures in telling stories, Marie-Laure Ryan defines narrative in cognitive terms, as a mental image constructed by the reader in establishing causal relations between represented events, even when such relations are not communicated explicitly (2004, 9). As a combination of words and images, the photo-essay avails itself of the narrative power of language, such that narrative form in photojournalism bears many resemblances to narrative film, which should give a clear indication that Kubrick's four-and-a-half-year tenure at *Look* magazine represented much more than "a good opportunity to learn and experiment with the photographic aspects of cinema" (Kagan, 1).

Among the many features of narrative form that apply to both film and photojournalism, we can identify common plot patterns and methods of narration. Stories are usually characterized by a central conflict, a problem that needs to be resolved, thus motivating the narrative to move from an initial situation to a positive or negative resolution (Kobré, 141). In terms of length, the photo-essay is best compared to a short story, and due to a magazine's limited space and a journalist's limited time in following real-life stories, there is a tendency for journalists to select topics or events that have a built-in or imminent resolution. Kenneth Kobré provides the example of "an athlete preparing for the big match. Here the *complication* is the athlete's desire to win. The story follows the athlete through the rugged, sweaty, training regime. Finally, the athlete wins or loses the big contest (*resolution*)" (Kobré, 150). We might illustrate this description with Kubrick's profile of celebrated boxer Rocky Graziano, published on February 14, 1950. *Look* had assigned Kubrick to cover the popular athlete on his road to regaining the middleweight championship. In a narrative structure echoing the one used for the 1949 photo-essay on boxer Walter Cartier, the Graziano article begins with the fighter training and relaxing in his Brooklyn home, followed by the preparations on the day of the fight in Cleveland, Ohio. The essay culminates with two pages of action pictures as Rocky defeats his opponent in a ten-round decision.

Subtitled "he's a good boy now," the article suggests that Graziano has moved beyond his troubled past, which includes an underprivileged youth, jail time for hitting an Army officer, and an unfair suspension from New York rings. Family life has softened the former street fighter, who now enjoys playing with his baby daughters, as depicted in a small picture under the headline. The opening page's dominant photograph is a close-up of an unshaven Graziano, his head covered with a towel, relaxing after a workout. It is not a flattering portrait, but one that strives to remind us of the high-profile athlete's working class roots.

The second page's headline states that "the day of the fight is a long day," a claim supported by five photographs illustrating events leading up to the boxing match. This would prove to be a recurring narrative trope in Kubrick's boxing stories, including his documentary and fiction films. In fact, *Day of the Fight* (1951) became the title of his first film. Three small photographs show a shirtless Graziano eating a simple breakfast, making a long-distance phone call to his wife in Brooklyn, and touching the tip of his nose with his eyes closed. Despite the importance of this test of balance, there is implicit humour in the picture, as it contrasts the brutal physical requirements of a boxing match with the delicate act of touching one's nose. The page's largest photograph shows Rocky sitting next to his opponent Sonny Horne, along with a third boxer, waiting to appear on a radio show to promote the fight, while the managers and promoters stand in the background. The caption highlights Graziano's "savoir-faire" in his choice of a "contemplative toothpick and sport sweater," perhaps meant to contrast with his opponent's particularly gaudy pair of checkered socks.

The third page's headline increases the suspense by pointing out that "the time of battle finally draws near," which is supported by a picture of Graziano and his manager walking to the arena, wearing winter coats on December 6, 1949. The dominant photograph is a dramatic top-lit portrait of Rocky leaning forwards, hands taped, waiting anxiously for the call to the ring, another recurring image in Kubrick's boxing stories. The next spread exhibits a clear progression in picture sizes, beginning with a small long shot of Graziano making his way to the ring, assisted by ushers and policemen while the crowd sits in anticipation.

The progression may be compared to a zoom-in, as we get closer to the action, thus likening this layout to a filmic device. The second photograph takes place in the ring, as Rocky's right punch appears to have missed the mark, whereas Horne connects with a left jab to the jaw. The headline explains that Rocky is still rusty on his comeback, and "gets off to a slow start." Consequently, the third and largest picture, which overlaps on both pages, shows Graziano in another typical boxing shot, on his bench between rounds, looking a bit punch drunk as his trainer and manager express concern.

The article's concluding page is a bit anti-climactic, due to the fact that the fight did not end with a knockout. A large action photograph thus shows the two fighters hitting away, with no clear favourite. The caption explains that Graziano ended up accumulating more points. A smaller inset photograph shows Rocky in a medium-shot, talking to reporters in his bathrobe after the match. He does not have a celebratory expression, and this downbeat ending is in keeping with the article's opening claim that Graziano has matured, and that he is no longer a wild street fighter.

The Graziano profile combines two basic kinds of narrative patterns: goal-centred, and character-centred plots. The goal may be an investigation, meeting a deadline or winning a match, whereas the character portrait is more concerned with revealing information about the subject's psychology. Some photo-essays may only focus on one pattern, such as Kubrick's one-page sequence of 12 shots titled "A Woman Buys a Hat" (July 11, 1946). Featuring a woman on a mission to find the right hat, the story ends indecisively when the protagonist suddenly looks in our direction, as if asking us for help, unsure what to do next. Many more photo-essays will profile an individual by using a series of brief events as pretexts, in order to highlight aspects of the subject's personality. A related pattern is the "day in the life of an average person" narrative, described as one of *Life* magazine's most common conventions (Kozol, 134). Kubrick's profile of writer Emily Kimbrough illustrates this strategy, as representative samples of the author's routine are assembled from different locations on the lecture tour.

Kimbrough was the former editor of the *Ladies Home Journal* and author of several best-selling books of non-fiction as well as television and film scripts. The profile titled "Lady Lecturer Hits the Road," produced by Patricia Coffin and published in the February 28, 1950, issue of *Look*, explains that the lecture tour is not particularly lucrative in itself, but that Kimbrough travels 18,000 miles a year to promote her name and hopefully increase book sales. Twenty-one photographs are included in this four-page photo-essay, which follows the lecturer in St. Louis, Missouri, Des Moines, Iowa, and York, Pennsylvania, both on stage and behind the scenes, and reveals that Kimbrough is targeting the Women's Clubs lecture circuit exclusively.

The first spread focuses on morning activities, and is dominated by an oddly unflattering medium close-up of Kimbrough applying lipstick in a Des Moines hotel, framed in the background by a hot-water bottle hanging on the left, a dress being steamed on the right and a shower head, which appears to grow out of Emily's own head. A small inset photograph in the top left-hand corner shows her standing in the St. Louis train station with her bags and pet poodle at 7 am. Above the essay's main title on page right is a medium-shot of Kimbrough addressing the Des Moines Women's Club, as she stands between the current and former Club presidents. On page three, the essay's narrative structure follows Kimbrough after her lecture in Des Moines, as she boards the train for St. Louis. The page begins with the headline: "One-night stands have taught her travel tricks." The first four photographs show Kimbrough to be a seasoned traveller, as she tells the porter where to put her luggage on the train, feeds her pet poodle and reads a mystery novel before going to sleep. The body copy informs us that she "always travels with a jar of Sanka coffee, her eye-shade, hot water bottle and a flask of Dubonnet." Additional text elaborates on her clothes: street dresses, evening wear, lingerie, shoes, and so on, information no doubt considered de rigueur for a professional woman's profile in 1950. On the bottom part of the page, we return to the stage, with a medium long shot of Kimbrough standing behind a lectern, facing a wide shot of a female audience smiling as they listen to the speech. The two shots contain matching eyelines, and could represent the starting and ending points of a left-to-right panning movement, an impression that is enhanced by the use of a particularly narrow interior margin between both photographs.

The concluding page abandons the chronological structure for a thematic one, focusing on Kimbrough's relationship with the press, although the complete absence of men echoes the essay's opening spread, which suggests a segregation of women's issues, particularly as representatives of the media covering this lecture tour are also women. Kubrick used a similar combination of thematic and "day in the life of" narrative strategies for his first two documentary shorts, followed by the goal-centred plot of *The Killing*, the character-centred plot of *Barry Lyndon*, and a combination of character portrait and narrative intrigue via the flashback device in *Lolita*.

One could argue that the definition of narrative as a "chain of events in time and space" only applies to goal-centred plots, and that an important element is missing if we wish to account for character-centred plots. The causal chain in the vast majority of narratives is attributed to the actions of characters, including anthropomorphized agents such as machines, animals and nature. Moreover, characters are usually the main conduit for providing narrative information, and they are crucial in the audience's ability to identify emotionally with the diegesis or story-world. As practitioners of personal journalism, the major photo-magazines recognized that the general public relates best to stories about or involving people, regardless of the narrative point of view (first- or third-person perspective). In fact, if the photo-essay was primarily a social study, there was a tendency to narrativize it by including a token protagonist as a point-of-entry. One of Kubrick's last assignments for *Look*, titled "How to Check Your City's Health," provides a useful example.

Submitted on June 26, 1950, and published in the November 21 issue, after Kubrick had left the magazine, this story concerns free public health tests conducted in Richmond, Virginia, in temporary clinics to check the population for chronic diseases. Continuity is provided through the use of a person or character whose presence is maintained in all the images, a strictly visual link that helps to hold the photo-essay together. A woman named

Rosemary Howren, most likely a local model, was hired to serve as a protagonist with whom readers could identify, in a mini-narrative of her taking the 15-minute test. Howren's presence in all but one out of nine photographs provides a form of visual continuity for a story that is not about her. The opening spread lists the various types of tests that are conducted. This is reminiscent of the fighter's preparations in Kubrick's boxing stories: the waiting room, getting registered, weighed in, blood tests, eye drops and an electrocardiogram on the full-page overlap picture. The image of the eye test also may have inspired Kubrick in visualizing Alex's ordeal in *A Clockwork Orange* (1971).

The health story adopts third-person narration to follow Rosemary's physical, and we have seen first-person diary mode used for the Portugal travel story (August 3, 1948), much as *Lolita* (1962) would feature excerpts from Humbert Humbert's personal diary as voice-over narration. The interaction between formal and stylistic systems, namely narrative point of view and camera framing, is mentioned in Kenneth Kobré's textbook, when he argues that the "medium shot tells the story," including the relationship between characters, and the close-up enhances drama, intimacy and "elicits sympathy in the reader" (12–5). The health story's opening spread includes a medium-shot of Rosemary surrounded by nurses, waiting for test results at the blood station, followed by a full-page bleed picture of her taking the electrocardiogram test, which functions as a close-up by virtue of the picture's printed size. The character appears anxious to receive the test results in the medium-shot, as she looks off-frame, away from the nurses, and sports a neutral, almost resigned look in the larger picture, expressing the patient's role as a passive subject.

Categorical form

One of the four non-narrative formal systems discussed by Bordwell and Thompson, categorical form is characterized by "common-sense sortings of examples" (Bordwell 1997, 131). In the classical photo-essay structure, this translates as thematic groupings of pictures, with each category usually displayed within single pages or two-page spreads. For instance, FSA photographer Dorothea Lange's essay "Irish Country People," published in *Life* magazine (March 21, 1955), shows "many facets of country living, layed out in separate spreads: farm and town dwelling, fairs and market days, games of field hockey and church-going every Sunday" (Hoffer, 148). Much as the layout style of Lange's essay proves to be important to categorical form, Wendy Kozol's description of *Life*'s typical essay, framed by half- or full-page photographs containing "a series of smaller and larger photographs display[ing] various aspects of the situation," also highlights the relationship between formal and stylistic systems by including references to image sizes (Kozol, 43). We can turn to Kubrick's May 11, 1948, profile of Columbia University to illustrate categorical form.

Kubrick was assigned to cover three large educational institutions during his tenure at *Look* magazine, including the Mooseheart (Illinois) vocational school for orphans, Columbia University and the University of Michigan. Kubrick may have been chosen to photograph these institutions because of his age, under the assumption that he could work inconspicuously, fitting in more easily with the student population. One wonders how he must have felt walking down the hallways of Columbia University in Manhattan, not having been able to study there or at New York University (NYU) due to poor grades in high school and the G. I. Bill (Bernstein 2006, 315). He certainly made up for it by providing *Look* magazine's editorial staff with at least 550 photographs (archived at the Museum of the City of New York), 29 of which were selected to accompany Don Wharton's nine-page article.

The opener is a medium close-up photograph of a smiling Dwight D. Eisenhower, who had recently been appointed the new president of Columbia University. The original negative at the Museum of the City of New York reveals that this portrait was cut out due to a distracting background. Printed on page right, the portrait was flipped vertically, perhaps because *Look*'s editors wanted Eisenhower to face the centre fold, thus making it appear as if he was endorsing their sponsor on page left, Philco radios, and also to invite readers to remain on that two-page spread a little longer. Next to Eisenhower's head is a bird's-eye view of a mass examination, highlighting the regimented nature of such exercises. The analogy with the military seems apt, particularly given Eisenhower's new responsibility as General of the University, so to speak. The dehumanizing geometric patterns created by rows upon rows of individuals would feature prominently in Kubrick's film *Paths of Glory*, nine years later. The young photographer was clearly quite taken by this perspective, as it appears 56 times in the archives, representing one tenth of the entire job.

In line with the principle of categorical form, the following spread's theme is articulated by the headline: "Columbia's libraries encourage study, but students jam dining, recreation halls." The centre of the two-page spread is taken up by four equally sized and fairly nondescript establishing shots of students occupying the dining hall, the bookstore and a university hang-out known as the Lion's Den. These pictures are framed by two more serious, book-related scenes. On the left, a long shot of an English PhD candidate reading in the main library contains an internal caption in the form of a sign on the student's table, which demands "Silence." The sign almost appears to be directed to the cacophonous crowd in the centre pictures. We are reminded of Kubrick's long-standing habit of including signs as commentary, whenever possible. On the right, a posed photograph features a representative from Columbia University Press standing behind hundreds of books piled up waist-high and holding up a sign that reads: "In one year Columbia Professors wrote this many books." Ironically, the wordless photographs are read as "noisy," whereas those containing signs are mute.

The third spread describes Columbia's elitist nature, by pointing out that "only one from every 40 applicants" is admitted to the College of Physicians and Surgeons, and that its Law school has produced two American Presidents, two Chief Justices, members of the Supreme Court, and so on. According to the headline, Columbia's faculty likes to boast that "the best in brains are here." The spread is dominated by a photograph overlapping both pages, which appears to illustrate the concept of forming superior minds. Kubrick has placed himself behind the instructor in a lecture theatre at the College of Physicians and Surgeons. A medium close-up profile of the lecturer in the foreground shows him pointing to something beyond the left edge of the frame. A sea of students in the background look straight ahead at their instructor and the photographer's camera. By eliminating other depth cues and keeping both planes in sharp focus, Kubrick creates the slightly surreal and humorous impression that the lecturer is a giant head pointing to one of the smaller heads on display, that is, one of the students sitting on a tiered seat. Is the lecturer identifying one of the aforementioned "best brains," albeit an ironically small one, or does that status apply only to faculty, whose job is to inflate young minds until their size reaches their instructors'? Kubrick repeated this type of deep-focus composition on a number of occasions, for the purpose of creating interesting, and cheeky, contrasts in scale. The other large photograph, on page left, is an establishing shot of an art class in the School of General Studies, meant to offset the alienating impression of elitism at Columbia, while also including a female nude to satisfy the magazine's cheesecake quota. The model sits on a chair, posing for the students busily at work at their easels, some of them wearing business suits or smoking a pipe, while their instructor supervises the art in progress.

The penultimate spread focuses on science and technology, an area of interest to Kubrick who produced some evocative photographs. The headline informs us that "scientific research thrives at Columbia, a center of early atomic bomb experiments." A high-angle establishing shot of three men posing next to, and overwhelmed by, a huge cyclotron is recycled in several scenes from *2001: A Space Odyssey*, in which technological structures have become society's new cathedrals (Crone 2005, 223). This link between science and religion is underlined by the name of the "Bethlehem" steel company, which appears three times in large print on the structure's walls (Duncan, 20). Moreover, the man identified in the caption as the director of Columbia's nuclear physics research centre, "E. T. Booth," has a name that evokes the extraterrestrial theme in Kubrick's *2001*.

In the centre of the spread, overlapping both pages, is a medium-shot of five first-year students from the School of Engineering with their instructor, examining the results of a compression test on a cement cylinder, placed in the foreground. We see the men's faces as they lean forwards behind the cylinder to get a closer look at the experiment. Rainer Crone's perceptive analysis of this photograph points out the deliberate placement of the students on either side of the cylinder, a claim that is supported by the presence of similar photographs in the archives at the Museum of the City of New York (2005, 12). The alternate shots basically represent before-and-after pictures, while the cement cylinder is still intact, and once it has been partially crushed. In all cases, the students are placed in an identical position. Crone speculates that Kubrick may have deliberately staged the image in order to offer a subtle critique of Columbia University's failure to integrate the student population, since the four men on the left of the cylinder are fair-looking Caucasians, graphically separated from the two on the right who are slightly darker, particularly a bearded Indian man wearing a Sikh turban (2005, 12). However, this analysis overlooks the notion that the prominent appearance of an Indian student at Columbia University contrasts with *Life* magazine's practice during the post-war era of only showing members of non-European social groups as poor and illiterate (Kozol, 13). Another photograph, albeit an unpublished one, of two smiling Asian women sitting under a world map includes the inscription "they have *many* foreign students" written in grease pencil on the back of the contact sheet, which at least indicates an interest on the part of *Look* magazine's editors to acknowledge if not openly embrace diversity in America.

The last of the large pictures on this spread is a top-lit close-up of a Psychology Professor conducting an experiment on a rat in a cage (Crone 2005, 227). The psychologist's face is seen through the glass cage with the rat in the foreground, looking fairly ominous thanks to the use of single-source lighting from above, akin to an interrogation scene in the film noir genre. The contrast in scale between the man's head and the rat's body reminds us of the picture on the previous spread opposing the lecturer and his medical students, with the difference that the contrast is "real" in the psychology experiment, whereas it is manufactured in the classroom photograph. This combination of real and contrived contrasts in scale within the same photo-essay appears in Kubrick's Circus photo-story as well, published in the following issue of *Look*, indicating that he was, despite his young age, a thinking man's photographer, consciously framing and setting up his photographs to manipulate various formal parameters.

Three small photographs on page right illustrate various activities at Barnard College, Columbia University's undergraduate school for women. The third in this series, featuring two musicians and two tea-drinkers, uses composition in depth in a very deliberate way. The tea-drinkers are in the centre background, framed by a cellist in the left foreground and a harpist in the right middle ground. Spatially, the women are thus positioned in a triangle, echoed by the harp's shape, which frames one of the tea-drinkers in the background, seen behind or through the strings. The harp's forepillar also divides the image vertically in half, highlighting a mirroring effect created by having the women in each half face the centre of the image, that is, each other. This highly formalized composition focused on classical music and tea appears to support the caption's contention that Barnard College's "academic and social standards are high." Kubrick's photographs on the second-to-last page of this photo-essay are mostly small portraits of Columbia's sports team coaches, providing illustration for the final spread's headline, which states that "Columbia wants to build minds, not winning teams." One exception is a medium-shot of a bespectacled man conducting a simple chemistry experiment, printed below the photographic credit. This image shows a scientist feeding a fire by pouring chemicals out of a jar, creating a large flame akin to a sculpture of light that partly obscures the man's face (Crone 2005, 225).

Categorical form in film is more easily identified in the documentary mode; however, narrative fiction film does employ editing conventions, which reveal a categorical impulse. An instructive example is Christian Metz' characterization of two non-narrative syntagmas: he first defines the "bracket syntagma" as "a series of very brief scenes representing occurrences that the film gives as typical samples of a same order of reality, without in any way chronologically locating them in relation to each other in order to emphasize their presumed kinship within a category of facts that the filmmaker wants to describe in visual terms" (Metz, 126). The categorical logic in the bracket syntagma is thus more visual and conceptual than temporal or spatial, and is typically used to exemplify a concept or feeling, such as the "masturbation" fantasy sequence from Kubrick's *A Clockwork Orange*, and perhaps the Stargate sequence from *2001: A Space Odyssey*, to the extent that it is not simply meant to be read as a literal representation of a trip through space and time. The "descriptive syntagma" is then defined by Metz as one "in which the relationship between *all* the motifs successively presented on the screen is one of simultaneity … [and where] the only intelligible relation of coexistence between the objects successively shown by the images is a relation of *spatial* coexistence" (Metz, 126–7). While still non-narrative in the strictest sense, this type of sequence helps to establish a location and activities that occur in that space, and is thus more common in mainstream fiction than the bracket syntagma. Kubrick has used this form of categorical editing on many occasions, including for the training of gladiators in *Spartacus*.

Rhetorical form

In addition to describing a subject thematically, categorical form may be used as a means of listing items in an argument, thus simultaneously functioning as a rhetorical device. The discursive function of rhetorical form is "to convince the viewer of something of practical consequence" (Bordwell 1997, 139). This purpose is usually located within documentary modes of expression, commercial advertisements or propaganda, but it is useful to bear in mind that narrative fiction "is in fact a patchwork, or a more or less homogenized amalgam, of heterogeneous elements borrowed for the most part from reality," that may include referential statements inviting us to act upon learning the moral of the tale, for instance, as told by the storyteller-rhetor (Genette, 49). In fact, Roger Odin argues that it is precisely thanks to the playful and non-deceptive nature of fiction that viewers become more susceptible to being impressed, touched, convinced by the storyteller, and that a serious (i.e., real) speech act is in fact occurring under the guise of a simulated one (1988, 128). There also exist relatively more overt, transparent referential genres and poetic devices such as allegory and didactic fiction, which are clearly designed to exemplify a thesis by using narrative as a rhetorical tool. For example, the ideological novel, or *roman à thèse*, has been defined as "a novel written in the realistic mode … , which signals itself to the reader as primarily didactic in intent, seeking to demonstrate the validity of a political, philosophical, or religious doctrine" (Suleiman, 7). The clearest example of rhetorical form in photojournalism may be didactic, how-to articles that were fairly popular in the 1940s and 1950s, and which we can illustrate with Kubrick's essay "Don't be afraid of middle age," published in the January 31, 1950, issue of *Look*.

Written by Jacques Bacal, the article begins with a list of top-ten tips on how to enjoy middle age. The second spread features the first of two photographs staged by Kubrick with models portraying a married couple injecting romance in their life by dining and dancing the night away. Despite their purely illustrative function, the staged photographs are interesting in that they provided Kubrick with the opportunity to create a mise-en-scène and to direct actors, which brings us a step closer to fiction (cf. Figure 41). The blissfully waltzing couple may be usefully contrasted with Nicole Kidman and the greasy Sandor Szavost (Sky Dumont) in *Eyes Wide Shut* (1999), a film thematically focused on married life (Castle, 242). The concluding spread shows the middle-aged couple enjoying each other's company. The caption reads: "Re-courting and second honeymoons often help prepare couples for happy and productive middle age – at the same time, check urge for a 'fling.'" It may be significant that this is exactly the conclusion reached in the film *Eyes Wide Shut*, when Kidman's character suggests to her husband that in order to settle their relationship problems, all they need to do is have sex.

The relationship between the photo-essay and the advertisements demonstrates some forethought. The advertisement included in the opening spread offers another tip to add to the top-ten list on how to enjoy middle age: drink Blatz beer. The star of an NBC radio show, "Duffy's Tavern," helps to sell the product. Opposite the waltzing couple in the second spread, a life insurance advertisement features a similar white, upper-middle class couple and their children, representing the magazine's target audience. Both *Look* and *Life* magazines' advertisers were interested in reaching people who had money to spend, the beneficiaries of the post-war boom, which mostly excluded African Americans, Latinos and Asians (Kozol, 67–69). The last spread's headline reads: "As children grow up, parents should develop new interests." These new interests should no doubt include buying expensive cars like the one on page right. In the post-war era, consumerism was considered a patriotic way of contributing to the economy.

The adoption of similar rhetorical strategies in articles and ads can both create a seamless continuity, the photo-magazine's invisible style of editing, and potentially surprise readers who assumed there was a difference between features and commercials. As previously mentioned, photography's indexical power is used in both magazine genres to "prove" the

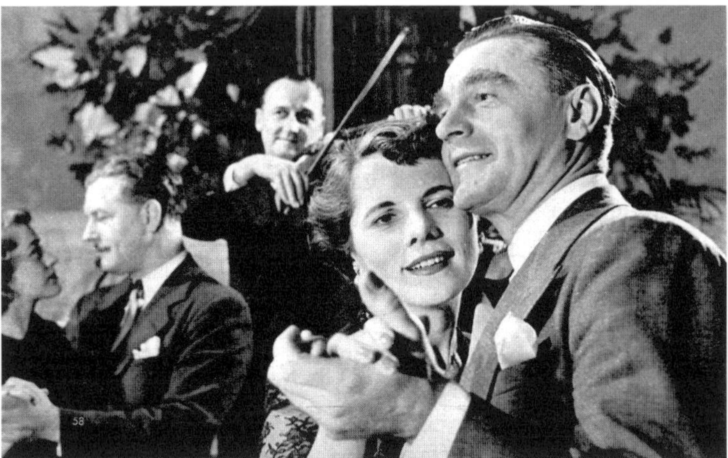

Figure 41: "Don't be afraid of middle age" (January 1950).

informational assertions provided by the accompanying verbal text, with the difference that the photograph legitimizes the word in photo-essays, and merely supports it in advertisements (Schaeffer, 99). Indexical proof may be photojournalism's chief rhetorical weapon, thus explaining the adoption of stylistic practices designed to ensure that photographs will not be perceived as doctored or manipulated. For instance, Wendy Kozol indicates that by the end of the 1930s at *Life* magazine, "layouts became more sober as they depended exclusively on a grid format that did not break the rectangular integrity of the photographic frame," which was deemed important as it served to enhance the perception that images were not manipulated (43). In their 1951 textbook on picture editing, Kalish and Odom recommend that photographs should go to the art department for possible retouching, but that the result should not look like it was retouched, for fear that it may undermine the reader's faith in the publication's accuracy and honesty in documenting community life (122).

This concern for the appearance of authenticity, as a rhetorical device, may be compared with Kubrick's fastidious attention to detail during the production of *2001: A Space Odyssey*, specifically regarding special visual effects. To achieve an impression of realism, Kubrick aimed for a "single-generation look," which ruled out conventional process shots such as travelling mattes, in order "to have each scene look as much like 'original' footage as possible" (Lightman, 98). As a science-fiction rhetor, Kubrick wanted to convince his audience that what they were seeing was possible, if not actually real. In terms of traditional or content-based expressions of rhetorical form, it has been argued that most of Kubrick's films tend to be ambivalent about the issues they raise, but that *A Clockwork Orange* is perhaps his most didactic regarding the question of free will, which is voiced explicitly by the prison chaplain, acting as a mouthpiece for the filmmaker's views (Shaw, 222).

Abstract form

Of the five formal systems, abstract form is the one that is most closely identified with the stylistic system, and Bordwell acknowledges that it is difficult to write about abstract form without involving style (1997, 373). It is therefore useful to bear in mind that the stylistic system is composed of medium-specific techniques (film, photojournalism, literature, etc.), which serve a given formal system's discursive function, whether it is storytelling or expressing abstract qualities of movement. *A Clockwork Orange* features several scenes depicting the protagonist Alex's mental subjectivity, including the aforementioned "masturbation" fantasy sequence, which uses abstract form. It is a quickly edited sequence that "begins with a montage of a dancing Jesus sculpture set to Beethoven's Ninth Symphony. … The sequence presents violent images of explosions, hangings, Alex as a vampire, and a patently 'movie' image of an avalanche crashing down on several prehistoric characters" (Falsetto, 121). The sequence may be described as Alex's private music video, with "poetic" imagery edited to Beethoven's music. Of course, the most abstract imagery, in a literal sense, in Kubrick's films must be the Stargate sequence in *2001: A Space Odyssey*, including

Douglas Trumbull's Op Art slit-scan cinematography and extreme close-ups of swirling chemicals, made to look like exploding supernova. In the context of a narrative film, however, "an abstract pattern becomes a means to an end, always subordinate to the overall purpose," which in this case happens to be primarily storytelling, relating a trip through time and space (Bordwell 1997, 146). In fact, avant-garde film scholars have been quick to point out the narrative function of *2001*'s Stargate corridor, specifically as a means of downplaying its significance as art (Le Grice, 82).

A similar analysis may apply to photojournalism, which is mainly rhetorical in aim but can contain narrative and lyrical elements as well. Magazine photo-essays will then not normally adopt a global structure of theme-and-variations in a musical or poetic fashion, but may include local metaphorical relations between consecutive photographs and visual progressions or crescendos (James Peterson, 41). However, Kenneth Kobré advises against the use of "visual homonyms," pictures that look similar but carry different meanings, arguing that it can lead to editorial confusion (197). In other words, the suggestion is that abstract form may work against or distract from rhetorical form rather than support it, even though picture editors would never rule out an opportunity to produce an expressive or stylish layout that may, in fact, enhance the photo-essay's argument. For example, the previously discussed photo-essay "How to Check Your City's Health" functions rhetorically as a public service announcement, encouraging readers to participate in free public health tests should clinics be set up in their city. This message is overlaid with a global narrative structure following Rosemary Howren's 15-minute examination, with the occasional visual link or contrast at a local level. The only picture without the protagonist, at the top of the essay's third and last page, is a stiff, posed photograph of civic leaders who planned the health testing. It features the oppressive, symmetrical composition that Kubrick would later use in his feature fiction films, and is also compared with the following photograph of Rosemary having her blood pressure taken. Both images are composed in depth, looking down a table with similar perspective lines, with the difference that the civic leaders are all lined up, looking at the photographer, whereas the nurses and patients in the health test "action" picture are oblivious to the camera's presence. Kubrick's stylistic decision regarding camera placement was put to use by the layout artist, emphasizing a graphic or visual similarity between two otherwise dissimilar subjects. This aesthetically pleasing use of abstract form is designed to contribute to the essay's visual continuity and readability, especially since the protagonist is absent in one of the photographs.

Paradoxically, continuity can also be achieved by including visual contrasts, provided they are integrated into a larger configuration. A good example can be seen in a June 8, 1948 essay titled "Mooseheart – The Child City," concerning a vocational school for orphans, situated 38 miles west of Chicago. The essay's third and fifth pages both feature a vertical series of three medium-sized photographs contrasting camera angles and diagonal lines. The third page begins with a low-angle perspective of the Cadet Corps engaged in formal exercises, followed by a regular angle shot of a budding sculptor working on a bust of Lincoln, ending with a high-angle portrait of a woman surrounded by a group of children, posing for the photographer. The same pattern is repeated on the last page, with a low-angle shot of teenage girls performing a sword dance, a regular angle view of more teenagers at the side of an indoor pool, and a slightly higher angle of a young couple sitting in front of a lake. The contrast is in the first and last shot of each series, although the intermediate pictures create a progression, which can be likened to a crane shot cutting to different images as it moves up. The second series also displays a contrast in diagonal lines anticipating Sergei Eisenstein's "A Dialectical Approach to Film Form," published in *Film Form* in 1949. The orderly rows of teenage girls in the first two pictures are slightly angled, facing the spread's centre fold on the left. The contrast is in the perspective lines, which are angled downwards in the first image and upwards in the second. Also, the teenagers themselves are leaning forwards for the sword dance and leaning back by the pool, with the exception of one girl who leans forwards as if to plunge, thus mirroring the sword dancers. The third picture is an idyllic medium-shot of a couple by the lake, slightly angled to the right, in contrast with the previous photographs, with two people facing each other rather than lined up side by side. Careful layouts such as this one demonstrate the art director's eye for abstract form that Kubrick would not have failed to miss.

Associational form

While abstract form focuses strictly on graphic, visual properties, associational form compares and contrasts images in terms of content, inviting conceptual links akin to metaphors (Bordwell 1997, 154). Such links may help to reveal aspects of transmediality alluded to at the beginning of this chapter, that is, the process of matching the expressive resources of two signifying systems, as a means of mapping Stanley Kubrick's creative journey from photojournalism to film (Andrew, 102). It has been argued that among Kubrick's films, *2001: A Space Odyssey* provides the most systematic attempt at transmitting story information and creating meaning through symbols and metaphors rather than a linear cause-and-effect narrative (García Mainar, 136). *2001* features perhaps the most celebrated graphic match-cut in film history that links a prehistoric bone and a futuristic spaceship, thereby eliding four million years of human history. It also creates a metaphor that can be translated literally as: the spaceship is to contemporary humankind what the bone was to the Australopithecus, namely another form of technology that can be both destructive and a key to our survival. The conceptual nature of metaphors may also be useful in the development of a journalistic argument, and so we note that associational form is more common in the magazine photo-essay than abstract form.

Photo-essays are often framed by half- or full-page photographs, serving narrative or rhetorical purposes such as establishing a space, introducing characters and proposing a solution to the essay's problem (Kozol, 43). They can also exhibit aspects of associational form, as they contrast two different images, placed strategically at the beginning and at the end of an essay, and related by subject matter. For instance, the September 2, 1947, photo-essay "The 5 and 10" observes shoppers at a discount store. It is an ad-free, four-page social study containing 32 pictures, the highest number of Kubrick photographs published by *Look* in a single essay. We are informed in a brief introductory text that "the nation's 5 and 10's do an annual business of more than a billion dollars," a huge sum at the time that has led to the current success of corporations such as Wal-Mart, which began as Walton's Five and Dime in the late 1940s. The 5 and 10's "attract all types and ages," as illustrated by Kubrick's photographs. The essay is framed by two large photographs, placed in the top left corner of the first spread and the bottom right corner of the second spread. They are printed as bleed pictures, and echo each other in their content. The opener shows a young girl yawning for the camera while her mother simultaneously carries her and examines some stockings laid out on a table in front of them. In contrast, the closing photograph's "wide-eyed little girl has a field day," according to the caption, whereas the accompanying parent, perhaps a grandfather, looks quite bored as he holds on to some balloons and smokes a short, drooping cigar. This pairing of photographs features different individuals yet dramatizes the human reality of shopping with relatives, especially conflicting levels of interest in the activity itself.

A major social study that tapped into Kubrick's interest in jazz music was "Dixieland Jazz is Hot Again," written by noted music critic and *Look* editor Joseph Roddy, and published in the June 6, 1950 issue. The seven-page photo-essay breaks down into three sections: an opening spread with body copy providing reasons for the musical genre's current revival, three pages with portraits of "Dixieland luminaries" and a concluding spread focusing on the history of Dixieland and current hardcore practitioner, clarinetist George Lewis. The opener is a full-page bleed picture, which overlaps on the right page by three inches, showing the George Lewis band in action at a New Orleans cabaret. Trumpet player Elmer Talbert stands in profile in the foreground, likely taking a solo, silhouetted against the harshly lit middle ground where the band sits. He splits the image in half, with his African-American band mates on the left and Caucasian jazz aficionados on the right. This photograph contrasts with a portrait of Lewis' band on the last page, engaged in a "backyard recording session." The location is familiar, more relaxed than the formal cabaret setting, and the lighting shows lower contrast, perhaps because it was shot on an overcast day. The article establishes a parallel between the rough quality of Dixieland jazz and the rough lives of the New Orleans musicians, who seldom make a living from playing music, as Lewis' humble backyard indicates. Joseph Roddy ends with the hope that Dixieland's surging popularity in Chicago and New York will translate into a revival in New Orleans along with economic benefits for the local musicians who created or nurtured the genre. The paired photographs both exemplify the writer's thesis (rhetorical form) and implicitly contrast other themes (associational form) such as social inequities, the public and commercial spheres, versus a private, personal and safe environment consisting of family and friends.

Links between photo-essays and commercial ads are primarily designed to function rhetorically to help the sponsors, but they also reveal associational properties in terms of visual and thematic congruence. The following examples both feature the trope of parent–child relationships. In the October 12, 1948 issue of *Look*, we are introduced to five-year-old Wally Ward who was struck by polio at age two, paralyzed from the waist down, and has been gradually recovering the use of his legs thanks to daily therapeutic exercises and the use of walking sticks. Kubrick's opening picture is a low-angle full shot of Wally walking gingerly on a sports stadium field, holding on to a football and wearing a helmet, while his father kneels behind him delightedly urging him on. It is a touching picture, and certainly taps into normative ideas regarding father–son relationships. The opposite page echoes this idea with an illustrated advertisement for Chevrolet including a man holding a football, getting ready to play with his son who is putting on a helmet. Until Jonas Salk licenses his vaccine in 1955, the cure for polio may thus consist in driving a Chevy to the football field for a little game with junior.

On the second page of Kubrick's October 10, 1950, staged photo-essay titled "What Teenagers Should Know About Love," a picture of a young girl, perhaps five years old, shows her sitting on a bench and looking up adoringly at her father who remains mostly off-frame while he holds her hand (cf. Figure 42). The photograph illustrates the caption's banal assertion that "the father plays an important part in the child's early love life." It also provides a link to another image, an advertisement for a television set by Arvin Industries, on the same page. The ad shows a man and his daughter watching an episode of Howdy Doody on their new Arvin TV, mirroring Kubrick's photograph of a father–daughter relationship.

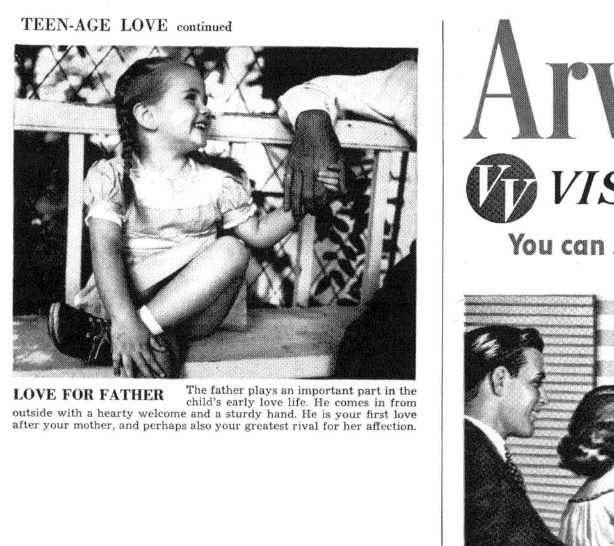

LOVE FOR FATHER The father plays an important part in the child's early love life. He comes in from outside with a hearty welcome and a sturdy hand. He is your first love after your mother, and perhaps also your greatest rival for her affection.

Figure 42: "What Teenagers Should Know About Love" (October 10, 1950).

They could easily be listening to an LP record on "the best hi-fi set that you ever saw," as Humbert Humbert promised his stepdaughter Lolita in Kubrick's 1962 film. The relationship between photo-essays and advertisements is one that any photojournalist would inevitably become familiar with, and likely informed Kubrick's future practice of including commercial references both as product placements and for the sake of creating a realistic representation.

Stylistic System

Style refers to the ways in which medium-specific techniques are used in a given text or group of texts (those of a particular genre or artist), forming a pattern which is both separate from, and designed to serve the discursive requirements of, one of the formal systems analysed above (Bordwell 1997, 357). Examining techniques that are specific to film and photojournalism helps us to determine precisely what kinds of stylistic adjustments Kubrick was forced to consider when he began making films during his last year of employment at *Look* magazine. In some cases we find exact correspondences between the two media (particularly in framing and lighting), and in other cases equivalences or substitutions must be entertained (camera movement and sound). Bordwell and Thompson identify four areas in the analysis of film style, namely mise-en-scène, cinematography, editing and sound (1997, 168).

Mise-en-scène

This area refers to staging events for the camera's benefit, and "includes those aspects of film that overlap with the art of the theatre: setting, lighting, costume, and the behaviour of the figures" (Bordwell 1997, 169). The analysis of mise-en-scène applies to both intentional and accidental stagings, that is, the unscripted unfolding of a documentary event also has sets, lights and actors, objects of various kinds appearing within the camera's field of vision. Among the aspects of mise-en-scène examined by Bordwell and Thompson, we may focus on setting, lighting and acting. Setting concerns an image or a scene's interior or exterior location, the relationship between foreground and background characters and sets, the use of objects as props, and so on. In his textbook's chapter on portraits, Kenneth Kobré highlights elements of setting such as background and props, arguing that they "can transform an ordinary snapshot into a revealing portrait" (Kobré, 81). For instance, for a two-page article titled "New York: World Art Center," Kubrick contributed a portrait of German expressionist painter George Grosz, printed as a full page (June 8, 1948). The essay argues that New York has replaced Paris as the capital of the Art World. Grosz straddles a chair on a Fifth Avenue sidewalk, in a symmetrically framed shot, wearing a pin-striped suit and smoking a cigar. In Kubrick's films, symmetrical compositions usually communicate a sense of uncontrollable fate, as in the execution scene from *Paths of Glory* (1957). Here, the

German artist is presented as a man very much at ease and in control of his destiny. This is accomplished through the use of composition in depth and props, with Grosz placed in the foreground, confidently looking at the camera while the background includes the buildings of Manhattan, pedestrians and street traffic. Props feature the cigar, the office chair and a strategically placed "no parking" sign next to Grosz, commenting ironically on the subject. The caption under Kubrick's photograph states that the portrait of Grosz "symbolizes world artists who find stimulation and peace to work in New York. Unaware passerby [sic] typify public oblivious that city is now world art center." This unusual mise-en-scène stands out when compared with the article's second page, which includes eight smaller portraits of artists taken by other *Look* photographers: they all feature the painters and sculptors in their studios, a more conventional approach to the portrait of an artist, whereas Grosz is cast against type, so to speak, as a successful businessman who parks anywhere he likes.[1]

Another portrait demonstrates a use of setting that will be further developed in Kubrick's later film work, thus revealing the ultimate link and indebtedness of Kubrickian aesthetics to photojournalistic practice. For the August 2, 1949, issue of *Look*, Kubrick caught up with London, Ontario native Guy Lombardo, the famous bandleader best known for his New Year's Eve rendition of the traditional song "Auld Lang Syne". Lombardo was earning $250,000 a year from his recording contract with Decca, a success that is confirmed by a half-dozen photographs of the musician's luxurious home in Freeport, Long Island. A full-page portrait of Lombardo on the essay's opening page shows him smiling to the camera, sitting in front of a portable record player set on the floor, and next to a most intriguing prop, a towering pile of 800 records that looks like a cylindrical version of the black monolith from Kubrick's film *2001: A Space Odyssey*. The bandleader is leaning forwards, his elbows resting on his knees, and Lombardo's smile might indicate a teasing suggestion for Kubrick, the former high school jazz drummer, to audition for Lombardo's orchestra. The other photographs mainly show Lombardo at home with his wife, but there is a slightly subversive aspect to Kubrick's framings. He uses establishing shots in order to highlight the décor in which the Lombardos live, which includes a zebra-themed living room (rug, pillows and piano!) described as spectacular by the caption. Another picture features the Lombardos dining alone at home, at the end of a long table with over a dozen conspicuously empty chairs seen in the foreground. The short essay's concluding page includes a photograph titled the "Lombardo zoo" by the caption, showing the Lombardos on the edge of a king-size bed covered with six pet animals sleeping peacefully. Mr. and Mrs. Lombardo look even less significant as the bed and its occupants only fill the lower half of the frame, while the upper half reveals the room's high ceiling and bare wall, covered with broad-striped wallpaper. This use of a monumental setting to overwhelm human figures, such as the physicists dwarfed by the cyclotron in the Columbia University essay, is an expressive form of mise-en-scène, which will be rearticulated many times in Kubrick's films. For example, a high-angle establishing shot of the court martial scene in *Paths of Glory* highlights the checkered pattern of the chateau's floor, thus turning the accused into pawns in a deadly game of chess, rather than human participants in a legitimate military tribunal (Falsetto, 40).

Lighting is sometimes taken for granted as an element of mise-en-scène, yet it may be argued that it is the single most important technical aspect of photography, as expressed in the title of cinematographer John Alton's classic book, first published in 1949, *Painting With Light*. Kubrick's lighting style owes much to his training as a photojournalist, where he developed a taste for naturalistic lighting. When indoors, he used available light as much as possible, using windows as natural sidelights or backlights. For example, in the July 18, 1950, photo-essay of model Betsy Von Fürstenberg, the concluding spread features a full-page, backlit composition highlighting Betsy's bare legs as she self-consciously stretches them out on a windowsill while reading a script. Merle Armitage's art direction has the photograph spilling over onto the left page by an inch, except for Betsy's feet, which continue past the frame edge as if her legs were just too long to fit into a square image. Rainer Crone suggests that Kubrick's "constructivist" composition focuses on an empty centre space outside the window, thus undermining the star, whereas the layout and backlighting clearly make every effort to enhance the woman's lower limbs (2005, 163).

A singular experiment at *Look* was to have eight of its photographers, each producing a portrait of film noir actress Jane Greer, who had starred in the 1947 film *Out of the Past*. Each picture includes a caption ostensibly stating the photographer's intention, and includes information regarding the equipment used, which is useful for comparative purposes. Greer herself also comments on the eight photographs in the magazine's table of contents. The photo-essay's brief opening text claims that none of the photographers had seen one of Greer's films, which seems doubtful in Kubrick's case, given his voracious viewing habits. This puts into question the caption under Kubrick's photograph, which explains that he sees Greer as "a young actress, worried over a job, whose most familiar expression is one of anxiety." Greer's column on the contents page explains that she was completing a crossword puzzle: "Stanley Kubrick's picture . . . caught me during a moment when I was trying to think of a three-letter word for 'North African sandarac tree.'" Kubrick's portrait of Greer, which appears in the December 21, 1948 issue of *Look*, is a full-page photograph printed as a bleed picture. Greer is shown in a medium-shot, sitting at a desk, with an unfocused glance to her left. The caption mentions the completion of the crossword, which explains the presence of a pencil in Greer's right hand, the eraser end resting on her lower lip. The wistful look and the use of natural light are similar to the portrait of Montgomery Clift sipping coffee, leaning on the windowsill. Greer's comment implies a relatively candid picture, since she was "caught" doing the crossword, but we can safely assert that it was a deliberately staged shot. A simultaneously posed and naturalistic-looking picture was becoming a Kubrick trademark. The technical information provided confirms that natural light was used, as well as a Rolleiflex camera, with an exposure of 1/25th of a second at an f-stop of 3.5. The Rolleiflex produces a 2″ × 2″ negative, and f3.5 was the widest aperture this camera normally allowed, indicating Kubrick was pushing his equipment to capture natural light. On this assignment, all the other *Look* photographers used larger cameras producing 4″ × 5″ negatives, and apertures ranging from f8 to f32, along with studio lights or bright sunlight and reflectors, indicating a concern for high-quality enlargements suitable for a movie star.

Kubrick's early tendency to use faster lenses would become well documented and publicized during the release of his film *Barry Lyndon* (1976), which was partly shot by candlelight with a special Zeiss lens offering an aperture of f0.7 (LoBrutto, 378).

With the exception of sound and movement, acting may have represented Kubrick's most challenging obstacle, in successfully completing the transition to feature fiction filmmaking. For magazine assignments, photographers would either ask their subjects to pose, or engage in a simple activity in order to provide a natural-looking "action" picture, but seldom would a sustained performance involving dialogue ever be required. Ironically perhaps, the most interesting facial expressions tend to be captured in spontaneous, candid moments, when the subjects are not performing someone else's script. We might contrast Kubrick's earliest staged essay with a more standard journalistic assignment. An entertaining gag titled "A Short-Short in a Movie Balcony," published in the April 16, 1946 issue of *Look*, was carefully orchestrated to look like a piece of candid camera. According to biographer LoBrutto, Kubrick had two friends from school and his sister Barbara meet him at a theatre in the Bronx before the first matinee, to shoot a mise-en-scène during a screening involving a boy attempting to make a move on a girl, who then slaps him (25). It seems Kubrick instructed the boy, fellow high school photography club member Bernard Cooperman, to simply make a move on the girl, while unbeknownst to Bernard, she was told to slap him when he got too close. Only the top of Barbara Kubrick's head appears in the foreground, to create the illusion of a crowded theatre. The first three pictures are printed vertically in a column, and one must turn the page for the spectacular conclusion as a full-page shot reveals Cooperman getting hit across the face. The text refers to a freelance photographer who used "infra-red" film to capture this scene unobserved. While *Look* magazine lied about the candid nature of this short story and the photographic technique employed, they did publish two letters in the June 11 edition, which react to this alleged event: one woman feels emboldened to strike wise guys who annoy her in theatres, while a man is doubtful that unaccompanied girls would react in such a way. Kubrick's personality story appears to have resonated with the movie going public. Of course, there is little acting involved here, as the three pictures leading up to the slap feature fairly expressionless faces, ending with a violent action and a genuine look of pain on Cooperman's face.

For the March 30, 1948, issue of *Look*, Kubrick was sent to Connersville, Indiana, to illustrate an article titled "The Boss Talks It Over with Labor," in which the general manager of a company that produced kitchen appliances decided to talk to his employees about the new Taft-Hartley labour law. The essay's second page includes ten small close-up portraits of the manager during his speech, lined up like a film strip from an instant-photo booth, as he grimaces, coughs, wipes his face and drinks, all in a comical effort to impress his employees (cf. Figure 43). The humorous dimension to the serial photos of boss Johnson's facial contortions can be usefully compared to the slightly low-angle medium close-ups of George C. Scott as a gum-chewing General Buck Turgidson in the War Room set of *Dr. Strangelove*. The General argues for the advantages of a first strike approach to nuclear war by gesticulating, pouting and grimacing, a scene that highlights the advantages of the long-take, fixed camera

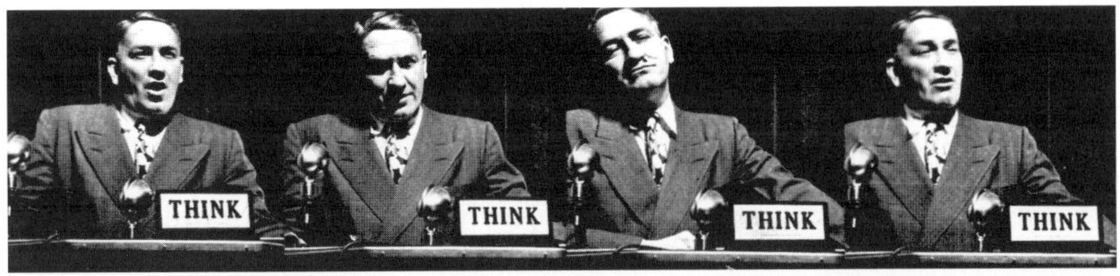

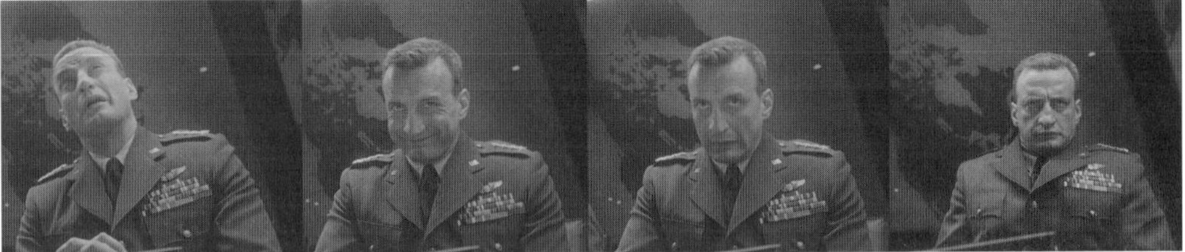

Figure 43: "The Boss Talks It Over with Labor" (March 1948) and *Dr. Strangelove* (1964).

technique. Even though the labour meeting represents something of a performance from Boss Johnson as a social actor, it remains a "real," documentary event, whereas Scott's performance is entirely scripted and fictional in nature. And yet, both situations yielded similar results from a photographic perspective.

This fact may initially have led Kubrick to underestimate the direction of actors as a specialized field in the dramatic arts warranting more attention if not research. While he could rely on collaborators for screenwriting and music, for instance, directing actors is a most theatrical skill that is not required of photojournalists, yet is essential for live-action, narrative fiction film and is not normally assigned to someone other than the director. This must have represented a handicap for a young Kubrick, when he came to realize that his primary job was not so much to photograph the film (the cinematographer's responsibility) but to direct the actors, according to the industry's traditional breakdown of tasks. Published interviews with Kubrick tend to highlight his comments regarding the primacy of a photographic background to film, while downplaying remarks concerning the direction of actors, although there are indications that learning about the importance of acting was a difficult but key turning point in his career. Filmmaker Curtis Harrington, who attended a preview of Kubrick's first feature *Fear and Desire* (1953), reports that "the film was not well received. In particular, Paul Mazursky's performance was laughed at. There were giggles in the wrong places, and it all seemed a bit overdone and overwrought. And afterwards, Stanley was in tears" (Baxter, 54). A few years later Kubrick admitted to Jeremy Bernstein: "I didn't know anything about directing *any* actors. I totally failed to realize what I didn't know" (2001, 25). Obviously, the ex-photojournalist had learned the hard way that most audiences care more about character performances than cinematography.

Framing

While acting is an essential ingredient in engaging filmgoers, it remains no less true that cinematographic style has an enormous impact on our enjoyment of movies, and Kubrick was one of the film medium's most accomplished stylists. Bordwell and Thompson refer to this aspect of mise-en-scène as cinematography, but from our transmedial perspective, we may simply designate it as framing, underscoring the common technical features shared by photography and film, with the exception of camera movement. Framing thus includes the following four areas: issues of distance or proxemics, camera height and angle respective to the image's content, composition in depth and deep focus, and the mobile frame.

Life magazine encouraged its photographers to follow "the formula," a list of eight types of photographs designed to ensure enough variety for the photo editors to produce a visually interesting essay (Kobré, 147). The first three types of photographs are identical to the shot scale developed by the film industry, representing photojournalism's implementation of the principle of analytical editing. The long shot is favoured as a means of establishing the story space, often appearing as the essay's first picture; the medium-shot summarizes the story by identifying the main actors and their relationship to each other; the close-up can either convey information by showing a significant detail or add drama by focusing on a single character's face (Kobré, 10–15). This exemplifies the interaction between the photo-essay's stylistic system and its formal system, as the shot sizes are usually associated with a particular narrative or rhetorical function. Kubrick's films tend to use medium to medium close-up shots either in long takes or in slightly unusual formulations of the shot/reverse-shot technique, whereby one party in the conversation gets more airtime than the other (García Mainar, 15). His other strategy is to contrast carefully composed, oppressive long shots with close-ups, by suddenly cutting in to the tighter shot "to reveal the true natures of characters" (García Mainar, 38). This is not inconsistent with standard photojournalistic practice, especially if we consider the medium's ability to crop and print pictures in different sizes in order to create expressive contrasts on a two-page layout.

We may note that the photo-magazine use of the long shot as an opener applied more to social studies than personality profiles, since the portrait of an individual can be narrowed down visually to a relatively small space. Kubrick's 1947 photo-essay "Life and Love on the New York Subway" follows this pattern as it opens with an establishing shot of Grand Central Station. In contrast, his profile of composer-conductor Leonard Bernstein, titled "Boy Wonder Grows Up" and published on March 14, 1950, begins with a close-up. It is a right profile of Bernstein, with a strong key light coming from the right, overlapping on the second page. Bernstein is framed on the left side of the photograph, while the right side contains sheet music on a piano's music rest, out of focus in the background. Kubrick seldom used the shallow-focus technique, no doubt due to the fact that it is a clichéd way of creating an aura of glamour, which is inconsistent with his realistic approach. However, having the out of focus sheet music next to Bernstein's profile may be a way of suggesting that he is not so much looking at the music, since there is nothing in the foreground, but thinking about it. In other words, the photograph includes a narrative element of mental subjectivity.

Salient techniques stand out due to their infrequent use. When photographers are encouraged to "avoid the 5′7″ syndrome" and produce high- and low-angle shots rather than eye-level ones, they might also be reminded that it is the zero-point of photojournalistic style or the unmarked norm that allows for the unusual angles to be meaningful in the first place (Kobré, 15). When Kubrick uses extreme low-angle shots in *Dr. Strangelove* and *The Shining*, for instance, it is to establish the psychological instability of Jack Ripper and Jack Torrance in a way that creates a sense of estrangement from the characters, partly due to the stylistic artifice or deviation from the norm. A low camera height, on the other hand, can work to enhance our identification with children, one of the enduring tropes of photojournalism (Kobré, 141). Kubrick in fact adopted this technique and used it throughout his career at *Look* and beyond. The second page of his photo-essay "While Mama Shops," published on March 18, 1947, begins with a ground-level shot of three young children in a crouching position, as they play with a pile of sawdust on a Manhattan sidewalk. Kubrick would often get low to the ground in order to be at eye-level with children, much like the Steadicam follow-shots of Danny in the hallways of the Overlook Hotel in *The Shining*. A more pictorial/abstract and less psychological/narrative use of the low angle can be seen in Kubrick's "Family Full of Health," a four-page photo-essay published in the August 19, 1947 issue of *Look*, depicting the training habits of the Jantzen family from Bartelso, Illinois. Although the muscle-bound physiques of bodybuilders can be a spectacle in itself, the editors of *Look* chose not to include standard beefcake portraits or shots of the couple jogging, swimming or sharing a meal, which Kubrick had included as part of his assignment. Instead, they elected to print more striking exercise routines reminiscent of a circus act, such as Gene Jantzen doing handstands on his wife's back, balancing her on one hand and catching her in mid-air as she leaps off the ground. Kubrick took these pictures as low-angle shots from the ground, with a neutral overcast sky in the background, emphasizing the athletes' bodies and physical prowess. Years later, Kubrick would have his crew dig holes in the ground for similar low-angle shots of gladiators training in the film *Spartacus* (LoBrutto, 177). As for the high-angle perspective, it is often combined with a long shot, in order to situate characters in a larger narrative and social context, usually one over which they have little or no control. We might compare the aforementioned high-angle shot of a mass examination in Kubrick's profile of Columbia University with a different kind of exam from the film *Eyes Wide Shut*, namely Tom Cruise's interrogation by the Red Cloak in a menacing, circular mise-en-scène (Castle, 255). Another circular composition appears in Kubrick's September 30, 1947 essay "Walkathon – The World's Wackiest Show," a high-angle establishing shot of a dancing endurance test with couples and referees standing in a circle on the dancing floor, in the middle of the arena with stadium lights shining from above (cf. Figure 44). An ominous dance with death, so to speak, is featured in a high-angle view of the circular War Room set from *Dr. Strangelove*, as well.

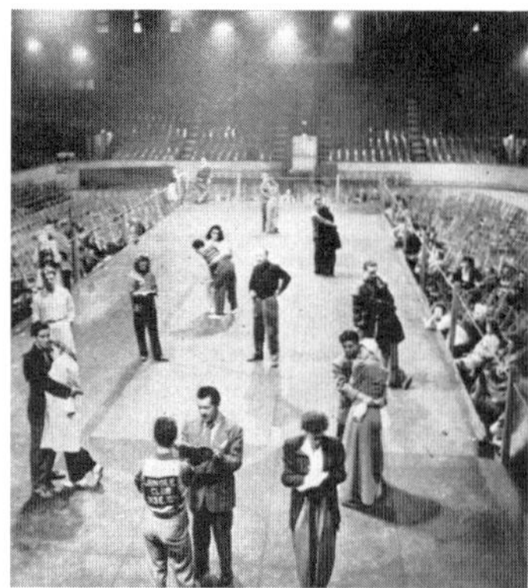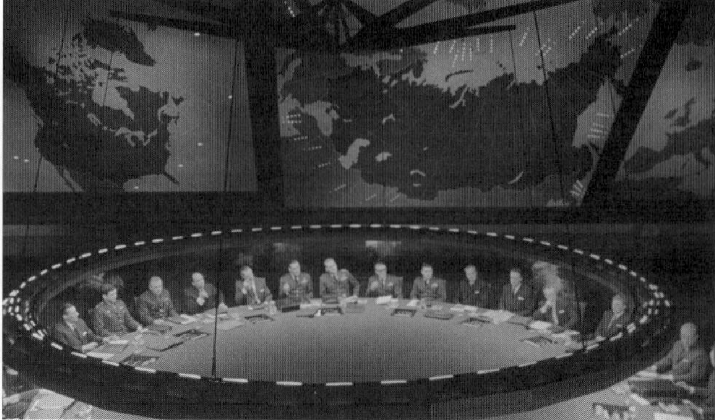

Figure 44: Circular compositions in "Walkathon" (1947) and *Dr. Strangelove.*

Photojournalism's default adoption of realist aesthetics is partly due to the need to catch as many elements as possible within the frame, at a moment's notice. This requirement will often dictate the use of short lenses with deep focus, whereas a long lens' shallow depth of field would isolate the subject from the background and create a more formal and less natural-looking image. We might contrast Bert Stern's shallow-focus publicity photographs of Sue Lyon with the way she appears in the film *Lolita* (Nessel, 70). Exceptions to this general "rule" include telephoto or zoom lenses that can create a candid, illicit surveillance quality, and low lighting conditions, which affect the depth of field, most noticeably in the candlelit scenes from Kubrick's *Barry Lyndon*, which were singled out for their realistic look. Kubrick generally stuck with deep-focus photography, although he also included fairly stylized compositions in depth, as if to benefit from a realist look even in a formal mise-en-scène. By combining deep space and deep focus, he could create slightly surreal or satirical images that simultaneously complied with and distorted conventional perceptions of realistic or documentary photography (García Mainar, 41).

One of Kubrick's favourite devices, as mentioned previously, was the "trick shot" technique of combining deep focus with no depth cues, to contrast two or more elements in a humorous way. This device was used to good effect for the essay on the Ringling Brothers and Barnum & Bailey Circus, featuring president John Ringling North yelling to his seemingly miniature trapeze artists. On the first page of the 1948 photo-essay "Holiday in Portugal," Kubrick frames American traveller Jan Cook in a full shot, standing in the centre of the image with her back to the camera, framed by a windmill in the left background and miller Joaquin Rodriguez in the right middle ground (Crone 2005, 131). The perspective lines are eliminated by having the ground line coincide with the horizon, in other words by setting the camera on ground level. As a result, Jan Cook is made to look as large as the mill itself, towering like a giant over a diminutive miller. The slight spatial disorientation highlights the deliberate manipulation of depth perspective and thus the photographer's discourse, using trick photography of *The Incredible Shrinking Man* variety to make a statement about power relations between characters. The Circus president is entitled to give orders to his employees, but what of American tourists travelling to countries that are struggling economically as they rebuild in the wake of World War II?

A slightly more subtle version of this deep-focus technique appears in a profile of Columbia Broadcasting System (CBS) radio host Arthur Godfrey, published in the February 1, 1949 issue of *Look*. While the essay broadly pays lip service to Godfrey's folksy public image, some of the text's information along with Kubrick's photographs suggests a discrepancy between image and reality. Several pictures present Godfrey at home with his family, yet we are also told that the radio star spends most of his time at work, and that his job provides him with an annual income of $500,000. One might argue that his "real" family is displayed on the article's third page, a medium close-up of a smiling Godfrey who stands out from the CBS morning show staff of 21, posing in the background. This deep-focus formal picture isolates the star from his team, undermining his reported gregarious nature. Kubrick's use of deep focus is reminiscent of Gregg Toland's cinematography in *Citizen Kane*, and one wonders whether Kubrick was implicitly comparing Godfrey and Charles Foster Kane, in terms of their personalities. It may be that Kubrick could see through Godfrey's affable façade: a few years after *Look* published this profile, the radio host's controlling and occasionally abusive behaviour began to manifest itself, affecting his reputation as a gentle man of the people.

In Kubrick's June 1950 essay on Dixieland Jazz, portraits of Dixieland "luminaries" are featured in the article's middle section, including jazz legends Louis Armstrong and clarinetist Sidney Bechet, along with other musicians such as guitarist Eddie Condon, trumpeters Phil Napoleon, Muggsy Spanier, Red Nichols and Sharkey Bonano. Most of these portraits appear to have been taken during live performances, with the notable exception of The Hot Five, a jazz quartet (!) led by pianist Art Hodes. The archived negatives at the Library of Congress include a dozen slight variations on this particular image, a deliberately staged and carefully composed Wellesian deep-focus shot: in the left foreground is Hodes sitting at the piano, pretending to play as he looks back at the photographer, while the clarinetist, trumpeter and trombonist stand behind the piano in the middle ground, also in mock performance (cf. Figure 37). The portrait stands out by virtue of its Kubrickian combination of theatricality and hyperrealism, contrasting with the other slightly grainy action pictures, as well as being the largest printed photograph on the page.

Kubrick was also clearly aware that, in addition to its expressive qualities, deep space could enhance the perceptual realism of two-dimensional images. By including figures or objects in the foreground, middle ground and background, he increased the number of depth cues, which heightened the illusion of three-dimensionality, and helped to provide black-and-white photographs with a dynamic impact more easily obtained from colour photography or a mobile frame. The stillness of the photographic image is its most obvious difference with film, one that photo-story producers tried to overcome by using a number of different techniques that directly address the issue of transmediality and highlight the photojournalistic medium's self-consciousness regarding its immobile frame. The adoption of such techniques underscores film's influence on the photo-magazine and its photographers, some of whom either dabbled in cinema or switched career paths, such as Gordon Parks and Jerry Schatzberg. Kubrick's colleague Earl Theisen had been a lecturer on cinematography at USC prior to joining *Look*'s team of photographers (Cooperman, 182). Camera movement is certainly one of Kubrick's trademarks as a film stylist, and its origin may be traced back to the photo-essay genre's efforts at dynamizing its own images.

Imitating the kinetic quality of film could be accomplished within the single picture via deep space as well as blurred imagery, the photographic equivalent to the comic strip's motion lines. However, blurring was mostly interpreted as a technical mistake or a poetic effect, and thus reserved for amateur and art photography. As a rule, professional journalistic photography strove for a clean, sharp focus look. Minor blurring was only allowed if it highlighted the spontaneity of the documentary moment. An example can be seen in Kubrick's portrait of the New York Yankees shortstop Phil Rizzutto, titled "The Yankee Nipper" and written by *Look* Sports Editor Tim Cohane (May 9, 1950). The third page features a medium close-up profile of Rizzutto playing cards with Yogi Berra in the Yankee clubhouse and waving off Yankee pitcher and kibitzer Vic Raschi, in the background. The caption includes dialogue for Rizzutto as he allegedly tells Raschi: "Stick to your pitching!" If accurate, this information would have been noted by the writer accompanying Kubrick, perhaps Cohane, and provides a film-like immediacy to this "clubhouse action" picture. Adding to the documentary flavour is the grainy texture of these photographs, relying as they do on available light, which also reduces their depth of field, and the blurring caused by Rizutto's dismissive hand wave to Raschi.

Creating the illusion of a mobile frame or simply movement within the image was more often achieved with multiple photographs, laying out in space what the film presents in time. Along the top edge of "The 5 and 10" photo-essay's second spread is a series of eight two-inch square medium close-ups of a young girl reading six Donald Duck and Katzenjammer Kids comic books at the magazine counter. The girl is clearly engrossed by her reading, as is Kubrick in capturing the event. The composition remains identical, enhancing the serial nature of these photographs, in addition to one key detail identified by the caption: the girl reads while eating a foot-long stick of liquorice out of the side of her mouth. The stick grows gradually shorter if the reader scans the pages from left to right, until the candy disappears in the last frame, replaced by a smile as the girl appears to have reached the comic book story's happy ending.

A forward travelling shot broken down into its component parts is featured in the January 20, 1948 issue of *Look*. A brief one-page essay titled "Bubble-Gum Contest" shows children competing to blow large bubbles with chewing gum, as part of a nation-wide promotional event organized by a gum company. A circus clown is on hand to measure the results with a "bubblemeter." As Kubrick biographer LoBrutto points out, the article includes "a four-shot sequence of a young boy in a sailor's hat blowing a bubble. The effect is similar to a zoom or tracking shot in a film. … The influence of cinematography is starting to show" (LoBrutto, 39). Based on the archived prints at the Museum of the City of New York, it is quite clear that the zoom-in effect achieved by the progressively tighter shots of the young boy, culminating with a burst bubble, was in fact the result of the layout, not Kubrick's compositions. The photographs were thus printed in gradually closer framings, increasing the size of the image grain, which makes this technique comparable to an animation stand zoom-in rather than an optical zoom. In any case, bringing the reader progressively closer to the ill-fated bubble gum is an idea that could have originated from anyone at *Look*, including Kubrick. Cinematography was indeed an influence on photo-magazines, and Kubrick's colleagues were also susceptible to thinking in filmic terms.

Editing

A photo-essay's layout displays separate photographs on a two-page spread. The physical co-presence of the photographs makes the process of image selection visually explicit, akin to the film production practice of storyboarding. In contrast, film has the option of minimizing if not eliminating "the coordination of one shot with the next" by letting the camera roll as long as desired (Bordwell 1997, 271). One could argue that, from a technical perspective, there is no editing in Aleksandr Sokurov's one-take film *Russian Ark* (2002), despite the fact that when combined with camera movement, the long take may "present continually changing vantage points that are comparable in some ways to the shifts of view supplied by editing" (Bordwell 1997, 260). Moreover, even when a film is highly edited, the dominant practice is to present only one image at a time, since multiple-frame imagery is quite rare in mainstream cinema. Consequently, one of the major aesthetic decisions in filmmaking is basically rhythmic in nature as it opposes quick editing to the long take, if we put aside the rhythmic qualities of the mobile frame and the movement of mise-en-scène elements within the frame. Kubrick's films are well known for exemplifying the long-take aesthetic, either with or without camera movement (Falsetto, 23). This predilection for the long take may find its origin in a number of magazine layout strategies designed to influence the reader's rhythm in scanning the photographic spreads and turning the pages. This may seem surprising to the extent that editing in the photo-essay is accomplished in space, not in time, yet this is precisely what a transmedial analysis entails, the identification of semiotic equivalences, which in this case influenced a photographer's transition to filmmaking. We can therefore focus on photojournalistic techniques mirroring the filmic categories of the long-take aesthetic, continuity and discontinuity editing.

One approach to gauging the dominant editing practices in film has been to chart the Average Shot Length in Hollywood features, which reveals that "in the late thirties and early forties [the ASL] was 9–10 seconds, and there was an increase in this average of a few seconds through the latter part of the forties as more and more directors strove for longer takes" (Salt, 21). In fact, the late 1940s witnessed a handful of films experimenting with 5–10 minute takes, such as *Rope* (Alfred Hitchcock, 1948), *Lady in the Lake* (Robert Montgomery,

1947), *Dark Passage* (Delmer Daves, 1947), *Casbah* (John Berry, 1948) and *Gun Crazy* (Joseph H. Lewis, 1949), a development that the cinephilic Kubrick could not have ignored during his tenure at *Look*. If the language of photojournalism was indeed influenced by the movies, it follows that magazines would also attempt to emulate new trends such as the long take and the mobile frame. The photo-essay offers two basic strategies in order to simulate the long take: a series of images, or a single image printed large. It could be argued that the image series is better suited to conveying an impression of duration than of movement, particularly if the composition remains the same. An example of this technique in the "celebrity genre" occurs in the June 21, 1949 issue of *Look* when Kubrick met comedian Milton Berle and his three-year-old daughter Vickie. In a series of four medium close-ups, Berle mugs for the camera while hugging his daughter who appears to enjoy her father's sense of humour (cf. Figure 23). Similar sequence pictures, shot from the same vantage point, were regularly used in photo-essays to illustrate the changing expressions of individuals, and Kubrick often adopted this technique to capture the most interesting moments in an otherwise dull visual event, rather than taking shots from different angles. Such series remind us of frames lifted from a strip of film, confirming the notion that photojournalists were generally thinking in terms of motion pictures at this time. One of Kubrick's assignments, a profile of CBS-TV entertainer Peter Lind Hayes (October 24, 1950), includes series photographs taken by colleague Frank Bauman. On the essay's third page, Bauman's sequence of six pictures shows Hayes doing an impersonation routine, highlighting the fact that it was not an uncommon photojournalistic practice to print photographs in this fashion, and that Kubrick may have been equally influenced by his colleagues at *Look* and by Hollywood.

The cinematic long take may also be suggested via the large printed photograph, described by Clive Scott as the first of several factors affecting the reader's perception of time. Comparing newspaper layouts to the comic strip, he argues that "[t]he large, panoramic vignette – often used, for example, as the opening 'shot,' for its informational capacity – has more spectatorial duration in it … than the smaller vignettes, which diminish in proportion as the pace of the action quickens" (Scott, 120). A good example is the opener to Kubrick's staged essay "What Teenagers Should Know About Love," an excerpt from the new pop psychology book by Evelyn Millis Duvall, which appeared in the October 10, 1950, issue of *Look*. The picture's size, as well as its visual and thematic irony and ambiguity, invites the reader to linger on its significance, as if it were indeed a long take. The word "love" from the article's title is capitalized and printed in larger type on the first page, and rhymes visually with the large picture above it, in which a girl has written the phrase "I HATE <u>LOVE</u>!" on a door with her lipstick (cf. Figure 45). The teenager seems to be responding negatively to the author's call for knowledge, rejecting the very photo-essay in which she appears as a character. Rainer Crone's elegant formal analysis of this particular photograph focuses on the ironic and ambiguous mise-en-scène, which anticipates Kubrick's films and their aesthetics of ambiguity (2005, 8). Crone points out the contrast between the teenager's left arm, leaning against the door with a

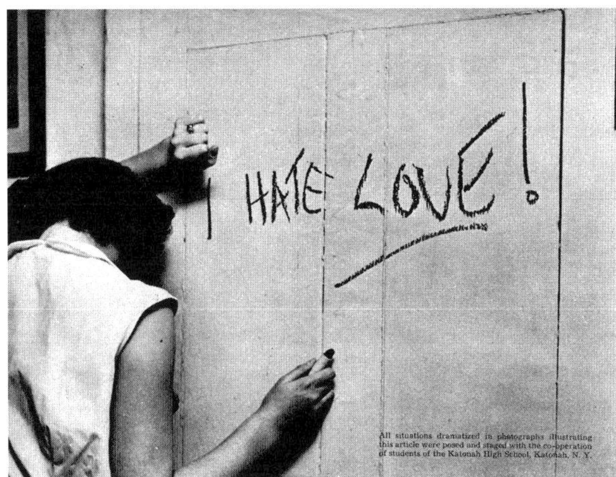

Figure 45: "What Teenagers Should Know About Love" (October 1950).

clenched fist, described as a "gesture of desperation," and the right arm that rests below the paradoxical phrase "I hate love," in a fashion suggesting resignation or uncertainty (2005, 9). However, this contrast is in keeping with the caption, which argues that "mixed up feelings are a normal part of everyone's development," again highlighting the notion that expressive ambiguity was not unknown to the editors of *Look* magazine. Thirty years later, this photograph will echo rather strikingly in a Kubrick film, which also features mixed up feelings, *The Shining*, specifically when the young boy Danny writes "redrum" on the bathroom door with his mother's lipstick (Nelson, 218).

Another version of the long take combines large photographs strategically placed at the beginning and the end of the essay, with characters facing in the page, that is, towards the spread's centre fold or gutter. Kubrick's essay "The Boss Talks It Over with Labor" (March 30, 1948) is framed by two large pictures showing the beginning and the end of boss Johnson's speech, with his eyeline directed towards the gutter in both photographs. The 1951 textbook *Picture Editing* states that a "standard practice is to have the halftones face 'in' when possible to keep the reader's eye in the page" (Kalish, 146). An off-page glance might be interpreted as an invitation to turn the page, while sponsors would like readers to spend as much time as possible on their advertisements. In addition, the closing photograph of "The Boss Talks It Over" is an expressive picture of employees leaving the room after Johnson's lecture that functions as a lingering coda or pedal point (Crone 1999, 193). The boss is silhouetted in the foreground with his back to the camera. Visually, we're encouraged to identify with the speaker, who remains standing as his audience files out of the room, as if regretting that the meeting has ended so soon. The picture has a melancholy quality, similar to a person watching a train leave the station carrying friends or family into the distance. In fact, on the page opposite to Johnson, an advertisement for Sentinel Clocks and Watches includes a drawing of a man watching helplessly as a train he wanted to catch leaves the station, visually mirroring the photograph's deep space composition. Unpublished contact sheets of the Eric

Johnson photograph reveal the event's step-by-step progress in a cinematic way, as workers gradually disappear through the back doors.

Continuity editing in film refers to editing techniques developed prior to World War I and designed to serve the narrative clarity of a story's spatial and temporal articulations (Bordwell 1997, 285). Spatial continuity is maintained thanks to the 180-degree system and its corollary devices such as analytical editing, shot/reverse-shots, eyeline matches, matches on action, and so on. These devices are primarily based on the establishment of an axis of action, film's version of frontal staging in theatre. As noted previously, the photo-essay is basically rhetorical in form, although it also makes frequent use of categorical and narrative strategies. Consequently, continuity editing in photo-magazines includes film-like devices such as establishing shots and reverse angles, but also avails itself of non-narrative techniques like thematic groupings and strictly visual links based on a number of stylistic parameters: "variations in framing; position of the image on the page; size, age and quality of the photograph; ... proxemics (varying distance of subject from viewer); angle of vision; etc. ..." (Scott, 291). Regarding the position of photographs on the page, for instance, it is recommended that "[w]henever possible, the layout should unfold from left to right, from top to bottom – in the orderly pattern of reading matter" (Kalish, 136). Much like cinema, "the basic purpose of the [photojournalistic] continuity system is to create a smooth flow from shot to shot" (Bordwell 1997, 285).

Kenneth Kobré lists the common devices employed to achieve visual consistency: "With a visually unified essay, the viewer sees in almost every picture either the same (1) person, (2) object, (3) mood, (4) theme, (5) perspective, or (6) camera technique" (132). Using the same person as a visual link occurs frequently in photo-magazines, and not only in personality or celebrity profiles. In Kubrick's fashion photo-essay "The Mid-Century Look Is the American Look" (January 3, 1950), 19-year-old model Ann Klem appears in all the pictures. The spread begins with a full-page cut-out profile of Klem in close-up, apparently smiling at the rest of the layout on page right. Among the six other pictures are three staged images of Klem going to a modelling shoot, which may be read in sequence. Kubrick takes an interior shot of Klem opening the door to the building, followed by a profile of the model looking up at the building's directory. The sequence ends with Klem again in profile, this time sitting on a stool in a photography studio, wearing a striped dress and holding on to a telephone receiver, as if waiting for instructions from the photographer. A studio light is visible in the background, identifying this picture as a behind-the-scenes look at fashion photography. The other pictures show Klem having coffee with her boyfriend, on horseback and singing in a church choir, all designed to illustrate the article's contention that Klem possesses the American look on the basis of her physical appearance, her birthplace (Brooklyn) and profession, in that order. This sort of picture series is similar to cinema's montage sequence, wherein habitual or repeated activities occurring over a period of time are shown in a summarized form (Bordwell 1997, 300). Kubrick made use of this technique in several films, including *Full Metal Jacket*, to illustrate the training of Marines on Parris Island.

Explicit thematic links between photographs is an equally common device in the photo-magazine continuity system, as mentioned in our previous discussion regarding categorical form. A good example involving a Greenwich Village laundromat illustrates this editing technique. "Wash Day in a Self-Service Laundry" is a three-page essay featuring 13 photographs, which appeared in the April 27, 1948 issue of *Look*, a month before Kubrick himself moved to Greenwich Village with his first wife Toba Metz. The structure is thematic, beginning with three wide shots inside the laundromat, followed by a second page focusing on women and a third page featuring men as they all wait for the washing machines to complete their cycles. The three opening photographs present the laundromat as an informal and almost chaotic place, a temporary playground for young children accompanied by their mothers and a dumping ground for bags of clothes waiting for machines to be emptied. A small inset cartoon from the New Yorker magazine is included for humour, to reassure readers that laundromat customers are not quite as informal as the woman in the cartoon who removed all her clothes for the wash.

The layout for the last two pages is identical: each page is split in half vertically, with Kubrick's photographs on the left and an advertisement on the right. A medium-sized photograph occupies the top half of the page, with four wallet-sized pictures in the bottom half. In typical telegraphic style, the second page's headline announces: "Women Watch Clothes Look Bored." The same two women appear in the first and last photographs, but are referred to as "girls in slacks" in the first picture and as "yawning young women" in the last. Kubrick catches a woman looking at the camera in the second image, while she holds on to various packages including a clothes-filled "chenille bedspread." The top picture's caption informs us that the customers "watch dial on top of machine click around, indicating how much longer they must wait." Next to the photograph, appropriately enough, is an ad for Westclox electric clocks, including a picture of an alarm clock and a wall clock, visually reinforcing the theme of waiting patiently for the clothes to wash.

The last page's headline states the theme: "Men Read, Wait Idly, Mind Children." The first two photographs show men from the same angle, leaning on a washing machine to read a book or simply to rest for a while. An advertisement on the right side of the page features a cartoon with a large man resting in a hammock being held up by transparent Scotch tape, perhaps the ideal way to kill time. One father has no such luck as he "serves double duty" by washing clothes and carrying a young child. Most sharply dressed is noted actor John Carradine who sits on the laundromat's bench reading the newspaper while his wife holds on to their baby boy.

Kobré's sixth device for visual continuity is a consistent camera technique, an extreme version of which might be the visually dull "Meet the People" feature, consisting exclusively of wallet-sized medium close-ups printed in a regular grid-like pattern similar to a family photo album. Otherwise, the aforementioned mise-en-scène and framing techniques could all contribute to a stylistic consistency and the photojournalistic ideal of invisible editing, including naturalistic lighting, sharp focus, establishing shots, and so on. Finally, the most film-specific editing strategy may be the shot/reverse-shot pattern combined with eyeline matches, designed to create a clear narrative space based on an axis of action. The photo-essay adapted this editing pattern for its own purposes, namely a centripetal reading strategy focused on the two-page spread as a relatively self-contained signifying unit. For instance, the opening layout of Kubrick's profile of composer Leonard Bernstein appears to use eyeline matches of Bernstein looking "at himself" on the opposite page, which provides the spread with an intriguing solipsistic quality. Both pictures on the left page feature Bernstein at the piano looking right, then looking left on the next page in a medium-shot of the musician wiping himself after a swim. Similarly, the concluding spread of Kubrick's portrait of Brooklyn Dodgers pitcher Don Newcombe (April 11, 1950) features informal pictures of Newcombe in the locker room, facing each other on opposite pages. He sits waving to someone off-frame in the first picture, and stands shirtless drinking a coke and eating a sandwich in the second picture. The "eyeline match" makes it look like Newcombe on page left is waving to himself on page right. It is a framing device that encourages the viewer to dwell on the essay's final spread, rather than turn the page.

Discontinuity editing in film has been defined as "[a]ny alternative system of joining shots together using techniques unacceptable within *continuity editing* principles. Possibilities would include mismatching of temporal and spatial relations, violations of the *axis of action*, and concentration on graphic relationships" (Bordwell 1997, 478). The term discontinuity itself implies a negative conception of editing styles, which are then described in terms of how they violate continuity editing. Referring instead to other editing techniques as alternatives can highlight their own formal logic in a more positive fashion, without forgetting that the Hollywood style has remained dominant and influential. Also, listing continuity editing principles or ideals may constitute a narrow or prescriptive definition of editing, while actual filmmaking practices would require a broader definition attuned to the historical evolution of style and the expressive realities of techniques once considered to be mistakes. For instance, jump cuts, flaring the lens and cutting across the axis are techniques that have become more common and are no longer necessarily perceived as anomalous, confusing or amateurish, which broadens the filmmaker's expressive vocabulary. Moreover, even during Hollywood's Golden Age, there were practices that did not follow the ideal of continuity editing to the letter, such as the cheat cut, which provided the director "some freedom to 'cheat' mise-en-scène from shot to shot, that is, to mismatch slightly the positions of characters or objects" (Bordwell 1997, 295).

Taking such liberties is always at the service of the film's narrative logic, revolving around character psychology, which explains and justifies the bolder departures from continuity one finds in dream sequences and musical numbers, based as they are on revealing character subjectivity. In addition, the growth of international film festivals after World War II helped in establishing the art cinema genre, premised in part on the principle of authorial expressivity, which further encouraged directors to engage in formal experimentation (Bordwell 1979, 57). Kubrick was certainly no exception to this trend, and his editing style has been succinctly described as a "mixture of adherence to and distortion of classical cinematic strategies" (García Mainar, 15). It should perhaps come as no surprise that photojournalists were not immune to the appeal of discontinuity, as it not only represented an opportunity for photographers and art directors to express themselves in a more artful way, but for magazines to be more competitive by innovating and becoming trend-setters, including the possibility of adapting the devices of the popular cinematic medium. During the last year of Kubrick's tenure at *Look*, Associate Editor Fleur Cowles spearheaded the production of a classy arts and culture magazine titled *Flair*, a monthly that ran for only a year due to high production costs and insufficient advertising revenue (Cowles, 114). Its stylish design and bold use of graphic arts devices such as pull-outs, holes in the cover, pages cut horizontally and others vertically, has perhaps never been duplicated on such a scale (Cooperman, 164). At least, there was an interest and willingness among the editors of *Look* to push the envelope and experiment with the photo-magazine format, an attitude that had to trickle down to all of *Look*'s staff.

Discontinuity may manifest itself via the artistic trope of ambiguity, normally eschewed by reader-friendly photojournalism, but which can work to the photo-essay's advantage if it is eye-catching or otherwise encourages the reader to pause and reflect (Bordwell 1979, 60). The second page of Kubrick's aforementioned article titled "The Boss Talks It Over with Labor" (March 30, 1948) features a singular layout: the dominant photograph is a reverse-angle cut-out of ten employees in medium close-up, sporting poker faces as they listen to their boss. It is framed on the top and right edges of the page by ten small close-up portraits of the manager, lined up like a film strip from an instant-photo booth. The strip is introduced by the headline "Management talks about labor legislation ...," followed by "Labor listens ..." The headline's meaning is ambiguous, particularly in its relationship with the images: we may infer, for instance, that the lot of workers is to listen, that only the boss has the power of speech, namely to dictate his terms. Furthermore, on a visual level, one boss is implicitly worth ten workers, a superiority that is enhanced by the sign "think," which rests on the table in front of Johnson, next to his microphone. The sign faces the audience, as if to suggest that workers do not normally think, and must be prompted to make an unusual effort. On the other hand, the sign may be directed at Johnson himself, who grimaces, coughs, wipes his face and drinks, perhaps unsuccessful in his own attempts to "think." Also, there is a discrepancy in the layout between the workers' large size and their boss, confined as he is to two-inch square images on the edges of the page. A further contrast highlights the stalwart quality of the workers, who remain still while the serial photographs of Johnson show him emoting in an almost comical fashion, as if desperately trying to impress his employees. His efforts do not appear to inspire the ten workers, who all look suspiciously to the right edge of the page at their boss's facial contortions.

One young man at the top of the cut-out image is an exception, a fly in the ointment who may be listening to Johnson but is more curious about the photographer, and looks straight at the camera, undermining the journalistic ideal for an invisible, non-reflexive mode of presentation. His head could easily have been left "on the cutting room floor," but was included by the photo editor, indicating a willingness to overlook conventions in order to produce a more memorable layout. We might point out Kubrick's later habit of including shots of characters in a brief direct mode of address, such as Jack Nicholson's dirty look to the camera as he storms out of the apartment after berating his wife in *The Shining*.

Reflexivity can therefore qualify as a discontinuity device, to the extent that it highlights the discursive apparatus at the expense of the essay's argument or story. However, it is fair to point out that the subversiveness of reflexivity can be a matter of degree, and that there exists a "Hollywood formula of minimal demystification at the service of a greater mystification" (Stam, 112). In other words, mainstream cinema has devised strategies allowing films to reveal the functioning of the apparatus as a pretense, when in fact they are a celebration of illusionist fiction filmmaking. Such films may be nostalgic love letters to the history and process of filmmaking or affectionate parodies of genre films, for instance. Photojournalism has its equivalents, like Kubrick's essay on seven-year-old Jere Whaley from Chattanooga, Tennessee, who entered a *Look* photography contest and won "a free trip to New York with his dad and tickets to the World Series as *Look*'s Junior Photographer." Who else better than *Look*'s salaried junior photographer to cover the event? The one-page essay published in the December 6, 1949 issue of *Look* shows Jere enjoying a hot dog in the baseball stadium, but also taking pictures with the camera that won him the prize. In the background is Jere's father, and one wonders whether Kubrick could identify with this camera-wielding young boy whose dad encouraged his photographic pursuits, just as he had received a Graflex camera from his father Jack for his thirteenth birthday (Baxter, 20). As regards picture editing in general, it should be noted that it was a two-step process, including a preliminary selection from the photographer's output, and that the final layout was the art director's responsibility. Moreover, depending on the type of assignment, a shooting script might have determined the layout's themes, but the photographer's selection of subject matter could also affect the essay's ultimate form. In any case, *Look*'s approach to group journalism provided many learning opportunities for creative picture editing.

Sound

In addition to the mobile frame and the long take, sound is the third stylistic parameter, which distinguishes film from photojournalism, but for which magazines sought to develop equivalences in their efforts to emulate the immediacy of cinema. There are three kinds of sound in the cinema: dialogue, music and sound effects. While sound effects and music could theoretically appear in photo-essays in the form of onomatopoeia or a musical staff, borrowing from the comic book technique, they basically remain absent in photojournalism, unless the text or captions explicitly print the musical score or quote lyrics from a well-known song, for instance. Kubrick's innovative use of music for film is well known and could not have been learned from *Look* magazine. However, there are two basic analogies between film music and photojournalism, which suggest a relevant influence. Firstly, film music can function both as underscoring, supporting or revealing the characters' emotional states, and as counterpoint, providing a running commentary on narrative events. The latter function is analogous to a story's narrator, including the possibility of offering ironic observations on the action, albeit musically. Kubrick has done so in several films, including *A Clockwork Orange*, which features the protagonist's sarcastic voice-over narration and the equally satirical use of Rossini's *William Tell Overture* for the fast-motion orgy scene. These qualities boil down to the general aesthetic principle of contrast, and *Life* magazine's executive editor Wilson Hicks has argued that the combination of words and images in the photo-essay could be achieved through ironic counterpoint, one of Kubrick's favourite rhetorical devices which were perfected during his years at *Look* (Hicks, 20). Secondly, the photo-essay's mode of production bears a resemblance to film music. In contrast with newspapers, the dominant photo-magazine practice is always to give priority to pictures in the layout, after which "type can squeeze in wherever there is a hole" (Kalish, 138). The writer must wait until a layout has been approved, because "[t]he layout indicates exactly how much text and caption space he has to work with and the copy must be written to fit" (Cooperman, 188). The writer is therefore in a position similar to the composer, who must wait until a fine cut has been edited before cue sheets are drawn up indicating precisely how much music is needed, and where.

There remains dialogue, to which we may add voice-over narration and intertitles, even though the latter is technically part of the image-track. Dialogue between characters or social actors featured in the photographs normally takes the form of quoted direct speech, either in the block of text (body copy) or as captions. Since the body copy is relatively self-contained and separated physically from the pictures, the photographs will appear to illustrate the main text when the quoted speech appears, as if the relationship between the images and the text were intermittent and thus slightly distanced. In contrast, captions typically hug the bottom edge of each photographic frame, which suggests a more dedicated and constant link between text and pictures when the dialogue is situated there. This placement falls just short of the comic book speech balloon on its way to replicating the immediacy of sound film. Some of Kubrick's photo-essays include dialogue as captions, such as the previously discussed "Bronx Street Scene" as well as several entries in the "Meet the People" series. An interesting case is his very first published essay, titled "Kids at a Ball Game" (October 16, 1945), in which he demonstrated his ability in capturing a crowd's emotional expressions at sporting events. Kubrick submitted photographs of two boys at a baseball game when he was still in high school, and the editors at *Look* selected eight of them, printing several as mirror images, emulsion side up, to provide reverse angles. The brief caption explains that the kids' "emotional range – from dark despair to elation – mirrors a close but exciting victory for the home team. Write your own dialogue for these eight photographs." This invitation to supply "missing" dialogue both highlights the soundtrack's absence and represents an opportunity to engage readers in the production of a short movie scene. Similarly, Kubrick's street photography essay "While Mama Shops" (March 18, 1947) includes a close shot of a small girl sleeping in a pram, sucking her thumb and wearing a toque. The caption simultaneously points out the absent soundtrack, by mentioning that "traffic noises fail to disturb her," and provides a linguistic substitute in order to complete the film-like multi-sensory illusion.

In contrast to dialogue, voice-over narration in both documentary and fiction film functions non-diegetically, and is characterized by a lack of specific spatial and temporal markers, which neutralizes some of its acoustic properties and makes it relatively more consonant with a literary approach to narration. Thus, the magazine equivalent to the voice-over, that is, a self-sufficient essay written in the third person, with occasional references to the images, is the most common type of photojournalistic text in both body copy and captions. The objective, journalistic nature of such text aligns it most closely to documentary film, which traditionally uses voice-over more than fiction film. The authoritative quality of such narration is evident in Kubrick's three documentary shorts, as well as in *The Killing* and *Barry Lyndon*, that feature an impersonal voice-over narrator rather than a fictional character's subjective diary, as in *Lolita* and *A Clockwork Orange*. Despite its non-diegetic status and more overtly reflexive nature, the photojournalistic text may nevertheless be compared to the film soundtrack in terms of its ability to suture the image–text relationship and produce the medium's version of unheightened, realist discourse. Filmmakers employ continuity devices such as the sound bridge and sound mixing strategies designed to reproduce the "cocktail party effect." Magazine editors produce a reader-friendly photo-essay by using the text to interpret the photographs and minimize potential ambiguities, as well as pointing out details considered significant, the photo-magazine equivalent to analytical editing. Even though the end result comes across as "natural" or "realistic," it is communicated through deliberate representational practices, which work at denying the differences or gaps between media. In photojournalism, words and images are intended to fuse into a single expressive statement, much like cinema practices a form of ventriloquism, designed to mask the fact that the voices we hear were not produced by still photographs projected 24 times per second (Altman 1980, 75).

A good example of the text telling us how to read the pictures in a seamless fashion is Kubrick's portrait of debutante Betsy Von Fürstenberg, particularly as art historian Rainer Crone offers a different interpretation of the photographs. Von Fürstenberg, who made the July 18, 1950 cover of *Look* thanks to Kubrick's work, was a rich German count's daughter and a movie star hopeful. The illusory or misleading nature of the celebrity's persona is the central trope in Crone's analysis of Kubrick's photo-essay on the aspiring model-actress. It seems hardly surprising that someone aiming for a career in show business would become adept at constructing a public façade, especially when posing for an article in a popular photo-magazine. But when the person in question happens to have been born into privilege and endowed with good looks, the temptation may be great to expose her success as fleeting and unremarkable, as well as unfair when her status is compared to that of struggling artist and burgeoning genius Stanley Kubrick. Crone thus posits Kubrick as the subversive artist whose mission is to unmask the shallow and vain débutante (2005, 163). While it is true that Von Fürstenberg would only appear in one film, she did enjoy a consistently successful acting career on Broadway and on television in the 1950s and 1960s. An analysis of Kubrick's work, which systematically adopts an artistic approach explicitly opposed to the perceived formulaic and commercial aspects of photojournalism, is bound to downplay the influence of *Look* magazine genres to Kubrick's development as a visual storyteller, including the contributions of colleagues such as staff writer Patricia Coffin, who penned the text titled "The Debutante Who Went to Work." Reading Kubrick's photographs in their original intended context requires us to consider how the 16 pictures interacted with each other as well as with the body copy and the captions.

If we choose to ignore the photo-essay's text, the overall impression created by the photographs, with one or two exceptions, is that of a happy young woman leading a charmed life. While Coffin's article provides information regarding Von Fürstenberg's affluent background, it also argues that unlike her fellow debutantes, Betsy has sought to support herself by modelling and acting in Europe, after studying under Sanford Meisner at the Neighborhood Playhouse. Admittedly, the editors of *Look* chose not to include pictures of Betsy falling off her bicycle, a slapstick moment that Kubrick dutifully captured on film and Crone included in the catalogue of a Kubrick photography exhibition that he curated in Milan (Crone 2010, 136). Nevertheless, *Look* did select a potentially critical photograph of the young actress slouched on a sofa during a party at a rich friend's mansion, looking tired as she sips on a drink, while a former boyfriend leers at her. Hanging above the couple is Picasso's 1903 portrait of studio mate Angel de Soto, a man of little means who assumed the role of a dandy and organized parties to attract the ladies. Picasso's painting expresses a certain malaise in Angel's dilettantism, which Kubrick was able to exploit as it appears to comment on the subjects sitting on the couch below. While he smokes and drinks an absinthe in a bar, Angel's direct mode of address invites the viewer to compare his decadent lifestyle to Betsy's, as if the photo-essay's image of the debutante is all glitz and no substance.

A more explicit form of internal commentary in photography is the use of signs, which we may liken to film's intertitles, even though they are not part of the soundtrack. Film scholar Michel Chion identifies intertitles as one element from Kubrick's features that reveal his documentary training and his enduring interest in the real and the accuracy of details (12). Among Kubrick's photographs, we might mention the first one he submitted to *Look*, which uses the newspaper headline "FDR Dead" as a means of explaining the vendor's glum expression, as well as the ironic portrait of George Grosz, showing the German artist sitting next to a "No Parking" sign. Similarly, Kubrick ends his film *Barry Lyndon* with a title card belittling moral evaluations of the historical characters since "they are all equal now." In *The Shining*, Kubrick spoofs film conventions by using otherwise meaningless intertitles that pompously announce the day of the week, and "mock our desire for temporal sense and rational sequence" (Nelson, 209).

A photo-essay that includes signs as commentary is the November 26, 1946 profile of 20-year-old Johnny Grant, who had developed an early morning radio programme titled "Johnny on the Spot," featuring himself as a fearless reporter committing interviews to a wire recording device for later broadcast. The essay's body copy argues that Grant's daring and humour make for adventurous reporting, which perfectly matches the New York scene. The opening page is dominated by a large, carefully staged photograph, composed in depth, showing Grant interviewing a Latin Quarter chorus girl backstage, with two other dancers framing the shot in the foreground. The interviewee has her back exposed to the camera, having undone her top, while the other chorus girls are about to do the same. This risqué backstage photo is designed as an attention-grabber as well as an example of Grant's willingness to conduct his reportage in spaces normally off-limits. The "exit" and "no smoking" signs directly above Grant's head are implicit reminders that he is trespassing, albeit in a friendly and enthusiastic way. The photo-essay's second page has a vertical row of three photographs, highlighting Grant's sense of humour as he feeds a hippopotamus and interviews two babies after they lost a race at the Palisades Amusement Park. Grant gets on his knees to collect reactions from the babies after their loss, and Kubrick similarly uses a ground-level angle to capture the moment. In his book *Drama and Shadows*, Rainer Crone includes six unpublished photographs from this assignment, arguing that Grant, like Kubrick, "transcends the boundaries of official assignments to follow his own ideas" (2005, 52). It should be mentioned that photojournalists are in fact encouraged to think outside the box. *Look* Photographic Department Head Arthur Rothstein has stated that "the picture editor expects initiative, creative thinking, avoidance of clichés, and the unusual approach from the photographer" (1979, 131). Moreover, *Look*'s editors knowingly included many of Kubrick's "transgressive" photographs in the published photo-essays, rather than discarding them or firing the photographer!

This chapter has borrowed Bordwell and Thompson's diagrammatic characterization of film form in order to systematically map the formal and stylistic dimensions of film and photojournalism. Similarities and differences between media have been noted, as well as photojournalistic efforts at providing transmedial equivalences to popular filmic practices and conventions. A summarized version of this comparison is provided in the table below, and is intended to ascertain more precisely the extent to which budding filmmaker Stanley Kubrick either had to learn new skills, modify his journalistic technique to suit a new medium, or simply transfer already acquired knowledge in visual storytelling.

Technically, camera movement and sound are the filmic elements most obviously absent in photojournalism, yet the direction of actors appears to have confronted Kubrick with his steepest learning curve, since social actors are not required to provide a sustained dramatic or comic performance in journalism, only pose for a still picture. The next challenge was the soundtrack, which Kubrick may initially have taken for granted, considering his unwillingness to record sync sound on his first two features. Post-synchronization proved to be a costly mistake and a learning experience after he fired his soundman from *Killer's Kiss* (LoBrutto, 96). In contrast, Kubrick adopted the camera movement – long-take aesthetic more easily, perhaps due to its documentary connotations and the photojournalistic practice of using film-inspired techniques such as serial pictures. Continuity and discontinuity editing form an intermediate category, since both exist in photojournalism and film, but are articulated differently due to the media's unique substances of expression.

The remaining stylistic elements and the five formal systems are fully shared by both media, identifying a related argument, namely the scope of the aesthetic influence exercised by *Look* magazine on a young wannabe filmmaker. These factors include aspects of framing (proxemics, angle, depth) and mise-en-scène (setting, lighting) that show the Kubrick film style to be consistent with magazine practices, particularly a realistic concern with sharp focus and composition in depth. As for the five formal systems, they are organizational principles that may be equally applied to journalism and film, despite the photo-magazine's tendency to favour rhetorical form and the fiction film's focus on narrative. Concerning rhetorical form, it should be further noted that Kubrick's transition from photography to feature fiction film included three documentary shorts, where *Look*'s influence is, not surprisingly, even more evident, as we shall see in the next chapter.

Transmedial equivalences between photojournalism and film

FORMAL SYSTEM

Narrative	Plot patterns (goal or character-centred) and point-of-view (1st or 3rd person)
Categorical	Thematic groupings of pictures. Ex: layout (magazine) or bracket syntagma (film)
Rhetorical	Photos as proof, how-to photo-essays and didactic film genres (allegory and realism)
Abstract	Non-representational or geometric patterns (serving narrative or rhetorical purposes)
Associational	Metaphor: compare two images or signifying systems (photojournalism and film)

STYLISTIC SYSTEM

Mise-en-scène	Setting	Sets and props define characters in photography and film	
	Lighting	Natural or available light vs. flash or studio lighting	
	Acting	*Candid vs. staged pose*	Performance: style and type
Framing	Distance	Establishing shot, medium-shot, close-up (analytical editing)	
	Angle and Height	Consistent use of high and low angles in photography and film	
	Depth	Realistic and stylized use of deep focus and deep space	
	Mobile Frame	*Blurring and image series*	Camera movement and zoom
Editing	Long Take	*Image series, large size*	Above average shot duration
	Continuity	*Centripetal layout*	180-degree rule
	Discontinuity	*Novelty is marketable*	Poetic license
Sound	Dialogue/Music/Effects	*Speech and narration only*	Musical counterpoint
		Photojournalism	**Film**

Note

1　On page 238 of Crone's *Drama and Shadows*, two portraits of Henry Koerner and Jacques Lipchitz are incorrectly identified as Kubrick's, when in fact they were taken by his colleague Bob Hansen, according to *Look* magazine's credits as well as the stamp on the contact sheets at the Museum of the City of New York's Look Archives.

Chapter 9

Photography in Film: Photographic and Documentary Aspects of Kubrick's Films

Our comparative study of Kubrick's style as a visual storyteller and of the impact of photography on his film career may turn to photographic moments in his films, including both the documentary shorts and the better-known feature-length fiction films. Such an exercise reveals the "after the fact" nature of the analysis, in the same way that we looked for the filmic aspects of magazine photo-essays, as a means of explaining a mindset that historically encouraged photographers to migrate to motion pictures. This time we revisit Kubrick's films in light of his background as a photojournalist, but always mindful that our prior knowledge of the "Kubrick film genre," that is, an auteurist construct bent on identifying the narrative and stylistic trademarks of the Kubrick signature, did not usually consider his photographic output. Including specifically photojournalistic qualities in our examination of Kubrick's films will both highlight differences between the documentary shorts and the feature films and reveal an ongoing commitment to certain journalistic practices. It remains important to maintain an analytical distinction between fictional and non-fictional modes of expression, but this should in no way imply that Kubrick's training as a journalist is necessarily more relevant to his early films shorts, on the grounds that he had recently resigned from *Look* magazine, and was fresh out of photojournalism school. Indeed, there is a tendency in biographical accounts of Kubrick's career to assume a chronological progression from photojournalism to documentary film, and then to feature fiction filmmaking: "With three short documentary subjects behind him, 25-year-old Stanley Kubrick took the next logical step to move into feature films" (Howard, 33). In fact, the production of Kubrick's first and third documentaries overlapped with his tenure at *Look* and his initial feature filmmaking efforts: *Day of the Fight* was shot in April 1950, while he was still working for *Look*, and *The Seafarers* was filmed in June 1953, long after he had shot his first feature, *Fear and Desire*, in March 1951. The impact of photography and journalism on Kubrick's career extended well beyond the transitional period of the early fifties, and represented nothing less than a life-long interest. In December 1998, he sent Vicki Goldberg's recently published volume on Jacques Henri Lartigue's photographs as a Christmas gift to friends and colleagues such as Alexander Walker, Gene D. Phillips, Michael Herr, Frederic Raphael and no doubt many others, a further indication that he continued to think in photographic terms (Ciment 1999, 39).

This chapter will map salient photographic and photojournalistic aspects of Kubrick's filmic oeuvre, in order to evaluate their enduring influence. Photographic moments will include the presence of photographs within the story, the freeze-frame as an explicit reminder of cinema's photogrammatic basis, the zoom as a means of analyzing a static composition and further flattening the visual field, and specific features of Kubrick's photographic style such as deliberate forms of mise-en-scène involving sets and props, symmetrical framings, mirrors and frames within frames, unusual camera angles, composition in depth and naturalistic lighting. The photojournalistic dimensions of Kubrick's films will highlight the rhetorical and categorical structure of his documentary shorts, descriptive montage sequences, didactic narration, title cards and diegetic signs as commentary, ironic relationships between image and sound/text, and journalistic themes and tropes including reflexivity and iconography directly related to *Look* magazine photo-essays.

Photography

Inset photographs and the freeze-frame

Perhaps the most explicit manifestation of film's photographic basis consists in the "phototropic poles" described by Garrett Stewart, namely "quoted photos" and the "stop-action image" (9). The inset photo and the freeze-frame are two ends of a spectrum within which film can reveal its photogrammatic nature, two representational practices described as "tropes (synecdochic figures) of the whole cinematic process in its relation to photography" (Stewart, 17). Inset photos are either framed within the film image or shown full-frame, at which point they may be indistinguishable from the freeze-frame. If the photo is presented full-frame, a photopan may be introduced, as a lateral movement or a zoom. As for the freeze-frame, it may not necessarily suspend movement within the image more than a live-action shot from a fixed camera position would, specifically when there are no noticeable changes within the frame. While both poles evoke the photographic, from a technical perspective the full-frame photo is not a photograph but a filmed photograph, and the freeze-frame does not actually interrupt the projection as such. Like motion pictures, they still require 24 frames per second to be seen, the only difference is that it is the same frame that is replicated many times. This factor may not always be relevant from a phenomenological point of view, to the extent that a series of projected film stills is similar to a slide-show, as Chris Marker's film *La Jetée* (1963) suggests. The main difference between the two representational practices is logical in nature: the inset photograph is a pro-filmic and diegetic object, one which is part of the fictional world that the characters may have access to, whereas the freeze-frame is a non-diegetic intervention, which stops the story, and is attributed to the film's enunciative logic, that is, the filmmaker's explicit attempt to make a point. A notable exception would be fantasy or science-fiction narratives in which time is suspended through magic or technology, and the freeze-frame becomes a means of representing the fictional world, as in Kubrick's *2001: A Space Odyssey*, discussed below.

Inset photographs in Kubrick's films appear to serve standard narrative functions, such as revealing a character's interests or family portraits, and describing the history or space of a fictional location. In addition, they may resonate metaphorically with the unfolding story, tapping into cultural perceptions of, or connotations regarding, photographs. In *Killer's Kiss*, the mirror above Davey's dresser in his apartment has many family snapshots stuck in its frame, deliberately displayed in a series of closer views designed to establish the boxer's rural background (cf. Figure 46). Charlotte Haze in *Lolita* also has standard portraits of her daughter and late husband, while the walls in Lolita's room are covered by typical posters of teen idols. In this case, however, the still images relate ironically to protagonist Humbert Humbert's obsession with the teenage girl (Castle, 78). When he laughs triumphantly upon learning of Charlotte's desire to marry him, for instance, the camera pans ominously to a poster of Clare Quilty in Lolita's room, undermining Humbert's "victory" to the extent that the teenager's attention is already focused on the sleazy TV writer. Similarly, Humbert later makes love to Charlotte while looking at the portrait of Lolita on the nightstand, confirming the notion that photographs contain a truth absent from the superficial appearance of the motion picture's unfolding action. A more straightforward use of the photograph as proof can be seen in *2001: A Space Odyssey* during the moonbus ride to the black monolith in the lunar crater Tycho, when Heywood Floyd is presented with a series of 8 × 10 glossy prints as scientific evidence regarding the magnetic anomaly.

But among Kubrick's films it is *The Shining* that exploits most systematically the photograph's nature as indexical sign and its association with documentary realism, in contrast with fictional film's dominant link with fantasy (Stewart, 176–87). *The Shining* dramatizes the gradual defeat of cinematic illusion (movement) by the photograph's authentic stillness, which signifies death for the protagonist. Jack Torrance's present life with his family is thus revealed to be all smoke and mirrors, in contrast with his role as former caretaker of the Overlook Hotel, which asserts itself in the film's final scene. In a speeded-up version of Michael Snow's film *Wavelength* (1967), the camera tracks in to a close-up of a photograph,

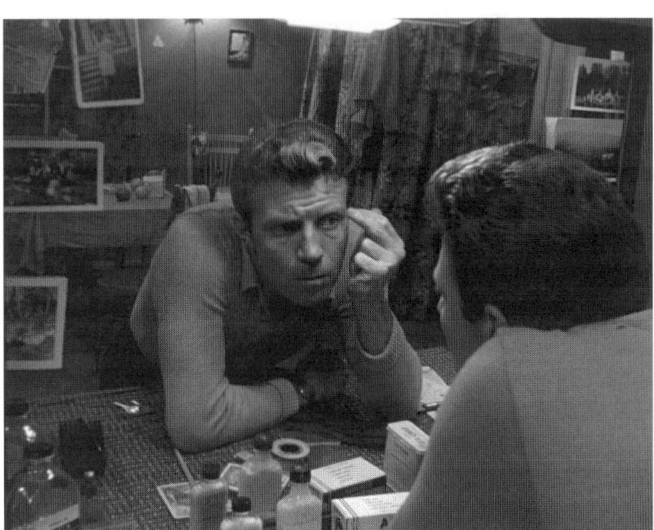

Figure 46: Informational function of the inset photo in *Killer's Kiss*.

which fills the frame and confirms Jack Torrance's "pastness" or presence at the Overlook in 1921 (Stewart, 361). A more subtle reference to photography as the contaminant that gradually dissipates the mirage of moving pictures is a prop that appears in the foreground during the scene where Jack expresses his displeasure at being distracted while he is working (Castle, 198). The prop is a scrapbook, a collection of newspaper articles and photographs sitting on the table next to Jack's typewriter. Featured more prominently in the 1997 TV movie version of *The Shining* written by Stephen King, the photojournalistic scrapbook is the object that appears to trigger Jack's growing paranoia leading to his homicidal mania. A photographic portrait also creates a sense of foreboding for pianist Nick Nightingale in *Eyes Wide Shut* when his college buddy Bill Harford visits him at the Sonata Café nightclub. The black-and-white picture is a standard advertisement included in a glass case by the nightclub's entrance, along with portraits of the other featured musicians. While the carefully posed portraits are reminiscent of Kubrick's *Look* job "Dixieland Jazz is 'hot' again" (June 6, 1950), one can't help but feel that Nick's association with Victor Ziegler highlights some of the photographs' negative connotations, namely a sense of entrapment, stillness and powerlessness.

The freeze-frame represents an overt intervention by the filmic storyteller, although it is not considered disruptive when it functions as a "photo finish" (Stewart, 48). Kubrick has only used the conventional freeze-frame in *Barry Lyndon*, when Barry is shown entering a coach on crutches at the end of the film, and the image pauses. It is not a literal photo-finish since a brief coda follows, but it is the last image of Barry. More interesting perhaps are the four half-second still images of astronaut Dave Bowman grimacing in his space suit as he travels through the Stargate in *2001: A Space Odyssey*. Rhythmically, these still images are like hiccups or intermittent pauses, and they may either be read as non-diegetic interruptions of temporal continuity, or a representation of the science-fictional theme of the relativity of time and space. In other words, Bowman's trip through the Stargate is presented in a different time scale, slowed down to the point where he appears frozen in time, whereas the light show proceeds at an agreeable pace.

Visually similar to the freeze-frame of Bowman, although technically live-action footage, are several examples of the trademark Kubrickian "crazy stare" in *The Shining* and *Full Metal Jacket*. Private Gomer Pyle has been driven insane by the merciless drill instructor in Kubrick's Vietnam War film, and he shows it by staring blankly into space as his graduation from the Marines is announced. More desperate is young Danny in *The Shining* who opens his mouth as if to scream, but remains silent and motionless (Castle, 214). His brief appearances wearing this mask of terror occur when he "sees" the murdered Brady sisters and cook Halloran, as well as the door with "redrum" written in red lipstick and the blood gushing through the elevator doors. The crazy stare as mask in Kubrick's films may thus both symbolize a paradoxical "fear and desire" for knowledge and Otherness, and represents a metadiscursive comment on film's "specular unconscious," the reality of the medium's photographic origin which it normally seeks to deny (Stewart, 5). When Otherness, for a self-conscious film character such as Danny, signifies death (photography as the death-mask), then a fearful grimace expresses a desperate desire to create "a boundary between us and the

Other, saving us from falling into the greater abyss where there is no distance between us and Otherness" (Marriott, 99). In Jack Torrance's case, he loses the battle against photography and freezes to death in the Overlook Hotel's hedge maze, providing us with a pun on the term freeze-frame (Castle, 217).

Analytical zoom

Variations on the Kubrick crazy stare include a slow forward zoom, such as when Jack stands in the hotel's Colorado Lounge looking outside with his mouth slightly open, staring without blinking for almost half a minute. Technically speaking, this is no longer a still shot, which we may liken to a photograph; however, the kinship remains due to the fact that the forward zoom "does not alter the aspects or positions of the objects filmed," it simply magnifies a central portion of the image (Bordwell 1997, 248). The French refer to the zoom as an optical travelling shot, another reminder that the illusion of movement is the result of a gradual change in the lens' focal length. In the telephoto range, the image's depth of field decreases and creates the impression that the visual planes are closer together. The zoom lens' ability to progressively flatten the image and compromise its sense of depth is what provides a reflexive, two-dimensional photographic quality, again reminiscent of the avant-garde film *Wavelength*'s 45-minute deconstruction of Renaissance perspective. While the reverse-zoom or zoom-out reveals space and restores a naturalistic sense of depth, the zoom-in does the opposite, analyzing the image as an image, and pushing film towards still photography as it eliminates the foreground and compresses the middle ground and background together. This is certainly not to suggest that photographs are only characterized by the use of telephoto lenses, but rather to point out that by decreasing its depth of field, film loses some of the depth cues that, combined with the mobile frame, can give it an "advantage" over photography in creating a three-dimensional illusion.

Kubrick's use of the zoom-in appears to boil down to four basic functions: displaying the aforementioned crazy stare, offering a character's perceptual point of view, providing a shocking revelation and presenting realistic details. Both Danny in *The Shining* and Gomer Pyle in *Full Metal Jacket* are shown wearing the crazy mask with a slight zoom-in on two occasions, although in Danny's case it is a sign of his extra-sensory perception, whereas Gomer simply sports a thousand-yard stare that isolates him from the rest of the platoon. Slowly zooming-in on a character's face may also trigger a zoom-in point-of-view shot, which occurs in *A Clockwork Orange* after Alex has been rejected by his family: he contemplates suicide by staring at the river. A similar pattern is used in *The Shining*, when Halloran is giving Wendy a tour of the kitchen and simultaneously "shining" with Danny. Lady Lyndon is introduced in *Barry Lyndon* through a zoom-in from Barry and the Chevalier's point of view as she walks in a garden with her family. In *Eyes Wide Shut*, the camera zooms in on Bill's face on two occasions when he takes a cab, triggering his mental subjectivity as he imagines Alice having sex with the Naval officer. The shocking revelation function is accomplished either with a crash zoom or with a jump cut on the axis. The latter technique is closer to photography, and recalls Kubrick's *Look* essays in which the image is cropped in order to simulate the zoom effect. It can be seen in *2001: A Space Odyssey*, when one of the space pods turns on Frank and the killer is revealed thanks to a quick series of jump cuts to a close-up of HAL's eye. It might be noted that James Whale's *Frankenstein* (1931) uses the very same technique to introduce the monster. The crash zoom as revelation is used in *The Shining* when Danny sees the Brady sisters for the first time in the games room, and as Wendy witnesses what appears to be a costumed act of fellatio. The zoom-in for realistic detail occurs in *Dr. Strangelove*, to illustrate the bomb-run check on board the B-52, in *Barry Lyndon* when the Lady is signing cheques to pay for Barry's expenses, and in *Eyes Wide Shut* when Bill reads an article in a tabloid about prostitute Mandy's overdose.

Static mise-en-scène

Aspects of Kubrick's compositions that do not involve camera movement are directly indebted to his training as a photographer, to the extent that they reveal representational strategies in framing the image and staging the scene, which can be traced back to his *Look* photo-essays. Kubrick displayed a tendency to create a very deliberate and controlled photographic mise-en-scène, in the form of static compositions. Three such strategies include the use of large sets that overwhelm the characters, props that comment symbolically on the action, and overhead establishing shots of characters in a circular composition.

Davey in *Killer's Kiss* is often isolated in his environment, whether it is waiting for a train at Penn Station or running away from Rapallo's thugs in the deserted back streets and the rooftops of Manhattan's garment district. The French Army officers in *Paths of Glory* may appear to be in control, but an early interior shot of the chateau shows Broulard and Mireau walking around in circles, lost or ensnared in their own plotting as they grow smaller and dominated by the large room. Kubrick's ambivalent attitude towards technology finds an expression in long shots of Mandrake surrounded by mainframe computers or hiding behind a computer printout in *Dr. Strangelove*, as well as Heywood Floyd dwarfed by the ships he takes en route to moonbase Clavius in *2001: A Space Odyssey*. Large machines towering over insignificant humans were also featured in Kubrick's 1948 photograph of three men posing in front of Columbia University's huge cyclotron (Duncan, 20). Related to the theme of technology is Buck Turgidson's precious Big Board in *Dr. Strangelove*, a wall-sized, computer-fed display screen that provides the political elite with an illusion of control over the world, a likely parody of James Bond films (cf. Figure 47). A similar image appears in *The Killing*, a large board displaying relevant information about racetrack results, and most strikingly in *The Seafarers*, where a man is silhouetted against a blue and yellow board in the Union's Hiring Hall. The inspiration for this imagery may be an unpublished photograph

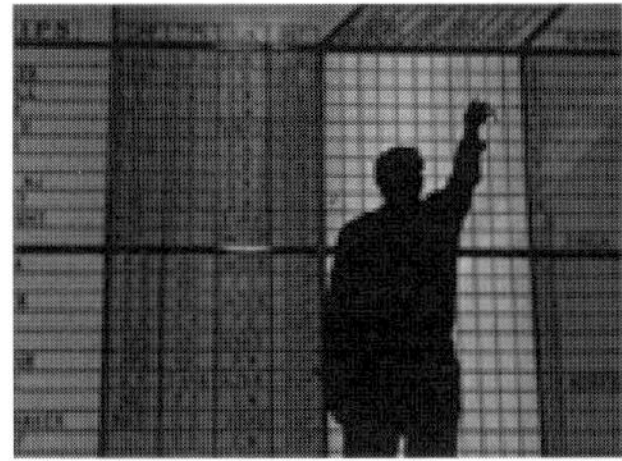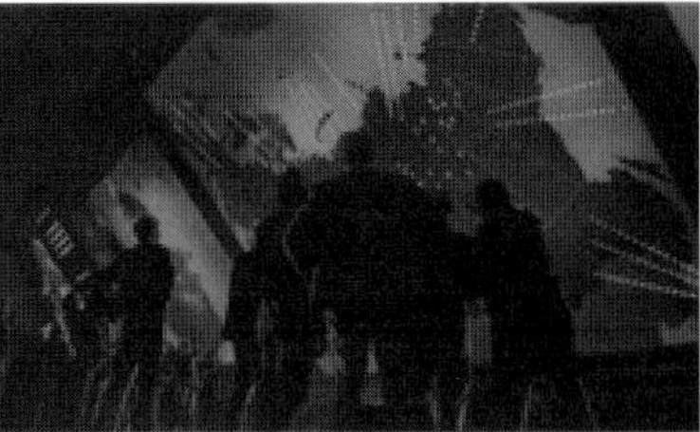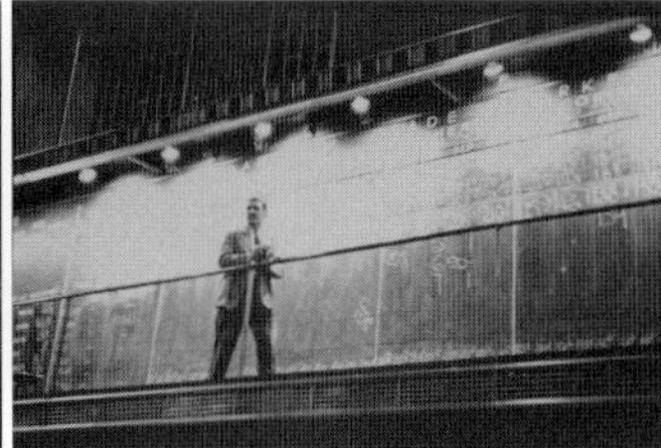

Figure 47: The "Big Board" in *The Seafarers, Dr. Strangelove* and the "Chicago Story" (1949).

from Kubrick's Chicago story (April 12, 1949), showing yet another man silhouetted against a large board at Chicago's Stock Exchange.

Paintings are sometimes used as props by strategically positioning characters below them, in order to benefit from an implicit form of ironic commentary. *Eyes Wide Shut* features a scene in which a painting of a nude, pregnant woman ("Paula in Red" by Christiane Kubrick) is compared with naked model/prostitute Mandy who has overdosed on drugs while having sex with the wealthy Victor Ziegler: "These two contrasting representations of female nudity enunciate the difference between the artworks with which men appropriate visions of a higher sense to female nudity and the exploitative reality of what they are doing, while underscoring how both act to contain and objectify female bodies" (Whitinger). Similarly, Kubrick's essay on the 1949 Philadelphia Beaux-Arts Ball includes a large overlapping photograph featuring a group of socialites at a pre-Ball party, sitting under an original Van Gogh painting, *Mother Roulin with Her Baby* (1888). The mother and child in Van Gogh's painting look comparatively normal next to the society ladies wearing goofy costumes.

A frequent device in Kubrick's early work was to place characters behind bars, to suggest some kind of narrative or existential entrapment even when the protagonists were not (yet) in prison. For instance, Davey and Gloria in *Killer's Kiss* are framed by the vertical bars of a bedframe, to imply that their relationship may be doomed (cf. Figure 48). George Peatty in *The Killing* is first seen as a cashier at the racetrack, serving customers behind a barred window. This recalls Kubrick's August 20, 1946 two-page essay "How a Monkey Looks to People … and How People Look to a Monkey." The first page is a picture of a chimpanzee taken by another photographer,

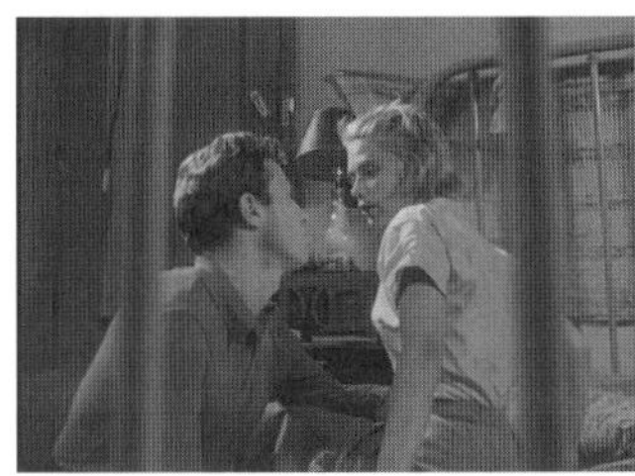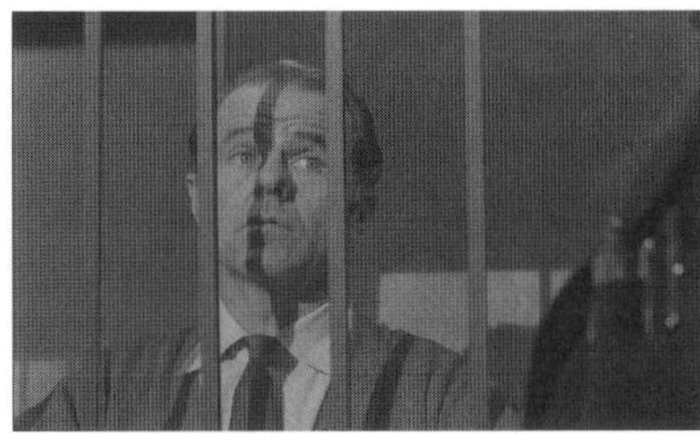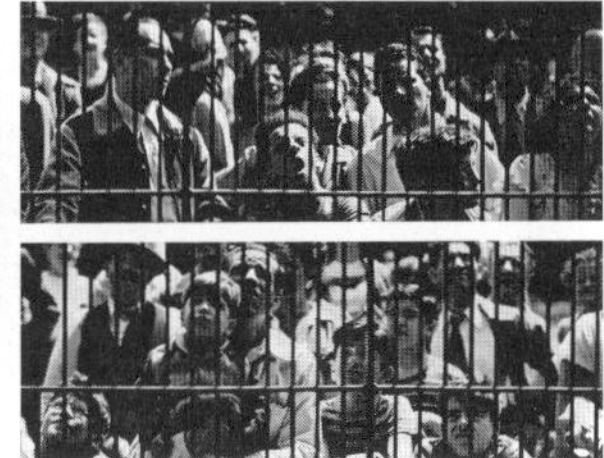

Figure 48: Behind bars in *Killer's Kiss, The Killing* and "How People Look to a Monkey" (1946).

followed by three Kubrick shots of people ostensibly looking at the monkey from the previous page. Taken more or less from the monkey's perspective inside the cage, the photographs are cropped as widescreen-formatted medium close-ups of the visitors, thus giving the impression that the people are behind bars. An unusual aspect of these reaction shots is that visitors are not smiling, recognizing the monkey's human behaviour, but looking up and wincing due to the sun. One might read these expressions of concern as the worried look of prisoners directing their gaze upwards to their jailors. Kubrick would use a similar kind of reversal at the conclusion of *The Killing* (1956), when the stolen money is dispersed on the airport's tarmac, and protagonist Johnny stands behind a wire fence, looking like he is already back in prison (Castle, 34).

A singular composition that appears intermittently throughout Kubrick's work is the high angle long shot of a group of people standing or sitting in a circle, usually conveying a sense of ritual or social control. One such picture appears in the September 30, 1947 essay "Walkathon – The World's Wackiest Show," concerning a Kansas City, Missouri arena show that included a dance marathon, various other refereed endurance tests, intermissions featuring singers, comics, and other vaudeville acts, as well as door prizes. A group of slow dancers attempting to remain awake is observed by a few referees, all standing in a rough circle on the arena floor, shown in a high-angle establishing shot (cf. Figure 44). A similar composition is applied to recently freed gladiators in *Spartacus*, who gather in a circle in the training school's arena in order to plan their next move (cf. Figure 49). The circle is thus also associated with rational thought, and *Dr. Strangelove*'s War Room is presented as a centrally lit, large circular table where the military and political elite will decide humanity's fate: "From a high angle, the camera reveals a world encircled by darkness but internally organized" (Nelson, 92). Gilles Deleuze uses the same example to support his argument that "it is the brain which is *mis en scène*" in Kubrick's cinema, "as in the great circular and luminous table

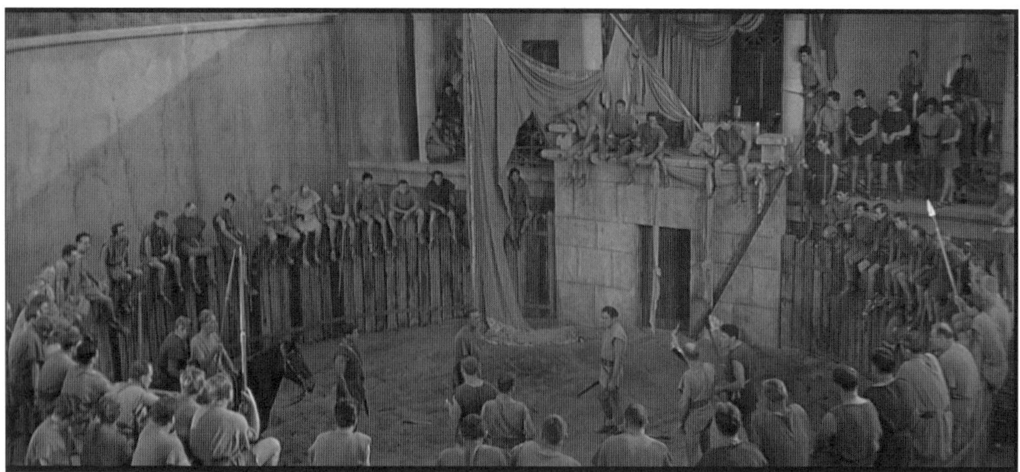

Figure 49: The circle as a symbol of centralized power in *Spartacus*.

in *Doctor Strangelove...*" (Deleuze, 198). In addition to rational thought, the circle represents an underground or secretive expression of the Establishment's power base, as illustrated by the circle of young women in the Somerton mansion from *Eyes Wide Shut* (albeit presented at eye-level), at the centre of which a sectarian leader issues ritualistic directives (Castle, 251).

Symmetry

More common in Kubrick's photographic and filmic work is the presence of symmetrical compositions, which split the image down the middle, violating the conventional rule of thirds. Such compositions may come across as unnatural or staged; however, they gain in strength as deliberate visual statements. One cannot pretend that the framing, that the perspective is accidental: the viewer is confronted with an image that insists on being acknowledged as an image, bearing an idea which must be identified. The initial impression created by the symmetrical frame may be claustrophobic or oppressive, and from an axiological perspective, this form of mise-en-scène does tend to be recognized as negative. It may simply represent an ominous foreshadowing of narrative events or, as with the circle, convey a general critique of social and political conditioning and control. In fact, the conflict between individual free will and societal laws, values and institutions constitutes a running theme in Kubrick's work, with the institutions often symbolized by symmetrical compositions, and thus made to look bad or threatening for the protagonist. A striking early example is included in the August 5, 1947 issue of *Look*, for a three-page essay on 15-year-old Polish war orphan Jack Melnik, titled "I Found Freedom in America." The concluding page's second picture is a dramatic, symmetrical composition looking down a shiny wooden table, which catches Jack's reflection as he writes a letter wearing a simple white undershirt. The teenager stands out in his YMCA room thanks to a top light and a plain, dark table and background, which creates an austere, Spartan impression. Broadly speaking, then, symmetrical framings in Kubrick's films most commonly reference a formal or ritualistic expression of institutional authority, occasionally a danger of a more personal nature for the protagonists, and in the case of *2001: A Space Odyssey*, an ill-defined natural or universal law.

Among the social institutions targeted by Kubrick's symmetrical camera are the military, judicial, medical, political and religious institutions, along with the technology they use to assert their power and impose their authority. The dehumanizing nature of the French military during World War I is revealed in *Paths of Glory* thanks to a rigorous system of narrative, thematic and visual oppositions (Eaton, 71). Symmetrical compositions are employed to chilling effect when Major Saint-Auban declares the three "randomly" chosen soldiers guilty of cowardice during the court-martial scene, and later when they are lined up in front of the chateau, facing a firing squad. *Full Metal Jacket* also avails itself of the symmetrical frame when drill instructor Hartman abuses the recruits in their barracks, when the soldiers lie on their bunk beds holding their weapons and reciting the rifle creed, and when a deranged Gomer Pyle executes a rifle drill perfectly in the washroom prior to murdering the drill instructor. The authoritarianism, intimidation and fear that characterize the training of Marines are conveyed in part by uncompromising symmetrical compositions. The judicial institution is portrayed as similarly authoritarian during scenes taking place in prison in *A Clockwork Orange*, while Alex is being processed for admittance by the Chief Guard and later in the prison courtyard where prisoners are allowed to walk around in circles for some fresh air. Both scenes use symmetrical framings that Kubrick may have remembered from a January 6, 1948 issue of *Look* (to which he contributed a portrait of Doris Day), which features a striking photo-essay by Frank Bauman of the infamous Illinois State Penitentiary near Joliet. Symmetrically composed photographs of Joliet's guards lined up for inspection and prisoners during visiting hours, printed full page, must have stood out for Kubrick (cf. Figure 50). The heavy hand of the law also catches up with Johnny in the last shot from *The Killing*, when two detectives emerge from the airport terminal, framing him to preclude any lateral escape. The finality of this composition is underscored by Johnny's admission of defeat, even as girlfriend Fay urges him to run: "What's the difference?," he mumbles, expressing typical film noir "*apatheia*, the acceptance of one's fate, as recommended by the Stoics" (Sanders, 153).

Hospitals can be prisons of a different sort, and when Lolita suffers from the flu, Humbert admits her into a hospital, later complaining that it is run like a prison when he cannot have her released without a doctor's permission. He then refuses to accept news that his daughter was released to an Uncle Gus (a.k.a. Clare Quilty), and proceeds towards her room without authorization, which forces the attendants to wrestle him to the ground and escort him out of the hospital. This last scene is presented in a symmetrical composition, highlighting the strict security which is enforced at the hospital and supporting Humbert's comparison with a prison. The line between the two institutions becomes thinner in *A Clockwork Orange*, when Alex is strapped into his theatre seat for multiple sessions of brainwashing. As the patient/prisoner's pain increases, he protests against the use of Beethoven on the soundtrack and his face becomes gradually more distorted, as if in a desperate effort to impart some dissymmetry into the tyrannical composition. Political authority is critiqued in several films, including *2001:*

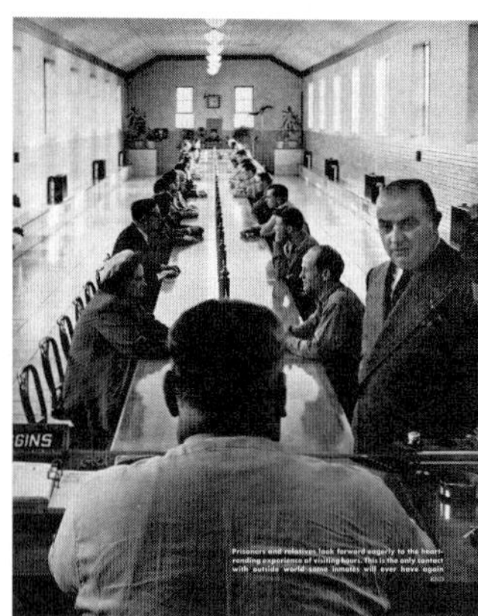
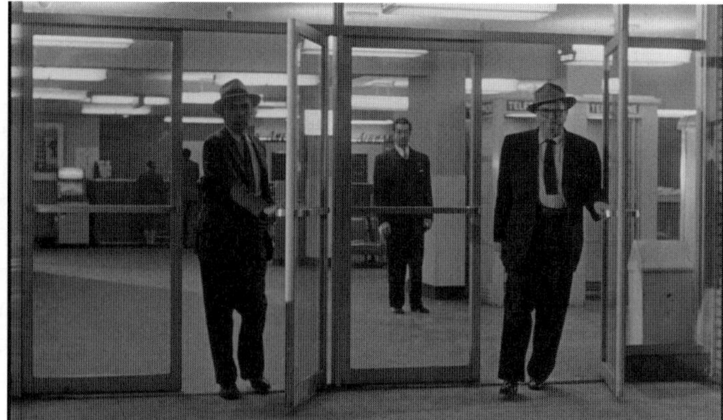

Figure 50: Symmetry in prison (F. Bauman, 1948) and in Kubrick's *The Killing* (1956).

A Space Odyssey, when NASA's administrator Heywood Floyd is sent to Moonbase Clavius essentially to clamp down on those who are unhappy about being kept prisoner with no visiting hours. During his brief preliminary speech, Floyd's manner is casual and even goofy, but there is no mistaking his euphemistic "hope" that everyone will "accept the need for ab-so-lute secrecy" and his directive for all on Clavius to sign formal security oaths. Once again, Kubrick employs a symmetrical composition with Floyd as the authority figure in the middle of the Cinerama frame (Stewart, 197). A more satirical presentation of an influential politician sees the British Minister of the Interior in *A Clockwork Orange* walking down the prison hallway to the tune of Elgar's *Pomp and Circumstance*. In *Barry Lyndon*, the title character is offered a job as a spy by Captain Potzdorf and the Prussian Minister of Police. While Barry stands at attention in a symmetrical framing, Potzdorf remains off-screen, describing the nature of Barry's new mission.

The power of technology is featured prominently in *2001: A Space Odyssey*, through countless interior and exterior shots of spaceships, orbital stations, landing platforms, docking bays, hallways, cockpits, airlocks, and so on, many of which are framed symmetrically. The presence of corporate logos such as IBM reminds us of the economic and political collusion in the military–industrial complex. Technology not only provides power to those who have the means to acquire and use it, but it also possesses the power to impose a certain behaviour upon the human characters, who, to a certain extent, must conform to and serve the needs of the technology itself. As a result, astronauts Dave and Frank seem barely more human than their onboard computer HAL. Recurring symmetrical close-ups of HAL's cyclopic yet ubiquitous eye, akin to an Orwellian Big Brother, is a disconcerting reminder that the machine has access to knowledge, which could theoretically make it a formidable enemy. HAL's inaccurate fault prediction of the spaceship's antenna leads to a secretive discussion between the two astronauts regarding the computer's fate. A symmetrical composition presents Frank and Dave in profile, facing each other, with the pod's porthole visible between them, revealing HAL in the background. On occasion they turn their heads in HAL's direction, the porthole functioning as an additional frame, temporarily containing a problem which they will have to deal with once their conversation has ended (Castle, 124). The mise-en-scène recalls a similar composition from *Spartacus*, when four gladiators are selected for a private performance at the training school, and are briefly placed in a holding area before the pairings are announced. The four men are also shown in profile, glancing at the arena when the door is opened, framing General Crassus' box in the background, in the same central position as HAL (cf. Figure 51).

Symmetrical framings can also boil down to the expression of a direct or implied threat to the fictional characters, such as in *Killer's Kiss* (Rapallo's thugs), *2001: A Space Odyssey* (HAL), *A Clockwork Orange* (Mr. Alexander), *The Shining* (Room 237) and *Eyes Wide Shut* (Red Cloak). Davey leaves his apartment at the same time as Gloria in *Killer's Kiss*, and both acknowledge each other as they walk towards Rapallo's car parked at the front entrance. The high-angle shot is symmetrically composed, with the film's romantic leads unknowingly heading for trouble as they approach bad guy Rapallo at the top of a triangle. During the BBC news broadcast in *2001: A Space Odyssey*, a symmetrical shot of the Discovery's

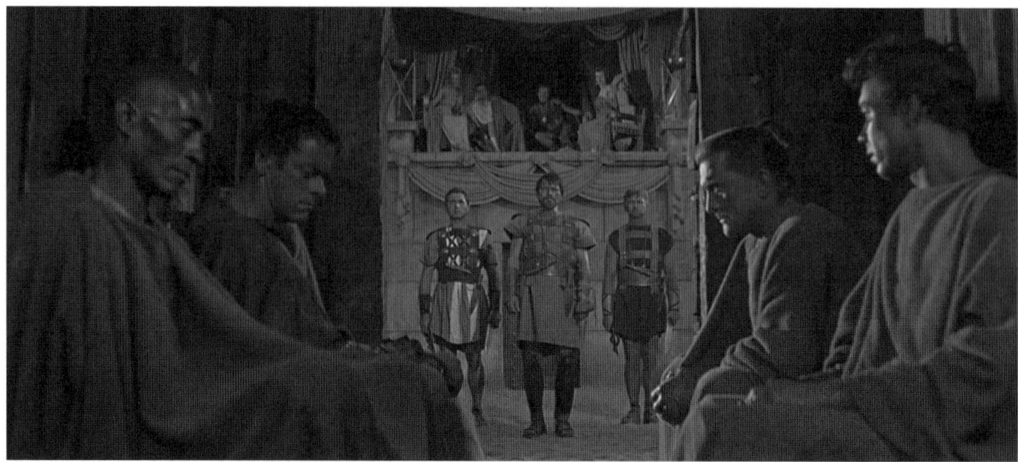

Figure 51: Protagonists frame the real source of power in *Spartacus*.

survey team in hibernation underscores the resemblance of their hibernacula to coffins or sarcophagi, suggesting that the astronauts would never survive the journey. In *A Clockwork Orange*, a rather ominous-looking symmetrical shot of Alex eating spaghetti by himself in Mr. Alexander's house hints at a dire fate for the story's narrator. The most systematic and frequent use of the symmetrical frame as foreboding, however, occurs in *The Shining*, sometimes accompanied by a slow and creepy forward track, or a faster follow-shot in the maze of the hotel, particularly as Danny rides his tricycle. The music also contributes to our interpretation of these symmetrical shots as menacing, and we build up the sense that there is an unseen, evil spirit or presence in the hotel, and that shocking events will follow.

A particular kind of symmetrical framing, specifically a vertical alignment of objects, performs a different function in *2001: A Space Odyssey*, one which does not express danger as such or other social constraints to personal freedoms. *2001* features five major alignments: (1) The sun emerging behind the earth and moon, followed by the title "The Dawn of Man"; (2) A low-angle shot of the black monolith with the sun and crescent moon above it, when Moon-Watcher "invents" the weapon; (3) A low-angle view of the monolith with the sun and crescent earth, when it emits a radio signal from the moon, followed by the title "Jupiter Mission: 18 months later"; (4) A "magical" alignment of Jupiter's moons with the monolith, following the title "Jupiter and Beyond the Infinite" by four minutes and immediately preceding the Stargate sequence; (5) An alignment of a dying Bowman with the monolith, Bowman reaching out to touch the monolith, like Moon-Watcher and Heywood Floyd before him (Castle, 140). The geometrical alignments of the monolith with other natural objects, such as planets, function as a repeating visual motif or leitmotif, as well as a structuring device. This alignment of stellar bodies as symptom of a narrative transition is strengthened by the fact that the three non-diegetic titles support three out of the five alignments, either by preceding or following the alignments. They do not symbolize a threat so much as fate or an order to the universe, in contrast with the principle of entropy, an order which may also be extraterrestrial in origin and suggests an evolutionary milestone for the human species.

Mirrors and frames within frames

Like the freeze-frame, creating an additional frame within the film camera's frame is a reflexive device, that is, a means of drawing attention to the film itself as an act of enunciation. It is a fairly common technique in Western art, if one considers paintings that include a proscenium arch or other framing devices such as trees or columns. Multiplying the frames in the image is also a way of highlighting the importance of that which is framed, as well as enhancing a sense of depth. Favoured devices in photography and film are openings in buildings such as doors and windows, particularly as the window duplicates the camera frame's aspect ratio. For his July 4, 1950 story titled "12 Children – $75 a Week," concerning the large Bova family from Stamford, Connecticut, Kubrick produced a portrait of Mr. Bova kneeling in front of his 1933 Plymouth with one of his daughters, while seven of the youngest children look out three of the car windows, similar to picture frames (cf. Figure 12). Alfred Hitchcock's *Rear Window* (1954) is a celebrated film example in which the numerous apartment windows function like little movies within the movie, reminding us that we are looking at a film that is framed in a specific way, where we can only see a portion or a fraction of diegetic space at a time. *Killer's Kiss* features a scene similar to *Rear Window*, as Davey looks out his window and sees Gloria through her apartment window. Davey's face is shown through a fishbowl, distorted and metaphorically trapped in a similar predicament to the fish he is feeding. *Full Metal Jacket* also includes frames within frames, such as the point-of-view shot of the sniper who looks through a window and spots the Marines, unaware of her location. More striking is a large circular door in the Buddhist temple when Joker is reunited with Cowboy. The door frames the two men, not unlike the circular hallways on board the Discovery in *2001: A Space Odyssey*.

Mirrors may be considered a case of frames within frames, providing different perspectives on a given character, or perhaps a single perspective on someone who is off frame. The conclusion of Orson Welles' *Lady from Shanghai* (1948) features a chase scene in a hall of mirrors, a self-conscious play on appearances, on the lack of reality of film images. In addition to being a self-referential comment on the artifice of representation, the mirror is also a means of articulating the doppelgänger theme, as an expression of the Kubrickian struggle between reason and emotion, described by Joker in *Full Metal Jacket* as "the duality of man, the Jungian thing." The presence of boxer Walter Cartier's twin brother Vincent throughout the photo-essay "Prizefighter" and the documentary film *Day of the Fight* provides these two texts with an eerie sense of being able to see the same person from two angles simultaneously. For instance, on the second page of "Prizefighter," a picture shows Vincent sleeping in the foreground while Walter stands in the background, stretching prior to his morning jog (cf. Figure 32). The theme of the double also features prominently in Kubrick's

The Shining, as a vision of two dead sisters likely inspired by a Diane Arbus photograph, taken in New Jersey in 1967, showing twin girls standing side by side (Castle, 193). We should not discount the possible influence of *Look* colleague Doug Jones' April 29, 1947 essay "Twins Capture Washington," profiling the debut party of 21-year-old Betty and Virginia Baker, focusing on the confusion created by identical twins. In Kubrick's "Prizefighter," a portrait of Vincent applying Vaseline on his brother's face almost looks like a mirror image, and in the opening scene from *Killer's Kiss*, a mirror provides Davey with a false twin as he checks his brow and nose for signs of injury (cf. Figure 46). During the BBC television report in *2001: A Space Odyssey*, a two-shot of Dave and Frank eating their TV dinner presents them as mirror reflections: each has his own video monitor angled towards him, and both hold their forks with different hands to complete the illusion of a reflection, even though other scenes establish that they are both right-handed.

The unreality or metaphysical quality of the reflection is used for practical purposes, paradoxically, in the vampire film genre, in order to confirm whether or not a character has a soul, since vampires do not produce reflections. In *The Shining*, the mirror suggests multiple personalities, which can be read metadiscursively as a comment on the logical status of fictional characters. The Torrance's bedroom in *The Shining* includes a strategically located mirror allowing the image to be split in half, with Jack's reflection on the left, and Wendy's "real" self on the right. When she brings him breakfast, her eyeline is directed offscreen to the right, which is where Jack is, except that the viewer only has access to his reflection on the left. We therefore get the impression that Wendy is talking to someone else. The shot then slowly zooms in to the mirror on the left and a two-shot of the couple, as Wendy sits next to her husband and the reflection fills the frame. Suddenly, the two-shot flips left to right as the film cuts to a "real," non-reflected image of the characters, as if the camera had crossed the axis of action. This spatial confusion subtly accentuates our sense that something is wrong with Jack. This feeling is confirmed 15 minutes later when Danny visits his father in the same bedroom, except that this time, the mise-en-scène includes both Jack and his reflection, with poor Danny literally stuck in the middle (Castle, 202).

Among Kubrick's initial photographic explorations into the mirror was a two-page photo-essay titled "First Look at a Mirror Bewilders the Baby," featuring a one-year-old baby interacting with his double. This series of six pictures, published in the May 13, 1947 issue of *Look*, is a literal depiction of the Lacanian scenario of the mirror phase, and art historian Alexandra Von Stosch analyzes it as such in *Drama & Shadows* (246–9). Von Stosch's analysis points out Kubrick's use of the low angle as a means to encourage our identification with the child, and argues that the mirror highlights the artifice of representation (the reflection) as well as the realism of intersubjectivity (multiple views on a subject) (248). Direct forerunners of *The Shining's* Brady sisters might include children from *Look's* two-page spread titled "Deaf Children Hear for the First Time" (May 25, 1948), in which radio and opera star Risë Stevens hosts a party in her New York City apartment for 12 deaf children. They are outfitted with hearing aids courtesy of inventor Leland A. Watson, whose device received a patent in 1952. One little girl adjusts the earpiece while checking herself in the mirror, interacting with a twin version of herself, and another picture features the same girl with a similarly dressed little friend, possibly her sister, anticipating Danny's playmates from *The Shining*.

Camera angle

Michel Cieutat quite rightly argues that Kubrick's training as a photographer led him to experiment judiciously with extreme high and low camera angles in order to convey specific information regarding fictional characters, such as General Ripper's insanity in *Dr. Strangelove* (Cieutat, 87). A related yet distinct formal property of framing the image is its level, that is, the degree to which the horizontal edges of the frame are parallel to the horizon. Canted images are rare, and are stereotypically used to suggest psychologically unstable characters, as in the sixties *Batman* television series. In *2001: A Space Odyssey*, however, Kubrick deliberately creates a spatially disorienting sequence with canted frames during the extravehicular activity scenes when Frank and Dave fix the Discovery's antenna. The result is a figure of estrangement characteristic of the science-fiction film genre, one that reminds us that notions of up and down are meaningless in the absence of gravity (Mather, 196).

As for camera angles, the extreme low-angle shot of Ripper chomping on his cigar distorts his facial features, which, combined with his fanatical speech about the "international Communist conspiracy to sap and impurify all of our precious bodily fluids," confirms his status as a lunatic. Even lower angles, looking straight up at characters' faces, are featured in *A Clockwork Orange* and *The Shining*. When Mr. Alexander hears Alex belting out "Singin' in the Rain" and realizes that the young man is none other than his belated wife's rapist, he appears to suffer an epileptic fit in his wheelchair. *The Shining*'s Wendy Torrance manages to lock up her violent husband in the hotel's pantry, but Jack nevertheless gloats about having cut off their means of communication and transportation, and laughs like a madman. A sharp switch from an extreme-low to an extreme-high angle stands out in *A Clockwork Orange*, when the government aims to demonstrate that their brainwashing programme works. Alex is tempted by a topless woman, whose breasts stand out in a provocative fashion, in a low-angle point-of-view shot. Alex becomes nauseous in the reverse high-angle shot, withdrawing uncontrollably from the woman.

The high-angle perspective is usually combined with a long shot that establishes the location, often one that dominates the characters. For instance, a high-angle shot during the court-martial sequence in *Paths of Glory* highlights the checkered flooring, which turns the soldiers into chess pieces. Similarly, the four gladiators selected for a fight to the death at the training school in *Spartacus* are presented in a high-angle long shot, alone in their compound like the condemned soldiers from *Paths of Glory*. Maze patterns are showcased in *The Shining*, particularly Jack's unnatural bird's-eye view of the hedge maze, combined with a slow zoom-in which reveals Danny and Wendy at the centre. The maze becomes a metaphor for the photographic apparatus, a machine which traps or captures its subjects forever, immobilizing them like Jack himself who both freezes to death in the maze and is immortalized by the film's last photograph.

Deep space

Kubrick did occasionally resort to conventional shallow focus for character close-ups, but his preference was for shots carefully composed in depth, and in deep focus. He would thus use short focal length lenses in order to oppose characters in the foreground and the background, creating a self-contained mise-en-scène or narrative within a static composition. This strategy also enhanced a sense of depth in the image, an important consideration for black-and-white photography, and helped to maintain the sharp focus required for quality reproductions in a large photomagazine. For instance, a photograph from an unpublished story concerning the Keeley Institute (added to *Look*'s library on April 1, 1948) features three men from the Institute composed in depth, waiting for a train at the Dwight, Illinois station (cf. Figure 52). *Paths of Glory* also includes compositions with single characters deliberately positioned in the foreground, middle ground and background, such as Corporal Paris, Private Ferol and Private Arnaud in the condemned soldiers' cell.

Kubrick used deep focus to separate the visual planes in narratological terms in his essay "Jealousy: A Threat to Marriage" (October 24, 1950) and in *Lolita*, when Clare Quilty is spying on Humbert and his "lovely, tall, pretty, little small daughter." The *Look* photo-essay's third spread features a middle-aged man in a business suit sitting on the corner of his smiling secretary's desk in the foreground, while his suspicious wife happens to look around the open door in the background. Expressing this information gap by contrasting visual planes is reprised in *Lolita*, when Humbert checks in with Mr. Swine, the receptionist at the Enchanted Hunters Hotel. He is positioned in the foreground, while Quilty hides behind a postcard stand in the middle ground, listening in on Humbert's sleeping arrangements. A reverse-angle confirms Quilty's illicit activity, as the foreground becomes the site of knowledge. Moments later, Humbert returns to the hotel lobby and stands briefly at the

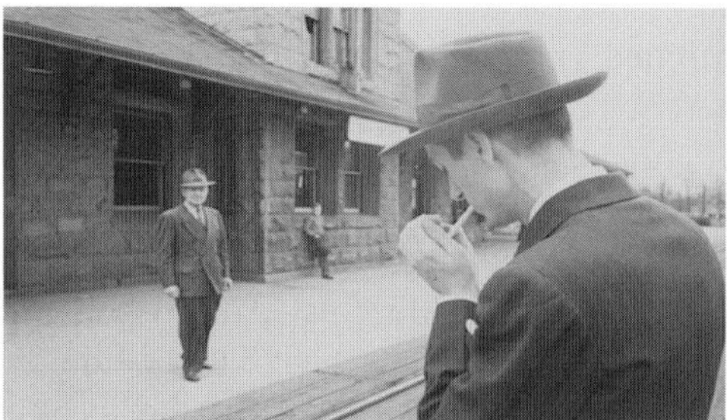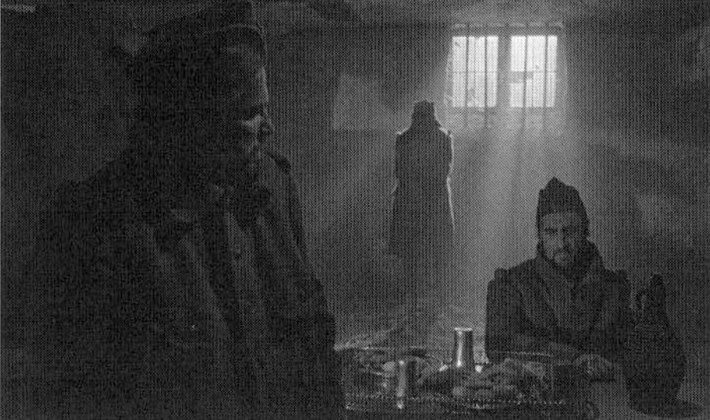

Figure 52: Composition in depth in the "Keeley Institute" (1948) and *Paths of Glory* (1957).

reception desk in the background, while Quilty and his partner Vivian Darkbloom hide behind newspaper comics in the foreground. It is perhaps no accident that postcards and comics, both media related to photojournalism and film, are used diegetically as devices to conceal information, and metadiscursively to reveal the illusory nature of film, which consists of single photographs (postcards) organized sequentially (comics). A related use of deep space that involves concealing and revealing information occurs when Bill Harford and Victor Ziegler engage in a dance of sorts at the end of *Eyes Wide Shut*. Bill has been summoned to the billiards room, and maintains a physical distance by remaining in the foreground and keeping his back turned to Victor, who stays in the background. Bill wants information concerning Mandy, but also wishes he did not know about Victor's involvement in the secret society. Similarly, composition in depth characterizes a shot in *The Shining* when Wendy expresses her shock upon realizing that Jack has likely injured Danny again. Jack remains sitting in the foreground, in the hotel's Colorado lounge, as Wendy looks at him accusingly and retreats into the background.

A striking composition that anticipates Ingmar Bergman's formal experiments in films such as *Persona* (1966) features two enemy officers in *Fear and Desire* sitting at a 90-degree angle to each other. The General is shown in profile in the foreground, musing on the paradoxes of war in a 30-second take, and his aide-de-camp listens in the middle ground, facing the camera. Two young men in white shirt and tie strike a similar pose in an unpublished photograph from Kubrick's Chicago story (added to the *Look* library on January 27, 1949), with the difference that the man in the foreground is turned slightly towards the camera and his left eye stares at us like Nicole Kidman in the poster for *Eyes Wide Shut* (Crone 2005, 39). *Dr. Strangelove* also includes static shots composed in depth, when General Ripper uses the PA system to personally issue orders to his troops to seal off the base. Two men silhouetted in the foreground and middle ground are standing under a large jet engine inside an aircraft hangar. A shot featuring the sign "Peace is our profession" hanging on a barbed wire fence includes a soldier in close-up on the left, two other men in the middle ground next to the sign, and a path along the fence leading into the distance.

Realist/noir lighting

Although "Kubrick never forsook his predilection for the natural or 'practical' lighting he had used as a photo-journalist," his simultaneous attraction to lighting styles described by some as expressionistic may seem paradoxical (Naremore, 54). The paradox is only apparent, however, since realistically motivated sources of light often produce expressive effects, which contrast with Hollywood's dominant high-key studio style. Therefore, it should come as no surprise that Kubrick's penchant for single-source lighting (top, back, side or underlighting) and available light (windows, candles, etc.) is both a feature of expressionistic film noir as well as a mark of "the black-and-white street photography of the New York school" (Naremore, 54). For instance, backlighting and underlighting are often interpreted as menacing, since we either can only see a silhouette or else the character's features are distorted by the light's unusual direction, even though it may be perfectly justified diegetically. A good example of ominous backlighting from Kubrick's photo-essays was produced for the Walkathon story (September 30, 1947), as part of a series of four numbered pictures showing the ordeal suffered by Johnny Makar, who agreed to be "frozen alive in a hollow ice tomb." He spends over half an hour in this transparent ice-coffin, is then removed once he has lost consciousness, revived with an oxygen pump and hot coffee, then sent to the dance floor where he fares poorly, not surprisingly. The first photograph in this series focuses on the 1200-pound ice-coffin, with the caption explaining that Makar must periodically operate a switch, turning on a light which indicates to the audience that he is still conscious. One of the unpublished images, available at the Library of Congress, is a dramatic backlit shot of the ice coffin, taken without a flash (cf. Figure 53). The result looks ethereal and otherworldly, highlighting the danger of putting one's life at risk in such a fashion. Kubrick would reprise similarly cold hibernation coffins in *2001: A Space Odyssey*.

After Rapallo's thugs mistakenly murder Davey's manager in *Killer's Kiss*, they emerge as menacing silhouettes from a back alley, in the same way that Alex and his droogs approach a helpless old tramp in *A Clockwork Orange*, their long shadows virtually announcing their ill intentions. Later, it is the State's turn to be violent, as Alex is abused by a stage actor who forces him to lick his boots. The scene is introduced by a backlit shot on stage of Alex and the actor, reminding us of the previous beating perpetrated by the droogs (Castle, 158). After the bomber wing has been successfully recalled in *Dr. Strangelove*, Buck Turgidson leads the War Room in prayer, and when he makes a reference to the Angel of Death, the camera cuts to an eerie shot of Strangelove himself, silhouetted against the big board (cf. Figure 53). Danny's imaginary friend Tony is a source of information in *The Shining*, specifically regarding the evil power that lurks in the hallways of the Overlook Hotel. It is fitting, then, that Wendy's conversation with Tony, following Jack's discussion with Delbert Grady in the red bathroom, should include a backlit shot of Danny's mother, obviously anguished by the young boy's behaviour.

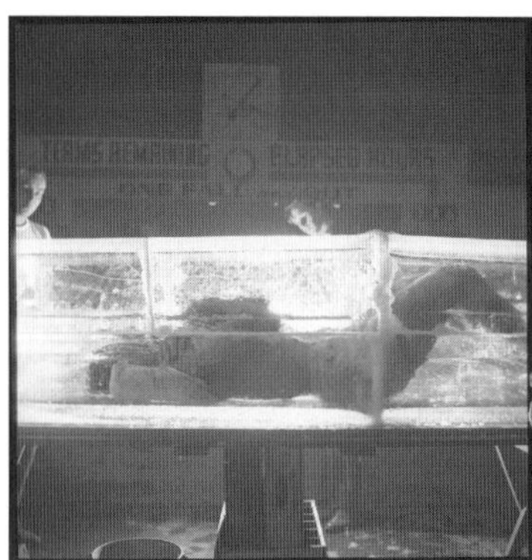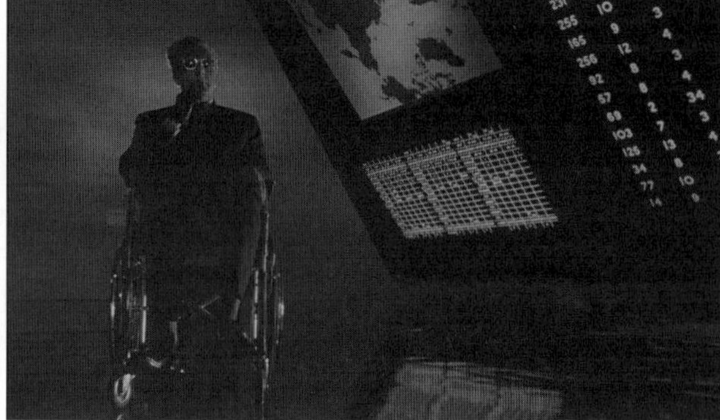

Figure 53: Backlighting in "Walkathon" (1947) and *Dr. Strangelove*.

Photojournalism

Rhetorical/categorical structure

Strictly speaking, only Kubrick's documentary shorts avail themselves of rhetorical form, although they also use narrative strategies, with the exception of *The Seafarers*. It is possible to argue that some fiction films may also possess an overall didactic structure, which overrides narrative exigencies, particularly in allegorical genres such as science fiction, but for the purpose of the present analysis, those journalistic aspects will be examined as more localized or punctual effects. Generically, Kubrick's first two shorts are "straight" documentaries based on photo-essays, which had previously appeared in *Look* magazine, and the third short is an industrial or promotional film commissioned by the Seafarers Union International. *Day of the Fight* and *Flying Padre* thus share specific photojournalistic sources, whereas *The Seafarers* reveals a slightly broader range of influences. It is also a non-fiction film, but differs from Kubrick's previous shorts in its general avoidance of narrative form and "personal journalism." As for Kubrick's first two films, it could be argued that they are not only adaptations of his January 18, 1949 essay "Prizefighter" and the October 15, 1946 essay "Flying Priest" (photographed by George Heyer), but are also exemplifications of photomagazine genres, which were popular during the post-war era. The sports personality profile and the portrait of a rural or small-town professional were essay topics commonly seen in *Life* and *Look*. As it is standard journalistic practice for editors to assign stories based on their photographers' areas of interests, young sports fan Kubrick got the opportunity to cover boxing events on several occasions, many aspects of which can be seen in the film *Day of the Fight*. As for *Flying Padre*, it follows in the tradition of photo-essays such as Arthur Rothstein's "Flying Doctor" (*Look*, November 25, 1947), Eugene Smith's famous "Country Doctor" (*Life*, September 20, 1948), John Vachon's "Country Preacher" (*Look*, June 21, 1949) and "Woman Doctor" (*Look*, December 20, 1949), as well as the wartime story "Invasion Heroine: The Flying Nurse," photographed by *Look*'s Harold Rhodenbaugh (Mich, 90). We may surmise that what attracted Kubrick to the flying priest story was his own enthusiasm for aviation as well as photojournalism's explicit goal to inform and entertain their readership, a dual purpose which explains the selection of unusual or surprising personalities for magazine profiles. The contrast that piques our curiosity in the "Flying Priest" comes from "putting modern technology at the service of an ancient calling." The story thus acquires a news peg or timely quality, which Kubrick would have recognized as marketable, with the added bonus of being able to do some aerial photography.

Both *Day of the Fight* and *Flying Padre* adopt a photojournalistic "day in the life of" structure, in line with essays such as Kubrick's "Prizefighter" and "Rocky Graziano – He's a Good Boy Now," as well as *Look* colleague Maurice Terrell's profile of a college football player, titled "Day of the Game" (November 23, 1948). The only difference is that Father Fred Stadtmueller's story features two days in his life, and boxer Walter Cartier's story begins after a four-minute prologue describing boxing as a social phenomenon.[1] The prologue thus adopts rhetorical form, much like *The Seafarers*, and may have been partly based on another *Look* boxing story, titled "Fight Night at the Garden" (February 15, 1949), which does not feature the athletes, but focuses instead on audience reactions to the match, as well as the journalists covering the event. Perhaps the most consistent feature of the "day in the life of" structure in Kubrick's boxing stories is the creation of suspense by adopting a flashback structure, which confronts us immediately with the inherent drama of a fight, followed by a gradual build-up to the main event thanks to a systematic chronicle of the fighter's preparations on the big day. On the second page of "Prizefighter," five small pictures list the events leading up to the fight, including Walter and his twin brother Vincent waking up, breakfast with Aunt Eva, the weigh-in and the physical exam, and waiting at home for a ride to the arena. Most of these events are reprised in *Day of the Fight*, and their function is to indicate a careful and meticulous preparation, as well as to build up tension. When the fighter is left to wait, the documentary's voice-over narrator refers to "the pressure of the last waiting," and the photo-essay's text informs us that "time drags heavily."

Tension may also be triggered suddenly, as on the second page of Rothstein's "Flying Doctor," where the last picture's caption, in the bottom right corner, provides a narrative hook by informing us that the doctor's help is often solicited after hours, for instance in a diner where the waitress relays an important phone call: we are invited to turn the page. Similarly, the *Flying Padre*'s montage sequence ends with the priest being interrupted while he works on his plane's engine. A young man conveys an urgent message about a mother whose child is ill at a remote farm. This launches the film's longest and concluding sequence, in which Kubrick plays up Stadtmueller's qualities as a man of action. The voice-over narration stops, with only music and occasional sound effects to assist the image-track in building suspense: Father Fred runs to his plane, starts the engine, handles the throttle and checks the time. Narration and music are also absent from the concluding sequence of *Day of the Fight*, in order to convey the immediacy of Walter Cartier's fight with Bobby James as an unheightened documentary event. After having been paged in the diner, the doctor from Rothstein's essay is shown already at the scene of a farming accident. The caption introduces dramatic tension by explaining that moving the patient might have proven fatal if the doctor had not examined him in a timely fashion, and that if necessary, he could also be flown directly to the hospital, much like in the Father Stadtmueller story.

Montage sequences

Rhetorical form in photojournalism manifests itself most clearly in specific types of image sequences or magazine spreads that form signifying units, according to their spatial, temporal and semantic properties. It may be useful in this context to apply three of Christian Metz' syntagmatic figures, even though they concern narrative film, as a means of identifying filmic montage sequences which can be assimilated with photojournalistic practice. The "descriptive syntagma" is commonly used to situate the action, and is included by Metz among the non-narrative figures, even though its images are presented as temporally simultaneous (not consecutive) and spatially contiguous (127). Metz' example is "the description of a landscape (a tree, followed by a shot of a stream running next the tree, followed by a view of a hill in the distance, etc.)" (127). The second figure is the "episodic sequence," one that "strings together a number of very brief scenes, which are usually separated from each other by optical devices (dissolves, etc.) and which succeed each other in chronological order" (130). The presence of a chronology lends a narrative quality to the episodic sequence, which otherwise has "many characteristics in common" with the third syntagmatic figure, the non-narrative and conceptual "bracket syntagma" (130). The bracket syntagma entertains no precise spatio-temporal unity, only a thematic or logical one, in order to "sketch a global picture of 'modern love'" or convey "the idea of the 'Disasters of War'" (Metz, 126). Film scholar Geneviève Jacquinot has adapted the Metzian typology of syntagmas for the documentary mode, which amounts to variations on the bracket syntagma, since the documentary's structuring principle is not based on the representation of time and space but on conceptual and rhetorical logic (77). The two basic forms, dubbed the "monstrative" and "demonstrative" syntagmas, refer to illustrative and argumentative strategies, respectively, within rhetorical form (Jacquinot, 78).

The descriptive syntagma is most commonly found at the beginning of films or sequences that require the establishment of a narrative space. *Flying Padre* begins by establishing the space of the semi-arid terrain of Harding County, New Mexico, over which Father Fred Stadtmueller flies before conducting a funeral in the town of Gallegos (cf. Figure 54). Father Fred is responsible for 11 parishes and uses a small plane to cover 4,000 square miles. Establishing the space with a slow pan is a standard documentary device, and was repeated in the opening shot from Kubrick's first fiction film, *Fear and Desire*, as well as for the remote landscape of Southwest

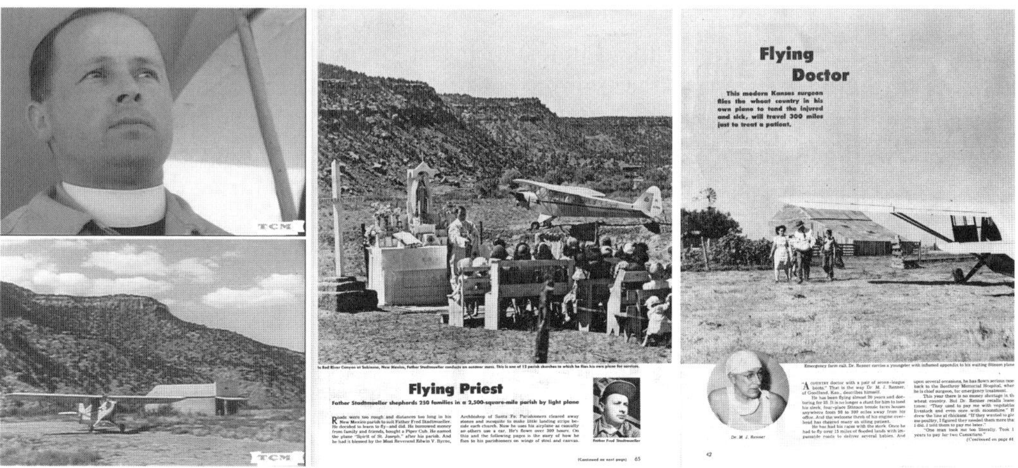

Figure 54: *Flying Padre* (Kubrick), "Flying Priest" (G.Heyer), "Flying Doctor" (A.Rothstein).

Africa during the inaugural "Dawn of Man" sequence from *2001: A Space Odyssey*. Kubrick then includes a medium close-up of Father Stadtmueller and a shot of a modest landing strip in the canyon, as does George Heyer's 1946 photo-essay version of this story, highlighting the rough terrain and inserting a small portrait of the title character on the first page. Arthur Rothstein's 1947 essay "Flying Doctor" displays an identical layout on its opening page.

Following *The Seafarers'* opening credits, a brief sequence establishes the location of the new Union Headquarters in Brooklyn (675 Fourth Avenue, now an Islamic school), by first showing an image of the nearby port, then panning on the city rooftops, before ending on a general view of the new building and a closer tilt shot of its main entrance. This descriptive syntagma reprises Kubrick photographs of city rooftops in the unpublished "Shoe Shine Boy" assignment, as well as establishing shots of Chicago by day and by night, in the April 1949 "City of Extremes" essay (Crone 2005, 69). Further examples of introductory long shots providing a spatial context in which to frame the story include the high-angle exterior pan on the chateau in *Paths of Glory*, when General Mireau arrives in his vehicle, and a series of four shots describing the Air Force base in *Dr. Strangelove*: a swivelling radar antenna, planes taking off, and so on. The documentary quality of such descriptive montage sequences is most apparent in *Killer's Kiss*, a film in which "Kubrick documents his New York environment, the city that shaped his consciousness as an artist and a person" (LoBrutto, 103). A montage of Times Square by night includes a hot dog stall, ice cream sundaes on a carousel, a portrait photography store window, a toy baby in a water basin, and other candid images that "capture the reality and resonance of New York City in the fifties" (LoBrutto, 103).

The episodic sequence focuses on habitual, recurring activities in compressed form, an early example of which appears in Kubrick's *Flying Padre*. After a narrative episode in which a dispute between two children is resolved, a 40-second segment illustrates the priest's other duties and hobbies. Rhetorically, this sequence represents a pause in the narrative, so that we may be informed about the subject's day-to-day routine. The boxer's training regimen and preparations for the fight unfold in a similar fashion in "Prizefighter" and *Day of the Fight*, with the difference that the training routine may be perceived as a chronological series of vignettes, a crescendo rather than a frequentative. *The Killing's* title sequence is combined with an episodic sequence illustrating typical events leading up to the start of a horse race. Variations on this sequence are repeated at least twice during the course of the film, including helicopter shots of the racetrack, high-angle views on the crowd, telephoto images of the horses racing, and so on. Kubrick had been assigned to New York's Aqueduct Race Track in September 1947, and took many crowd pictures and individual portraits, none of which were published in *Look* magazine, although 21 were printed in *Drama & Shadows* (Crone 2005, 133–45).

Episodic sequences involving physical training are featured in *Spartacus* and *Full Metal Jacket*, enhancing the photojournalistic quality of both films, particularly *Full Metal Jacket* since the Vietnam War was covered by the major photomagazines, allowing the film to tap into and be read through this contemporary intertext. A variety of high and low angles are included in the training of gladiators in *Spartacus*, along with different martial disciplines. A chronology is implied when baffles are removed from the swivelling swords, thus confirming the episodic nature of the syntagma. In *Full Metal Jacket*, a first episodic sequence focuses on the training of Marines, including marching, climbing, running in mud, overcoming various obstacles, and instructor Hartman subjecting Gomer Pyle to a barrage of verbal abuse. A second montage sequence concerns Pyle being taught by Joker how to assemble a gun, lace a pair of boots, make a bed, and so on.

There is no implied narrative space–time continuum in the bracket syntagma, which may be described as a conceptual montage sequence. Thematic rather than strictly narrative groupings of images are common in the photo-essay format, and in Arthur Rothstein's "Flying Doctor" (*Look*, November 25, 1947), the second spread provides an additional suturing device through the constant presence of the protagonist, in order to enhance the thematic coherence with a visual continuity from one photograph to the next. A few moments after the opening establishing shots in *The Seafarers*, a 50-second bracket syntagma is designed to support the narrator's argument that the Seafarers' Union Hall is "big, modern, efficient and safeguarding the rights and interests of those who go to sea, but never forgetting that the machines and the files and the figures are there to serve the seafarers, and not the other way around." The sequence is framed by six images of technology: four brief close-ups of adding machines and two close-ups of computer printers. Four longer shots show the staff interfacing with the machines and a large card catalogue. Biographer Lobrutto observes that a "montage of machines is framed with Kubrick's exacting photojournalist eye and makes the point that machines serve man, a theme he would later confront head-on in *2001*" (LoBrutto, 74).

Didactic narration

Narration in the fiction film may only be considered journalistic if it incorporates the goals of rhetorical form, namely an attempt to inform and persuade the viewer regarding a particular issue. David Bordwell identifies "historical-materialist" narration as one of the major modes of narration whose purpose is explicitly didactic, in contrast with classical narration, based on "psychologically defined individuals who struggle to solve a clear-cut problem or to attain specific goals," and art-cinema narration, characterized by open-ended causality, expressive realism and authorial commentary (Bordwell 1985, 157). To what extent, then, do Kubrick's films adopt historical-materialist strategies in conveying narrative information, thereby betraying a journalistic influence? It is fair to say that the films exhibit a range of narrational practices, revealing the director's reluctance to deny himself an expressive resource or tool. Not surprisingly, the clearest instances of didactic narration occur in the three documentary shorts.

The Seafarers is the most explicit, including an on-screen narrator, whose appearance frames the film. He announces that "it's the story of the SIU," that is, the Seafarers International Union, although there is no story as such, not even a history of the union. Instead, a list of all the services that the union offers its members is intended to impress potential recruits. *Day of the Fight*'s prologue includes images linked in a series of dissolves and wipes to support the narrator's arguments concerning the boxing fan's enthusiasm for violent action, particularly a montage sequence of knock-out punches which appears to be stock footage not filmed by Kubrick. Similarly, the *Flying Padre*'s third sequence is a narrative episode designed to demonstrate the narrator's contention that "the wise and friendly counsel of the priest is always available to his flock." It bears mentioning that Kubrick considered including a prologue to *2001: A Space Odyssey*, consisting of edited clips from interviews he conducted in 1966 with 21 prominent scientists. The goal was "to establish that the question of extraterrestrial life *was* a legitimate subject for scientific investigation," and thus convince the viewer of its plausibility and importance (Frewin, 129).

The rhetorical status of narrative fiction is always more complex, a patchwork of heterogeneous speech-acts, to use Gérard Genette's description (49). In terms of voice-over narration, Kubrick has used either first- or third-person narration in nine feature films, sometimes neither (*2001: A Space Odyssey, The Shining, Eyes Wide Shut*), and both on one occasion (*Fear and Desire*). First-person narration is considered a realist device because it authenticates the imagery: this really happened to me, dear viewer. Third-person narration is anonymous and thus further removed from the diegesis, which allows it to enjoy a more objective status as a disinterested and reliable source of information, the closest to non-fictional discourse. The most consistent use of third-person narration in Kubrick's films occurs in *The Killing* and *Barry Lyndon*. Today, the masculine and authoritative voice-over in *The Killing* may come across as a parody of film noir or post-war documentary "voice of God" narration; however, its compliance with conventions of the time allowed it to provide a reassuring familiarity to the potentially disorienting non-linear narrative structure (Falsetto, 3). Mario Falsetto has convincingly argued that a number of discrepancies in the narrator's official explanation of the film's timeline may be attributed to a subtle critique of "the conventional faith in the authority of the voice-over" (5). He adds, quite accurately, that undermining the impersonal narrator's alleged neutrality "may have its roots in Kubrick's early years as a nonfiction filmmaker and photographer. He, better than most, knew the extremes of manipulation inherent in both these forms" (Falsetto, 103).

Title cards and signs as commentary

Michel Chion has suggested that Kubrick's training as a photojournalist shaped his use of voice-over commentary and titles in film, specifically as if they were magazine captions for photographs (25). The result has been a reflexive or self-conscious relationship between image and word, an explicit tension between the word's assumption that it can automatically explain and ennoble the image, whereas the image always hopes to assert its own irreducible, self-evident visual meaning (Chion, 26). This tension is symptomatic, according to Chion, of Kubrick's filmic language, one which remains true to the classical style but repeatedly exposes its discursive mechanisms (30). The titles in *The Shining* are a good example of this strategy, similar to the quasi-parodic use of voice-over in *The Killing*. The chronology displayed by the inter-titles becomes increasingly pointless, as it portentously announces unrelated days of the week and times of the day with a crash of cymbals on the soundtrack. This can again be read as a genre parody, or Kubrick's effort to undermine "an audience's faith in the narrative machinery of exposition – and its cause/effect logic … [and] mock our desire for temporal sense and rational sequence" (Nelson, 208–9).

Lest we adopt a knee-jerk auteurist stance regarding the origin of alternatives to the classical style, it is helpful to bear in mind that such critiques may be attributed in part to the photojournalistic medium's interplay between text and images, as Chion points out, as well as deliberate editorial explorations of both continuity and discontinuity montage. For instance, Kubrick's August 16, 1949 profile of popular jazz bandleader Vaughn Monroe begins with a superlative description of the musician's success. We are told that Monroe "topped all bandleaders in earnings" in 1948, despite an admission that the post-war era is witnessing "melancholy days for dance bands." Monroe's success is attributed to good looks, a pleasant baritone voice, and gruelling cross-country touring. Kubrick's photographs appear to subtly undermine some of the article's assertions.

The opening photograph is a wide overlap close-up of Monroe blocking his ears with his fingers, a somewhat unglamourous pose. Furthermore, one would think that a musician such as Monroe would keep his ears open during a recording session, to identify his band's mistakes rather than deliberately ignore them. The caption explains that Monroe is attempting to "feel the beat of one of his recordings," but the picture remains cheeky. The first spread's second picture undercuts Monroe's good looks further, as he looks in Kubrick's direction with his mouth full, eating at a diner. Amusingly, Monroe is shown sharing the meal with a female vocalist from his band, which may have prompted *Look*'s editors to include a shot of Monroe with his wife at home, lest readers think that something fishy was going on. Interestingly, this last picture is the only one in which Monroe is seen smiling.

The photo-essay's closing spread features Monroe in three different settings: in a recording studio, on stage wearing a cowboy outfit, and on the bandstand as adoring female fans look up at him. In each case, he looks serious, as if he were never enjoying himself, contradicting the article's claim that he possesses "a broad and ready smile." The teenage fans are gathered at the foot of the bandstand, exhibiting the kind of worshipful gaze that had become more common in the post-war era, notably with Frank Sinatra's bobby-soxers. Monroe looks quite distinguished in his suit, which contrasts with the childish and goofy-looking cowboy outfit he wears for a closing production number, although the caption finds that it adds "fillip to the tunes." We are led to wonder whether the text's positive spin was due to unofficial sponsorship from Monroe's record company, RCA-Victor, as opposed to genuinely "disinterested" journalism, in which case Kubrick's persona-deflating pictures would be the photojournalistic equivalent of Arthur Godfrey's commercial-kidding technique. Godfrey was a radio personality who pioneered the practice of gently poking fun at the product being advertised, and whom Kubrick photographed on assignment in November 1948.

The above comments concern titles, that is, non-diegetic graphical elements within the film. Signs may be viewed as a clever attempt by the image to caption itself, to pre-empt the non-diegetic text with its own devices. Auteurists may be tempted to see this as an example of Kubrick defending the artistic integrity of his photographs, before insensitive picture editors and layout designers have a chance to ruin his work. In fact, photojournalists have always been encouraged to include signs, plaques, posters and other written words within the frame in order to comment, sympathetically or ironically, on the represented action. Kubrick seized this principle earlier than most, considering that he was 16 when *Look* published his first photograph, the famous portrait of the newspaper vendor in Brooklyn on the day after Roosevelt's death, which is based on the interaction between newspaper titles and a human face. Kubrick bookended his career by including a scene in his last film, *Eyes Wide Shut,* that shows Tom Cruise standing in front of another New York City newspaper vendor, buying a tabloid with the headline "Lucky To Be Alive" that comments on his character's predicament (Schaesberg, 243). Cruise is situated where a teenage Kubrick might have stood half a century earlier, allowing us to step back and witness this primal scene, the birth of the artist (Castle, 260).

Diegetic signs feature quite prominently in several Kubrick films, mostly for satirical purposes. For instance, when Humbert picks up Lolita at summer camp, he approaches a sign announcing "Camp Climax for Girls Drive Carefully." Several characters in both *Lolita* and *Dr. Strangelove* have explicitly humorous names, and some of them appear as name tags or desk nameplates, such as hotel night manager George Swine or General Jack D. Ripper. Ironic posters concerning the military are also highlighted in *Dr. Strangelove* and *Full Metal Jacket,* including the Strategic Air Command motto "Peace Is Our Profession" and a sarcastic

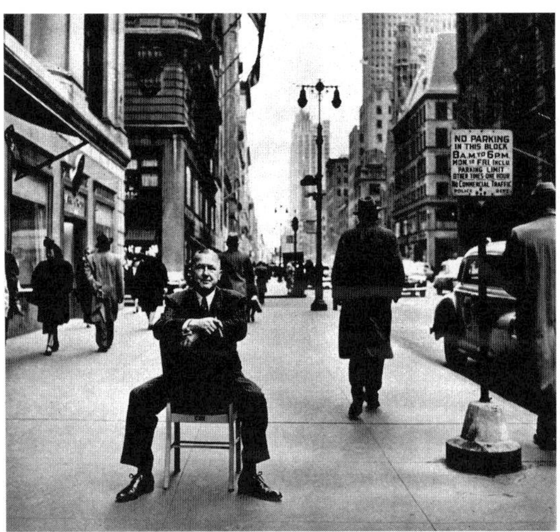

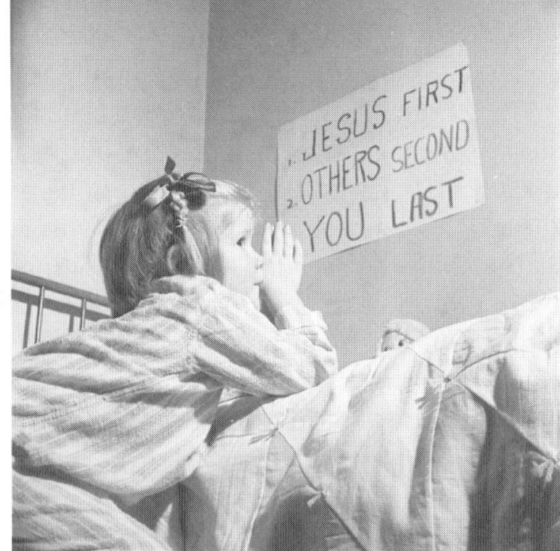

Figure 55: Signs as commentary in "New York – World Art Center" (June 1948) and "Orphanage Story" (January 1947, unpublished).

banner in the Marines media room reading: "First to go last to know. We will defend to the death our right to be misinformed." Warning signs immediately relevant to the plot may be observed in *Killer's Kiss* and *Eyes Wide Shut*, when Gloria walks down the stairway from the dancehall past the sign "watch your step," and Bill Harford notices a man following him, who stands conspicuously next to a stop sign (Castle, 260). We are reminded of Kubrick's portrait of German expressionist painter George Grosz straddling a chair on a Fifth Avenue sidewalk next to a "no parking" sign (Crone 2005, 239). Also, a series of photographs from an unpublished assignment concerning an orphanage in Lake Bluff, Illinois (January 1947), shows a small girl saying her prayers at bedtime (cf. Figure 55), under an authoritative sign dictating whom one should pray for: "Jesus first, others second, you last."

Ironic sound/image relationships

While didactic narration is technically non-diegetic, there are also instances of diegetic sound, including sound effects, dialogue and mental subjectivity, that reflect the photojournalistic tendency to create meaning thanks to a productive tension between its two channels of information, images and text. Even though the narrator in *Flying Padre* is non-diegetic, meaning also arises from an ironic juxtaposition with the image, rather than being an unambiguous statement in the didactic style of narration. We are told that Father Fred raises canaries and is a crack shot, and that he likes to hunt deer and other game. One may recognize Kubrick's trademark impish sense of humour, nurtured at *Look* magazine, by placing Father Fred behind bars while his canaries fly in the foreground, and making it appear as if he were going to shoot his own birds by editing the images together. The ironic contrast between the subject's profession and his hobbies may also be noticed in *Look* colleague John Vachon's "Country Preacher" (June 21, 1949), where the quiet and reserved Reverend Cagwin is shown hunting squirrels. He aims a rifle skyward, perhaps at a tree off-frame infested by the arboreal rodents, setting a good example for his ten-year-old son who stands next to him and watches with interest. Humour also appears in *The Seafarers* when Kubrick's camera visits the SIU building's art gallery, and the narrator confidently asserts that union members "take a look at works of art by fellow seafarers, carvings and paintings done aboard ship, some good enough for any gallery." The narration's encouraging art criticism comes across as cheeky when Kubrick includes two female nudes, which echo an earlier nudie pin-up calendar photograph used as a satirical introduction to the SIU barbershop.

Flying Padre ends with perhaps the most traditional photographic genre, the camera pose, combined with a backward dolly shot and an ironic juxtaposition of image and narration not unknown to photojournalism. As the priest poses proudly and the camera dollies away from him, the voice-over narrator concludes by stating: "There's no brass band here, no cheering crowds, no newspapermen clamouring for a headline, just an ambulance driver, an anxious mother, a sick baby and their priest. At the hospital, the baby will be treated and nursed back to health. And that, really, is the only reward ever asked of *The Spirit of St. Joseph*'s flying padre." There is a discrepancy between the priest's humility as described by the narrator, and the pride he expresses visually in Kubrick's mise-en-scène. This underscores the ironic claim regarding the absence of newspapermen, as we watch a Radio-Keith-Orpheum (RKO) newsreel on Father Stadtmueller, produced by former journalist Kubrick. Similarly, cheerful images in *Day of the Fight* of Walter Cartier playing with "his" dog contrast with the voice-over narrator's characterization of the boxer's devastating knock-out punch. We might be tempted to attribute such discrepancies to the auteur filmmaker's playful critique of mainstream documentary form, unless we also consider the fact noted by *Life* magazine scholar Wendy Kozol, for instance, that ideological contradictions were a common feature of text-image relationships in photojournalism (Kozol, 5). The *Flying Padre*'s narration may provide a fairly traditional and conforming portrait, but the ambiguous, polysemic quality of images may resist, to a certain extent, the soundtrack's attempt to impose specific meanings.

Ironic sound-image relationships in Kubrick's fiction films come in different flavours, according to their tone as well as the type of sound that is mobilized. During Dave Bowman's extravehicular activity in *2001: A Space Odyssey*, all we hear is the constant sound of the astronaut breathing in his spacesuit. The sound's volume remains the same, as if we were in close proximity to the action. We then cut to a noticeably distant perspective, an extreme long shot of the spaceship, while a few meteors drift by in the foreground, with no change on the soundtrack. This discrepancy between the image scale and the sound scale creates a sense of estrangement characteristic of the science-fiction genre, one which reminds us that sound scale is meaningless in the vacuum of space, and that in astronomical terms, the meteors depicted in this shot narrowly missed colliding with Discovery. A different example of sound effects either clashing with or forcing us to reinterpret the image may be heard in *The Shining*, when Jack has been locked up in the hotel pantry. Jack suddenly hears the voice of Delbert Grady, whom he had "met" in an earlier scene, a voice we assume to be imaginary, a product of Jack's deranged mind. We are then made to hear the sound of the door's lock being opened, shortly after which Jack is seen outside the pantry, pursuing Danny. The viewer is hard-pressed to explain this occurrence other than in supernatural terms, in keeping with Tzvetan Todorov's definition of the fantastic, characterized as "that hesitation experienced by a person who knows only the laws of nature, confronting an apparently supernatural event" (25). The off-screen voice of Grady and the sound of the door being unlocked gain a diegetic reality, which can be compared to the photojournalistic way in which a caption imposes its interpretation of an image.

A narratologically objective combination of sound and image, which nonetheless achieves a degree of surrealism, is the last scene from *Full Metal Jacket*, in which soldiers march past burning buildings in war-torn Vietnam by night, singing the Mickey Mouse Club song. It is a subversive recontextualization of a children's song comparable to Alex's use of "Singin' in the Rain" in *A Clockwork Orange*. More straightforward is Lieutenant Corby in *Fear and Desire* philosophizing about the insanity of war over a montage of dead enemy soldiers. It represents a poetic pause in the plot, which is patently journalistic in the way images illustrate a running commentary, sometimes ironically. A remarkable scene in *Spartacus* reveals Kubrick's ability at applying such photojournalistic devices to the historical epic genre.

Tony Curtis' character Antoninus recites a poem around a campfire, a nostalgic song about returning home, which is accompanied by a montage of images showing slave-camp family life during the day. While atypically sentimental for Kubrick, this sequence demonstrates a skilful use of expressive documentary techniques, unusual for a mainstream Hollywood genre film of the period. The use of a subjective acoustic flashback as counterpoint to the image provides *Eyes Wide Shut* with an ironic illustration of the theme of duality. Alice Harford is helping her daughter with school homework at the breakfast table, while Bill looks at his wife, mentally replaying her earlier confession about an adulterous dream. She smiles back at him in a medium close-up, creating a striking contrast between the caring mother and the sexually adventurous woman. Bill responds to Alice's smile in kind, but he has obviously been challenged to rethink his assumptions about married life.

Journalistic themes/tropes

In an article dealing with art historical allusions in *Barry Lyndon*, Ralf Michael Fischer itemizes different forms of intertextuality in the films of Stanley Kubrick, ranging from cross-references within films to general references to cultural history, although the numerous allusions to photojournalism and Kubrick's own work at *Look* magazine are missing from this list (170). If Kubrick is indeed "a director of the *déjà vu* and the *déjà lu*," then an examination of specific thematic and iconographic sources within the pages of *Look* is in order, particularly when we consider that Kubrick had personally kept many issues of *Look* as well as multiple copies of individual photo-essays, now available at the Kubrick Archives at the University of the Arts, London (Fischer, 171).

One of the most enduring conventions in magazine journalism is the cover girl, that is, a portrait of a female model on the publication's front cover, a practice ostensibly designed to satisfy the male editors' cheesecake quota. Kubrick produced three magazine covers during his tenure at *Look*, including a female talk-show host (August 15, 1950), and a young model (July 18, 1950). The model was Betsy Von Fürstenberg (cf. Figure 56), an aspiring actress whose cover picture shows her wearing a broad-rimmed hat similar to Lolita's, in the famous backyard scene when Humbert first sees Dolores Haze (Phillips 1975, 91). Betsy's photo-essay also highlights her legs in a backlit shot of her sitting on a windowsill, not unlike Lolita who stretches out her legs in front of the window when she visits Humbert in his study. One gets the sense that Kubrick was tapping into his *Look* magazine iconography, a personal reservoir of visual tropes that had proven their effectiveness to a readership of millions across North America. Kubrick's first cover, featuring a little boy playing in his bathtub (August 5, 1947), reminds us of another established photojournalistic trope, the "cute" factor, which includes animals and children. There is a minute-long sequence in *Flying Padre* in which Father Stadtmueller settles a dispute between two children in his parish village, which thematically falls under the human interest or cute category, which can be seen in *Look* colleague John Vachon's similar photo-essay "Country Preacher," about a clergyman whose "most important

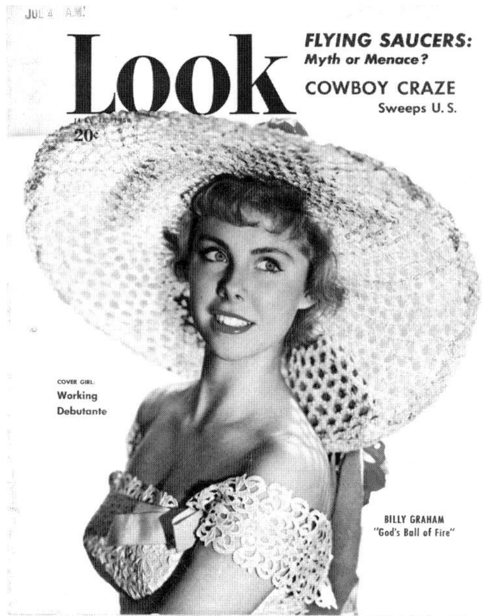

Figure 56: The broad-rimmed hat worn by Betsy Von Fürstenberg (1950).

job is work among young." *Eyes Wide Shut* includes the Harford's young daughter Helena, whose parents bring her to Macy's for Christmas shopping, unlike Kubrick's daughter Vivian in *2001: A Space Odyssey*, who had requested a bush baby. Admittedly, the Harfords are preoccupied with their adult problems, but they do not seem particularly interested in the toy department, which recalls the last picture in Kubrick's essay "The 5 and 10" (September 2, 1947), about a discount department store. A little girl wearing earmuffs and a cute hat looks around excitedly, while an older man, perhaps her grandfather, smokes a cigar and holds on to a balloon, visibly bored. Helena Harford then stands in front of a Barbie doll display, much like another little girl from an unpublished Kubrick photograph about "Sparkle Plenty" dolls from the Dick Tracy comic strip (added to *Look*'s library on July 29, 1947). Kubrick's photo-essay "A Dog's Life in the Big City" (November 8, 1949) includes an amusing profile of two dogs looking at each other nose-to-nose, a great Dane and a miniature pinscher. A similar profile is repeated in *Day of the Fight*, when boxer Walter Cartier is shown playing with his dog, and in *Fear and Desire*, when the enemy General talks to his dog Proteus.

Among the few Kodachrome colour photographs Kubrick took for *Look* was the portrait of a clown, included as an inset picture on the cover of the magazine's May 25, 1948, issue. The portrait was part of the circus story assignment, concerning the Ringling Brothers – Barnum & Bailey Circus. It is possible that Kubrick may already have been thinking in terms of the symbolic meanings of masks and the aesthetics of the grotesque discussed by James Naremore, since it reappeared as Johnny's clown mask from *The Killing*, disguises worn by the Droogs in *A Clockwork Orange* and "the ghostly figure who performs fellatio while wearing a pig mask in *The Shining*" (34). Perhaps more striking is a participant at the first Philadelphia Beaux-Arts Ball, who wore a cubist mask with a single oversized eye, captured by Kubrick and printed full-page in the September 13, 1949 issue of *Look*. This striking image is echoed in the brief montage of expressionist masks featured in *Eyes Wide Shut*, when Bill Harford manages to infiltrate an exclusive "party" at the Somerton mansion (cf. Figure 16). Related to the grotesque, arguably, are unpublished photographs produced for the Chicago story (April 12, 1949), which include a woman simultaneously smoking and modelling a girdle and a strapless bra, anticipating Alice Harford grilling her husband in her underwear while smoking pot in *Eyes Wide Shut* (Crone 2005, 37). The image of the woman smoking in her undergarments seems slightly funny and threatening at the same time, providing something of the shock value or tension that relates to the grotesque, in its combination of conflicting emotions such as laughter and fear (Naremore, 27). Another instance of the grotesque identified by Naremore is "the female statuary or 'furnishings' of the Korova Milk Bar in *A Clockwork Orange*" (34). While this erotic furniture may have been inspired by Allen Jones' installation art titled *Table, Chair and Hatstand* (1969), consisting of female mannequins wearing black stockings and undergarments, a more relevant source for our argument is an unpublished photograph by Kubrick's colleague Bob Sandberg, for a profile on surrealist artist Salvador Dalí, which appeared in the June 10, 1947 issue of *Look* (Lindgaard, 40). The photograph in question "captures a performance staged for *Look* in which a bizarre office environment is equipped with a water cooler, a telephone, and a human desk" (Albrecht, 30). The human desk, on which Dalí is writing, is a woman in her underwear bending her body backwards in order to offer her torso as a desk and use her four limbs as the table's legs, an awkward position which is also similar to the creepy "spider-walk" scene from the 2000 re-release of William Friedkin's *The Exorcist* (1973).

Sports is a perennial favourite topic in photojournalism, and Kubrick demonstrated his talent in producing profiles of two boxers in particular, Walter Cartier from Greenwich Village and the famous middleweight Rocky Graziano. Success with this topic spilled over into his career as a filmmaker, which included a number of boxing matches and images inspired by his *Look* photo-essays. For instance, good photo opportunities present themselves in the corner of the ring between rounds, since the fighters must stay put and regroup, with help from their trainers. This stage in a boxing match has been captured several times by Kubrick, including virtually identical compositions in "Prizefighter" and *Killer's Kiss*.

The topic of photojournalism itself could be an opportunity for publications to show off their employees' hard work and enhance their credibility with behind-the-scenes features. Kubrick's February 28, 1950 essay about author Emily Kimbrough on the women's club lecture tour shows the popular writer being interviewed by KRNT radio commentator Betty Wells and photographed by Des Moines *Tribune* journalist Ruth Hughes. Kubrick's name appears in the credits under the radio interview picture. His role as photographer is taken up by the reflexive shot of colleague Hughes, who happens to work for *Look* magazine's parent publication in Des Moines. The Library of Congress archives reveal that during this assignment, Kubrick took three photographs of himself in the mirror (Crone 2005, 4).

Another reflexive exercise that allowed Kubrick to consider his own position as a junior photojournalist was published in the September 27, 1949 issue of *Look*. "Teen-Age Columnist" featured 19-year-old journalist Pat White, the author of a successful teenage column in a New Jersey newspaper. The five photographs show Pat on the job, engaged in the various aspects of her duties as a reporter, including the essay's second picture, in which Pat lies in bed in her pyjamas, answering reader mail on a typewriter. She appears to give Kubrick a knowing smile, perhaps because he allowed her to borrow his camera and, in a role reversal, take unpublished and slightly out-of-focus pictures of the 21-year-old photojournalist. Kubrick included allusions to photography and journalism in his films on several occasions, including images depicting the newsroom of the *Seafarers Log* in *The Seafarers* and the *Stars and Stripes* in *Full Metal Jacket*. Although trained as a Marine, Joker is a war correspondent, and travels with his photographer Rafterman, not unlike Kubrick himself and a writer from *Look*, on assignment in the late forties. A documentary film crew records interviews with Joker's platoon in Hue City, in a series of brief medium close-up shots of the soldiers expressing their thoughts about their role in Vietnam. The formal interviews contrast with the rest of the mise-en-scène in the film's second half, highlighting the mediated nature of the imagery and a sense that the war is being packaged and edited for viewers in the United States. This set-up is reminiscent of *Look* magazine's "Meet the People" feature, consisting exclusively of medium close-ups and captioned quotes from the subjects.

This chapter has sought to illustrate the extent to which Kubrick's style as a filmmaker remained indebted to his training at *Look* magazine, both in terms of a photographic mise-en-scène involving deep focus, natural lighting and symmetrical compositions, as well as rhetorical journalistic practices designed to enhance the realism and believability of the material presented to the viewer. Kubrick's profile of New York cartoonist Peter Arno may further illustrate how the *Look* assignments had an enduring impact on the form and content of his later work as a filmmaker, including *Lolita* and *Eyes Wide Shut*. Peter Arno was an artist who used the tools of popular culture, specifically cartoons, in order to satirize New York aristocracy. "Sophisticated Cartoonist" is the oxymoronic title of an article by *Look* staff writer Patricia Coffin, which appeared in the September 27, 1949 issue of *Look*. Kubrick would presumably feel right at home photographing an artist who seemed to embrace contradiction. Educated at Yale, Arno's cartoons helped to define the *New Yorker* magazine's style of humour. Coffin's article hints at Arno's inner contradictions by suggesting that he was, in a sense, trapped by his own blue-blood upbringing. The son of a Supreme Court Justice in New York City, Arno had sophisticated tastes, and regularly indulged in the high class party scene. It is claimed that he also despised its hypocrisy, which found its way in his caustic brand of cartoon caricature.

Kubrick's photographs capture the middle-aged man's paradoxical personality, showing him alternately dishevelled and slick. The photo-essay's opening page shows Arno at the piano in his Park Avenue apartment, wearing an unbuttoned shirt and with a cigarette holder in his mouth. The shirt disappears in the second page's photograph of Arno doodling in bed, with newspapers scattered all over the sheets. He almost looks like Montgomery Clift's gag of the lonely drunken bachelor, and the antithesis of the polished Leonard Bernstein, two other artists photographed by Kubrick. Arno's apartment floor is littered with sketches on the article's third page, which features a full-page photograph of the cartoonist giving instructions to a nude model for a series of sketches. The model is standing with her back to the camera, a relatively risqué picture for the period which apparently caused *Look* magazine to lose a contract with Campbell's Soup, and is visually similar to Nicole Kidman's opening nude shot in *Eyes Wide Shut* (Cowles, 113).

Lest we should think Arno doesn't know how to dress, the photo-essay's concluding spread reveals that he does wear a tux when he goes on a date. The twice divorced man of 45, whose own daughter is 20, has dinner with 21-year-old actress Joan Sinclair, and the caption informs us that the artist dates "fresh, unspoiled girls." The article does mention the cartoonist's reputation as a wolf, and given the age difference, one cannot help but think of Humbert's relationship with Lolita. It is also intriguing to consider the spread in oedipal terms, since Kubrick was the same age as Ms. Sinclair, and Arno was old enough to be their father. The extent to which this concluding spread supports the essay's characterization of Arno as "sophisticated" is up for debate, which either highlights the importance of considering the argument in its historical context, or else provides us with another ambiguous text to feed Kubrick's view of the relationship between men and women.

Film critic Robert Koehler has argued that Kubrick's films are "docu-fictions" that exhibit "the documentarian's observational advantages of distance, commentary and overview, and the techniques to make an audience see things his way" (24). We not only find that Kubrick's photographic style and themes are inspired by his magazine assignments, but his much touted aesthetics of contingency or the grotesque are always based on the conviction that departures from a naturalistic base are effective or compelling only to the degree that the realistic grounding is factually solid and strictly believable. This is perhaps most clearly illustrated by *2001: A Space Odyssey*, a film exemplifying the science-fiction genre's intersection between fantasy and realism, that is, an estranged world based on logical and scientific extrapolations from a contemporary state of affairs. When BBC reporter Martin Aymer interviews HAL, we are shown an image of the computer's red eye framed by eight video monitors, four on each side. Aymer occupies one of the monitors, speaking to the viewer in a direct mode of address, until he turns slightly to his left for the interview with HAL, in typical TV news fashion. The image of the video monitors reminds us of a photomagazine layout, with the reporter looking in HAL's direction, his eyeline facing "in" the page, while the computer's eye is situated in the gutter. This example underscores the intertextual and specifically photojournalistic dimension of Kubrick's cinema.

Note

1   There are two versions of *Day of the Fight*, running 12 and 16 minutes respectively. The shorter version skips the opening four minutes, described by biographer LoBrutto as "a tabloid history of boxing," and includes minor variations in the voice-over narration (LoBrutto, 64).

Conclusion

It should no longer be possible to think of Stanley Kubrick without including *Look* magazine, if we are to uncover the photojournalistic pattern underlying Kubrick's filmic oeuvre. While the 16-year-old shutterbug had already displayed a penchant for storytelling in his portrait of the neighbourhood newspaper vendor, the discipline required of *Look* photojournalists to seek out visual story material, aided by a shooting script and prompted by a staff writer, would certainly enhance Kubrick's skills as a photographic narrator. In addition, the ever-present opportunity, over a five-year period, to contribute to the production of photo-essays at the preview stage, once the layout was completed, would further cement the photographer's appreciation for the relationship between images and text. It has also been argued that the photo-essay can be understood as a hybrid form that tapped into the widespread popularity of the movies, by pushing photography to represent unfolding events via image sequences. It should then come as no surprise that Kubrick's mastery of photojournalism, thanks to *Look* magazine, would entice the ambitious young man to consider transferring his skills to a closely related and more glamourous medium, the cinema.

In summary, how did *Look* magazine determine Stanley Kubrick's later development as a filmmaker? While Kubrick may not have been a model student in high school, his enthusiasm for the arts and his ability at absorbing new information quickly, coupled with the length and timing of his tenure at *Look*, during the formative years of young adulthood, made him particularly susceptible to being influenced in a positive way by the professional environment at the New York–based photomagazine. Kubrick's developing identity and worldview as an expressive person during the late forties and early fifties were the result of a patchwork of influences, many of which can be directly attributed to *Look* magazine, particularly as it affected the budding filmmaker's acquisition of professional skills and aesthetic values. This was enhanced by the magazine's relatively collaborative approach to photo-essay production, in addition to its informal mentorship of Kubrick during the first two years at least of his career at *Look*. The magazine's method of group or team-journalism provided ongoing opportunities for Kubrick to learn every aspect of the photo-essay production process from seasoned professionals, which was not limited to following work guidelines but also included the freedom to explore one's creativity in response to unfolding story situations. Moreover, photographers were expected to internalize *Look*'s norms and values as regards the practice of "personal journalism," which included narrative, documentary and "human interest" qualities that would directly inform Kubrick's future film aesthetic. Kubrick himself has acknowledged that *Look* was his default film school, and his steadfast commitment to photographic realism in film, as a minimal guarantor of viewer identification, confirms his indebtedness to a prevailing aesthetic in the thirties and forties that finds its roots in the work of FSA photographers, including *Look*'s long-time director of photography, Arthur Rothstein.

From a generic perspective, it has further been argued that Kubrick picked up his tendency to produce slightly unusual or striking images not from art photography, but from photomagazine journalism's need to inform and entertain its readership, which resulted in a creative balance between candid and staged representations. His training at *Look* thus influenced his adoption of a viewer-friendly film language that still allowed for poetic licence in the form of occasional moments of unconventional style. Such training was never limited to the technique of photography but included a number of relevant editing and storytelling skills, made necessary by the photo-essay's position as a transitional form between still photography and film. Photojournalism's formal and stylistic systems also reveal a number of transmedial equivalences that provided Kubrick with skills that could be applied to the cinema, such as the narrative dimensions of *Look*'s "personal journalism." Other factors included a realistic obsession with sharp focus and composition in depth, as well as the magazine equivalents to Kubrickian long takes, namely photo-series and the large picture, which implies a longer viewing time. A close textual analysis of Kubrick's films confirms the enduring presence of *Look*'s photojournalistic methods, as well as a number of formal and stylistic practices which reveal a photographer's training. Among these we can mention extreme camera angles, symmetrical framings, naturalistic lighting and didactic montage sequences, all of which contributed to establishing Kubrick's *Look* iconography.

This book's proposed method of analysis may also prove useful in examining the works of other photographer-filmmakers, such as Ken Russell, Howard Zieff, Dick Richards, Jerry Schatzberg and Gordon Parks (Monaco, 85). Even though their work appeared in post-war era illustrated magazines and they were all directing films by the 1970s, there are considerable differences between these photographers. Some were freelance documentarians (Russell), while others specialized in advertisements (Zieff) or fashion (Schatzberg). Parks was a regular photographer for *Life* magazine, not unlike Kubrick, but was the only African American on staff, and was in his fifties when he directed his first film. Given these differences, the parallels are perhaps even more striking. Focusing on Schatzberg, Kubrick and Parks, we may note that both Kubrick and Parks started making short documentary films based on their most popular photo-essays: in Kubrick's case it was "The Prizefighter," and Parks used his 1961 article about a destitute child from the slums of Rio, Flavio de Silva (*Flavio*, 1964). Parks and Schatzberg's first feature-length films dealt with topics inspired by their own personal experiences. In Schatzberg's case it was the story of a photographer making a film about the unhappy life of a fashion model (*Puzzle of a Downfall Child*, 1970), while Parks was encouraged by John Cassavetes to adapt his semi-autobiographical novel as a feature film, *The Learning Tree*, which was released in 1969 (Parks, 252). The critical response to *The Learning Tree* was the same as for Kubrick's first feature, *Fear and Desire*, combining praise for the film's polished cinematography and concern for the awkward and undramatic acting. Despite the argument that "it was [Schatzberg's] portrait photography that taught him how to deal with actors," *Puzzle of a Downfall Child* was widely considered to be a visually attractive film hampered by a clichéd script (Ciment, "Jerry Schatzberg Biography"). Such failings appear to confirm John Grierson's infamous phrase (originally aimed at Josef von Sternberg), claiming that "when a director dies, he becomes a photographer," although it may be more accurate to suggest that the three aforementioned films were rookie efforts revealing both their directors' background and growing skills. Parks' follow-up directorial project was *Shaft!* (1971), a film that includes some gritty New York City Street scenes comparable to Kubrick's second feature, *Killer's Kiss*. Schatzberg, who grew up near Kubrick's former High School in the South Bronx, also situated his second feature film in the unforgiving urban environment of Manhattan, in *The Panic at Needle Park* (1971).

The influences of 1930s documentary photography and film, as well as photomagazine-based codes of realism, manifest themselves differently for the three filmmakers. Before joining *Life* magazine, Parks was trained by Roy Stryker, when the FSA photography project was taken over by the Office of War Information in 1943 (Parks, 66). We have already seen that Kubrick was supervised by, and worked with, FSA alumni Arthur Rothstein and John Vachon at *Look* magazine. Although Schatzberg learned his craft as fashion photographer Bill Helburn's assistant in the mid-fifties, Helburn had been an Air Corps photographer and was thus well versed in the realist school of war photography (Loke). Schatzberg also did a lot of reportage and street photography, alongside his more commercial work in fashion and portraiture (Ciment 1982, 38–55). He deliberately employed a candid camera documentary style through his use of telephoto lenses for the film *The Panic at Needle Park*, in addition to the story being based on a series of *Life* magazine essays written by James Mills (Ciment 1982, 114–6). Similar observations apply to the influence of photomagazine aesthetics on the photographic and filmic work of Parks, Schatzberg and Kubrick. Philip Brookman, Curator at the Corcoran Gallery of Art (Washington D.C.), has argued that Gordon Parks was a photographic storyteller who brought to his film career an intimate knowledge of visual narrative as well as "photographic truth and fiction," which would include the respective benefits of candid and staged imagery (352). Michel Ciment has described Jerry Schatzberg's aesthetic approach as simple and direct, reminiscent of the dominant photojournalistic quest for simplicity in expression, an artistic version of Occam's razor (1982, 96). Schatzberg's style is also deemed to be less cerebral and satirical than Kubrick's, yet closer to *Look* magazine's ideal of personal journalism, ironically, without being sentimental (Ciment 1982, 101).

It is argued that "in more than forty years of photography and cinema, Schatzberg has achieved a delicate balance between [a] refined form of mise-en-scène and the rendering of true moments," yet another way of characterizing an intermediate position between stylization and pure journalism, the staged and the candid, the personal and the documentary (Ciment, "Jerry Schatzberg Biography"). Similar descriptions of Kubrickian aesthetics underscore the notion that photojournalism, in addition to being a kind of interstitial medium situated halfway between photography and film, broadly combined pre-war documentary realism with post-war modernist expression, an idea articulated in the art photography milieu by Keith F. Davis, Curator of Photography at the Nelson-Atkins Museum of Art (Kansas City, Missouri). Writing about the recently "rediscovered" work of Homer Page, who spent a year in 1949–50 as a Guggenheim Fellow capturing New York City street scenes, Davis makes the bold claim that this work represents nothing less than "a key missing link between two great eras of American photography: the humanistic, social-documentary vision of the Farm Security Administration and the Photo League of the 1930s and 1940s, and the more subjective, poetic, and expressionistic approach of a younger generation of 1950s street photographers. In essence, Page provides a previously unrecognized bridge between the artistic worlds of Dorothea Lange and Robert Frank" (7).

One could argue, as I have, that part of this "missing link" may be found in the pages of popular photomagazines, and that the photo-essay was a mainstream expression of this transitional period in American photography. The men and women working for *Life* and *Look* were not only graduates of the FSA school or inheritors of its philosophy, but also sensitive to the evolution of their medium, and intimately aware of new developments in photography as creative self-expression. At *Look* magazine, Arthur Rothstein was developing his darkroom acumen (pun intended), Frank Bauman was experimenting with strobe lights, editor Fleur Cowles was redefining the magazine format, and a young Stanley Kubrick was taking it all in and refining his craft at the same time. While Davis singles out Homer Page as a pivotal figure, he also points out that Page did not operate in a vacuum, and lists 16 influential photographers who worked in New York City circa 1950 and provided a context for Page's own contributions, although magazine photography is not mentioned (33). The case of Stanley Kubrick should make it equally clear that neither creative individuals nor photographic genres function in a vacuum. The success of photojournalism was due to its hybrid nature, to the fact that it was never limited to strictly functional reportage, but combined the ideals of the documentary project as well as the popular pleasures of storytelling and even the loftier pursuits of artistic self-expression. Similarly, art photography was never practised in an ivory tower, and cannot be fully understood apart from a rich visual culture that includes less prestigious media such as film and illustrated magazines. An exhibition held in 2007 at the Cinémathèque Française, titled "The Image to Come: How Cinema Inspires Photographers," reminds us of a constant process of cross-fertilization between media from seemingly different social strata, suggesting that genre-mixing in the twentieth century had become the norm, not the exception (Toubiana, 11).

Intermedial hybridity is apparent in one of Kubrick's first assignments, during his street-photography apprenticeship period, published in *Look* as "While Mama Shops," on March 18, 1947. The opening picture shows a young boy leaning against his younger sister's pram in order to read the latest adventures of *Superman*, while the little girl tries to occupy herself inside the carriage. One wonders whether Kubrick could identify with these children, since he not only grew up with a younger sister (Barbara), but is also likely to have enjoyed reading comic books at an early age. This specific boyhood interest in comic books suggests another relevant influence on Kubrick's development as a visual storyteller. The layout of comic strips is closely related to photo-essay spreads, a point which is highlighted in an advertisement for the RKO film *The Farmer's Daughter* (1946, H.C. Potter), next to the picture of the boy reading *Superman*. The ad uses a comic strip to summarize part of the plot, mirroring the spread of photographs on the opposite page which, in a mise-en-abyme, includes the aforementioned comic book. Moreover, Stanley Kubrick's assistant from 1965 to 1999, Anthony Frewin, informs us that Kubrick's "childhood reading in the 1930s was largely limited to the 'pulps' – the popular newsstand magazines of the 1930s such as *Amazing Stories*, *Astounding Stories* (both science fiction), *The Shadow* (detective), *G-8 and His Battle Aces* (spying, aerial combat), *Weird Tales* (occult, supernatural), and similar. . . . These magazines had a great influence on him and sixty years later he could still effortlessly quote phrases and recount story lines. SK thought that while the characterization was deplorable the narrative plotting was, by and large, exemplary" (Castle, 514). While these pulps were not comics, there were comic book versions of *The Shadow* and no doubt other titles whose use of "sequential art" would have provided Kubrick with an "instinctive" sense of how to edit images in a two-page spread.

While this book has focused on the social context of discourse, in methodological terms, it remains an auteurist study from its examination of the label "photographed or directed by Stanley Kubrick," recognizing a biographical person's creative output as the generic criterion. Referring to an author as a means of identifying the cause of discourse in texts is always only an option, given the reality of other sources of meaning, including economic, social, cultural, political and psychological ones. Moreover, as film scholar Janet Staiger usefully reminds us, there exist different theories of authorship, including approaches that avoid "the problem of causality for the *production*" of the text, by displacing the source of meaning to the reader or to a wider "site of discourses" (46). For instance, we find within auteurism significant differences of emphasis in terms of social theory, depending on one's views regarding the relative importance (or value) of individual agency versus structural determinations. One might assume that a balanced perspective would situate the analysis of personal creative work within the context of institutional and ideological influences, acknowledging the extent to which individuals can express themselves and communicate meaningfully with others by reflecting the impact of their historical and cultural upbringing. Critics often only pay lip service to such a perspective, as they tend to state their case in a polarized fashion, either favouring the creative artist's personality or the "genius of the system." For instance, Kubrick scholar Mario Falsetto explains: "I am not claiming that Kubrick is the only creative artist with significant input into the final film. I am arguing instead that Kubrick's overall contribution is the most significant and that his creative input essentially guides the other contributions" (169). Thus, significant influences or contributions from the social and historical context, including generic intertextuality and film or photo-essay production collaborators, are bracketed because they do not amount, even collectively, to the most significant contribution, according to this position. Perhaps the difference of emphasis here is not simply a matter of deciding what is more important in a text's production or its interpretation, but a reflection of alternative epistemologies. It may be the case that in order to conduct a more in-depth and thorough analysis of the authorial code, one should restrict the locus of meaning to a single person, that is, by adopting many of the assumptions of romantic aesthetics, basically those enumerated under Staiger's discussion of "authorship as *origin*" and "authorship as *personality*" (30–40). I have argued instead that, in addition to reflecting an artist's personality, acknowledging "authorship as a *sociology of production*" and as a "*site of discourses*" should gain in more adequately describing a complex socio-semiotic phenomenon, even though it broadens the scope of the study and thus represents a greater challenge. For example, adding generic concerns to our examination of Kubrickian authorship is a helpful way to link the production and reception ends of the communication chain, and the notion of "auteur-genre" usefully combines auteurism and genre, not unlike the "auteur as reading strategy" approach to authorship.

Beginning with magazine genres, we note that photojournalists such as Kubrick had to internalize the semantic conventions of personality profiles and social studies, as well as the syntactic categories of the photo-story and the photo-essay, all of which fed directly into the interpretive expectations of readers. These expectations also included the photomagazines' pragmatic mission to inform and entertain their readership, by adopting a realist aesthetic that allowed for formalist strategies, staged imagery supporting strictly candid photography. A closer examination of the photo-essay reveals a dual ontology positioning this genre as a transitional form linking documentary photography and fiction film, an ideal combination for a young professional seeking to apply his skills to one of the related media. Focusing more closely on a comparative analysis of photojournalism and film points to a range of formal and stylistic elements, which are either identical, or required a variety of transmedial equivalences in order for Kubrick to successfully complete his professional migration to the cinema. For instance, while the mobile frame is one of two key cinematic features absent from photography (the other is sound), it is germane to journalism's documentary and realist aesthetic and proves to be a friendly candidate for remediation. In contrast, directing actors appears to have been the most alien skill for a young photographer to acquire, due to acting's fundamentally fictional and performative natures. Finally, a detailed consideration of Kubrick's filmic output from a photographic angle leads us to argue and conclude that *Look*'s photojournalistic legacy is very much present and visible, and that the Kubrickian signature or aesthetic has inherited many stylistic and thematic features from post-war magazine photography. If Kubrick was ever to make the proverbial "bad" film, one would have to modify John Grierson's phrase to suggest that "when a director dies, he becomes a photojournalist."

Appendix

At the time of this writing (September 2012), photo-essays photographed by Stanley Kubrick are only available in back issues of *Look* magazine, which may be purchased from private collectors on Ebay and other sites. Regrettably, it has proven impractical to set up a companion website featuring scans of the essays analysed in this book, as originally envisioned, due to the complexity of the copyright situation. The following spreadsheet lists all *Look* magazine "jobs" assigned to Kubrick for which prints or negatives exist at the Museum of the City of New York (MCNY) and the Library of Congress (LOC) in Washington D.C., and jobs that only appear in print in *Look* magazine or are only included on the photographer's logbook at the LOC. Photographic archives of jobs concerning New York City were donated to the MCNY beginning in the fifties, and the rest was donated to the LOC shortly after *Look* magazine ceased publication in 1971. The archives for some jobs were split between the two institutions. For a few assignments, confirming the identity of a single photographer has proven impossible. The total number of photographs thus only represents the surviving and identifiable records. Recently discovered contact sheets at the Kubrick Archives in London (University of the Arts) indicate that approximately 2000 additional photographs belonging to the following eight jobs may be added to Kubrick's *Look* photographic corpus, pending further research: Chicago Story, 5 & 10, Naked City, Subway Story, Montgomery Clift, Walter Cartier, Rocky Graziano and Jazz Story. The total number of available photographs may then be closer to 27,000.

Look library	Published	Location	Look #	Job Title – Article	Prints
	1945/06/26			FDR Dead	1
	1945/10/16			Kids at a Ball Game	8
	1946/01/08			Psychoquiz: Are You a Fatalist?	1
	1946/04/02			Teacher Puts "Ham" in Hamlet	4
	1946/04/16			A Short-Short in a Movie Balcony	4
1946/04/11	1947/03/18	MCNY	10346	Children – When Mothers are Shopping	74
1946/04/11	1947/03/18	MCNY	11110	Shopping – What Children do When…	13
1946/04/16		MCNY	10343	Astor Hotel	12
1946/04/16	1946/06/11	MCNY	10345	Woman Trying on Hats	53
1946/04/17		MCNY	10344	Pigeons	11
1946/05/01		MCNY	10347	Park Benches – Love Is Everywhere	35
1946/05/13		MCNY	10358	Park Bench Nuisance – Bryant Park	7
1946/05/13		MCNY	10361 & 11717	Police Athletic League – Boxing	158
1946/05/15	1946/07/23			Meet the People: How Many Times… Propose?	5
1946/05/27	1946/08/20	MCNY	10323 & 11042	How People Look to Monkeys	117
1946/06/03	1946/10/01	LOC & MCNY	46-605 & 10322	Dentist Office Story	152
1946/06/07	1946/09/17			Psychoquiz: Do You Have Imaginary Illnesses?	1
1946/06/11	1946/09/17			Meet the People: What… Childhood Ambition?	10
1946/06/18	1947/06/24	MCNY	11294	Palisades Amusement Park	420
1946/07/08		Logbook	693	John Vislocky, High Jumper COLOR	
1946/07/16		MCNY	10336	Street Fight	35
1946/07/30		Logbook	2561	People Are Superstitious	
1946/08/21		Logbook	2586	Meet the People: … Men Who Use Cologne?	

1946/08/23	1946/11/26	MCNY	10296 & 11078	Street Conversations & Bronx Street Scene	320
1946/08/27	1946/11/26	MCNY	10334	Johnny Grant's Adventures	59
1946/08/30	1946/11/26			Meet the People: "Spend $1000 in a Week?"	4
	1946/09/03			Photoquiz: "Buy Victory Bonds" sign.	1
1946/09/11		Logbook	2620	Billboard	
1946/09/12		MCNY	10303	People Mugging	116
1946/09/12		Logbook	2622	Photoquiz – Typewriter	
1946/09/18		Logbook	2637	Cheer Leader Story	
1946/09/25	1947/03/04	MCNY	10292 & 11107	Subway Story	515
1946/09/25		Logbook	3010	*LOOK* employees: Mort Hunt and Barbara Kornfeld	
1946/09/26		Logbook	2656	*LOOK* Christmas Cover COLOR	
1946/10/21	1947/01/07			Meet the People: See America? Sobotka, Perveller	6
1946/10/23	1947/01/07	MCNY	11287	Television Show	35
1946/10/23	1947/01/07	MCNY	11093	Television Studio	1
1946/10/25	1946/12/10	MCNY	11068 & 11069	Meet the People: Harold Shaw & Nevin De Turk	2
1946/10/28	1947/03/18			Meet the People: Favorite Way of Loafing?	2
1946/11/01		Logbook	2723	Photoquiz – Pad and Pencil	
1946/11/19		LOC	46-2744	Shadow Story	14
1946/12/11		Logbook	2786	Meet the People: What Do You Carry in Your Purse?	
1946/12/11	1947/03/04	LOC	46-1016	How to Spot Communist: Foundations of Leninism.	1
1946/12/16		Logbook	2789	Radio Warming Up Story	
1946/12/17		Logbook	2792	Meet the People: Why... Decide to Get Married?	
1946/12/18		Logbook	2794	Kids Talking to Santa Claus COLOR	
1946/12/20		Logbook	2804	Psychoquiz	
1946/12/20		Logbook	2805	Cargo Story (Airplane)	
1947/01/07	1947/03/18	LOC	47-1051	Photocrime: Perry Mason: "Cobb Reasons It Out"	3

	1947/01/07			Psychoquiz: Distracted Couple Watching Movie	1
1947/01/20	1947/03/18	LOC	47-1092	Baby vs. Athlete	142
1947/01/20		LOC & MCNY	47-2850 & 11166	Orphanage Story, Lake Bluff, Illinois	265
	1947/01/21			Photoquiz: CU Jaguar Growling.	1
1947/01/28		Logbook	2878	Photoquiz – Card Hand	
1947/01/28		Logbook	2880	*LOOK* Book: Abe Lincoln	
1947/02/03		Logbook	2889	People in an Art Gallery	
1947/02/04	1947/05/27		2893	Furniture for Photoquiz	5
1947/02/13	1947/05/13	LOC	47-1139	War Orphans: Meet the People: Worst Experience	55
	1947/08/05			I Found Freedom in America: Jack Melnik	12
1947/02/18		MCNY	11684	Joe Louis	1
1947/02/18	1947/08/05		2952	Cover: Boy Splashing Water in Bathtub	1
1947/03/03		Logbook	2939	Jazz Jam Session	
	1947/03/04			Meet the People: Why Do You Wear a Mustache?	1
1947/03/05		Logbook	2943	Meet the People: What Is a Lovely Woman?	
1947/03/11		Logbook	2956	Antique Show	
1947/03/11	1947/05/13	LOC	47-1187	Baby Looking into Mirror	38
1947/03/13	1947/07/22		2963	CU "Scientific Toy Drinking Bird"	2
1947/04/01		Logbook	2996	Parades	
1947/04/01		Logbook	2997	Maxine Davis	
1947/04/10		Logbook	3046	Floating Bathing Suit	
1947/04/15		MCNY	10256	People Waiting	35
1947/04/22	1947/08/05	LOC	47-1263 & 1266	Psychoquiz – Knots & Flags	8
1947/04/23		MCNY	10254	Woolworth's Store	607
1947/05/08		Logbook	3093	Superstition Story	
1947/05/19	1947/09/30	LOC	47-A23	Walkathon	245
	1947/05/27			Meet the People: ...Desire to Go West?	11
1947/06/02	1947/08/19	LOC	47-A53	Strong Man's Family, a.k.a. "Family Full of Health"	103
	1947/06/10			Meet the People: ... Celebrity... Like to Marry?	5

1947/06/11		Logbook	A73	News Stand Sale of *LOOK*	
1947/06/12	1947/08/05	LOC	47-A76	Javelin Thrower	46
1947/06/13		Logbook	A79	Outdoor Movie Ad	
1947/06/13		Logbook	A80	It Happened Here: Eiffel Tower in Toothpics	
1947/06/19	1947/09/16	LOC & MCNY	47-A95 & 10798	Juvenile Jury & Radio – Children	25
1947/06/25		Logbook	B6	Pie Throwing Radio Show	
1947/06/25		MCNY	11278	Clark, Buddy – Singer	20
1947/06/30	1949/04/12	LOC	47-B14	Chicago Travel Story	1
1947/06/30		LOC	47-B17	Air Show	120
1947/07/07	1947/10/14	MCNY	11280	Radio Show, Teen-Age	114
1947/07/09		Logbook	B12	Children's Greeting Cards	
1947/07/28		MCNY	10262	"Naked City"	81
1947/07/29	1947/11/11	MCNY	B79	Sparkle Plenty (Dick Tracy Dolls)	28
1947/08/01	1947/11/25		B86	Meet the People: Who Stands Pain the Best?	9
1947/08/06		LOC	47-B94	Diaper Story	156
1947/08/10		Logbook	B87	Meet the People: Do Women Talk Too Much?	
1947/08/11		LOC	47-C3	King of the Hams	37
1947/09/00		LOC	47-1259	Irving Mondschein	
	1947/09/02	MCNY	10799	Five and Dime Store	146
1947/09/03		MCNY	12150	Advertising – Outdoor Advertising Sign	40
1947/09/04		MCNY	10647	Lynch, Christopher	24
1947/09/15	1948/03/30		C65	Lazy Ex-G.I.	1
1947/09/16		Logbook	C70	It Happened Here: Bow-Tie Man	
1947/09/19	1948/12/07	MCNY	10295	Aqueduct Race Track	173
1947/09/29	1947/12/09	MCNY	10821	Fans (Colour) – (also B&W)	4
1947/09/30		MCNY	10237	News Stand Picture	
	1947/09/30			LS Mother 2 Babies Playpen Philadelphia	1
1947/10/01		Logbook	D8	Look Handbag: Fashion	
1947/10/01		LOC & MCNY	47-D10	Music and Art in High School	145
1947/10/03	1947/12/09	MCNY	11306	High Button Shoes	7
1947/10/06		Logbook	D23	Christmas Story	
1947/10/06		MCNY	10368	Shoe Shine Boy	251

1947/10/06		Logbook	D29	Josh White Jr.	
1947/10/07	1947/12/09	MCNY	10236 & 10818	Coffee Drinking & Making	62
1947/10/14		MCNY	10522	*LOOK*'s Lord & Taylor Display	7
1947/10/15	1948/01/06	MCNY	10524	Day, Doris	6
1947/10/17		Logbook	D52	Seaman's Bank Display	
1947/10/20		LOC	47-D57	Foreign Car Contest	8
1947/10/21	1948/03/02	MCNY	10375	Advertising Sandwich Board	55
1947/10/24	1948/01/20	Logbook	D73	Appendicitis Story	1
1947/10/27		MCNY	10383	Abraham Strauss Display	12
1947/10/27		Logbook	D75	Career Girl	
1947/10/27		MCNY	10389	International House	41
	1947/10/28			Meet the People: Joseph L. Mankiewicz.	1
1947/10/29		LOC & MCNY	47-D83 & 11162	Boxing Story – Ruffin, Bobby & W. Beltram	136
1947/11/03	1948/01/20	LOC	47-D90	Bubble Gum	48
1947/11/10		Logbook	191	*LOOK* Employees: Lew Gillenson	
1947/11/14		MCNY	10523	Hurok, Sol – Impresario	7
1947/11/17	1948/04/27	MCNY	10875	Laundry (In Greenwich Village)	45
1947/11/17		Logbook	191	*LOOK* Employees: Paul Marcus	
	1947/11/25			Fashion: Model with Sheer Dress (Studio)	3
1947/11/26	1948/03/30	LOC	47-E26	Salvador Dali Art Show	28
1947/12/01		MCNY	10366	United Nations Children's Party	98
1947/12/01		MCNY	11304	Lizt, Eugene & Wife	20
1947/12/08		Logbook	E32	New Born Baby	
1947/12/08	1948/04/27	LOC	47-E43	Rheumatic Fever	84
1947/12/11	1949/08/02	MCNY	10379	Lombardo, Guy	105
1947/12/15		MCNY	10376 & 47-E53	Ives, Burl	95
1947/12/17	1948/03/30	LOC	47-E60	Labor and Management	228
1948/01/05	1948/03/16	LOC	48-E78	Miss America	71
1948/01/13	1948/04/13	MCNY	11302	Valdes, Miguelito	21
1948/01/16	1948/05/11	MCNY	10365 & 10871	Columbia University	550
1948/01/16		MCNY	12103	Van Doren, Mark	
1948/01/22		Logbook	191	*LOOK* Employees: Joanne Melniker	

1948/01/22	1948/05/25	MCNY	10364	Carnegie, Dale	127
1948/01/26	1948/05/25	MCNY	10511 & 10916	Stevens, Rise & Deaf Children in NY	170
1948/02/25		LOC	48-F73	Mason Story	7
1948/03/03	1948/05/25	LOC & MCNY	48-F80 & 11327	Circus Story	479
1948/03/03	1948/05/25	MCNY	11379 & 11376	Circus Story & Clown	19
1948/03/11	1948/10/26	LOC	48-G3	Ringling Art Museum	50
1948/03/18	1948/06/08		G20	Chicago Fashions	2
1948/03/24		Logbook	G32	Hat Check Girl	
	1948/03/30			Photoquiz: CU Bowl of Popcorn Balls	1
1948/04/01		LOC	48-G45	Keeley Institute	107
1948/04/01		Logbook	G46	South Bend, Indiana	
1948/04/01	1948/06/08	LOC	48-G48	Mooseheart, Illinois	234
1948/04/01		LOC	48-G49	Illinois Tech	32
1948/04/01		MCNY	10569	New York Central – 20th Century Ltd.	70
1948/04/08		Logbook	G67	Advertising Kits	
1948/04/12	1948/06/08	MCNY	10565 & 10914	Grosz, George – "New York – World Art Center."	20
1948/04/15		LOC	48-G82	Man vs. Mosquito	62
1948/04/23		Logbook	H4	Life Expectancy	
	1948/04/27			Meet the People: …Meet President Truman…?	3
	1948/04/27			"Musical Tycoon": Philanthropist Henry Reichhold.	1
1948/04/28		LOC	48-H15	Families First	261
1948/04/29		MCNY	10578	Two Sisters (Musicians)	20
1948/05/06		Logbook	H37	Autographing Charity Comforter COLOR	
1948/05/19	1948/08/03	LOC	48-H60	Portugal	542
1948/05/20		MCNY	10554	Franklin & Simon (Display)	12
1948/06/09	1948/08/17	MCNY	10564	Fashion – Men (Ballot Story Men's Wear)	47
1948/06/14	1948/08/17	MCNY	10559	School Children – Clothes of	160
1948/06/14		Logbook	191	*LOOK* Employees: Howard Mace	

1948/06/15		Logbook	191	*LOOK* Employees: Ab Sideman	
1948/06/15		Logbook	191	*LOOK* Employees: Felix Jager	
	1948/07/06			Sports: Track Star Roy Cochran.	1
1948/07/12	1949/01/18	MCNY	11122 & 12213	Cartier, Walter – Prizefighter	1272
1948/07/22	1948/10/12	MCNY	10653 & 10920	Art by Celebrities – Urban League	5
1948/08/09		MCNY	10558	Macy's	8
1948/08/13		Logbook	K11	Soap	
1948/08/23		Logbook	K23	Lord and Taylor Display	
1948/09/02		MCNY	10617	Bloomingdale's	12
1948/09/09		Logbook	K51	Love Life	
1948/09/13	1948/12/07	LOC	48-K56	Milk Train	5
1948/09/23		Logbook	K76	*LOOK* Travel Posters	
1948/09/30		Logbook	K90	Cerdan – Boxer	
1948/09/30	1948/12/21	LOC	48-K91	Greer, Jane	1
1948/10/01		MCNY	11168 & 10638	Children's Book Tryouts	221
1948/10/04		Logbook	K99	Haaren High School	
1948/10/05		Logbook	M8	*LOOK* Display – Kew Gardens	
1948/10/06		Logbook	M10	*LOOK* Can	
	1948/10/12			"Wally Ward Conquers Polio."	3
	1948/10/12			"What Makes Their Eyes Pop?" (ID Uncertain)	
1948/10/14		LOC	48-M28	Nelly Don Dresses	184
1948/10/18		MCNY	10621	Football Writers	29
1948/10/21		Logbook	M45	German Editors	
1948/10/25	1949/09/27	MCNY	10581 & 11715	Paddy Wagon [published 11 months later].	51
1948/10/27		Logbook	M48	Picasso	
1948/10/27		MCNY	10608	Chemist (Botany)	43
1948/10/28		MCNY	10607	National Business Show	36
1948/10/28		Logbook	M69	G.I. Watercolors	
1948/10/29		MCNY	10603	Men's Fashion Show	30
1948/11/01	1949/02/15	LOC & MCNY	48-M73 & 10593	Fight Night at the Garden	101
1948/11/01		Logbook	M81	Promotion Display – Bathing Suits	

1948/11/05		Logbook	K48	Extremities	
1948/11/15	1949/02/01	LOC & MCNY	48-M92 & 10609	Godfrey, Arthur - "America's Man Godfrey"	345
1948/11/16		Logbook	N16	Skeds Display	
1948/11/23		Logbook	N13	Debutante	
1948/11/23		Logbook	N18	Warm Modern	
1948/11/23		MCNY	10585	Hunter College	11
1948/12/06	1949/01/18	MCNY	11338	Kiss Me Kate	37
1948/12/08	1949/09/27	LOC	48-N69	Pat White – Teenage Editor	244
1948/12/09		MCNY	11336	Goodbye My Fancy	81
1948/12/10		Logbook	M9	Christmas Gifts	
1948/12/14	1949/07/19	MCNY	10583	Nightclubs – Copacabana Girl [N79 in logbook]	198
1948/12/29	1949/03/01	LOC	48-N82	Lobster Story Display (ID Uncertain)	6
1949/01/07		MCNY	12154	Radio Grand Slam Show	208
1949/01/07	1949/05/10	MCNY	12285	Harootian, Koren Der (Sculptor)	78
1949/01/07		LOC	49-O8	American Look	
1949/01/18	1949/04/12	LOC	49-O26 & 046	Chicago – City of Contrasts	1008
1949/02/14	1949/05/10	LOC	49-O77	University of Michigan	662
1949/02/16	1949/04/26	MCNY	12172 & 12195	Radio – Stop the Music (Bert Parks)	113
1949/02/16		LOC	49-O83	Hucksters Party	23
1949/02/28	1949/05/10	LOC	49-O97	Gridiron Club – "Gridiron Show" (St. Louis)	253
1949/03/08		Logbook	N29	Mens Colored Shirts and Ties	
1949/03/16	1949/06/07	LOC	49-P34	Resort Wear – "The 16-ounce Look"	75
1949/03/28		LOC & MCNY	49-P47 & 11169	Williams, Rosemary – Showgirl	85
1949/03/28		MCNY	11448 & 12302	Williams, Rosemary – Showgirl	616
1949/03/28	1949/07/19	LOC & MCNY	49-P53 & 12164	Montgomery Clift – "Glamour Boy in Baggy Pants."	330
1949/04/12	1949/08/16	LOC	49-P94	Poodles, Inc.	40
1949/04/13	1949/06/21	LOC	49-P97	Milton Berle and Children – Father's Day Feature	36
1949/04/15		LOC	49-R7	Bop City	31
1949/04/22		MCNY	12245	Celebrity Art Show	198

1949/04/27		MCNY	11811	Lighthouse for the Blind	54
1949/05/02	1949/09/13	LOC & MCNY	49-R37 & 11124	Philadelphia Beaux Arts Ball [published pix]	134
1949/05/06		LOC	49-R50	Roller Derby	58
1949/05/13	1949/08/16	MCNY	11807	Monroe, Vaughn	492
1949/05/23		MCNY	11800	Art in the Marketplace	122
1949/05/24		LOC	49-R78	Buddy Baer and May Mann	276
1949/05/27		LOC	49-R80	Sweater Cover	10
1949/06/13	1949/08/02		S10	"Miss Liberty" – Broadway Musical	7
1949/06/27		Logbook	S39	Dairy Award Luncheon	
1949/07/14	1949/12/20	MCNY	11821	TV Programs – Howdy Doody	5
1949/07/20	1949/09/27	LOC	49-S75	Peter Arno	29
1949/07/20	1949/09/27	MCNY	11817 & 12180	Peter Arno	275
1949/07/20		Logbook	S79	*LOOK* Brass	
1949/08/00		MCNY	11833	NYC Scene – Fashion Shots	74
1949/08/01	1949/10/11	LOC	49-S86	Baskerville – 1st Portrait of Indian PM Nehru	89
1949/08/03	1949/09/27	MCNY	12091	Theatre – Gentlemen Prefer Blondes	105
1949/08/10	1949/10/25	LOC	49-S95	Lou Maxon	54
1949/08/15	1950/01/03	LOC	49-S97	Fighters Skull	21
1949/08/15		LOC	49-S98	Fran and Ollie Kukla	114
1949/08/18		MCNY	12280	Pearson, Beatrice	292
1949/08/22	1950/03/14	LOC & MCNY	49-T10 & 12304	Leonard Bernstein	382
1949/08/23	1949/11/08	MCNY	12306 & 49-T11	Animals – Dogs (Dog Story)	352
1949/08/23		Logbook	T13	Sylvia Schur Painting	
1949/08/23		Logbook	T14	Kalart Camera	
1949/08/29	1949/10/25	LOC	49-T24	G.O.P. Story – "Meet the Chairman of the GOP"	23
1949/09/06	1949/12/20	MCNY	12063	Museum of Modern Art	44
1949/09/12		MCNY	12312	Gimbels Fashion Show	201
1949/09/15		Logbook	R30	Look Promotion Books	
1949/09/15		Logbook	S37	Change About Display	
1949/09/15	1949/11/22	Logbook	T40	Urban League Paintings (ID Uncertain)	
1949/09/15	1949/11/22	Logbook	T49	Divorced Woman (ID Uncertain)	3
1949/09/23		LOC	49-T65	Raccoon Story	61

1949/09/23	1949/12/20		T68	Sherman Billingsley	2
1949/09/27		Logbook	S19	Architects & Artists Design Fabrics	
1949/09/29	1950/05/09	LOC	49-T79	Phil Rizzuto	29
1949/09/29	1949/12/06	LOC & MCNY	49-T81 & 11678	Wedgewood Ball - "New York Society Ball"	66
1949/10/03		Logbook	T86	Bears – Cardinals Game	
1949/10/03	1950/04/11		T89	Don Newcombe: Next 30-game Winner?	11
1949/10/05		LOC	49-T95	Rutgers Tug-of-War	65
1949/10/06	1949/12/06	LOC	49-T97	World Series Junior Photographer	122
1949/10/10		Logbook	S41	Cheese Promotion	
1949/10/11	1950/08/01	LOC	49-T74	Gene Autry	46
1949/10/11		Logbook	U6	Henry Erlich & Dan Mich	
1949/10/17	1950/01/31	LOC	49-U20	Sinatra and Kirsten	268
		MCNY	11834	Night Clubs – Stork Club	9
1949/10/19		LOC	49-R94	Mrs. Fairington at Stork Club – Stockings, Dresses	30
1949/10/20		Logbook	S41	Cheese	
1949/10/20	1949/12/20	Logbook	U24	Luggage ("Portable Porter")	2
1949/10/21	1950/02/28	MCNY	12325	Art – Collectors ("Big Little Art Collection")	27
1949/10/25	1950/10/24	LOC	49-U31	Sadler's Wells Ballet (ID Uncertain)	
1949/10/28		MCNY	49-U31	Shearer, Moira	2
1949/10/26	1950/01/03	LOC	49-U34	American look (Ann Klem)	22
1949/10/27	1950/02/14	LOC & MCNY	49-U38 & 12284	Rocky Graziano	464
1949/10/28	1950/01/03		U40	I Predict – Robert Montgomery	1
1949/11/07	1950/01/31	LOC	49-U59	Senator Robert Taft	355
1949/11/09		MCNY	12281	Urban League – Paintings by Celebrities (ID ?)	
1949/11/09	FLAIR	Logbook	9	"Flair Contributors"	
1949/11/15	FLAIR	Logbook	17	Jewelry	
1949/11/16		Logbook	U73	Mary Blair	
1949/11/21		Logbook	U81	Lecture Bureau	
1949/11/21		Logbook	U83	Suspense	
1949/11/25	1950/03/14	LOC	49-U95	Traveling Saleswoman (ID Uncertain)	

1949/12/08	1950/02/28	LOC	49-V46	Lecture Tour – "Lady Lecturer Hits the Road"	395
1949/12/12		MCNY	12197	Mostel, Zero	11
1949/12/13		Logbook	V57	Luggage Display	
1949/12/22		Logbook	V82	Display – Groceries	
1949/12/28	1950/05/09	LOC	49-V87	Ken Murray – TV	183
1950/01/09	1950/03/28	MCNY	12219	Radio – Quick as a Flash	66
1950/01/16		LOC	50-W14	Furniture Convention	151
1950/01/17	1950/07/04	LOC	W20	Cheaper by the Dozen	6
	1950/01/31			Don't Be Afraid of Middle Age	2
1950/02/02		LOC	50-W49	Bone Bank	82
1950/02/03	1950/05/23	LOC	50-W48	Theodore Roosevelt III	18
1950/02/03		LOC	50-W50	Walter Reed Hospital	391
1950/02/06		LOC	50-W55	Supermarkets (ID Uncertain)	
1950/02/14		Logbook	W68	Pregnancy Test	
1950/02/15	1950/06/06	LOC	50-W69	Double or Nothing	121
1950/03/03	1950/06/06	LOC	50-W99	Jazz Story	487
1950/03/21	1950/06/06	MCNY	12217	Napoleon, Phil	6
	1950/06/20			NY Giants Broadcaster Russ Hodges	1
1950/03/09	1950/08/15	LOC	50-X5	Card Games – Canasta	1
1950/03/10	1950/07/18	LOC	50-X9	Peggy Lee - "The Ballad of Peggy Lee"	186
1950/03/16	1950/09/12	LOC	50-X19	Break the Bank	102
1950/03/29		Logbook	X46	Display: Magazine Rack	
1950/04/03	1950/07/18	LOC	50-X55	Cowboy Craze Among Children	2
	1950/08/01			What Every Teenager Should Know About Dating	12
1950/04/19		LOC	50-X85-A	Eddie & Stark Stanky – Baseball	
1950/04/19		LOC	50-X85-B	New York Giants – Baseball	
1950/04/24	1950/10/10	LOC	50-X89	What Teenagers Should Know About Love	4

1950/05/01	FLAIR		Logbook	325	Reginald Massey (Dean Acheson)	
1950/05/01	1950/07/18	LOC & MCNY	50-Y1 & 12268	Debutante Goes to Work: Betsy Von Furstenberg	236
1950/05/03		Logbook	Y4	Assassination of Lincoln	
1950/05/10		Logbook	Y17	Dog Food, Gaines – Promotion	
1950/05/15	FLAIR	Logbook	362	Flair Promotion	
1950/05/15		LOC	50-Y27	Farm Toys	77
1950/05/22		LOC	50-Y42	Ralph Kiner	59
1950/05/29	1950/08/15	LOC & MCNY	50-Y56 & 12264	Faye Emerson	218
1950/06/19	1950/09/26	LOC	50-Y90	Red Rolfe and Walt Dropo	22
1950/06/22	1950/12/05	LOC	50-Z4	Lionel Trains	55
1950/06/26		LOC	50-Z8	Richmond Health Story	54
1950/06/28	1950/09/12	LOC	50-Z13	Transoceanic TV – David Sarnoff, Chairman RCA	10
1950/06/28		LOC	50-Z14	Cerebral Palsy Angels	47
1950/07/06		LOC	50-Z23	Rochester Newsboy	61
1950/07/06		Logbook	Z26	Drugstore Promotion	
1950/07/10	1951/03/13	LOC	50-Z31	Narcotics	
1950/07/12		Logbook	Z37	Ruth Roman COLOR	
1950/07/12	1950/09/26	Logbook	Z41	Meet the People ("Mind Your Manners")	7
1950/07/23		Logbook	Z63	Walter Miles, Perfume	
1950/07/25		Logbook	Z58A	Christmas Cards	
1950/07/27	1950/12/05	LOC & MCNY	50-Z60 & 11703	CBS News Team	156
1950/07/28			Z61	Promotion Dept. – Globe	
1950/08/03		MCNY	12276	United Nations	34
1950/08/07	1950/10/24	LOC	50-Z42	Peter Lind Hayes	137
1950/08/07	1955/07/12	Logbook	Z74	Rogers & Hammerstein	1
1950/08/14	1950/10/24	Logbook	Z86	Jealousy: A Threat to Marriage	6
					Total 24210

Bibliography

Albrecht, Donald and Thomas Mellins. 2009. *Only in New York: Photographs from Look Magazine*. New York: The Monacelli Press.

Altman, Rick. 1980. "Moving Lips: Cinema as Ventriloquism." *Yale French Studies*, 60: 67–79.

———. 1992. *Sound Theory/Sound Practice*. New York: Routledge.

———. 1999. *Film/Genre*. London: British Film Institute.

Andrew, Dudley. 1984. *Concepts in Film Theory*. Oxford: Oxford University Press.

Arnett, Jeffrey Jensen. 2004. *Emerging Adulthood: The Winding Road from the Late Teens Through the Twenties*. New York: Oxford University Press.

Barth, Miles. Look Magazine Project Recordings. Audiotape. Rec. May 18, 1994. Library of Congress, Washington D.C., Recorded Sound Division. RYL 1859. Audiocassette.

Barthes, Roland. 1974. *S/Z*. New York: Hill and Wang.

———. 1981. *Camera Lucida*. New York: Hill and Wang.

Baxter, John. 1997. *Stanley Kubrick: A Biography*. New York: Carroll & Graf.

Bazin, André. 2004. *What Is Cinema?* Berkeley: University of California Press.

Berk, Laura E. 2004. *Development Through the Lifespan*. Boston: Allyn and Bacon.

Bernstein, Cal. Look Magazine Project Recordings. Audiotape. Rec. June 12, 1994. Library of Congress, Washington D.C., Recorded Sound Division. RYL 1866-7. Audiocassette.

Bernstein, Jeremy. 2001. "Profile: Stanley Kubrick." In: *Stanley Kubrick Interviews*. Gene D. Phillips (ed.). Jackson: University of Mississippi Press, pp. 21–46.

———. 2005. Interview with Stanley Kubrick. Audio CD. Rec. November 27, 1966. In: *The Stanley Kubrick Archives*. Alison Castle (ed.). Köln: Taschen, p. 1.

———. 2006. "Projected Greatness." *RPS Journal*, 146(7): 314–317.

Bocknek, Gene. 1986. *The Young Adult: Development After Adolescence*. New York: Gardner Press.

Bolack, Michelle Renee. 2001. "Constructed Images: The Influences of News Organizations and Socialization in Photojournalism." Diss. University of North Texas.

Bordwell, David. 1985. *Narration in the Fiction Film*. Madison: The University of Wisconsin Press.

———. 1989. *Making Meaning: Inference and Rhetoric in the Interpretation of Cinema*. Cambridge: Harvard University Press.

———. 1997. *Film Art: An Introduction*, 5th ed. New York: MacGraw-Hill.

Bouineau, Jean-Marc. 1994. *Le Petit Livre de Stanley Kubrick*. Garches: Spartonage.

Brennen, Bonnie S. 2004. "From *Headline Shooter* to *Picture Snatcher*: The Construction of Photojournalists in American Film, 1928–39." *Journalism*, 5(4): 423–439.

Bridger, Earle. 1997. "From the Ridiculous to the Sublime: Stereotypes of Photojournalists in the Movies." *Visual Communication Quarterly*, 4(1): 4–11.

Brookman, Philip. 1997. "Unlocked Doors: Gordon Parks at the Crossroads." In: *Half Past Autumn: A Retrospective*. Parks, Gordon. Boston: Little, Brown and Company, pp. 346–353.

Burch, Noël. 1973. *Theory of Film Practice*. London: Secker & Warburg.

Cahill, Tim. 2001. "The *Rolling Stone* Interview: Stanley Kubrick." In: *Stanley Kubrick: Interviews*. Gene D. Phillips (ed.). Jackson: University of Mississippi Press, pp. 189–203.

Campany, David. 2008. *Photography and Cinema*. London: Reaktion Books.

Cantor, Jeffrey A. 1995. *Cooperative Education and Experiential Learning*. Dayton, Ohio: Wall & Emerson.

Carlebach, Mike. Look Magazine Project Recordings. Audiotape. Rec. June 16, 1994. Library of Congress, Washington D.C., Recorded Sound Division. RYL 1862-3. Audiocassette.

Castle, Alison (ed.). 2005. *The Stanley Kubrick Archives*. Köln: Taschen.

Chatman, Seymour. 1980. "What Novels Can Do That Films Can't (And Vice Versa)." *Critical Inquiry*, 7(1): 121–140.

Chion, Michel. 2005. *Stanley Kubrick: l'humain, ni plus ni moins*. Paris: Cahiers du Cinéma.

Cieutat, Michel. 1999. "Précis d'initiation à l'esthétique kubrickienne." *Positif*, 464(October) : 86–90.

Ciment, Michel. "Jerry Schatzberg Biography." *jerryschatzberg.com*. n.d. Web. 11 May 2011.

———. 1982. *Schatzberg: de la photo au cinéma*. Paris: Chêne/Hachette.

———. 1999. "Entretien avec Alexander Walker: Une recherche de l'infaillibilité." *Positif*, 464(October): 37–40.

———. 2003. *Kubrick*. New York: Faber & Faber.

Cooperman, Gary Stanford. 1966. "A Historical Study of Look Magazine." MA thesis. University of Missouri.

Corrigan, Timothy. 2008. "'The Forgotten Image Between Two Shots': Photos, Photograms, and the Essayistic." In: *Still Moving: Between Cinema and Photography*. Karen Beckman and Jean Ma (eds). : Duke University Press, pp. 41–61.

Cowles, Gardner. 1985. *Mike Looks Back*. New York: Gardner Cowles.

Crone, Rainer. 2005. *Stanley Kubrick: Drama and Shadows*. London: Phaidon Press.

———. 2010. *Stanley Kubrick Fotografie: 1945–1950*. Milano, Italy: Giunti.

Crone, Rainer and Petrus Graf Schaesberg. 1999. *Stanley Kubrick: Still Moving Pictures, Fotografien 1945–1950*. Munich: Schnell & Steiner.

Crone, Rainer and Alexandra Von Stosch. 2004. "Kubrick's Kaleidoscope: Early Photographs 1945–1950." *Kinematograph*, 20: 19–27.

Davis, Keith F. 2009. *The Photographs of Homer Page: The Guggenheim Year: New York, 1949–50*. New Haven and London: Yale University Press.

Deleuze, Gilles. 2005. *Cinema 2: The Time-Image*. London: Continuum.

Dogra-Brazell, Julia. 2009. "The Quiet One: A Photograph in a Film in NY in 1948." Framing Film Conference, University of Winchester, 6 Sept. 2009.

Duncan, Paul. 2003. *Stanley Kubrick*. Köln: Taschen.

Eaton, Eric. 2008. "Patterns of Space, Sound, and Movement in *Paths of Glory*." In: *Stanley Kubrick: Essays on His Films and Legacy*. Gary D. Rhodes (ed.). Jefferson, North Carolina: McFarland & Co., pp. 71–81.

Eisenstein, Sergei. 1949. *Film Form*. New York: Harcourt Brace Jovanovich.

Evans, Gary. 1984. *John Grierson and the National Film Board: The Politics of Wartime Propaganda*. Toronto: University of Toronto Press.

Evans, Glen and Millicent Poole. 1991. *Young Adults : Self-Perceptions and Life Contexts*. New York: Falmer Press.

Falsetto, Mario. 2001. *Stanley Kubrick: A Narrative and Stylistic Analysis*. Westport, CT: Praeger.

Fischer, Ralf Michael. 2004. "Pictures at an Exhibition? Allusions and Illusions in *Barry Lyndon*." *Kinematograph*, 20: 168–183.

Fish, Stanley. 1991. "Biography and Intention." In: *Contesting the Subject*. William H. Epstein (ed.). West Lafayette: Purdue University Press.

Fleckhaus, Willy. 1972. "Overdesigned." In: *Photographic Communication*. R. Smith Schuneman (ed.). New York: Hastings House, pp. 110–115.

Foucault, Michel. 1980. *Language, Counter-Memory, Practice*. Ithaca: Cornell University Press.

French, Karl. 2004. *Art by Film Directors*. London: Mitchell Beazley.

Frewin, Anthony. 2004. "2001: The Prologue That Nearly Was." *Kinematograph*, 20: 128–135.

Fusco, Paul. Look Magazine Project Recordings. Audiotape. Rec. November 6, 1998. Library of Congress, Washington D.C., Recorded Sound Division. RYL 1874-5. Audiocassette.

García Mainar, Luis M. 1999. *Narrative and Stylistic Patterns in the Films of Stanley Kubrick*. Rochester, NY: Camden House.

Gelmis, Joseph. 2001. "The Film Director as Superstar: Stanley Kubrick." In: *Stanley Kubrick: Interviews*. Gene D. Phillips (ed.). Jackson: University of Mississippi Press, pp. 80–104.

Genette, Gérard. 1993. *Fiction & Diction*. Ithaca, NY: Cornell University Press.

Ginna, Robert Emmett. 1999. "The Odyssey Begins." *Entertainment Weekly*, 480(April): 16–22.

Goldsmith, Arthur. 1963. "Photojournalism." In: *The Encyclopedia of Photography* (Vol. 15). Willard D. Morgan (ed.). New York: Greystone Press, pp. 2761–2790.

Guimond, James. 1991. *American Photography and the American Dream*. Chapel Hill: University of North Carolina Press.

Hamilton, Edward A. (ed.). 1958. *School Photojournalism: Telling Your School Story in Pictures*. Washington, D.C.: National Education Association.

Hamilton, Edward A. and Charles Preston (eds). 1958. *Our Land, Our People*. Englewood Cliffs, NJ: Prentice-Hall, Inc.

Hamilton, Stephen F. 1990. *Apprenticeship for Adulthood: Preparing Youth for the Future*. New York: Free Press.

Hicks, Wilson. 1972. "What Is Photojournalism?" In: *Photographic Communication*. R. Smith Schuneman (ed.). New York: Hastings House, pp. 19–56.

Hoffer, Mary Jane. 1983. "Technical and Aesthetic Developments of the Photo-Essay." Diss. Columbia University.

Hopkins, William. 1972. "Art Direction in the Magazine of the '70's." In: *Photographic Communication*. R. Smith Schuneman (ed.). New York: Hastings House, pp. 104–109.

Houston, Penelope. 2001. "Kubrick Country." In: *Stanley Kubrick: Interviews*. Gene D. Phillips (ed.). Jackson: University of Mississippi Press, pp. 108–115.

Howard, James. 1999. *Stanley Kubrick Companion*. London: B.T. Batsford, Ltd..

Hurlburt, Allen. 1972. "Design in Photographic Communication." In: *Photographic Communication*. R. Smith Schuneman (ed.). New York: Hastings House, pp. 99–104.

Jacquinot, Geneviève. 1977. *Image et pédagogie*. Paris: Presses Universitaires de France.

Juntunen, Arthur. "Snap Hundreds, Says 'Boy Genius.'" Detroit Free Press (late forties, exact date unknown).

Kagan, Norman. 2000. *The Cinema of Stanley Kubrick*. New York: Continuum.

Kalish, Stanley E. and Clifton C. Edom. 1951. *Picture Editing*. New York: Rinehart & Company.

Kastner, Joseph. 1972. "Writing for the Picture Magazine." In: *Photographic Communication*. R. Smith Schuneman (ed.). New York: Hastings House, pp. 122–125.

Kobré, Kenneth. 1996. *Photojournalism: The Professional's Approach* (3rd ed.). Newton, MA: Focal Press.

Koehler, Robert. 1987. "Kubrick as Reporter – Distanced Docu-Fiction." *Los Angeles Times*, (July): 24.

Kohler, Charlie. 2000. "Stanley Kubrick Raps." In: *The Making of 2001: A Space Odyssey*. Stephanie Schwam (ed.). New York: The Modern Library, pp. 245–257.

Kolker, Robert. 2006. "Introduction." In: *Stanley Kubrick's 2001: A Space Odyssey: New Essays*. Robert Kolker (ed.). New York: Oxford University Press, pp. 3–12.

Kozol, Wendy. 1994. *Life's America: Family and Nation in Postwar Photojournalism*. Philadelphia: Temple University Press.

Kubrick, Christiane. 2002. *Stanley Kubrick: A Life in Pictures*. London: Little, Brown.

Kubrick, Stanley. 2005. "Words and Movies." In: *The Stanley Kubrick Archives*. Alison Castle (ed.). Köln: Taschen, pp. 338–339.

Lebeck, Robert and Bodo von Dewitz. 2001. *Kiosk: A History of Photojournalism*. Göttingen, Germany: Steidl Verlag.

Le Grice, Malcolm. 1977. *Abstract Film and Beyond*. Cambridge, Mass: The MIT Press.

Leonard, George. 1988. *Walking on the Edge of the World*. Boston: Houghton Mifflin Co..

Lerner, Richard M. 2002. *Adolescence: Development, Diversity, Context, and Application*. Upper Saddle River, NJ: Prentice Hall.

Life Magazine. 1972. "Preserving the Past." *Life*, 73(April): 63–66.

Lightman, Herb A. 2000. "Filming *2001: A Space Odyssey*." In: *The Making of 2001: A Space Odyssey*. Stephanie Schwam (ed.). New York: The Modern Library, pp. 94–105.

Lindgaard, Jade. 1999. "Science Vision." *Les Inrockuptibles*, 191(March): 40–42.

LoBrutto, Vincent. 1997. *Stanley Kubrick: A Biography*. New York: Da Capo Press.

Loke, Margarett. 2005. "Ted Croner, 82, Dies; Photos Captured New York Energy." *The New York Times* (August 17).

Lovell, Ronald P. 2002. *Pictures and Words*. Clifton Park, NY: Thomson – Delmar Learning.

Marriott, Stephanie. 2005. "Desire and Crisis: the Operation of Cinematic Masks in Stanley Kubrick's *Eyes Wide Shut*." *Lectora*, 11: 93–104.

Mather, Philippe. 2002. "Figures of Estrangement in Science Fiction Film." *Science Fiction Studies*, 29(2): 186–201.

McLean, Adrienne. 2003. "'New Films in Story Form': Movie Story Magazines and Spectatorship." *Cinema Journal*, 42(3): 3–26.

Metz, Christian. 1974. *Film Language: A Semiotics of the Cinema*. New York: Oxford University Press.

Mich, Daniel D. & Edwin Eberman. 1945. *The Technique of the Picture Story*. New York: McGraw-Hill.

Mitchell, W. J. T. 1994. *Picture Theory*. Chicago: University of Chicago Press.

Molina Foix, Vicente. 2005. "An Interview with Stanley Kubrick." In: *The Stanley Kubrick Archives*. Alison Castle (ed.). Köln: Taschen, pp. 460–463.

Monaco, James. 1975. "Why Still Photographers Make Great Directors." *Village Voice*, (December 22): 85–86.

Moran, Tom. 1974. *The Photo Essay: Paul Fusco and Will McBride*. Los Angeles: Alskog, Inc.

Morris, Charles W. 1938. *Foundations of the Theory of Signs*. Chicago: University of Chicago Press.

Mydans, Carl. Look Magazine Project Recordings. Audiotape. Rec. May 10, 1994. Library of Congress, Washington D.C., Recorded Sound Division. RYL 1857-8. Audiocassette.

Naremore, James. 2007. *On Kubrick*. London: British Film Institute.

Nelson, Thomas Allen. 2000. *Kubrick: Inside a Film Artist's Maze*. Bloomington: Indiana University Press.

Nessel, Sabine. 2004. "How Did They Ever Make a Movie of Lolita?" *Kinematograph*, 20: 66–73.

Newhall, Beaumont. 1982. *The History of Photography*. Boston: Little, Brown and Company.

Odin, Roger. 1987. "Cinéma, photographie et 'effet-fiction.'" *Pour la photographie II: de la fiction*. Ciro Bruni (ed.). Sammeron, France: GERMS, pp. 43–52.

———. 1988. "Du spectateur fictionalisant au nouveau spectateur: approche sémio-pragmatique." *Iris*, 8: 121–139.

———. 1995. "A Semio-Pragmatic Approach to the Documentary Film." In: *The Film Spectator: From Sign to Mind*. Warren Buckland (ed.). Amsterdam: University of Amsterdam Press, pp. 227–235.

Panzer, Mary. 2005a. *Things as They Are: Photojournalism in Context Since 1955*. New York: Aperture.

———. 2005b. "Eyes Wide Open." *Vanity Fair*, 535(March): 408–444.

———. 2005c. "Stanley Kubrick's Chicago." *Chicago Tribune*, 8(June): 6.

Parks, Gordon. 1997. *Half Past Autumn: A Retrospective*. Boston: Little, Brown and Company.

Peterson, James. 1994. *Dreams of Chaos, Visions of Order: Understanding the American Avant-Garde Cinema*. Detroit: Wayne State University Press.

Peterson, John. Look Magazine Project Recordings. Audiotape. Rec. April 9, 1997. Library of Congress, Washington D.C., Recorded Sound Division. RYL 1871. Audiocassette.

Phillips, Gene D. 1975. *Stanley Kubrick: A Film Odyssey*. New York: Popular Library.

———. 2002. *The Encyclopedia of Stanley Kubrick*. New York: Checkmark Books.

———. 2005. "Early Work." In: *The Stanley Kubrick Archives*. Alison Castle (ed.). Köln: Taschen, pp. 268–276.

"Photo-essay." *Merriam-Webster's Collegiate Dictionary*. 1993 ed.

Pollack, Sydney. 1999. Interview. *The Last Movie: Stanley Kubrick and Eyes Wide Shut*. Dir. Paul Joyce. Channel 4: Lucida Productions.

Reynolds, Charles. 1960. "Interview with Kubrick." *Popular Photography*, 47(6): 144–149.

Ritzer, George. 1981. *Toward an Integrated Sociological Paradigm*. Boston: Allyn and Bacon.

Ritzer, George and Douglas J. Goodman. 2004. *Modern Sociological Theory*. New York: McGraw-Hill.

Rosenbaum, Jonathan. 2006. "In Dreams Begin Responsibilities." In: *Depth of Field: Stanley Kubrick, Film, and the Uses of History*. Geoffrey Cocks, James Diedrick, and Glenn Perusek (eds). Madison: University of Wisconsin Press, pp. 245–254.

Rosten, Leo (ed.). 1975. *The Look Book*. New York: Harry N. Abrams, Inc..

Rothstein, Arthur. 1953. "The Leica in Photo-Journalism." In: *The New Leica Manual*. Willard D. Morgan and Henry M. Lester (eds). New York: Morgan & Lester, pp. 221–231.

———. 1979. *Photojournalism*. New York: AMPHOTO.

———. Unpublished article about Stanley Kubrick, ts. Box 3, Folder 7. Arthur Rothstein Papers. Library of Congress, Washington D.C.

Rothstein, Arthur and Douglas Kirkland. 1972. "The Editor-Photographer Team." In: *Photographic Communication*. Smith Schuneman, R. (ed.). New York: Hastings House, pp. 92–99.

Rupp, Carla Marie. 1978. "People-Watching Pastime Pays off for Photographer." *Editor and Publisher*, (April 22): 36–38.

Ryan, Marie-Laure. 1991. *Possible Worlds, Artificial Intelligence, and Narrative Theory*. Bloomington: Indiana University Press.

———. (ed.). 2004. *Narrative Across Media: The Languages of Storytelling*. Lincoln: University of Nebraska Press.

Salt, Barry. 1974. "Statistical Style Analysis of Motion Pictures." *Film Quarterly*, 28(1): 13–22.

Sanders, Steven M. 2007. "The Big Score: Fate, Morality, and Meaningful Life in *The Killing*." In: *The Philosophy of Stanley Kubrick*. Jerold J. Abrams (ed.). Lexignton, Kentucky: The University Press of Kentucky, pp. 149–163.

Schaeffer, Jean-Marie. 1987. *L'image précaire: du dispositif photographique*. Paris: Seuil.

Schaesberg, Petrus. 2005. "Stanley Kubrick: Inventor of Facts." In: *Stanley Kubrick: Drama and Shadows*. Rainer Crone (ed.). London: Phaidon Press, pp. 242–245.

Schuneman, R. Smith (ed.). 1972). *Photographic Communication*. New York: Hastings House.

Scott, Clive. 1999. *The Spoken Image: Photography and Language*. London: Reaktion Books.

Sgarbi, Elisabetta (ed.). 1994. *Stanley Kubrick: Ladro di sguardi, fotografie di fotografie 1945–1949*. Milano: Bompiani.

Shaw, Daniel. 2007. "Nihilism and Freedom in the Films of Stanley Kubrick." In: *The Philosophy of Stanley Kubrick*. Jerold J. Abrams (ed.). Lexington, KY: The University Press of Kentucky, pp. 221–234.

Stagg, Mildred. 1948. "Camera Quiz Kid: Stan Kubrick." *The Camera*, 70(10): 36–41.

Staiger, Janet. 2003. "Authorship Approaches." In: *Authorship and Film*. Gerstner, David and Janet Staiger (eds). New York: Routledge.

Stam, Robert. 1985. *Reflexivity in Film and Literature: From Don Quixote to Jean-Luc Godard*. New York: Columbia University Press.

Stang, Joanne. 1958. "Film Fan to Film Maker." *New York Times Magazine*, 12(October): 34–38.

Stewart, Garrett. 1999. *Between Film and Screen: Modernism's Photo Synthesis*. Chicago: University of Chicago Press.

Strick, Philip and Penelope Houston. 2001. "Modern Times: An Interview with Stanley Kubrick." In: *Stanley Kubrick: Interviews*. Gene D. Phillips (ed.). Jackson: University of Mississippi Press, pp. 126–139.

Suleiman, Susan Rubin. 1983. *Authoritarian Fictions: The Ideological Novel as a Literary Genre*. New York: Columbia University Press.

Theisen, Earl. 1947. *Making Your Pictures Interesting*. Chicago: Ziff-Davis.

Thompson, Kristin. 1985. "The Formulation of the Classical Style, 1909–28." In: *The Classical Hollywood Cinema*. David Bordwell, Janet Staiger and Kristin Thompson (eds). New York: Columbia University Press, pp. 155–240.

Todorov, Tzvetan. 1975. *The Fantastic: A Structural Approach to a Literary Genre*. Ithaca, NY: Cornell University Press.

Toubiana, Serge. 2007. *The Image to Come: How Cinema Inspires Photographers*. Göttingen & Paris: Magnum/Steidl & La Cinémathèque Française.

Tretick, Stanley. Look Magazine Project Recordings. Audiotape. Rec. June 2, 1994. Library of Congress, Washington D.C., Recorded Sound Division. RYL 1864-5. Audiocassette.

Trumbull, Douglas. 2001. Interview. *2001 and Beyond*. Dir. Michael Lennick. Foolish Earthlings Prod.

Vachon, John. Unpublished letters to mother, undated. Box 3, Folder 7. John Vachon Papers. Library of Congress, Washington D.C.

Van Citters, G.W. 1949. "Flying Football Cameramen." *Modern Photography*, 13(4): 74–124.

Von Amelunxen, Hubertus. 1999. "Imaginäre und reale Blickpunkte: Zu Stanley Kubrick Fotostories." In: *Stanley Kubrick: Still Moving Pictures, Fotografien 1945–1950*. Rainer Crone and Petrus Graf Schaesberg (eds). Munich, Germany: Schnell & Steiner, pp. 18–27.

Von Stosch, Alexandra. 2005. "Beyond the Looking Glass: Kubrick and Self-Reflectivity." In: *Stanley Kubrick: Drama and Shadows*. Rainer Crone (ed.). London: Phaidon Press, pp. 246–249.

Walker, Alexander. 1971. *Stanley Kubrick Directs*. New York: Harcourt Brace Jovanovich.

Walter, Renaud. 1987. "De *Killer's Kiss* à *2001: l'Odyssée de l'espace*." In: *Stanley Kubrick*. Gilles Ciment (ed.). Paris: Éditions Rivages, pp. 11–30.

Whitinger, Raleigh and Susan Ingram. 2003. "Schnitzler, Kubrick, and 'Fidelio.'" *Mosaic*, 36(3): 55+.

Wigginton, Eliot. 1986. *Sometimes a Shining Moment: The Foxfire Experience*. Garden City, NY: Anchor Press.

Willumson, Glenn G. 1992. *W. Eugene Smith and the Photographic Essay*. Cambridge: Cambridge University Press.

Zimmerman, Paul D. 1972. "Kubrick's Brilliant Vision." *Newsweek*, 79(1): 28–33.

Index

Photographic Credits

Cover photo & figure 19: © Estate of Phillip Harrington. Courtesy of the Library of Congress, LOOK Collection.

Figures 3, 4, 12b, 13b, 14b, 16, 18a, 18b, 18c, 20, 23, 26a, 29, 30a, 30b, 31b, 32a, 32b, 33a, 33b, 34b, 35, 36a, 37a, 37b, 38, 39, 41, 42, 43a, 44a, 45, 54b, 55a, 56: © Cowles Broadcasting, Inc.

Figures 5, 6: © SK Film Archives LLC. Courtesy of the Museum of the City of New York, LOOK Collection.

Figures 11b, 22a, 27a, 48c: © SK Film Archives LLC.

Figures 21, 47c, 52a, 53a, 55b: Courtesy of the Library of Congress, LOOK Collection.

Figure 25: Courtesy of the Museum of the City of New York, LOOK Collection.

Figures 17, 54c: © Estate of Arthur Rothstein.

Figures 8, 10, 15: © Estate of Arthur Rothstein. Courtesy of the Library of Congress, LOOK Collection.

Figures 11a, 12a, 13a, 14a: © Estate of Arthur Rothstein. Courtesy of the Library of Congress, FSA/OWI Collection.

Figure 24a, 34a, 50a: © Estate of Frank M. Bauman.

Figure 28, 31a: © Estate of John Vachon.

Figures 24b, 26b, 27b, 36c, 46, 48a: KILLER'S KISS © 1955

Metro-Goldwyn-Mayer Studios Inc. All rights reserved. Courtesy of MGM Media Licensing.

Figures 22b, 48b, 50: THE KILLING © 1956 Metro-Goldwyn-Mayer Studios Inc. All rights reserved. Courtesy of MGM Media Licensing.

Figure 52b: PATHS OF GLORY © 1957 Harris Kubrick Pictures Corp. All rights reserved. Courtesy of MGM Media Licensing.

Figures 49, 51: SPARTACUS © 1960 Universal Pictures Company, Inc. & Bryna Productions, Inc. Courtesy of Universal Studios Licensing LLC.

Figures 43b-e, 44b, 47b, 53b: DR. STRANGELOVE © 1964 COLUMBIA PICTURES (Sony Pictures Entertainment).

Every effort has been made to locate copyright holders for material contained in this book. If you have information pertaining to such copyright not already credited here, please contact the author at Philippe.Mather@uregina.ca.